NEW TESTAMENT HISTORY

NEW
TESTAMENT
HISTORY

RICHARD L. NISWONGER

ZondervanPublishingHouse
Grand Rapids, Michigan

A Division of HarperCollinsPublishers

New Testament History
Copyright © 1988 by Richard L. Niswonger
First softcover edition 1992

Requests for information should be addressed to:
Zondervan Publishing House

Grand Rapids, Michigan 49530

Library of Congress Cataloging-in-Publication Data

Niswonger, Richard L.
    New Testament history
      Bibliography p.
    Includes indexes
    ISBN 0-310-31201-9
    1. Bible. N.T.–History of Biblical events.
    2. Bible. N.T.–History of contemporary events. I. Title.
    BS1407.N57 1988
    225.9'5   88-6193
                                                 CIP

Edited by Gerard Terpstra
Designed by Stanley N. Gundry

Printed in the United States of America

96 97 /QG/ 10 9 8 7 6 5 4

To Grace

CONTENTS

LIST OF APPENDIXES

ILLUSTRATIONS

11

LIST OF MAPS

PREFACE

It has been my aim in this book to provide a survey of New Testament history that is marked by clarity, readability, and scholarship. The viewpoint expressed is conservative and evangelical.

A bibliography has been provided to lead the serious student to some of the important literature in the field. It is based on a wide theological spectrum, and the fact that a book is listed in the bibliography should not be taken as an indication that its theological position is endorsed by the author.

Special thanks are due several individuals who have contributed to the completion of this work. Some of my students—specifically Janet Schneider, John Miller, and Stanley Albritton—have helped keep my academic office in running shape while I have been involved in the writing process. At Zondervan Stanley Gundry, Ed van der Maas, and Len Goss have given helpful advice. I am indebted to a multitude of teachers and scholars whose influence and writings have helped direct my path. I willingly endorse the usual mandatory disclaimer that none of these people should share culpability for any of my errors. Most important, I express gratitude to my wife, Grace, whose patient encouragement, unfailing confidence, and tireless efforts helped bring this task to completion.

INTRODUCTION

Christianity is a faith rooted in historical events. By contrast, Hinduism, Buddhism, Confucianism, and most other great religious movements have been based more on an ideological foundation than on some dramatic series of events. For them a set of teachings or a philosophy is more important than the experiences of a key figure. Remove the Incarnation, the Cross, and the Resurrection from Christianity, and the result is a faith stripped of its primal elements. Because Christianity is so singularly based on historical events in a particular time and place, it can be apprehended more fully only by a careful study of these events in their context.

This work attempts to present both the historical milieu from which Christianity arose and a summary of the biblical events themselves. In other words, New Testament history as conceived here involves both a study of backgrounds and an overview of the historical content of the New Testament. To understand the works and words of Jesus one needs to know something about the political stirrings of Jews, Syrians, and Romans in the centuries preceding his birth. The religious beliefs and practices of Judaism are also an essential prerequisite for interpreting the message of Jesus and Paul. One needs to have some conception of the Roman philosophical and religious environment to understand the appeal of the Christian message as well as its uniqueness. Any historical investigation must also deal with issues of historical methodology either implicitly or explicitly. A study of New Testament history should at least consider the question of the reliability of the New Testament documents.

An overview of the life of Jesus, the ministry of Paul, and the other major historical events of the New Testament provides a brief survey of the historical content of the New Testament itself. As interesting and profitable as it might be to restrict this kind of study to background information alone, such an approach would lose sight of the most important reason for studying backgrounds. The events and ideas of the first-century Roman Empire have their interest for the Christian as a backdrop for the drama of the central figure of history—Jesus Christ. While a survey of his life can be only one part of a New Testament history, it is in fact the central event that gives real impact to all the rest. Similarly, the events of Acts and the apostolic era are a major part of New Testament history. The story of the spread of the gospel and the growth of the church must not be lost amid lengthy accounts of royal intrigues and the changing fortunes of armies. Yet in a survey that seeks to cover both backgrounds and biblical content, it is important that the amount of space given to the biblical material itself also be kept within bounds. The study of content can only be initiated here, and the serious Bible student will want to go far beyond the limitations of this volume.

The approach to the New Testament in this work is chiefly a chronological one. When we study biblical content, it is appropriate to place emphasis on those sections, such as the Gospels and Acts, that primarily contain historical narrative. This necessitates a lessening of emphasis on the epistles, since primarily they contain exhortation rather than narrative. Galatians 1 and 2 provide one obvious exception in that they record a historical account of Paul's early experiences. Admittedly also, the epistles provide many insights into the life of the early church, and these insights are extremely useful in seeking to create a picture of first-century times. The concern with chronological issues also explains the emphasis on topics such as the North Galatian theory versus the South Galatian theory. This debate, although never fully resolvable, is critical to any resolution of the question of the order of events in Paul's life as well as the relationship of the Galatians information to that in Acts.

Explicitly or implicitly, every historical narrative is shaped by a writer's frame of reference. To claim total objectivity is to be a victim of self-deception. Historians are very much aware of the extent of humanity's tendency to unconsciously distort and warp reality to conform to one's own prejudices and biases. The best course is to be aware of one's basic presuppositions, to admit them frankly, and then to seek insofar as one is capable to be objective and fair. The conceptual framework of this book is conservative and traditional. The Gospels are viewed as reliable historical documents. But there has been a conscious effort to present more than a one-sided picture. Students need to be aware that different viewpoints exist and to have some conception of what these views are. They need to be wary of an approach that claims to possess the sum total of truth and looks on other viewpoints as nothing more than the product of irrational or insincere writers. In other words, the aim here is to provide a balanced treatment rather than a one-dimensional polemic.

The scope of this work is vast. History encompasses an immense landscape of time, events, ideas, and individuals. Taking a historical description of the New Testament age with all its diverse themes involving politics, wars, philosophies, and religions and blending this with the varied approaches of biblical studies—such as introduction, survey of content, literary criticism, Judaic studies, the life of Christ, and apostolic history—is somewhat like taking on the role of a juggler who has decided to keep ten bowling pins in the air at once. Occasionally a few pins may drop, but the challenge is worth the effort. The result is a much more holistic way of viewing the New Testament message. It is approached through a study of the historical context that shaped its expression and form.

To set the scene for the story of the beginnings of Christianity, one could begin with Abraham or Moses, and the foundations of Judaism. Historians usually are tempted to trace any movement from as early a point of development as possible. Here it is assumed that one knows or will be interested to learn something of Old Testament history and the close of the exile period under the Persians. Because the Maccabean revolt had such a major influence on the thinking of first-century Jews, and in order to keep the narrative within bounds, the narrative begins with Alexander, the advent of the Hellenistic age, and the Maccabean independence struggle.

The magnificent ruins at Palmyra—a monumental arch in the foreground and the Grand Colonnade beyond. Roman influence reached far into distant lands; Palmyra lay about 120 miles (193 km.) northeast of Damascus. Courtesy Studium Biblicum Franciscanum, Jerusalem.

Chapter 1

Palestine and the Nations, 332–40 B.C.

Alexander's Conquests

When Jesus was born in Bethlehem, Rome had already dominated the land of his birthplace for nearly six decades. Roman forces continued their effort to pacify and stabilize this troublesome outpost of empire well beyond the era of New Testament history. In the centuries preceding Roman rule the Jewish people experienced a varied political history. It was the Persian Empire under Cyrus that granted permission (in 536 B.C.) to the first band of Jewish pilgrims to end their exile and begin their journey to the homeland. The Persians earned a reputation as beneficent rulers. Much like the later Romans, they believed a degree of magnanimity, respect for local customs, and a tolerance for varied ethnic and religious traditions would better cement a polyglot empire together than a policy of brute force and repression. The Persian era of control over Palestine ended suddenly with the conquests of the ruler of Macedon, Alexander the Great.

The advent of the Macedonian conqueror would signify much more to the Jewish people than a simple exchange of political masters. The young general and his successors brought Greek culture and language to the Near East. The collision of new ways with the varied patterns of life existing in the Near East produced a new amalgam of cultures—Hellenism. Pious Jews perceived in this blend of oriental and Greek ideas a threat to their cherished faith and way of life. Alexander was not a son of Hellas himself, and the Greeks looked askance at his homeland, Macedonia, as culturally inferior. Nevertheless, Macedonia, and Alexander in particular, drank deeply at the well of Greek learning and literature. When the young prince reached thirteen, Aristotle personally tutored him and apparently had a major role in stimulating Alexander in his lifelong zeal for poetry, philosophy, ethics, science, and literature. During

Alexander's military adventures in Asia Minor, he kept Homer's *Iliad* close by so that he might find time for reading and comparing his own exploits to those of earlier conquerors. But it required more than a brilliant mind to disseminate the Greek way of life to the East; it also necessitated a military genius who could subdue vast regions, and Alexander was capable of fulfilling both prerequisites.

A drawing of Alexander the Great, from a mosaic found at Pompeii (c. 300 B.C.).
Courtesy Carta, Jerusalem.

When Alexander was twenty years old, he assumed the throne of Macedonia in 336 B.C., after the assassination of his father, Philip II. his father. Although Philip had already subdued the Greek city states, Alexander reasserted the dominance of Macedonia by brutally crushing a revolt in the Greek city of Thebes. After leveling the rebel city and enslaving its citizens, Alexander turned his vision eastward toward the empire of Persia. With 35,000 soldiers he crossed the Hellespont in 334 B.C. and overcame the Persian defenders at Granicus. He led his army through the Cilician gates to Tarsus and won another strategic victory at Issus.

Darius the Persian emperor fled in haste, abandoning his bath tub and harem to the Macedonians.

Alexander chose to lead his troops directly south toward Egypt instead of pursuing Darius. Along the Palestinian coast, Tyre and Gaza fell after fierce resistance. The Jewish historian Josephus, who lived in the first century A.D. and is an important source for New Testament history, records an intriguing story of a meeting between the Jewish high priest Jaddua and Alexander. According to Josephus, Jaddua had spurned Alexander's call for submission and reaffirmed his loyalty to Darius. When news of Alexander's army marching from Gaza to Jerusalem came to Jaddua, he joined the people in making sacrifice and praying to Jehovah for deliverance. God's answer came to Jaddua in a dream. He must open the city gates and welcome the Macedonians. When the army drew near Jerusalem, the high priest had already led a welcoming party out of the city to beseech Alexander's mercy. After the two leaders met, Alexander surprised his comrades by revealing that in Macedonia he had seen a vision of this same high priest. In his dream, the God whose name Jaddua wore on his forehead had challenged him to take up arms and subdue Persia. The Macedonian general followed the high priest back to Jerusalem, offered sacrifice in the temple, and listened to the prophecies of Daniel that had foretold his victories. Most historians dismiss this story as legend. Josephus stands as the only witness, and a late one, to the event. But Alexander often did show respect to local religious shrines for political reasons

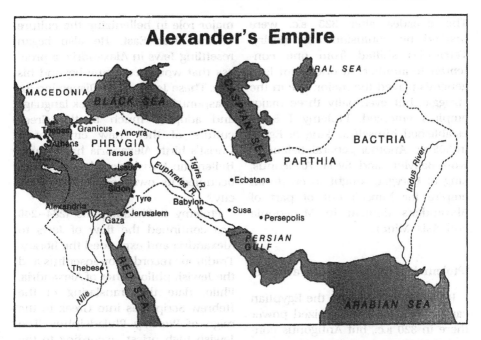

Alexander's Empire

and could have offered a sacrifice in Jerusalem. Although Josephus' story may reflect some exaggeration, it is likely that an encounter between Alexander and the high priest did occur.[1]

Continuing southward, Alexander took Egypt without a struggle. The priests of Amon acknowledged him as the son of God. Although divinity was one of the perquisites of office for the Pharaohs, Alexander did not utilize this new-found status as a device to unify his growing empire. He established no empire-wide cult. But he did later seek deification in Greece as a political device to pull that disunified peninsula together. The use of the "emperor worship" cult by Domitian and other Roman emperors as a stabilizing force was not the invention of the Macedonian. Alexander founded the city of Alexandria, one of many with that name, in the Nile Delta in 332 B.C. During the New Testament era this city was second only to Rome in population. Because of the large influx of Jews, it became an influential center for Jewish studies. Leaving Egypt, Alexander pursued Darius across Syria and Persia. But the harried Persian met death at the hands of one of his own supporters. With Persia vanquished, Alexander led his armies eastward as far as the Indus River. He would have driven his weary men farther into India had they not rebelled at the thought of continuing the long struggle. Returning to Persia, Alexander began to adopt the high style and pageantry of the oriental despots. But before he could create a unified empire out of his conglomeration of lands and peoples he died suddenly in 323 B.C.[2]

With Alexander's death, the empire disintegrated, and the fallen leader's generals contested with one another to inherit the largest slice of territory.

The decades after 323 B.C. were marked by confusion and rivalry. Territories shifted from one contender to another. At one point four generals played the major role in the struggle, but eventually three major empires emerged. Ptolemy I Soter established himself as king of Egypt in 305 B.C. Another general, Seleucus, won Babylon and Syria. Antigonus, king of Phrygia, sought to create an empire for himself out of part of Alexander's domain in Macedonia and Asia Minor.

Ptolemaic Domination of Palestine

Palestine first fell into the Egyptian camp when Ptolemy I seized power there in 320 B.C., but Antigonus contested the Egyptian rule with armed force, and Ptolemy did not regain full control of Palestine until 301 B.C. During the course of the third century B.C. the Ptolemies dominated the region and brought an era of relative stability and peace. They permitted the high priest in Jerusalem to exercise some political power as well as religious power, and the Jews seemed to generally accept the rule of their Greek overlords.

Ptolemy I, drawn from a tetradrachma.
Courtesy Carta, Jerusalem.

Ptolemy I established the famous library of Alexandria, which played a major role in hellenizing the culture of the Near East. He also began resettling Jews in Alexandria, a process that would continue beyond his day. These Jews of the Dispersion (or Diaspora) learned the Greek language and adopted much of the Greek culture of their new city. Before Christ's birth Alexandria had a large Hellenistic Jewish population, which occupied its own area in the Greek city.[3]

Ptolemy II Philadelphus (284–246 B.C.) continued the flow of Jews to Alexandria and expanded the library. Traditions recorded by Josephus and the Jewish philosopher of Alexandria, Philo, date the translating of the Hebrew Scriptures into Greek in the reign of Ptolemy Philadelphus. The Jewish high priest, according to the traditional account, sent seventy-two scholars, six from each tribe, to Alexandria to translate the law. The translation is known as the Septuagint (Latin for seventy) because of the story that seventy or seventy-two men were engaged in the translation. The Roman numeral LXX serves as a convenient symbol for the Septuagint. Scholars believe the translation of the Pentateuch probably did occur about 275–250 B.C. but not in the manner suggested by the legend. It is more probable that the translation was the work of Alexandrian Jews who, without the aid of a Palestinian contingent, recognized the need for a version that could serve the needs of Greek-speaking Jews and proselytes. Many of the Jews returning from the Babylonian exile had learned Aramaic and lost their facility in the ancient Hebrew language. During the time of Christ, Aramaic had become the commonly spoken language among Palestinian Jews. Contrary to earlier views, however, some Bible scholars now believe that the use of Hebrew in Palestine during the New Testament age was not uncommon and, in fact, shared currency with Aramaic and Greek. But in the areas of the Dispersion the greater force of Greek influence would make familiarity with Hebrew the preserve of scholars. The Septuagint translation became the common version for Jews of the Dispersion who were scattered widely in the Roman Empire and was the Bible of the early Christians. New Testament writers frequently quoted or alluded to the Septuagint.

Seleucid Domination of Palestine

The Seleucids brought an end to Egyptian control of the Jewish homeland in 198 B.C. The new ruling dynasty had been founded by Seleucus I (312–280 B.C.), one of Alexander's commanders. He built the city of Antioch along the Orontes River in the plain between the Taurus and Lebanon ranges in Syria to serve as his capital. Along with a population of Greeks and Macedonians, an early nucleus of Jews grew to a significant segment of the community. Antioch in the Book of Acts later became a major Christian center and the home base for Paul's missionary journeys. Seleucus I originally held only Babylonia but also wrested Syria from Antigonus in 301 B.C. After a brief exile in Egypt he regained his throne and added part of Persia and Asia Minor to his growing empire. Somewhat like the polyglot Austro-Hungarian Empire of modern history the Seleucid domain was a congeries of unassimilable races and tongues.

Palestine fell under Seleucid domination in the era of Antiochus "the Great." By 223 B.C. when he came to power, he ascended the throne of a weakened Seleucid empire. The rulers preceding him had lost Asia Minor after numerous conflicts with the Ptolemies. Anxious to regain the lost territories, he pressed into Asia Minor and even to Greece. There he fell prey to the rising power of Rome. Returning from a defeat at Thermopylae, he was again subdued by the Romans at Magnesia in western Asia Minor. As a pledge to stand by the peace settlement with Rome after Magnesia, he sent his son, the future Antiochus IV, as a hostage to Rome. Despite these setbacks, Antiochus III had revived the flagging empire. He had restored much of eastern Asia Minor to the empire, defeated the Parthians and Bactrians to the east, and successfully contested the Ptolemies for control of Palestine.

In the Seleucid-Ptolemaic contest for control of Syria, Palestine frequently served as the battleground. The Ptolemies and later Napoleon himself regarded Palestine as essential for defense of the Nile. At Panium (Paneas), in the New Testament era called Caesarea Philippi, just south of Mount Hermon, the armies of Antiochus III finally routed the force of the Ptolemaic general Scopas in 198 B.C. With this engagement the land of Israel passed into the hands of the Seleucid rulers. Antiochus III gave the Jews a period of relative calm. He also upheld the traditional freedom of worship granted by Hellenistic rulers to subject peoples. Yet the Seleucids did not bring permanent serenity to Palestine. The continual intrigue and treachery of rivals for the throne, and the battles to suppress invasions at the frontiers of the empire inevitably drew Judea into a vortex of strife. Very few Seleucid monarchs after 300 B.C. had enjoyed the luxury of dying in bed. Nearly all met their end on the battlefield or as victims of the assassin's knife. It was the murder of Seleucus IV Philopator (187–175 B.C.), the successor of Antiochus III, that gave Antiochus IV an opportunity to claim the throne in 175 B.C. The new king's title, Epiphanes, suggested the appearance or manifestation of a deity, but with a slight change in spelling his opponents labeled him Antiochus "Epimanes" (the madman). Pious Jews resented the worship of this Antiochus as the Olympian Zeus.

The Rise of Hellenistic Influences

Tensions between the Hellenistic Jews, who favored adaptation of Judaism to patterns of Greek culture, and those stalwart defenders of the Jewish law and customs came to a head during the reign of Antiochus IV. But Hellenistic influences in Palestine did not originate with Antiochus. The Ptolemies had earlier built cities in imitation of the Greek model; Philadelphia (modern Amman, Jordan) and Philoteria at the southern end of the Sea of Galilee were carefully planned urban areas with Greek names and also a Greek way of life. During the era before Christ, cities such as Joppa, Ptolemais, Ascalon, Samaria, and Gadara were built on the model of the Greek *polis*. A labyrinthine street system characterized most oriental towns, but the Greek *polis* adopted the pattern proposed by the Greek architect Hippo-

damus. This system called for rectangular blocks, paved roads, and large open plazas on the main streets. The creation of Greek towns signified more than an external architectural change. A true *polis* would adopt Greek styles of political and financial management and would provide fertile ground for social, intellectual, and business contact between Jew and Greek.[4] Many Jewish priests and aristocrats were enamored of Hellenistic culture and their pressure for liberalization increased during the era leading up to Antiochus Epiphanes.

The Greek verb *hellenizein* meant "to speak Greek." It was used of non-Greek peoples who would not normally be expected to use the language. In a broader sense, "hellenization" refers to the acceptance of Greek culture outside of Greece. In addition to an appreciation for the Greek language and literature, a Jewish Hellenist also absorbed something of the spirit of Greek culture. Hellenists shared the Greek love for athletics, and they hoped Jerusalem itself might have a gymnasium. Athletes ran and wrestled nude in the sports stadiums, and, in fact, the word *gymnasium* was derived from the Greek word *gymnos* meaning "naked." This display of the body in public repelled those Jews who took seriously the frequent condemnation of nudity in the Old Testament. As early as the third chapter of Genesis, in the account of Adam and Eve, the Scriptures depict nakedness as something shameful. But nudity was not the only offensive aspect of Greek sports. The Greeks dedicated the athletic games to their gods. To participate in a contest honoring a Greek deity would be idolatry. Some of the young men of Jerusalem adopted the typical dress of the Greek athletes and the sight of their broad-brimmed hats on Jerusalem streets provoked disgust and rage.[5] Such Greek practices may have seemed innocuous to some Jews, but the defenders of Moses perceived that they were merely the outward visible form of a way of life that threatened to undermine the foundations of Jewish law.

Along with the spread of Greek athletics came a new interest in various oriental gods. Deities once worshiped within a single region—such as Isis, Serapis, and Atargatis—now became popular all across the Hellenistic world. The author of the apocryphal book, Wisdom of Solomon, written in Egypt a century before Christ, condemns the spread of idolatry: "For the worship of idols, whose names it is wrong even to mention, is the beginning, cause, and end of every evil." The writer also offered his explanation for the origin of the deification of emperors. When men could not pay homage to a king because he "lived far away, they made a likeness of that distant face, and produced a visible image of the king they sought to honor."[6] One group of Jews vehemently opposed the Hellenistic infiltration of their faith. The members of this puritan sect, known as the Hasidim (pious ones), were the spiritual ancestors of both the Pharisees and the Essenes.

Background of the Maccabean Revolt

It was not long before the assumption of the Seleucid throne by Antiochus IV Epiphanes was viewed by the Hasidim as a fateful event in Israel's history. His reign brought a spiritual and political crisis that precipitated a Jewish revolt and the creation of an independent nation that lasted a century.[7] The struggle for national freedom obsessed Jews from the time of Antiochus until the rebellion of Simon Bar Cocheba (A.D. 132), when such hopes flickered out. Only after an eighteen-century hiatus would Israel aspire to nationhood again. The nationalistic fervor awakened during the Maccabean Era (168–143 B.C.) helps explain why it was so difficult for Israelites of a later day to heed Jesus' teaching that his kingdom was not of this world. They were still looking for a political and nationalistic leader rather than one who would call on people to set aside hate, pride, and earthly ambitions, and to seek instead a kingdom of love.

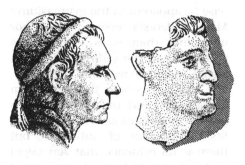

Antiochus Epiphanes (left) and his son Antiochus, drawn from a coin and a bronze mask respectively. Courtesy Carta, Jerusalem.

Antiochus IV unwisely embroiled himself in the political manipulations of those seeking to gain the office of high priest in Jerusalem. Jason, the brother of the reigning high priest, Onias III, offered the king a large sum of money to appoint him to the office in his brother's place. Antiochus apparently perceived in Jason an advocate of a more zealous Hellenizing policy. The latter had substituted the Greek name Jason for its Hebrew form, Joshua. The Syrian ruler could appreciate Jason's Hellenistic tendencies. After his release from Rome, Antiochus had spent some time in Athens before returning to Antioch. He had even held an Athenian office during his stay in Greece. Having a high regard for Greek culture as well as a need for the promised money, he appointed Jason.

The new high priest constructed a gymnasium in Jerusalem and encouraged the adoption of Greek ways of behavior. First Maccabees records that the king gave authority to "renegade Jews" to establish non-Jewish laws and customs. Some youthful Jews even tried to disguise their circumcision, which would otherwise be apparent in the gymnasium.[8] Many Hellenists received the honor of calling themselves Antiochenes and thus had the same privileges in Jerusalem as citizens in a Greek city. But it is not certain that Jerusalem actually received the name Antioch as some historians assert. Such an act fits the practice of Antiochus, but there is no evidence that Jerusalem had a change in form of government or name. To the consternation of Jason a new competitor outbid him for the high priesthood by offering three hundred talents above the sum Jason had agreed to pay. The usurper, Menelaus, did not meet the biblical standards for the office because he was not a descendant of Aaron.

Before the final chapter of the high priestly intrigues could be written, news of a Ptolemaic plot to recover Palestine for Egypt now diverted Antiochus. He invaded Egypt in 170–169 B.C., and tried to establish himself as the real power and protector of Egypt, but he could not subdue a strong force at Alexandria. Since Antiochus needed to build up his war chest for an anticipated second strike against Egypt, he plundered the gold furnishings of the temple in Jerusalem during his return journey to Antioch. First Maccabees 1:20–24 records this first outrage in the temple and lists the booty taken. Menelaus, the high priest, accompanied the king and thus condoned the sacrilege of a Gentile's entering the sacred precincts. The profaning of the sanctuary horrified faithful Jews and set the stage for the later revolt by casting Antiochus in the role of an enemy of Judaism. But the Judeans had also antagonized and wearied Antiochus by their volatile priestly politics. Before Antiochus' journey to Jerusalem and his sacrilege in the temple, he had heard news of a rebellion there. With a rebel force Jason had seized Jerusalem, ousted Menelaus, and invested himself again in the office of the high priest. The ouster of Antiochus' own appointee smacked of defiance of Seleucid authority. Thus not only avarice but also the necessity of keeping Jerusalem stable and loyal motivated the expedition to Jerusalem.

In 168 B.C. Antiochus led his army into Egypt for his second adventure there. He planned to assert more firmly his influence in the area, but a new force blocked his path. Popillius Laenus, a Roman envoy, arrived near Alexandria to deal with the ambitious

Seleucid conqueror. Rome had established itself as a power in the Near East by victories in a recent Macedonian campaign. The envoy demanded a disavowal of any Syrian pretensions in Egypt. Antiochus hoped to sidestep the issue by requesting time to ponder his response. In a dramatic scene Popillius Laenus drew his sword, traced a circle on the ground around Antiochus, and demanded an answer before the Syrian crossed the line. An embittered and angry Antiochus had to surrender to the growing power of Rome and scrap his Egyptian dream.

Having been frustrated by his eviction from Egypt in 168 B.C., Antiochus determined to pour out his wrath on Judea. He sent his revenue officer (apparently the Apollonius referred to in 2 Maccabees 5:24 as a leader of mercenary forces) to launch a surprise Sabbath Day assault on Jerusalem. The attackers slaughtered thousands of men, enslaved women and children, burned the city, and destroyed the walls. To keep Jerusalem in subjection the Seleucid forces built the citadel (or Acra), a walled fortress with high towers. Archaeologists cannot be certain of the exact location of the citadel, but it was apparently not far from the temple site and was meant to hold in check any rebellion that might rally about the holy shrine. Hellenistic Jews now fled to the citadel to join forces with the enemy garrison.

By placing Jerusalem under the domination of the citadel, Antiochus IV in effect repudiated the traditional Seleucid practice of allowing the Jews to enforce the Mosaic law. Idolatry and Sabbath breaking had been illegal in the temple-state of Judea, and the aristocratic priestly leadership had possessed the authority to require religious obedience. Antiochus not only revoked the religious independence of Israel, but by 167 B.C. he also began a policy of religious oppression. His attack on Judaism itself may have been motivated by a desire to unify his empire politically, but to the Jews it was an attempt to destroy their faith. The Macedonian rulers in the Hellenistic world were polytheists and had difficulty understanding the exclusiveness of the Jews. Possibly Antiochus did not anticipate the resolute defiance that would greet his introduction of new deities into the temple. The king by decree prohibited possession of the Torah, circumcision of children, observance of festivals, and the offering of sacrifice to Jehovah. He ordered the Jews to erect altars and offer sacrifice to pagan deities. Defiance of the decree meant capital punishment. In December of 167 B.C., the Syrian ruler dedicated the Jewish temple to the Olympian Zeus by sacrificing a sow on the altar of burnt offering.

The Book of 1 Maccabees is a valuable source for reconstructing the history of the Jewish revolt and the struggles in the period 167–135 B.C. Historians also make use of but give less credence to 2 Maccabees, which records the rebellion up to 160 B.C. The meaning of the term *Maccabee* is not certain, but it possibly meant "hammer." The Jewish people designated Judas, their brave guerrilla commander, "the Maccabee." The plural form, *Maccabees*, refers to the Jewish forces who fought against the Syrians.

Beginning of the Insurrection

An incident in Modin, about eighteen miles northwest of Jerusalem, sparked the Maccabean revolt. Seleucid officials were visiting the towns of Judea to supervise compliance with an edict from Antiochus ordering the Jews to make sacrifice to pagan gods. At Modin the king's agent appealed to a respected elderly Jew named Mattathias to step to the altar before his fellow villagers and make the first offering. When the resolute Mattathias refused, another Jew stepped forward and made the sacrifice. Full of indignation, Mattathias rushed to the altar and slew both the renegade Jew and the king's officer. With the war cry "Follow me, every one of you who is zealous for the law and strives to maintain the covenant," he led his sons—John, Simon, Judas, Eleazar, and Jonathan—their wives, and other supporters into the bleak Judean wilderness region.[9] A large number of other zealous Jews joined the rebels in the wilds. The Syrians, finding one group hiding in caves, slaughtered nearly one thousand men, women, and children. Because this assault came on a Sabbath Day, the Jews suffered death rather than resist. Mattathias decided that in the future he would be ready to fight seven days a week.

The Leadership of Judas

The guerrilla movement was not only a revolt against Seleucid religious innovations but also a civil war among the Jewish people. Mattathias' warriors forcibly circumcised children whose parents had complied with the prohibitions. The rebels tore down the pagan altars and killed Jews who practiced idolatry. Before Mattathias died (about 166 B.C.) he appointed his son Judas as military commander. Judas wore down the Seleucids by hammering away at their forces with continual guerrilla attacks. The Book of 1 Maccabees compared the new leader to a "lion in his exploits, like a lion's whelp roaring for prey."[10] When Antiochus sent larger forces into Judea to subdue the Maccabees, Judas began organizing his guerrillas into an army that could hold its own on the field of battle.

Remains of the tombs of the Maccabees at Modi'in. Courtesy Zev Radovan.

After winning a series of victories, Judas enjoyed one of his greatest triumphs at Beth Zur, in 164 B.C., on the southern boundary of Judea. Antiochus had appointed Lysias governor of Syria and had placed him in charge of the Judean war. Because Lysias' generals had suffered several defeats, the governor personally led sixty thousand select infantry and five thousand cavalry through Idumea to attack Judea from the south at Beth Zur. With a smaller force of ten thousand men, Judas routed the Syrian army. In the fall of the same year, 164 B.C., Judas captured Jerusalem, but he was unable to drive the Syrian garrison from the citadel. The Jews tore down the altar to Zeus that had been constructed over the altar of burnt offering and rebuilt it with new unhewn stones. After lighting the menorah (the lamps on the lampstand), placing the Bread of the Presence on the table, and restoring the other furnishings, he reconsecrated the temple to the worship of Jehovah. This restoration of the sacrifice occurred on Kislev 25, 164 B.C. (December 14), exactly three years after the altar was desecrated. The Gospel of John (10:22) makes reference to the annual Feast of Dedication (or Feast of Lights), which celebrated the reconsecration of the temple. Known today as Hanukkah, the eight-day festival's activities include the rekindling of the menorah each evening.

Judas now extended the war beyond the confines of Judea. When the Jewish high priests presided over the temple-state under the Ptolemies and Seleucids, they did not exert political influence south of Beth-zur, in the trans-Jordan area, in Samaria, or in the coastal plain. Now Judas ordered his warriors to enter those regions and to subdue hostile Gentile peoples who opposed the rising power of the Maccabees. After sending forces to Gilead, Galilee, Idumea, and the coastal plain, he turned his energies toward capturing the only Syrian fortification in Jerusalem, the citadel. Besieged by Judas' army, the Hellenistic Jews holding the fortress sent a desperate appeal for help to the governor. The Syrians under Lysias now reversed the tide of battle by laying siege to the fortified temple area.

Fragment of a bone object from Beth Zur, showing Egyptian influence on Canaanite art. Courtesy Israel Department of Antiquities and Museums.

Judas and the defenders of Jerusalem might have been forced to surrender had not the Syrians been diverted by one of their recurring internal quarrels. Antiochus IV had willed that his young son and heir, Antiochus V, be under the care of Philip, a high-ranking member of the king's court. Lysias, ignoring the will, had taken custody of the boy and seized the empire, but now word came that the legitimate regent was returning from Persia to assert his

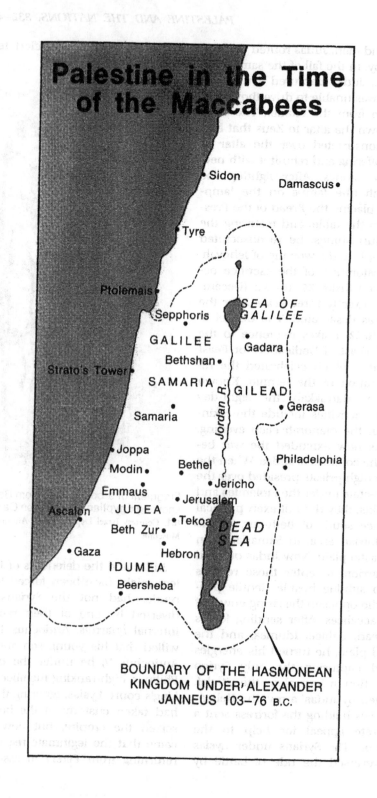

Palestine in the Time of the Maccabees

- Sidon
- Damascus
- Tyre
- Ptolemais
- Sepphoris

SEA OF GALILEE

- GALILEE
- Gadara
- Bethshan
- Strato's Tower

SAMARIA

GILEAD

- Samaria
- Gerasa

Jordan R.

- Joppa
- Modin
- Bethel
- Philadelphia
- Emmaus
- Jericho
- Ascalon
- Jerusalem
- JUDEA
- Tekoa

DEAD SEA

- Beth Zur
- Gaza
- Hebron

IDUMEA

- Beersheba

BOUNDARY OF THE HASMONEAN
KINGDOM UNDER ALEXANDER
JANNEUS 103–76 B.C.

authority. Syrian instability often proved to be a providential means of delivering the Maccabean rebels. The surprising success of a small rebel Judean band in asserting itself against a major power can be partially understood in the context of the intrigues and rivalries that diverted Syrian attention. The situation is reminiscent of that of the United States as a young republic gaining diplomatic victories over its powerful European rivals by playing one against another. The distresses of great powers offer opportunities for small ones to advance their interests. Lysias had no choice but to end his siege of Jerusalem, and in the bargaining Judas was able to secure a treaty in 163 B.C., guaranteeing the traditional religious freedoms of Judea. But Judas did not win a total victory; the Syrians demolished the walls of Jerusalem and retained control of the citadel.

The treaty did not end the conflict. Not satisfied with religious concessions alone, Judas set out to obtain political independence for Israel. A new Syrian ruler, Demetrius I, sought to end the rebellion by capturing the Jewish leader. But he failed to snare Judas in his net. Demetrius I had taken power in what had become almost the normal Seleucid manner, over the slain bodies of the enemy— this time of the boy king, Antiochus V, and Lysias.

Judas Allies With Rome

Believing that Judea needed powerful friends, Judas sent an envoy to Italy to appeal to the Roman Senate for an alliance. The ambassadors returned with an agreement inscribed on bronze tablets. Both parties contracted to give aid to the other if attacked, especially arms, ships, money, and food supplies. Judas evidently recognized the growing power of the Roman Empire, which had earlier driven Antiochus III the Great from western Asia Minor at the Battle of Magnesia and had thwarted Antiochus IV in his ambitions to dominate Egypt. But Rome's power was not yet sufficient to deter Demetrius I from his determination to check Judas' ambitions. By this time in history the Romans had reached only the fringes of the Near East. They needed to stabilize western Asia Minor and North Africa before trying to expand into the Seleucid regions. Since Rome would not be able to move its legions into Palestine for another century, it does not appear that the Roman alliance helped Judas in any material way. The Syrians, after suffering further defeats at the hand of Judas, finally sent a massive force to Elasa (exact location uncertain) in 160 B.C. to dispose of the Maccabee. Although many of Judas' soldiers deserted in the face of such a large army, leaving a force of only eight hundred, he courageously went out to battle. The Syrians routed his army, and Judas himself fell in the battle.

The Leadership of Jonathan

The loss of the Maccabean leader brought a period of renewed Syrian and Hellenistic power. Some of the Jewish resistance forces melted away, and some reverted to guerrilla-type warfare from their wilderness bases in Tekoa. The choice of Judas' brother Jonathan to deliver Israel from its enemies is described in 1 Maccabees in terms reminiscent of the rise of the Old Testament judges.[11] In times of oppression God had provided a judge to bring the land rest. Internal dissension in Syrian politics again came to the rescue for the Jewish freedom fighters. Two rival claimants to the Syrian throne, recognizing their need for support from Judea, tried to outbid each other in offering concessions to Jonathan in exchange for his backing. Jonathan cast his lot with Alexander Balas, who emerged victorious in a long struggle with the other factional leader, Demetrius. Alexander Balas appointed Jonathan high priest, gave him the title "King's friend," and sent him a gold crown and purple robe. The acceptance of such honors indicated that the Maccabean leaders were willing to enmesh themselves in the tangled web of Syrian intrigue in order to secure political power. They would exploit a revolt forged in the fires of religious zeal to gain secular power and worldly ambitions. Because of their increasingly political outlook, the Maccabees lost the support of the Hasidim. The appointment of Jonathan as high priest was significant in that it led to the linkage between the office of high priest and the office of king. Many of the Jewish rulers after the time of Jonathan would become priest-kings. This linkage seriously injured the spiritual and moral standing of Israel's high priesthood. The office would become an instrument used by unworthy men who sought political leadership.

Jonathan rebuilt his army, strengthened his control over Judea, constructed a wall in Jerusalem to hold in check the Syrian garrison in the citadel, reaffirmed the alliance with Rome, and entered into a new agreement with Sparta. But his increasing military power and his support of Antiochus VI (the current ruler of Syria) incited the wily Trypho, one of a new series of contestants for the Seleucid throne, to plot the death of the Judean leader. Trypho led his army to Bethshan but feared to attack the larger force of Jonathan. He then lured Jonathan to a peace parley at Ptolemais (Acco) on the seacoast, where he treacherously murdered the Judean escort and put Jonathan in chains. The leadership of Israel fell to Simon, the last surviving son of Mattathias. Although Simon paid a ransom for his brother's release, Trypho eventually executed the guerrilla leader during a campaign east of the Jordan.

The site of Tekoa, birthplace of the prophet Amos. It lies four miles south of Bethlehem. Courtesy B. Brandl.

Independence Established Under Simon

In 143 B.C. an assembly of the citizens of Jerusalem acknowledged Simon as their leader. The new defender of Israel rejected the claims of

Edom, a land of rugged mountains and plateaus; it extends from the Dead Sea to the Gulf of Aqabah. Courtesy Studium Biblicum Franciscanum, Jerusalem.

the upstart Trypho to the Syrian throne. Although Trypho did manage to seize power, his claim was weakened by the fact that he was not descended from the line of Seleucus I. As the price for joining the ranks of Trypho's rival, Demetrius II, Simon secured a treaty, in 142 B.C., that virtually established the independence of Judea from Syria. The concession by Demetrius II granting exemption from all tribute and taxation inaugurated an era of national freedom that endured until 63 B.C. when Pompey subjected the Jews to Roman rule. Simon tightened his grip on Judea by capturing the citadel. Jerusalem would no longer endure the hostile gaze of this fortress that had harbored Syrian mercenaries and Hellenistic Jews. During the ensuing brief era of relative peace and stability, the nation struck its own coinage and confirmed the right of Simon and his heirs to rule in perpe-

tuity. An inscription on bronze tablets deposited in the temple declared him to be "high priest, general and ethnarch of the Jews."[12] Simon's rule over an independent nation, although he did not formally receive the title of king, may be considered the beginning of the Hasmonean Dynasty. The term *Hasmonean* derives from the name of an obscure ancestor of Mattathias. This dynasty held control until Pompey's invasion of Judea.

The Reign of John Hyrcanus

Simon's own son-in-law, Ptolemy, murdered him and two of his sons in a quest for power. But another son, John Hyrcanus (135–105 B.C.), eluded Ptolemy, established himself as ruler, and gave Judea a long era of territorial expansion and relative stability. But even prosperous reigns were not fully free of turmoil in the Hasmonean era, and the independence of

Judea endured a brief eclipse early in John Hyrcanus' reign. The current ruler of Syria, Antiochus VII, laid siege to Jerusalem for a year and retired after forcing the Jews to accept terms that included an alliance with Syria and payment of tribute for certain cities on Judea's boundaries.

John Hyrcanus freed himself of these limitations when Antiochus VII died (128 b.c.). He regained the coastal cities lost to Antiochus VII and pushed his boundaries eastward beyond the Jordan to include Moab. Seizing Idumea, to the south of Judea, he forcibly circumcised the males and required obedience to the Torah. A crusade for religious liberty now deteriorated into a movement for religious oppression. This subjection of the Edomite people linked Israel's fortunes with Idumea and bore strange fruit later when a despised Idumean, Herod the Great, became Rome's puppet and ruled over a nation of Jews who loathed him. In 128 b.c., John Hyrcanus led an army into Samaria and destroyed the rival Samaritan temple on Mount Gerizim. Near the end of his long reign he leveled the city of Samaria itself after a one-year siege.

The Rise of the Pharisees and Sadducees

According to Josephus' *Antiquities of the Jews* (XIII. X. 5,6) the Pharisees and Sadducees made their first appearance in the reign of John Hyrcanus. It is not clear whether the terms *Pharisee* and *Sadducee* were actually used in the late second century, or if Josephus used the designations anachronistically. But, regardless of when the terms might have first appeared, the two parties were clearly in existence during the second century b.c. The Pharisees probably were an outgrowth of the Hasidim, who had supported the Maccabees and were a strict orthodox Jewish group. The etymology of the term *Pharisee* is uncertain, but it is generally believed to have meant "separatist." Like the Puritans of modern history, the Pharisees viewed themselves as separated from the corrupting influences of those who were lax in following God's Law. The origin of the term *Sadducee* is also shrouded in obscurity. The most common opinion holds that the designation derived from Zadok, the name of Solomon's chief priest, who was the progenitor of a long line of revered priests. The fact that the Sadducees were associated with the priestly and aristocratic class in Judea lends some weight to this etymology. But it does not seem likely that the Hasmonean high priest would adopt a name that reminded the people of the Zadokite priests. Antiochus IV Epiphanes terminated the rule of the Zadokites when he removed the high priest Menelaus. In the Maccabean period the Zadokite line was reestablished only at a rival temple in Leontopolis, Egypt. The Hasmoneans who acquired the office of high priest and derived their power from it were not in the Zadokite line. It is not likely they would encourage the use of a name that called into question their fitness for the position. Because the Sadducees identified themselves with the ruling class in Judea and were more concerned with power and political stability than with the resolute defense of the fine points of the Law, they bear more resemblance to the Hellenistic Jews than to the Hasidim.[13]

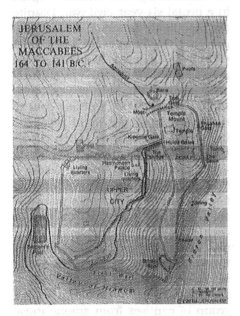

JERUSALEM OF THE MACCABEES 164 TO 141 B.C.

In the time of John Hyrcanus the two parties debated the basis for interpreting the law. The Pharisees insisted on the validity of an oral tradition that interpreted and exemplified the Torah. Jesus later condemned their ostentatious scrupulosity in tithing even mint, anise, and cummin because in trying to so precisely apply the law in a detailed and legalistic manner they missed the major spiritual lessons of the law. Some Pharisees were surely sincere and devout men, such as Nicodemus and Joseph of Arimathea in the New Testament, but a well-meaning devotion to a mass of regulations could easily deteriorate into hypocrisy and mock piety. In contrast with the Pharisees, the Sadducees rejected any external oral accretions to the written word and observed only the authority of the Mosaic Law itself. John Hyrcanus, during most of his reign, enjoyed a close alliance with the Pharisees. They pronounced him "entirely virtuous," and their moral approbation gave him much satisfaction, but he eventually sided with the Sadducees. According to Josephus, Eleazar, an influential Pharisee, challenged John Hyrcanus' worthiness to hold the office of high priest. Eleazar repeated a false tale that cast doubt on the legitimacy of John's lineage. This incident suggests an uneasiness on the part of the more scrupulous Jews with the high priestly rule of a man like John Hyrcanus, whose concerns were more political than pious. Although John's successors sometimes allied with the Pharisees, their Hellenistic and secular temperament seems more in line with the Sadducean character.

The Rule of Alexander Janneus

The death of John Hyrcanus in 104 B.C. initiated seven decades of decline and degradation for the Hasmonean Dynasty. John intended for his wife to succeed him as ruler and for his eldest son, Aristobulus, to be high priest. But Aristobulus imprisoned three of his brothers, had a fourth murdered, and starved his mother to death in prison. According to Josephus, he claimed kingship as well as the high priesthood. After a one-year reign he died unmourned.

Aristobulus' widow, Salome Alexandra, married one of the younger brothers who had been imprisoned, Alexander Janneus, and placed him on the throne. Janneus took the title of king, and during his unpopular reign he earned the hatred of the Jews for his barbarous excesses. Perhaps Josephus, our major source of

35

information, has been guilty of distortion in emphasizing the brutality of this "king." Because Janneus allied himself with the Sadducees during an era when that party was involved in bitter rivalry with the Pharisees, and since Josephus as a Pharisee would naturally be prejudiced against Janneus, it is possible that his record contains exaggerations. But even allowing for some distortion, the era of Janneus still emerges as a time of trial for the nation. At the very outset of his rule he murdered one of his surviving brothers. A series of endless campaigns, battles, and civil eruptions disturbed Judea in his time. There were serious thrusts into his domain, on different occasions, by the Egyptians, Armenians, Syrians, and the Nabatean Arabs, but he survived the crises and even enlarged his kingdom. Under Janneus the Hasmonean territory reached its farthest extent, equaling the bounds of Solomon's kingdom. His acquisitions included Gaza and Raphia in the coastal plain and Gadara, Gerasa, and Pella east of Galilee.

An incident that occurred while Janneus officiated at the altar during the Feast of Tabernacles illustrates the nation's dissatisfaction with their priest-king. During this festival the people traditionally carried palm branches and citrons, a yellow citrus fruit somewhat larger than a lemon. Shouting that he was unfit to offer sacrifice, the angry masses tossed their citrons at Janneus. This demonstration sparked a popular uprising, which the king tried to extinguish by the slaughter of six thousand of his countrymen. Later his army fell victim to a devastating Nabatean Arab ambush in Gilead, and when Janneus

returned to Jerusalem with his shrunken army, the nation erupted in a brutal six-year civil war. Despite the bloodbath, Janneus still clung to power. The Pharisees, in a last-ditch effort to bring down the irksome high priest, entered into a strange alliance. They secured the help of Demetrius III Eucerus of Syria, a descendant of the Syrian Antiochus Epiphanes who had defiled the temple. When Demetrius destroyed Janneus' mercenary army, the Pharisaic leaders feared a loss of the nation's independence. A force of six thousand Jews switched allegiance and came to the aid of their king. With reinforcements and new moral support, Janneus repelled the Syrian incursion. Then, according to Josephus, he marched back to Jerusalem bringing with him a large group of captives from among those Jews who had gone over to the Syrians. While feasting publicly with his concubines, the vengeful Janneus had eight hundred of these rebels crucified. He also ordered that the dying rebels witness a horrible scene during the ordeal of their slow death. Their wives and children were to have their throats cut before the crosses as a final spectacle for the condemned insurgents.

Two Brothers Vie for Power

Eventually Janneus himself met death on the battlefield, and his wife, Salome Alexandra, replaced him as ruler. She gave the nation nine years (76–67 b.c.) of peace and stability, but this was only a brief hiatus in an otherwise turbulent era. Salome reversed the policy of alliance with the Sadducee party and, possibly on advice of Janneus before his death, turned to the Pharisees for support. Because a woman could not serve as high priest, she chose her elder son Hyrcanus II to fill the office. He was a quiet, unassuming man with little desire for the hurly-burly game of politics, but his younger brother, Aristobulus II, ingratiated himself with the disgruntled Sadducees and used them as a lever to dislodge Hyrcanus from power. While the elderly Salome was ill and dying, he organized his forces to seize power. Although at Salome's death, Hyrcanus II inherited the kingship, Aristobulus II seized the title for himself and defeated Hyrcanus' army near Jericho. Hyrcanus, despairing because many of his followers had deserted to the side of his more aggressive brother, fled for refuge to the walled area of the temple. But Aristobulus moved his forces to Jerusalem and induced his older brother to relinquish both the office of king and the office of high priest and to retire to the life of a private citizen.

The settlement might have marked the conclusion of Hyrcanus' role in Jewish history except for the intervention of a new political force, a crafty Idumean leader named Antipater. His father, who had the same name but sometimes is referred to as Antipas, had been governor of Idumea during the reigns of Janneus and Salome Alexandra. This family, although not actually Jewish, would eventually give the Jews a kingly line in Herod the Great and his descendants. Antipater, the younger, deftly engineered events in a manner designed to secure power for himself behind the façade of a restored king, Hyrcanus II. Using his considerable powers of persuasion, Antipater maneuvered Hyrcanus into approving a movement to bring down Aristobulus. The defrocked priest took refuge in the Arab capital of Petra, where Aretas III took him in and agreed to an expedition against Aristobulus. In exchange for the alliance Hyrcanus and Antipater promised to restore to Aretas twelve cities in Moab that had been taken by Alexander Janneus. Many Jews who had fought for Aristobulus now deserted him for Hyrcanus, and the combined Arab and Jewish army pursued the bold usurper. When Aristobulus took refuge on the temple hill in 65 B.C., Aretas laid siege to the fortified area.

The Entrance of Roman Power

The unseemly power struggle for the Hasmonean throne made Judea easy prey for the voracious appetite of the Roman eagle. Only a few years before the two brothers clashed, Mithridates VI of Pontus represented the major bulwark that delayed further Roman penetration of the Near East. He expanded his realm to include areas on the eastern and northern coasts of the Black Sea and formed a solid front with Tigranes, king of Armenia, against the Romans. The decision of Mithridates to make satellites of Bithynia and Cappadocia provoked a long conflict with the Romans, who considered the area their protectorate. Lucullus, Roman governor of Asia, finally drove the Pontic adventurer westward into Armenia in 69 B.C. but could not follow up his successes because of mutiny in his army. Pompey, a popular military hero, now replaced Lucullus, and in 66 B.C. the senate authorized him to exercise almost unlimited power in the continuing crusade against Mithridates. Pompey's appointment came, in part, because he had used similarly broad powers to sweep pirates from the eastern Mediterranean. After Rome had disposed of Antiochus III (190 B.C.) at Magnesia, she had allowed her navy to deteriorate, and the pirates gained sufficient strength to prey on Rome's life-line, the crucial grain shipments from Egypt to Italy. Pompey disposed of the pirates within three months. With similar skill he brought Mithridates and Tigranes to their knees. Mithridates fled to his territories north of the Black Sea, where he later committed suicide, and Pontus became a Roman province. Tigranes lost areas in Cilicia and Syria, but he accepted an alliance with Rome and continued to rule as king of Armenia.

In the person of Pompey, Rome now moved from the wings onto the center stage of Palestinian politics. The Roman general easily seized the anarchic Seleucid realm in 63 B.C. and established Syria as a province. The two Jewish rival princes, Aristobulus II and Hyrcanus II, now appealed to Pompey to support their claims to the Judean kingdom. Pompey's legate to Syria, Scaurus, preceded his leader to Damascus, where he met the contenders. After receiving bribes from the aspiring Hasmoneans, he opted for Aristobulus and forced Aretas to end his siege of Jerusalem, but when Pompey arrived in Damascus, he reversed the decision of Scaurus and determined to install Hyrcanus as high priest. While Pompey delayed announcing his intentions, Aristobulus correctly anticipated an adverse decision and quickly moved south to

a fortress at Alexandrium in the Jordan Valley where he tried to organize a resistance. But he abandoned this fort at the insistence of Pompey and fled to Jerusalem for a final stand.

As Pompey's forces drew near Jerusalem, Aristobulus recognized the hopelessness of his cause, went to the Roman general's camp, and made an agreement to open the gates of the city to him. But the Jewish partisans in Jerusalem ignored Aristobulus' promise and refused to lay down their arms. As Pompey viewed it, the Jewish prince had betrayed him. He imprisoned Aristobulus and laid siege to the temple fortress for three months. With mechanical engines brought from Tyre the Romans hurled huge stones at the fortifications. A battering ram finally weakened a large tower, which upon collapsing ripped open a breach in the wall. Through the opening the conquerors swarmed into the city and slaughtered twelve thousand of the terrified defenders. Pompey and some of his officers entered the Holy of Holies. Although his act profaned the temple, since only the Jewish high priest was permitted to see the sacred chamber, he did not plunder the temple treasures. He permitted the cleansing of the sanctuary and the resumption of the worship of Jehovah.

Changes Under Roman Rule

Pompey appointed Hyrcanus II as high priest but denied him the title of king. Aristobulus II did not fare so well; the proud Roman took him back to Italy to be one of his trophies in a victory parade down the streets of Rome. Hyrcanus did not exercise effective power as high priest, but Antipater, because of his close political attachment to the Roman leaders, did wield considerable influence. Thus, for all practical purposes, ended the Hasmonean Dynasty. Later, Aristobulus and his heirs raised the standard of revolt but failed to reestablish the dynasty permanently. The independent status that Judea had enjoyed for eight decades was now lost as Judea became a part of the Roman province of Syria. The Romans removed many of the Hellenistic cities in the Decapolis (a region located mainly east of Jordan) from Judean administration. Some years after the time of Antipater these cities formed an alliance to ward off Arab attacks from the desert country to the east. By the time of Jesus this region had the name Decapolis, meaning literally "ten cities." The Romans also withdrew from Judean control the cities in the coastal area and Samaria, but Idumea, Perea, and most of Galilee were retained. The areas lost were primarily Gentile-populated lands that had been acquired by John Hyrcanus and Alexander Janneus. These Hellenistic cities gained independence from the Jewish religious community but fell under the direct control of the province of Syria. Syria's second Roman governor, Gabinius, divided what remained under Judean dominion into five administrative districts.

The two decades following the installment of Gabinius (57 B.C.) as governor of Syria witnessed a confused and tumultuous period in Judea. Aristobulus II and his heirs embroiled the country in a series of rebellions aimed at ousting Antipater along with his compliant stooge Hyrcanus II and restoring the more popular rule of Aristobulus' family. But the twenty-year period would end with victory for Antipater's son, Herod the Great, who captured Jerusalem and successfully established himself as king in 37 B.C. Beginning in 57 B.C. over the course of three years, the Hasmonean revolts became annual affairs. One Hasmonean heir, Alexander, managed to avoid the Roman net that had carried both his father, Aristobulus II, and a brother, Antigonus, captive to Rome. This Alexander initiated the first rebellions against Roman rule. Gabinius crushed the insurrection but unwisely released Alexander. The next year Aristobulus II escaped from his Roman confinement along with his son Antigonus, but father and son met defeat in a second revolt. Finally, Gabinius had to return from a military venture in Egypt to put down a third assault, led again by the rebel he had set free, Alexander. The people of Judea were restive under Roman rule, and their backing of these hopeless risings indicated that the Maccabean spirit of nationalism remained a glowing ember in the Jewish consciousness.

Rise of the Herodian Family

To the Romans the Judean turmoil must have seemed like a minor scuffle in the wings of a theater. At the center of the Roman stage powerful military commanders vied for ultimate control of the Republic. Originating with Marius at the beginning of the first century B.C., the generals began to recruit from the poorer classes, massive armies whose chief loyalty was not to the Republic but to the military commander who could provide them pay and the spoils of war. The round of contests did not cease until Octavian (Augustus) defeated Antony in a naval battle at Actium in 31 B.C. Judea's own troubles became inextricably enmeshed with the internecine strife of the clashing generals. Antipater and his son, Herod the Great, nimbly shifted alliances as they quickly abandoned Roman contenders whose fortunes were sinking and deftly maneuvered their cockboat into the wake of whatever commander seemed to be riding the crest. Both father and son had a knack for ingratiating themselves with the leader of the moment. Antipater's allegiance to Pompey made him suspect after Julius Caesar defeated the latter at Pharsalus in the summer of 48 B.C. But Antipater quickly won Caesar's favor by personally leading troops to Egypt to aid him in a venture there and by enlisting support for Caesar from the Jewish community at Alexandria.

Aristobulus II also hoped to make friends with Caesar and regain his lost influence. He had been returned to Roman captivity while Pompey was still in control of affairs. With Julius Caesar's rise he agreed to lead and command a pro-Caesar force against Pompey, but the mission aborted when Pompey's supporters poisoned the unfortunate Aristobulus. Pompey also ordered the execution of Aristobulus' son, Alexander.

Caesar rewarded Hyrcanus II and Antipater for their loyalty. Antipater received the office of governor of Judea and became a Roman citizen, while Hyrcanus became "ethnarch" of the Jews, a recognition of his role

as symbolic leader of the Jewish people both in Judea and in the Diaspora. Caesar guaranteed freedom of religious practice for the Jews, ended the division of the country into five districts, restored Joppa and some other areas lost under Pompey's tenure, and authorized the rebuilding of the walls of Jerusalem.

A drawing of a bust of Julius Caesar.
Courtesy Carta, Jerusalem.

Despite Caesar's concessions, the Jews despised the Romans and their vassal, Antipater. The Judeans also resented Antipater's appointment of his older son, Phasael, as governor of Jerusalem, and of Herod as governor of Galilee. Urged on by the Pharisees and the priesthood, Hyrcanus II brought charges before the Sanhedrin against Herod for his execution of a robber band in Galilee and its leader Ezekias (or Hezekiah). It was illegal to execute a man without the judgment of the Sanhedrin. Although

Herod made an appearance before the Sanhedrin, his power overawed Hyrcanus, and the charges were dropped. The swift and courageous manner in which Herod as governor had rooted out Ezekias' bandits and restored tranquility to the Syrian coast won the favor of the Syrian governor Sextus Caesar. The latter appointed Herod governor of Coele-Syria. The term *Coele-Syria* was a somewhat vague term referring to the southern portion of Syria. After the Sanhedrin had questioned his conduct in the execution of Ezekias, Herod considered retaliation against Jerusalem to humble the religious leaders, but Antipater restrained the young firebrand. Antipater's restraint was not to be available, however, after Rome entered its next leadership crisis period in 44 B.C. A group of conspirators arranged the assassination of Julius Caesar to save the Republic from his increasing monarchial tendency. After the stabbing of Caesar in the senate, one of the leaders of the *coup*, Cassius Gaius, became governor of Syria. Although Antipater quickly aligned himself with Cassius, he was poisoned in the ensuing power struggle.

The Romans under Cassius had failed to subdue the Parthian kingdom to the east of Syria. The intervention of Parthia in Palestine in 40 B.C. aroused discontented Jews to seize the opportunity to resist the power of Herod. The Parthians installed Antigonus II, son of the popular Aristobulus II, as king of Judea. In this new king, the Hasmoneans returned for a last brief interlude of power. Antigonus determined to rid himself of potential rivals. He cut off Hyrcanus' ears so that he could not regain the high priesthood (Leviticus 21 prohibits a mutilated person from serving at the altar). Phasael committed suicide rather than endure the vengeance of Antigonus.

Herod now headed for Rome to seek aid in recovering his office from Antigonus and the Parthians. Before he could make the trip Octavian and Antony had supplanted Cassius and Brutus as the dominant force in Rome, and the dexterous Herod had won Antony's confirmation of his position as tetrarch of Galilee. In Rome Herod, with the support of both Antony and Octavian, secured appointment as king of Judea by the senate in 40 B.C. But legal recognition did not mean actual possession of his kingdom. That would require a lengthy war. Herod landed at Ptolemais and began a desperate two-and-one-half-year struggle to oust Antigonus. Initially the Romans gave him little aid, but in the end they helped evict the Parthian invaders. Sosius, governor of Syria, joined Herod in a five-month siege of Jerusalem, and in 37 B.C. Herod finally possessed the kingdom. Mark Antony, at Herod's request, had Antigonus beheaded, and thus the brief resurgence of Hasmonean power ended. The political independence so valiantly wrested from the Seleucids had been lost for all practical purposes three decades earlier. Under Herod's firm rule, the Jews' visions of liberation seemingly dissolve into nothing more than hopeless fantasy. But few could have perceived that during the coming reign of Herod, little Bethlehem would see the birth of a Messiah who would proclaim deliverance from spiritual bondage for the people of Judea—and for all mankind.

Herod's palace, as shown in a model of Jerusalem in A.D. 66. This model is located in the Holyland Hotel, Jerusalem. Courtesy Israel Government Press Office.

Chapter 2

Herod the Great

Herod's Role as Client King

Herod successfully retained power as king in Judea from 37 to 4 B.C. by consistently making himself useful to the Romans. From the viewpoint of Rome he reliably fulfilled the role of a client king whose power ultimately derived from Rome but whose cultural ties with the people he ruled made Roman influence more palatable. The Jews were an individualistic people with an exclusive religion and deep dedication to their traditions. Because this region tended to be one of the more turbulent dependencies, the Romans preferred to rule indirectly through an allied king. The use of client kings in the less secure fringe areas of the Republic was not uncommon.

Despite Rome's confidence in him, Herod's link with the Jews was actually quite fragile. Not only did his Idumean ancestry identify him with the hated Edomites of Old Testament days, but his religious stance also aroused suspicion. Like his father, he maintained an association with Judaism that was only nominal. Herod's lack of genuine commitment to Judaism is demonstrated by an incident that occurred while he was in Rome. He received word at the senate of that body's ratification of his kingship, and immediately he accompanied Antony and Octavian to the Forum to offer sacrifice at Jupiter's shrine. Although Herod usually avoided any affront to the religious sensibilities of his subjects, his personal devotion to the God of Israel must have been very superficial. His outlook was more secular, cosmopolitan, and Hellenistic than that of the people he ruled. Herod's displacement of the popular Hasmonean line also offended the Jews. Despite such disadvantages, the Romans perceived in Herod a native ruler who could reliably carry out their own policies in Palestine and who had at least some understanding of the traditions and temperament of the people he governed. His stern grip on the kingdom rewarded the Romans with the stability and order they desired on their eastern borders, and consequently he enjoyed the favor of Rome.

An Evaluation of Herod's Character and Personality

Jewish history has seldom recorded the life of a ruler more paradoxical and intriguing than Herod. Most Christians know of the paranoid and brutal aspects of his character. They recall his slaughter of all the children under two years of age in Bethlehem (Matt. 2:16). This incident is not mentioned by Josephus, but such behavior is clearly consistent with the record of a ruler who ruthlessly put a host of enemies, rivals, and even members of his own household to death on the slightest rumor. Herod's order to the Magi to return after they had found the Child so that he might worship him reveals the cunning of a king who was ever alert to any political winds that might affect his control of the throne. Like a tightrope walker who skillfully manipulates his balancing pole, Herod cautiously wielded his scepter of power, always ready to adjust to any political shift that might threaten to topple him. During the struggles for control of the Republic, he nimbly switched allegiance from Cassius to Antony and then from Antony to Octavian.

Cunning and savagery were only the darker side of a complex personality. Herod also possessed a certain charisma that charmed others. Josephus described him as proficient with the javelin and bow, a skilled horseman, and an excellent hunter who on one outing "captured forty wild beasts."[1] He could skillfully per-

suade his Roman overlords to deal favorably with him whenever opponents charged him with misconduct. Some writers have extolled his intellectual and political capacities. He has even been described by a modern scholar as "far and away the most able and competent ruler the Jews ever had."[2] One of his biographers, Michael Grant, rates him as possibly the most gifted of all the Roman client kings, and as a ruler who had spectacular success in achieving prosperity and security for the Jews while maintaining a harmonious bond with Rome. But Grant sees Herod's goal of reconciling Jews to Rome as ultimately an unobtainable one, even for a remarkable leader. After Herod's death, his structure of Roman-Jewish cooperation crumbled with the Jewish Revolt of A.D. 66.[3] There can be little praise for Herod's performance as a father and husband, especially during his later years. In his last decade his mental and physical health deteriorated, his savagery intensified, his family turmoils escalated, and his firm grip on the helm of state loosened.

One might evaluate Herod's record from various vantage points, but the biblical perspective on his reign is seen in the story of the flight of Joseph's family to Egypt. The angel warned Mary and Joseph to take Jesus and escape the sword of Herod. Leaving by night, they did not return until the king had died. Herod may have offered security and prosperity for those who accepted the Roman yoke, but his designs on the infant Jesus meant that Christ would not live in Judea during his rule.

As soon as Herod had captured Jerusalem (37 B.C.) and was able to rule as king in fact as well as by the law of the Roman senate, he displayed his harsh character by executing forty-five aristocratic supporters of Antigonus. At the same time he also sharply curtailed the political influence of the Sanhedrin and the Sadducees. The Pharisees did not thrive under his regime, but according to Josephus they gained some favor at the outset because two of their leaders had advocated opening the gates of Jerusalem to Herod's army.

Three Major Challenges to Herod's Power

The Challenge From the Hasmoneans

During the first seven years of his reign Herod had to cope with major threats to his authority from three sources: the Hasmonean heirs, Cleopatra, and finally from the rise of Octavian to dominance after the battle of Actium (31 B.C.). The ambitions of the Hasmoneans created bitter conflict that centered in Herod's own palace because of his marriage into that family. Herod set aside Doris, the first of his ten wives, in order to marry a Hasmonean princess, Mariamne. This second marriage took place while Herod was besieging the supporters of Antigonus in Jerusalem. Since Mariamne was the granddaughter of Hyrcanus II, the alliance seemed politically advantageous for the Idumean, who needed some semblance of legitimacy. This match, however, involved more than a politically expedient union; Herod was deeply devoted to Mariamne. She, on the other hand, seemed something

less than enthralled with her husband, whose rise meant the eclipse of her family's authority. Her mother, Alexandra, looked upon Herod's clan with disdain and bitterness.

Alexandra especially resented Herod's appointment of a little-known Babylonian to the high priesthood instead of her own seventeen-year-old son, Aristobulus. Ananel, the new high priest, could claim descent from the respected Zadokite line, which had served as a source of Aaronic priests until Maccabean days. Herod did invite the former Hasmonean high priest Hyrcanus II to return from exile to Judea, but because Antigonus had cut off the old priest's ears, Hyrcanus could not be considered again as a candidate for the high priesthood. Bowing to pressure from Mariamne and her mother, Herod finally deposed his Babylonian appointee and, although appointment was supposedly for life, invested his brother-in-law, Aristobulus, with the sacerdotal office. Many of the Jews wept with joy at the sight of Aristobulus, a Hasmonean prince, officiating at the Feast of Tabernacles in the sacred vestments. Because this popular acclaim for a Hasmonean chagrined Herod, he arranged an "accidental" drowning incident at Jericho for the young priest. In what appeared to be a playful ducking party some young men held the priestly bather under water too long. The murder of Aristobulus disposed of a potential rival claimant to Herod's throne and left only the weak Hyrcanus II as a possible danger.

The Challenge From Cleopatra

The apparent "accident" did not deceive Alexandra. She saw the sinister hand of Herod in the death of her son, and in a vengeful fury she appealed to Cleopatra of Egypt for aid. Mark Antony had by this time fallen under Cleopatra's spell and might use his authority to the disadvantage of Herod. At the Egyptian queen's insistence, Antony summoned Herod to appear before him at Laodicea to answer the charges against him. The Idumean knew Antony could take his life and, given the latter's lustful reputation, even seize the beautiful Mariamne for himself. To prevent his wife from falling into Antony's hands, Herod secretly arranged with his uncle Joseph, who was also married to his sister Salome, to slay both Mariamne and Alexandra if he did not return from the trial. But to the surprise of the family he did return, with his powers intact. Herod's sister Salome resented the haughty Hasmoneans and informed Herod that Mariamne had committed adultery with Joseph during his absence. Because Joseph had revealed to Mariamne the secret of his orders to kill her if Herod was executed, the king assumed, and possibly incorrectly, that the malicious rumor about adultery must be true. He spared Mariamne this time but executed Joseph.

Herod failed to stifle the ambition of Cleopatra for Judean territory. Although she would be the last of the Ptolemies to even hold power, she entertained visions of restoring Ptolemaic control over Palestine. The worst setback for Herod came when Antony granted to her the Jericho area, prized for its balsam trees. These trees exuded a medicinal gum highly valued for its healing properties. Herod now had to pay rent for use of the lands. Antony also gave his consort part of Herod's Mediterranean coastal lands as well as Arab regions east of Galilee. He gave Herod the task of collecting rent for Cleopatra from Malchus I for the latter's Arab lands.

The Challenge to Herod's Power From the Rise of Octavian

Herod's responsibility for collections from the reluctant Nabatean Arabs indirectly saved him from the wrath of Octavian. If Antony had not ordered Herod to lead an expedition to subdue the rebellious Arabs, the Idumean would have taken his forces into battle alongside Antony against Octavian. The two leaders, Octavian and Antony, desperately competed for control of the Republic. When the showdown came at Actium in 31 B.C., Cleopatra fled the battle scene, and Mark Antony's fleet, unable without her aid to withstand Octavian's ships, also set sail for Egypt. Now that Octavian controlled the Mediterranean world, Herod pondered how he might ingratiate himself with the victor of Actium. Before he set out to confer with Octavian at Rhodes, he disposed of the one Hasmonean who could supplant him as king of Judea. Accusing Hyrcanus II of complicity with Malchus and the Arab rebels, he ordered his followers to strangle the elderly priest. At Rhodes Herod openly confessed his former loyalty to Antony but now swore to give the same allegiance to Octavian. Rome's new master accepted the offer and established a close relationship with Herod that continued until the latter's death. Not long after Herod switched his allegiance, Antony and Cleopatra committed suicide. Octavian displayed his support for Herod by returning to him the lands taken by Cleopatra.

Herod's rising political star was not accompanied by domestic peace. On his return from Rhodes his sister Salome and his mother Cypros again kindled doubts in his suspicious mind about the faithfulness of Mariamne. On this occasion he took action and had her executed (29 B.C.), but his remorse for the deed drove him to the brink of insanity. In 28 B.C. Herod fell sick, and Alexandra schemed to seize control of the fortresses in Jerusalem, but the king got wind of his mother-in-law's plot and arranged for her execution also. The three women—Cleopatra, Mariamne, and Alexandra—who had so often vexed him were now removed from the scene.

Herod's Achievements in an Era of Stability (27 B.C.–14 B.C.)

Except for a rebellion in 25 B.C., the period between 27 and 14 B.C. brought fewer challenges to Herod's authority, and his kingdom increased in wealth, size, and cultural achievements. He continued to maintain a good relationship with Octavian, who would usually be known after 27 B.C. by his title Augustus, meaning "worthy" or "honored." Augustus favored Herod by placing new territories under his rule. In addition to his original lands in Idumea, Judea, Galilee, and Samaria, he received Trachonitis, Batanea, and Auranitis in 22 B.C., and Iturea in 20 B.C. He eventually held sway over an area comparable to Solomon's domain.

Surrounding himself with men ed-

ucated in philosophy, literature, and art, Herod made his court a center for Greek culture. In the vanguard of the literati was Nicholas of Damascus, a historian whose voluminous writings on Herod's era became a major source for Josephus. Nicholas served the king as a trusted counselor, teacher, and friend. The influence of Greek-Roman culture became even more apparent to the Jews when Herod decided to celebrate the Olympic Games in Jerusalem. His cultural innovations offended the devout. The offering of daily sacrifices to Caesar may have won favor in Rome, but it angered many of Herod's subjects. Near the end of his long reign, when he was terminally ill, a band of angry Jews plucked up their courage and pulled down the Roman eagle that Herod had raised above the temple entrance. But the king's firm rule did bring some benefits to his people. He may have relied on a sinister spy network to maintain control, but he also ended the constant plundering of the land by bandits and insurrectionist gangs.

Herod's lavish building programs

A model of the three towers of Herod's palace. Courtesy Zev Radovan.

demonstrated his Hellenistic temperament. The Romans adopted Greek architectural styles and left their monuments throughout the Mediterranean world. King Herod followed the Roman model by constructing impressive structures, not only in Palestine, but also in other lands. The outlay of vast sums to build foreign projects has been condemned as an unwarranted drain on the resources of Judea, but it has also been justified on the grounds that it evoked in the Jews of the Diaspora a sense of national pride. The enhanced prestige for Herod may also have strengthened his political reputation in Rome. Josephus provides a lengthy account of his beneficence.[4] In Antioch of Syria he constructed a large polished marble plaza where there had been an expanse of dirt and squalor. Cities as distant as Athens, Pergamum, Sparta, Damascus, Byblos, Tyre, and Sidon received monuments or gifts. Some of Herod's grants aided the renovation of temples or shrines dedicated to pagan deities like Apollo. He also enlarged the city of Samaria and renamed it Sebaste, a Greek synonym for the Latin title Augustus. Herod also honored Augustus by dedicating a new temple to him in Sebaste.

One of Herod's most ambitious projects was the building of the city and artificial harbor of Caesarea. Since Palestine had no natural harbors on the coastline between Dora and Joppa, Herod decided to build an artificial one at a place called Strato's Tower. There, he positioned huge limestone blocks in the sea to create a protected area for ships. The Roman character of the city is apparent in its theater, amphitheater, hip-

podrome, and temple to Augustus. He also inaugurated "Caesar's Games," athletic contests to be held at Caesarea every five years. In the time of Jesus and Paul, this magnificent city served as the administrative capital, and Herod's palace in Caesarea became the official residence of the Roman prefects. Herod's other palaces, fortresses, and varied projects are too numerous to list.

The aqueduct built by Herod the Great to transport water to Caesarea. Photo by Richard L. Niswonger.

For Judaism the crowning structural achievement of the Herodean period was the erection of the third temple. Some Jews shrank back at first from any tampering with the hallowed old postexilic temple (Zerubbabel's temple), fearing that a renovated temple might even become a focus for introducing pagan idols, but eventually the new building evoked pride and awe among all those who made pilgrimages to the holy city. Herod encouraged priests to learn masonry and carpentry skills so that no Gentile need set foot on the most sacred areas. The craftsmen took up their tools in 20 or 19 B.C., and within eighteen months finished the shrine itself. During the first eight years of the project, the Jews built most of the temple area structures, but they did not complete the whole complex until A.D. 64, just six years before Titus' army destroyed it. During the time of Christ the project had been, for practical purposes, nearly finished. In the first year of his ministry, Jesus' critics referred to the temple building as having been under construction for forty-six years (John 2:20), but most of the work had already been completed over thirty years before. Herod refurbished the old Hasmonean tower on the northwest corner of the temple area and named it Antonia after his friend Mark Antony. An open courtyard of this new fortress became the scene for Christ's hearing before Pilate. Although the rubble of the temple today lies hidden beneath a Moslem mosque, one part of the complex is visible. Tourists and devout Jews often visit the Western Wall (or Wailing Wall), which is used as a place of prayer. Originally it had been one part of the large outer wall that Herod built around the temple area.

The Struggle for the Succession to Herod's Kingdom

After 14 B.C. Herod's troubles multiplied. His new wives and their sons spun webs of deceit and intrigue as they anticipated his death and the opportunity to inherit the kingdom. The harried king had married a total of ten women. His first wife, Doris, and her son Antipater had been sent away from the palace when the king married Mariamne. The latter had two sons who survived childhood, Alexander and Aristobulus. These two Hasmoneans believed they had a

greater claim to the realm than the sons of the non-Hasmonean women. After the execution of Mariamne, Herod had many wives in his palace at the same time, and the consequent jealousies and plots created a turbulent domestic life. Another wife with the same name, Mariamne, sometimes referred to as Mariamne II, bore Herod Philip. A fourth marriage, to a Samaritan woman Malthace, produced two sons who would eventually be victorious in the succession struggle—Antipas and Archelaus. The next wife, Cleopatra of Jerusalem, was the mother of Philip. Her son also inherited part of Herod's kingdom. Herod had other wives and children, but those named above became the major participants in the swirl of intrigues that plagued Herod's later days.

Part of the Wailing Wall in Jerusalem.
Courtesy Israel Government Office.

Not only did Alexander and Aristobulus believe the kingdom rightfully should devolve to them as sons of the Hasmonean Mariamne, but the people also preferred them to their half-brothers. Herod sent them to Rome to be educated and intended they should succeed him, but the two young men rashly aired in public their bitterness over the unjust execution of their mother. The king's brother Phreroras and sister Salome exploited for their own purposes the indiscreet complaints of the brothers. They suggested to Herod that something more serious than simple pity for their mother motivated the young men. Salome had hopes of displacing the two with her own son, and she lost no chance to bend Herod's ear with her malicious distortions. Believing the brothers needed a warning, Herod invited the exiled Antipater, son of his first wife, to return to the palace. At first, he intended to introduce this rival only as a means of curbing the insolence of Mariamne's sons, but Antipater shrewdly maneuvered himself into the place of preeminent favor with his father. Like Salome, Antipater sought to poison the king's mind against the two favorites in hopes of supplanting them, and he succeeded. Herod came to believe that Alexander and Aristobulus were plotting against him, and he appeared before Augustus in 13 B.C. to make an accusation against them. But Augustus managed to reconcile the father to his sons.

On his return to Jerusalem, Herod decided to designate all three sons as kings, but he appointed Antipater his first heir. The calumnies and plots only increased, and Herod's suspicions and his inability to discern between truth and rumor grew apace. A Greek from Lacedemonia, named Eurycles, now entered the court intrigues in an attempt to exploit them to his own advantage. Josephus describes this curious interloper as "a man of perverse mind, and so cunning in his ways of voluptuousness and flattery, as to indulge both, and yet seem to indulge neither of them."[5] Antipater bribed him to cultivate an intimate friendship with Alexander and Aristobulus. After hearing in confidence their bitter complaints against their father, Eurycles broke the trust by revealing all to the king along with some creative embellishment of his own. The news enraged Herod, and he sought permission from Augustus to execute the brothers. The emperor insisted on a trial at Berytus (Beirut), which was outside Herod's jurisdiction. There a jury consisting of Romans and members of Herod's family pronounced both Alexander and Aristobulus guilty of treason, and they were strangled to death at Sebaste.

Antipater did not enjoy his role of favored heir very long. The ever-vigilant Salome supplied her brother king with intelligence reports on the suspicious activities of the ambitious son. Antipater sensed the mounting danger and took refuge in Rome, but Herod now heard reports implicating Antipater in a plan to poison him. Trying not to arouse any apprehension on Antipater's part, he invited him to return to Judea for an ostensibly friendly reception. The father immediately imprisoned the returning son and later (5 B.C.) secured Augustus' authorization to execute him. Concerning the incident, Augustus remarked in jest that one might fare better as Herod's pig than his son. The play on words is evident in Greek since the words for pig (*hus*) and son (*huios*) begin with the same letters in that language.

Herod's Death and the Final Settlement

Herod died after an extended illness, just five days after he had executed Antipater. His maladies as described by Josephus included a fire that "glowed in him slowly," ulcerated entrails, colitis, and convulsions. When he was near death, his physicians sent him to bathe in the warm springs at Calirrhoe beyond the Jordan, but the waters did not assuage his suffering. Aware that Judea would rejoice at his passing and wishing to have the land grieving

The Herodium, built by Herod in 40 B.C. This fortress lies southeast of Bethlehem.
Courtesy Israel Government Press Office.

when he died, he ordered the principal men of the nation to be herded into the Jericho Hippodrome and shot with darts as soon as word came of his expiring. This madness was not carried out, and the nation exulted at being delivered from Herod.

Because of the many intrigues in the court and his own increasing mental instability during his last days, the suspicious monarch changed his will several times. Antipater had managed to alter the testament in his own favor but eventually overreached himself and met death. Herod's final will gave the monarchy to Archelaus, his son by Malthace the Samaritan.

But the kingdom did not remain entire. It would include Judea, the most important prize; Idumea; and Samaria, but Galilee and Perea went to another son of Malthace, Herod Antipas, whom Jesus later called "that fox." By this will a large block of Herod's kingdom fell under the rule of men who were born of a Samaritan mother and of a royal father who was mockingly called a "half-Jew." Herod Philip, son of Cleopatra of Jerusalem, received the racially mixed lands to the north and east of Galilee. These lands included Gaulanitis, Trachonitis, and Paneas. This Philip should not be confused with another Herod Philip, son of the second Mariamne, who received no territory, but who is mentioned in the New Testament as the husband of Herodias before she married Herod Antipas and arranged the execution of John the Baptist. Salome, the crafty sister of King Herod, received an inheritance that included a palace at Ashkelon and the income from three cities. The three inheriting brothers—Archelaus, Antipas, and Philip—went separately to Rome and lobbied for Augustus' ratification of the testament. Antipas left first, hoping for a larger share, but Augustus kept the will almost intact. He did deprive Archelaus of the monarchy, however, giving him instead the title of ethnarch with the provision that after proving his ability he might attain to kingship. But his reign was brief and turbulent, and he never received the monarchy. The other two rulers, Antipas and Philip, were named tetrarchs, a less prestigious title than ethnarch.

This division of Herod's domain occurred during the infancy of Jesus Christ.

Chapter 3

Judaism in the Christian Era

One cannot expect to have more than a superficial understanding of the New Testament era without some knowledge of Jewish faith and practice. Excluding possibly Luke, the writers of the New Testament were nurtured in Judaism, and the central figure of the Scriptures, Jesus, was taken by his parents on pilgrimages at festival time to the Jerusalem temple, where he amazed even the scribes with his knowledge of the ancient Jewish faith (Luke 2:41–52). Christianity rooted itself in Jewish history and doctrine. Although the Old Testament provides the greatest sourcebook for information on Judaism, a study of the continuing development of doctrine and practice at the end of the exile and during the intertestamental period also furnishes essential insights. After a brief outline of the events that ended the captivity and a summary of the major changes in Judaism that took place in Israel during and after the exile, this chapter will examine some of the major Jewish institutions, offices, and sects in more detail.

Three Bands of Returning Exiles

The main contingent of returnees from exile left Babylon in 538–537 B.C. Cyrus the Persian, who had defeated the Babylonians only a few years earlier, now encouraged the Jews to rebuild the temple. A group of over 42,000 returned under the leadership of Zerubbabel, a prince of the royal line of Judah. The former exiles rebuilt the altar and reinstituted the sacrifices. They laid the temple foundation at the outset of their second year, but opposition from surrounding peoples interrupted the project. In 520 B.C. Haggai and Zechariah stirred the people to resume the work after more than a fifteen-year delay, and the people completed construction of the postexilic (or second) temple in 516 B.C. A second group of over 1,750 exiles, led by Ezra, including priests and Levites, made the journey to Palestine in 458–457

B.C., with the approval of Artaxerxes I Longimanus. When word arrived back in Susa, the Persian capital, that enemies had burned the gates of Jerusalem with fire, the Persian king authorized Nehemiah to leave his exalted position as cupbearer and to direct the rebuilding of the city's defenses. In 445–444 B.C. he returned and began constructing the walls despite Samaritan protest.

The Cyrus Cylinder, which tells of Cyrus' capture of Babylon and his release of prisoners from Babylonia. Courtesy the Trustees of the British Museum.

Changes in Judaism
After the Exile

The postexilic era witnessed the evolution of new tendencies and new institutions in Judaism. The returning Israelites felt a greater sense of identity and nationalism. Having lost their religious and political independence, they had learned to cherish their spiritual heritage in the pagan environment of a foreign land. That which set them apart from their neighbors received greater emphasis than before. Idolatry became more abhorrent because unfaithfulness to Jehovah had caused their exile. Judaism became more exclusivist as the new sense of identity fostered an increased fear of racial mingling. The

mixed marriages of the Israelites with neighboring pagans deeply offended Ezra and Nehemiah. God's people must retain their religious and national identity by marrying within the Jewish community.

Another change involved a new emphasis on the study of the Torah (Law). During the exile it was not possible to make pilgrimages to the Jewish temple. Unable to participate in the levitical sacrifices prescribed in the Pentateuch, the Jew in a foreign land turned to the study of the law itself. The Torah took on an increased importance as an object of reverence and as a guide for life. Some of the reforms of Ezra and Nehemiah illustrate the renewed respect for the Torah. They insisted that the Feast of Tabernacles be celebrated in the proper manner. For the first time in Jewish history it was observed as prescribed by the law: by the people's dwelling in booths or tents. The reformers also strictly enforced sabbath restrictions and payment of the tithe for the support of temple worship.

Ruins of the ancient synagogue at Capernaum, with Corinthian capitals in the foreground. Zev Radovan.

Other changes included the creation of the synagogue. The origin of the synagogue is obscure, but this new institution apparently emerged during the exile as a partial substitute for the temple. It became a center for teaching and studying the law as well as a place of prayer and worship. The temple later regained importance, as the ministry of Haggai and Zechariah attest, but in the New Testament age, the Jerusalem shrine existed alongside these new locally accessible and widely scattered places of worship. With the rise of the synagogue and the increased interest in a study of the law came the institution of a new office, that of the scribe. This new lay leader was more than a copier of sacred texts; he was a scholar and teacher. His role as interpreter of the Scripture received great urgency from the cessation of divinely authorized revelations from the prophets. In the absence of a recognized prophetic office, after the time of Malachi, the scribe would apply the Torah to a multitude of contemporary questions by developing new oral interpretations. A detailed oral tradition grew up to supplement the Scriptures themselves. The Pharisees (a sect discussed both in chapter 1 and later in this chapter) became staunch supporters of the oral interpretation and taught their views in the synagogue. An office that survived from earlier times but underwent change was that of the high priest. In Old Testament days the chief priest led in the service of worship, but after the exile he would be increasingly a political leader also. The diversity of Judaism became apparent in the centuries after the exile. Although Jews sought to maintain their distinctiveness from other cultures, they could not find unanimity among themselves on some of the major questions confronting them. New parties and sects appeared: Samaritans, Pharisees, Sadducees, Essenes, and Nationalists (the latter did not come to be known as the Zealots until A.D. 66). Also non-Palestinian Jews increased both in numbers and in geographical distribution. These Jews of the Diaspora faced influences that tended to draw them away from more traditional Jewish practice.

The Scribes

A basic knowledge of some of the important institutions and offices of Judaism is necessary for an understanding of New Testament history. One of the most important offices was that of the professional scribe. Nehemiah and Ezra placed a great emphasis on the reading, study, and application of the Law. Not only was Ezra a priest, but, as is clear from Ezra 7:6, he also served as a "teacher well versed in the Law of Moses." He served as a prototype for future scribes who became guardians and expositors of the Torah. In Nehemiah 8:1 Ezra is depicted as standing before a large crowd at the Water Gate reading aloud from the Books of the Law of Moses "from daybreak till noon" (v. 3). The scribes were professional students of the Law. In the first centuries after the exile the office seemed to be most frequently held by priests. By the time of Jesus, priestly control over interpretation of the law had slipped considerably and most of the scribes were laymen. Mark 2:16 refers to scribes of the Pharisaic sect, and it is probable that in Christ's time most scribes belonged to that party, but one should not assume that all scribes were Pharisees. It is clear in Acts 23:9 that some of the scribes who served in the Sanhedrin in Paul's day were Pharisees, but the passage does not clarify whether any of the Sadducean members of the Sanhedrin might also have been scribes.

Two of the best-known scribes, Hillel and Shammai, lived in the half-century before Christ and represented opposing schools of interpretation. Shammai insisted on a rigid and rigorous interpretation of the law while Hillel's school argued for moderation in applying the Torah. Their opposing viewpoints were still being discussed during the time of Jesus and Paul. Out of the dialogue and teaching of such scribes developed a detailed body of interpretation, which faithful Jews passed on orally. It was because Jesus and his disciples violated the "tradition of the elders" that the Pharisees and scribes condemned them for eating with unwashed hands (Mark 7:5). Jesus charged that such interpretations did not have divine authority and were only human in origin. The scribes of Jesus' day believed their interpretations were consistent with oral traditions as old as Moses. The scribal traditions were preserved in written form in the Mishnah during the second century A.D., and eventually this collection of rabbinic dialogues became a part of a work called the Talmud.

The Synagogue

Much of the scribe's activity centered on the synagogue, because it existed for instruction in the Torah. Although the origin of the synagogue is obscure, it probably originated in Babylon during the exile. The synagogue became an alternative to the temple as a place for worship. It was not even necessary for a member of a priestly order to be on hand to direct services, for laymen led in the study and worship. The synagogue tended to supplant the temple for many Jews, but especially those of the Diaspora. After A.D. 70, the widely scattered synagogues, found in every land of the dispersion, replaced the temple as the chief place of worship for Jews. A synagogue could be established whenever as few as ten Jewish males banded together. When Paul journeyed through Asia Minor, Macedonia, and Greece, he found synagogues in many of the major cities, although some of the Roman colonies—i.e., cities with a large population of Latin colonists, such as Philippi—might not have a sufficiently large Jewish population for a synagogue. Jews of the dispersion founded many synagogues in Jerusalem to serve specific national groups. One of the first deacons, Stephen, preached Christ to one of these foreign gatherings. It was known as the Synagogue of the Freedmen. Scholars have disagreed on whether this group mentioned in Acts 6:9 might belong to a single synagogue or possibly as many as four or five. The passage may be interpreted to imply two synagogues, one for the "Jews of Cyrene and Alexandria," and one for those of "Cilicia and Asia."[1]

Synagogue services were held on the morning of the Sabbath and also on two nights during the week. The service began with the recitation of the *Shema* recorded in Deuteronomy 6:4, "Hear, O Israel: The LORD our God, the LORD is one."[2] Following a prayer came two readings from Scripture, one from the Torah and one from the Prophets. During a service in his home-town synagogue at Nazareth, Jesus read a selection from the prophet Isaiah and then proceeded to deliver the exposition or sermon that usually followed the reading (Luke 4:16–21). Jesus stood up to read the scroll, but when he assumed the role of teacher, he took the customary sitting position. One did not have to be a priest or scribe to take part in the services as reader or teacher. The synagogue rulers could invite anyone deemed qualified to give an exposition. In Antioch of Pisidia the leaders asked Paul and Barnabas to bring a "message of encouragement for the people" (Acts 13:15). In Acts 18:8 the leader in the business affairs and worship of the synagogue is called "the synagogue ruler." He also exercised judicial authority, since cases tried under the Torah would fall under his jurisdiction. Other officials included a board of twenty-three elders and an attendant or servant. The attendant functioned as custodian or janitor and sometimes as a teacher in the synagogue school for children. When Jesus read from Isaiah in the synagogue at Nazareth, it was probably such an attendant who carried the scroll to him (Luke 4:20).

The synagogue played an important part in the early development of Christianity. To some extent the services of the church followed the synagogue model: Scripture reading, prayer, praise, and the sermon can be traced to the synagogue. These houses of worship also served as convenient places for the proclamation of the message of Christ. Jesus and Paul frequently attended and ministered in the synagogue. Stephen, Apollos, and other early Christians found in these meeting places a ready-made and intelligent audience. In his missionary travels Paul preached first in the synagogues and abandoned them only after opposition forced him to turn to a private home (Acts 18:7) or some other available location. After being "publicly maligned" by those at the Ephesian synagogue, he began teaching in the "lecture hall of Tyrannus" (Acts 19:9).

Synagogue at Korazin—a reconstruction of the facade of this third-century structure. Courtesy L. Ritmeyer.

Temple Worship and Leadership

While there might be many synagogues, the Jewish people could have only one divinely authorized temple. The sacred shrine in Jerusalem evoked wonder, awe, and admiration among the Jews. Hellenistic Jews from many lands made pilgrimages to see the beautiful white stone sanctuary, which served as the central place for all Jews to worship. Nebuchadnezzar destroyed Solomon's temple with its sacred ark of the covenant in 586 B.C. We have already seen that the second temple, completed in 516 B.C., was desecrated by Antiochus Epiphanes in 167 B.C. and then rededicated three years later. Herod's refurbished temple was much more grandiose than the post-exilic structure.

Levites and priests ministered in the temple according to the pattern prescribed in the Pentateuch. All priests were Levites, but many Levites were not priests. Those Levites who were not priests served as assistants or attendants in the temple. The priesthood traced its descent from Aaron, who was of the tribe of Levi, and was divided into twenty-four courses, or families, each of which offered the temple sacrifice for one week in turn. Zechariah, the father of John the Baptist, belonged to the course of Abijah and was chosen by lot from his course to burn incense in the temple (Luke 1:5–10). Since there were eighteen thousand priests by Christ's time, it is clear that such an experience would have been the high point in the life of any priest.

The most important temple official was the high priest. According to the Levitical prescription, he must be descended from Aaron, but this was often ignored during and after Maccabean times. Only the high priest could enter into the Holy of Holies and offer the annual sacrifice for the nation on the Day of Atonement. He could also take part in any other sacrifice in the temple. Such an office would seem to demand a man of deep consecration, but a few centuries before Christ, as the position became increasingly politicized, it often harbored unworthy and ambitious men. Beginning with Simon, the son of Mattathias, the Hasmoneans

linked the offices of king and high priest. Until Alexandra's queenship both offices were held by the same person. The high priest, as presiding officer of the Sanhedrin, exercised both religious and political influence over the Jewish people. Although the Sanhedrin had governmental responsibilities only in Judea, many Jews in distant regions respected and obeyed the decisions of this council and its priestly moderator. Another temple official of importance was the captain (strategos, Acts 4:1; 5:24). He might replace the high priest if the latter were ceremonially defiled, but his usual duties involved commanding the temple guard. It is sometimes argued that the temple guard rather than a Roman band arrested Jesus in the Garden of Gethsemane, but John 18:12 seems to infer otherwise.

The Jewish Festivals

The priests offered daily sacrifices for the community in the temple at dawn and in the afternoon. Sacrifices could also be made for individuals. But priestly activity was at its peak during the seven festival seasons. (1) Passover at the beginning of the religious calendar commemorated the deliverance of Israel from Egypt. The Seven Days of Unleavened Bread following immediately after Passover should be classified as a fast rather than a festival. (2) Pentecost (in Greek the numeral fifty) came fifty days after Passover and celebrated the giving of the law to Moses at Sinai as well as the Spring harvest in Israel. It is sometimes also called the Feast of Weeks or the Feast of First Fruits. (3) The civil New Year for the Jewish people began with the Feast of Trumpets or *Rosh Hashanah* (Head of the Year). Thus the Jewish people had both a religious and a civil calendar. The religious year began in spring, and the civil year in the fall. Coming in the same month as *Rosh Hashanah, Tishri* (September/October), were (4) the Day of Atonement and (5) the Feast of Tabernacles. On the Day of Atonement the offering of blood brought into the Holy of Holies made expiation for the sins of the nation. During the Feast of Tabernacles, five days later, the Jews constructed booths with tree branches and during this camping-out experience commemorated the forty years of wilderness wandering. The last two feasts in the sacred year dated from postexilic times and are not mentioned in the Pentateuch. (6) The origin of the Feast of Dedication, also called *Hannukah* or Feast of Lights, has already been described in the story of Judas Maccabeus' cleansing and rededication of the temple. (7) The seventh of the annual festivals, the Feast of Purim, celebrated the deliverance of the Jews by Queen Esther from the genocidal scheme of Haman.

The Sanhedrin

While the synagogue ranked with the temple and priesthood as a major religious institution in the time of Jesus, another body, the Sanhedrin, functioned both as a leading religious authority and as a political force. The Sanhedrin acted somewhat like a supreme court for Judea. It was not an appellate court in the sense that any citizen involved in a criminal case before a lower court had a guaranteed right of appeal to the Sanhedrin. Rather, it considered cases it deemed of great importance or cases in which a local Sanhedrin could not come to a decision.

The Sanhedrin possessed legislative as well as judicial power. After A.D. 6 when Judea became a province, the Romans chose to delegate the governance of internal affairs to the Sanhedrin and its presiding officer, the high priest. Of course, the Roman prefect could assert final authority at any time, and it was understood that the Sanhedrin derived its authority from Rome. After the revolt of A.D. 66–70 the Sanhedrin ceased to exist as a political institution, although it did continue as a religious organization.

One of the more complex questions that has provoked much controversy among biblical scholars concerns the "competency" or authority of the Sanhedrin to mete out capital punishment. In John 18:31, after Pilate told the Jews to judge Jesus by their own law, they reminded him that they "had no right to execute anyone." Much evidence could be amassed suggesting that the Jewish council did have such authority, and also there is a significant body of testimony suggesting the opposite.[3] The evidence is contradictory, and some of the rabbinic sources used to document the theory that John erred are too late to be relied on. The author of the fourth Gospel demonstrates a detailed knowledge of the geography and physical features of Jerusalem, Judea, and Samaria, as well as an understanding of Jewish customs. It seems unlikely that a man so knowledgeable about Judaism lacked understanding of the Sanhedrin's jurisdiction. It is probable that the Sanhedrin's powers decreased or increased at different times during the first six decades of the first century A.D. Also historians should be aware that the existence of any statute, custom, or constitutional convention is not in itself evidence of consistent implementation. The history of colonial India records that several British governors-general abolished the practice of *suttee*, the burning of a widow on her husband's funeral pyre, but edicts cannot be assumed to establish practical realities. Evidently, at the time of Christ's crucifixion the Sanhedrin did not possess the power to sentence offenders to death, even though at other times in history it might have exercised such authority.

Three groups held positions in the Sanhedrin: priests, scribes, and elders. Total membership numbered seventy plus the high priest. The office of the latter had been traditionally held for life, but the prefects, like Herod in an earlier day, ignored this custom and made frequent changes in the leadership. The term *chief priests* refers to members of the Sanhedrin who either had once served as high priests or were members of a small and select group of aristocratic families from which the high priests were drawn. The scribes or lawyers were fewer in number, but because of their erudition and skill in the Torah they had an important influence. The masses had their representation in a group of laymen known as the elders, who like the priestly members came from the aristocratic classes. Both elders and priests aligned themselves with the party of the Sadducees whereas the scribal members were mostly Pharisees. This diversity frequently pro-

voked tumultuous conflicts in the body, a situation Paul found useful when he was being tried before the council. He incited a sharp doctrinal controversy between Pharisees and Sadducees concerning the resurrection, hoping perhaps to briefly divert attention from his own case and to elicit some Pharisaic support (Acts 23:6–10).

Diverse Parties of Judaism

Despite the unifying force of the Torah and the temple, one should not visualize Judaism as a homogeneous entity. Fringe sects like the Samaritans and the Jews of Leontopolis in Egypt established rival temples. Josephus, himself a Pharisee, spoke of four "philosophies" within Judaism: Sadducees, Pharisees, Essenes, and a patriotic group fiercely dedicated to Jewish national liberty. Because he was enamored of Graeco-Roman culture, he chose to picture the Jewish parties as somehow akin to Greek schools of thought like Epicureanism and Stoicism. But the groups described by Josephus were not comparable to the schools founded by peripatetic teachers in Athens. Most of the Jewish population did not belong to any one of the four groups. While the Pharisees and Sadducees formed a fairly distinct and identifiable party, the Essenes seem to have exhibited a variety of beliefs and practices. Possibly, Essenism could be thought of as a tendency toward puritanical separatism and exclusiveness, and it was manifested in a variety of forms. The term *sect* might be applied to both Essenes and Samaritans; Pharisees and Sadducees, while holding distinctive beliefs, are better described as parties. The patriots cannot be identified as a distinct party until the time of the Zealots in A.D. 66, though the spirit of rebellion and independence existed much earlier than that date.

The Samaritans

The origin of the people called "Samaritans" in New Testament days is uncertain. They were either Gentiles, Jews, or a mixture of both. Probably the majority of Bible scholars are correct in depicting them as a people of mixed Jewish and Gentile blood. Nevertheless, it is possible that the Jews of Samaria practiced miscegenation to no greater extent than their kinsmen of Judea. The Samaritans themselves have always claimed to be of pure Jewish blood. Although their assertion cannot be proved, a case can be made for it. No influence from Assyrian religious ideas seems to have affected Samaritan theology. But 2 Kings indicates that the Assyrians did replace the exiled northern tribes with men from Babylon, Cuthah, and other regions and that these people "worshiped the LORD, but . . . also served their own gods . . ." (2 Kings 17:33). Scripture does not really indicate whether the people who would be called Samaritans at a later time were descendants of these foreigners. Only a small minority of the population were deported from the ten tribes in 722 B.C. The upper class leadership had been removed, but a significant body of humbler Jews remained behind, and it is possible that these remaining Jews could have maintained a distinct identity side by side

with the Gentile colonists who became their neighbors.

On the other hand, evidence in the New Testament seems to go against the Samaritan claim. The New Testament views the Samaritans as a people distinct from Israel. Jesus, in commissioning the twelve disciples, charged them to go to the "lost sheep of Israel" and not to the Gentiles or Samaritans (Matt. 10:5–6). He also referred to a Samaritan healed of leprosy as a "foreigner" (Luke 17:18). Such statements clearly separate the Samaritans from other Jews, but the reason for the distinction is not so evident. It is possible that the Samaritans were distinct primarily because of historic conflicts between the tribes and theological aberrations rather than because of a large admixture of Gentile blood. The Jews of the first century A.D. probably erred in depicting the Samaritans as a wholly Gentile people. The epithet *Cuthean* for a Samaritan reflects this extreme view.[4] The term derives from 2 Kings 17:24 where the people of Cuthah are listed as one of the colonizing groups sent by the Assyrians to Samaria. The truth probably lies somewhere between the Jewish charge of wholly Gentile origins and the Samaritan claim to purity.

The proper site for the temple became a major point of dispute between the Samaritans and the Jews. When Jesus talked to the woman at the well in Sychar, she sought to initiate a theological discussion on this issue (John 4:21). According to Samaritan tradition, Joshua had established a place of worship for Jehovah at Mount Gerizim near Shechem, and Eli had apostatized when he made Shiloh the

Samaritans in prayer at a passover feast on Mount Gerazim. Courtesy S. Zur Picture Library.

worship center. The tradition positing the building of the Samaritan temple in the fifth century B.C. is contradicted by Josephus, who puts its construction in the time of Alexander the Great (332 B.C.), but the account of Josephus may be garbled. He tells the story of the high priest's relative Manasseh marrying Sanballat's daughter, of his expulsion from the priesthood for marrying a foreigner, and of the building of a temple for him at Mount Gerizim by Sanballat. Nehemiah says nothing of a rival temple but mentions briefly the marriage of a relative of the high priest to Sanballat's daughter and adds that he "drove" the offending relative out of Jerusalem (Neh. 13:28–29). Apparently Josephus expanded the Nehemiah account and placed it in the wrong time frame. It is also possible that there may have been more than one Sanballat and that thus Josephus was also correct in his chronology.

The Jewish people evidenced antagonism toward the people of Samaria as early as the division of Solomon's kingdom between Rehoboam and Jeroboam. Judean hostility toward the northern tribes increased through the centuries. Isaiah records that in his time Pekah, the king of Israel, allied with the Syrians against the southern kingdom of Judah (Isa.

7:1). In a later day (200–180 B.C.) the author of the apocryphal book of Ecclesiasticus, Jesus ben Sirach, spoke of the "senseless folk that live at Shechem" (50:26). John Hyrcanus' destruction of the Samaritan temple in 128 B.C. also illustrates the continuing hostility. Joachim Jeremias' researches reveal an ebb and flow of tensions during the centuries. He believes Herod's marriage to the Samaritan Malthace might have indicated a brief period of improved relationships. During Herod's reign Samaritans could enter the inner court of the Jerusalem temple, but tempers flared about A.D. 8 when the Samaritans defiled the sanctuary by littering it with human bones.[5] At the time of Christ's ministry relations remained very strained. Although Galilean Jews traveled through Samaria to Jerusalem at festival times, they avoided all social contacts. In the words of John's Gospel (4:9), "Jews do not associate with Samaritans."

Samaritan deviations in doctrine partially explain Jewish hostility. "You Samaritans," Jesus told the woman at the well, "worship what you do not know . . . , for salvation is from the Jews" (John 4:22). Three views deserve mention. (1) First, the failure to recognize the Jerusalem temple as a valid place for worship constituted the chief heresy. (2) Second, they had a divergent view on Scripture, a view roughly resembling that of the Sadducees. The latter did not accept all of the books of the Old Testament canon as having equal value. They gave greater weight to the Pentateuch as the only authority. The Samaritans rejected outright all writings except the five books of Moses, and they even had their own

edited version of that, known today as the Samaritan Pentateuch. This text contained a revision of Deuteronomy 27:4. While the Masoretic text (the traditional Jewish text) commands the erection on Mount Ebal of stone tablets containing the Law, the Samaritan version substitutes Gerizim for Ebal. The Samaritan text reflects both Septuagint readings as well as an early version of the text that lay behind the Masoretic text. Since the Samaritan text originated in the era of the Maccabees, it is not of extraordinary value in establishing the original text of the Pentateuch. (3) A third doctrinal distinctive of the Samaritans, and one echoed by the Sadducees, was the rejection of the bodily resurrection.

The Sadducees

While the Samaritans might be viewed as a fringe sect, the Sadducees occupied a central place in the Judaism of Christ's time. They could not command the same degree of respect from the masses as the Pharisees, but they did have a position of importance both in the temple worship and in the Sanhedrin. The Sadducees were members of the aristocratic families of Judea who provided some of the leaders in the priesthood. Not all Sadducees were priests, but they were from the highest stratum of society. By maintaining a close association with the Roman overlords, these noble families gained political influence along with sacerdotal supremacy. The party's spiritual roots go down to Seleucid times when the ancestors of the Sadducees were the pro-Hellenistic members of the priestly class. When the descendants of Mattathias lost their zeal for purity of faith and began to behave like Hellenistic rulers, the Sadducees found a natural affinity with them. John Hyrcanus (135–104 B.C.) and Aristobulus II aligned themselves with the Sadducees. Because the party encouraged Antigonus in his resistance to the claims of Herod the Great, victory for the latter meant a temporary loss of prestige for the Sadducees and the Sanhedrin. The establishment of direct Roman rule under a prefect in A.D. 6 brought greater influence to this elite group, but the destruction of the temple in A.D. 70 terminated the party's existence and left the more numerous and popular Pharisees to dominate Jewish culture.

A doctrinal description of the Sadducees, somewhat like that of the deists of the eighteenth century, must consist primarily of negatives. They rejected many of the Pharisaic concepts. (1) They denied the existence of angels and spirits, the immortality of the human soul, and the resurrection of the body. (2) They also rejected the elevation of the prophetic, historical, and poetical books as having the same authority as the Pentateuch, and (3) they opposed the Pharisaic belief in a traditional oral law that held equal authority with the written Torah itself. On a more positive note, the Sadducees (1) affirmed the free will of man, (2) defended the traditional regulations concerning ritual purity and liturgical practice in the temple, and (3) insisted on a literal interpretation of the Torah. Sometimes they have been viewed as the liberals of their day because of their materialistic and antisupernatural tendency, but they

demonstrated a conservative trait in their concern for maintaining the *status quo.* Because they wished to protect their wealth and power, they had little sympathy for anti-Roman revolts. The Sadducees were conservative in their literalist interpretation of the Pentateuch. They staunchly opposed later oral additions to the Law.

The Pharisees

The Pharisees, like the Essenes, appear to have originated from the Hasidim (the pious ones). Their name originated from the Hebrew verb *parash,* "to separate." Possibly they received their name because they separated themselves from those who were less rigid in observing the traditional oral additions to the Torah, but some scholars believe the term refers to a rupture between the Pharisees and the Hasmoneans. Josephus first mentions the Pharisees along with the Essenes and Sadducees in his discussion of Jonathan and the Maccabean era.[6] A rift occurred between the Pharisees and their Hasmonean rulers in the time of John Hyrcanus when one of the sect, Eleazar, accused the high priest of being the son of a captive woman and thus ineligible to serve as a priest. Hyrcanus' son, Alexander Janneus, crucified eight hundred of the Pharisees, but at the end of his life he instructed his wife and successor, Salome Alexandra, to align herself with them. In the time of Roman supremacy the Pharisees disdained the Sadducees for their obsequiousness to the foreigners, but rather than actively resist Roman rule themselves, the Pharisees turned away from politics to concentrate on religious interests. In the first century A.D. they still maintained religious influence and some political power through their representation in the Sanhedrin.

The Pharisees outnumbered the Sadducees and by Josephus' estimate had six thousand members. Scholars disagree about the degree of organization attained by the party. Some think that the Pharisees were a well—organized, tightly knit group with communal associations, officers, and regular meeting times. Others view the group as a less well-defined entity with similar religious views, who only occasionally banded together in anything like an organized manner. In the Jerusalem associations, at least, membership in the Pharisaic sect came only to those who proved their obedience to the Torah and the traditional rules during a probationary period.[7] Unlike the aristocratic Sadducees, the Pharisees belonged to the middle class. Most of the scribes and a few priests and Levites became Pharisees, but primarily the men who numbered themselves among the Pharisees were involved in business or the trades. They disdained the "people of the land" (*am ha-aretz*) who ignored the detailed legal prescriptions of the Pharisaic tradition. Some of the leading Pharisees reflected this attitude when they cursed "this mob that knows nothing of the law" (John 7:49).

According to Josephus' description of their doctrines, the Pharisees rejected both the Essene view that fate determines all human events and the Saducean view that man has absolute freedom. The Pharisees held a middle position, asserting that both God and man cooperate in human activities. Although Josephus used the Greek term for "fate" in his account, he seems to portray the Pharisees as believing in something quite different from Greek determinism. He sees them as supporting the concept of the providential working of God in human history. The Pharisees also held to the immortality of the soul, the uniting of just souls with their resurrected bodies in a future life, and the existence of angels and spirits. They accepted all of the Old Testament canon, which included the three traditional Hebrew divisions of the Law, the Prophets, and the Writings. But they added to this orthodox view a reverence for the oral interpretation of the law that elevated it as high or even higher than the Torah itself. By an allegorical method of interpretation they extended the meaning of the law so that it could be applied to almost any conceivable practical situation. Jesus accused them of in effect nullifying Scripture "for the sake of ... tradition" (Matt. 15:6). In their dedication to the law and oral traditions they closely resembled the scribes, and in fact a large number of the scribes identified themselves with the Pharisees. Their excessive dedication to outward form and their precise obedience to regulations affecting the trivial details of life sparked Jesus' criticism that they tithed "mint, dill and cummin," while neglecting the more basic requirements of "justice, mercy and faithfulness" (Matt. 23:23).

The Nationalists

In the *Antiquities of the Jews* Josephus describes a fourth "philosophic sect" in addition to the Sadducees, Pharisees, and Essenes. This fourth party might be described in modern terms as "patriots," "freedom fighters," or "rebels." According to Josephus, they had an "inviolable attachment to liberty."[8] Modern scholars question whether the "zealots" of the Jewish wars that began in A.D. 66 existed as a distinct party in the early part of the first century. But there is no doubt that Israel always had her feisty bands of patriots ready to support the struggle for national independence. Josephus sees the "fourth party" as originating with Judas the Galilean, who led a rebellion against Coponius, the first prefect or governor sent by Rome to rule Judea. Josephus had little sympathy for the extreme nationalists, and he blamed them for initiating a "distemper" that would bring insurrections, suffering, and death. He saw the work of men like Judas as an early manifestation of the spirit that would lead to the great rebellion of A.D. 66, a movement that Josephus believed to be misguided and catastrophic. Josephus did not use the term *Zealot* in his description of the fourth philosophy of the Jews. This designation does not appear until his discussion of the Jewish revolt. There he uses the term to describe the party of Menahem and John of Gischala, who sought to bring the direction of the Jewish revolt of A.D. 66 into the hands of extremists.

To trace the origins of the rebel nationalist spirit would involve a lengthy history, but a few brief examples may be cited. (1) Phinehas was one of the earliest examples of an Israelite who militantly defended the nation and the law. When adultery and idolatry threatened to pervert the nation, this angry priest took a javelin and slew a Jew and his pagan mistress (Num. 25:7–13). (2) When Mattathias killed the idolatrous Jew at Modin and called to battle "everyone ... zealous for the law," he appealed to pious nationalists whose jealousy for God and nation would be a prototype for later freedom fighters. (3) This was the tradition Judas the Galilean was following when he reacted against the establishment of Roman rule. Judea, Idumea, and Samaria had just come under the authority of the Roman prefect as part of the province of Syria (A.D. 6). Archelaus had been banished to Gaul for his inept administration. The Romans appointed Coponius as the first prefect in the area, and they charged Quirinius with the responsibility of administering a census that would establish the level of tribute that might be extracted from the region. These events led Judas the Galilean with the aid of a Pharisee, Sadduk, to resist foreign rule and taxation.

The patriots were often called bandits (*lestai*) by the populace as a term of admiration rather than contempt. Judas' father, Ezekias, had the respect of the Jerusalem Pharisees even though he led a robber band. When Herod the Great, as governor of Galilee, executed the popular Ezekias, the Sanhedrin reacted angrily. Probably some of those called bandits were in reality nationalists who used terror and violence to fight against Roman rule. When Barabbas and the two men crucified with Jesus are called robbers (*lestai*), they are possibly being identified as nationalistic rebels (John 18:40; Mark 15:27).[9] A Latin name used for insurgents by

Josephus, *sicarii*, suggests they were men armed with daggers. During the decade before the revolt in A.D. 66, the *sicarii* carried daggers concealed in their clothing and sometimes slipped into crowds, stabbed their enemies, then stole furtively away.

The Essenes

In his description of Jewish parties, Josephus gives detailed information on an ascetic withdrawal sect called the Essenes. Josephus himself might have had some personal experience with the Essenes during his teenage years. He tells of spending several years as a member of an unnamed desert sect before identifying himself with the Pharisees. Whether or not this particular desert group actually was Essene, Josephus does claim to have some knowledge of what he describes as the third sect of the Jews. Other sources of information on the group include (1) a brief description in Pliny the Elder's *Natural History* (died A.D. 79), (2) Philo's *Apology for the Jews* and *Let Every Good Man Be Free* (written before A.D. 50 in Egypt), (3) Hippolytus' *Refutation of All Heresies* written in Rome early in the third century A.D. apparently with reliance on Josephus' earlier account. The Dead Sea Scrolls may also provide information on the Essenes. The desert community that was located at Qumran on the northwest shore of the Dead Sea and produced the famous Dead Sea Scrolls cannot be proved without question to be an Essene group, but at any rate their belief and practice were similar to those of the Essenes. *The Manual of Discipline*, one of the scrolls found among others in the caves near Qumran, seems to be an Essene-like document.

The remains of a monastery of the Essene community, first century B.C. Courtesy Israel Government Press Office.

The New Testament never mentions the Essenes or Essaioi, but for more than a century some biblical scholars have tried to establish a link between New Testament Christianity and Essene practice. Although sensationalist books still appear announcing that Jesus and John the Baptist were Essenes and that Christianity drew heavily from the desert sect's doctrines and way of life, this overworked theme has been effectively discredited by more careful scholarship.[10] The lack of New Testament data on the movement is probably best explained by its relative obscurity. Josephus and Philo estimated a membership of only about four thousand. Since the sect demanded a rigorous rule of life and withdrew from normal social contact and intercommunication, it had less influence than other Jewish groups.

Like the Pharisees, the Essenes appear to have been an outgrowth of the Hasidim, but they were even more rigorous in their dedication to the Mosaic Law and righteousness.

Josephus says they observed the Sabbath more strictly than the other Jews did. The sect may have arisen in the second century B.C. after the time of Judas the Maccabee, when the staunch Hasidim reacted against the spiritual degeneracy of the nation and its rulers. Many of the early Essenes were priests, but the sect viewed the established priestly order and the temple leadership as morally bankrupt. According to Josephus, the Essenes preferred their own liturgical order to participation in temple sacrifice, although they did send offerings to the Jerusalem temple.[11] Having separated themselves from the religious leadership of Israel and from everyday social contacts, they looked to an apocalyptic deliverance to set the nation right again. Many of the Essenes separated themselves in a literal geographical sense by leaving Jerusalem and the other cities for a communal life in solitary places. Philo located them in villages where they engaged in agricultural and rural labor, but Josephus asserted that although "they have no certain city, . . . many of them dwell in every city."[12] Even those sect members who lived in the towns found themselves socially isolated by their exacting code of behavior.

The Essenes practiced strict asceticism. Usually they were celibate, though Josephus states that at least one branch did permit marriage. Those who remained single perpetuated their sect by adopting children and training them in the Essene manner. Spurning individual wealth, the members surrendered all property to the community and received equally from the common store to meet their needs. The community appointed a steward to handle all financial and business matters. A day in the life of an Essene began with prayers before sunrise, and no nonreligious topics could be discussed before daybreak. Hard work occupied much of the day, but there was also time for ceremonial bathing and changing into white robes for the communal meals. Since an Essene was not permitted to eat food prepared by those outside the order, excommunication could lead to starvation. Admission to the Essene community came only after a three-year probation. During the first year of the probationary period, a candidate had to demonstrate his willingness to live in accordance with the sect's regulations. A ceremonial cleansing marked his initiation into the final two years of probation, but he was still excluded from the communal meals. After proving his faithfulness during the final two years, he was admitted to full fellowship. His initiation included lengthy solemn oaths in which he promised to live righteously toward God, to deal justly with other men, and to guard the secrecy of the community's doctrines.

Josephus and Hippolytus disagree on the Essene view of the afterlife. According to Josephus it appears that the Essenes held, like the Greeks, that though the soul is immortal, the body is corruptible and will not be raised. As in Platonic doctrine, the body is a prison that holds the soul in check until death brings a joyous release from bondage. But Hippolytus asserts that, like the Christians, the Essenes believed in a physical resurrection of the body as well as in the immortality of the soul. It is not possible to determine which represents the authentic Essene teaching. Possibly Essenes in different locations held variant doctrines. Josephus may have erred in portraying them as denying the resurrection. His report may have been influenced by his desire to portray the Jewish sects as akin to Greek schools of philosophy, which denied a bodily resurrection.

The Dead Sea Scrolls

The Dead Sea Scrolls were discovered in the spring of 1947 at Wadi Qumran along the northwest end of the Dead Sea. They have provided light on one ascetic group that lived in isolation from the mainstream of Jewish life. The Qumran community, which was located near the cave area, cannot be proved to be an Essene group, but it seems to have been at least an Essene-like settlement. The famous leather scrolls were found by two Bedouin shepherd boys who were seeking a lost goat on the rocky hillsides along the Dead Sea. Finding a small opening in the rocky mountain, one of the boys tossed a stone into the cavern. The startling sound of broken crockery excited their curiosity. Squeezing through the cave opening, they found broken pottery littering the floor and several intact jars containing ancient parchment rolls. After authorities were made aware of the discovery, the documents passed through several hands, but eventually Archbishop Samuel of the Syrian Orthodox Church examined them in Jerusalem and recognized the writing as a form of Hebrew. E. L. Sukenik of the Hebrew University of Jerusalem, W. F. Albright of Johns Hopkins University, and a few other eminent archaeologists quickly perceived the scrolls to be authentic ancient Hebrew manuscripts. For Old Testament studies the most valuable find consisted of a complete text of Isaiah from the first century B.C., outdating by one thousand years the oldest copy of Isaiah known before the cave exploration. After the initial discovery, Bedouins and scholars combed the barren hills that overlook the Dead Sea. They eventually found ten more caves and numerous Greek, Hebrew, and Aramaic manuscripts or pieces of manuscripts. Almost every Old Testament book, many apocryphal books, and other significant writings were represented in the tens of thousands of manuscript fragments recovered. Some of the caves contained material placed there after the first century A.D., but a large portion of the documents were apparently copied or preserved by the Qumran community.

When news came of the early discoveries, scholars assumed that the ruins located nearby had no connection with the cave finds. But in late 1951, Lankester Harding and Pere de Vaux in excavating the Wadi Qumran site unearthed evidence contradicting the earlier assumption that the settlement had been a Roman fortress. Their study of the main building revealed a floor plan unsuitable for a fort or private home, but more likely adapted as a meeting place. In one of the rooms they found a jar of the same style as one of those in the cave. Archaeologists also found on the site a pottery kiln, which could account for the production of a distinctive type of pottery. This find indicated a probable connection between the scrolls and the ruins.[13]

The caves at Qumran where the Dead Sea Scrolls were discovered in 1947 by a Bedouin goatherd.   Courtesy S. Zur Picture Library.

The same two scholars were able to determine more precisely the time of occupation of the Qumran ruins when they resumed excavation in 1953. The buildings had been occupied by Jewish groups at three different times. (1) Coins found on the site indicated the first settlement began in the reign of John Hyrcanus (135–104 B.C.) and continued until possibly early in the reign of Herod the Great (about 37 B.C. or afterward). Josephus mentions the occurrence in 31 B.C. of an earthquake of sufficient magnitude to have destroyed the main building. (2) Millar Burrows dates the second occupation from the reign of Archelaus (4 B.C.–A.D. 6) to the Jewish revolt (A.D. 66–70). He believes the building was not restored until about the beginning of the first century A.D., since only two coins from the period of Herod the Great were found

whereas many from the first century A.D. were unearthed. The Roman suppression of the Jewish uprising brought an end to the second settlement. (3) A third and very brief Jewish occupation occurred during the second Jewish revolt (A.D. 132–135). The thirteen coins at the site from the early second century must have fallen from the hands of Jewish rebels who supported Simon Bar Cocheba's insurrection against Rome during the reign of Hadrian.[14] The archaeological evidence dating the occupation of Qumran has aided in the establishment of a date for the scrolls. Paleography, the analysis of writing style, has also been a significant factor in arriving at a rough date of about 150 B.C. to A.D. 50.

Some of the facilities at Qumran included a large two-story building with a defensive tower, meeting rooms, storage rooms, a kitchen, and a common dining area. Archaeologists also unearthed pottery works, aqueducts, cisterns for holding water, and a scriptorium that contained benches and tables. Probably many of the documents found in the caves had been copied by pious Jews in this scriptorium.

In addition to the valuable biblical and apocryphal texts, the scrolls include works casting light on the Qumran community's life and doctrine. One of the most significant books, *The Manual of Discipline* (or *Rule of the Community*), prescribes detailed ethical and ritual requirements for admission to and retention in the sect. It contains doctrinal discussions, stern exhortations to follow the path of righteousness, and lists of punishments for the wayward; it concludes with a psalm of praise to

God. *The War of the Sons of Light Against the Sons of Darkness* pictures the Qumran saints as God's valiant warriors, the children of light, in the struggle to defeat the Gentile nations, especially the hated "kittim." The identity of the kittim is unclear, but they could have been either the Seleucids or the Romans. The book gives a detailed prescription for the organization, weapons, strategy, and conduct of the combatants. They are to join in a holy crusade, fought for God's glory and led by a holy people. Prayers, exhortations, and hymns of thanksgiving were to be as much a part of the war scene as were spears and shields. The spirit of the warriors resembles that of the puritan rebels of seventeenth-century England whom Oliver Cromwell led into battle only after reading to them from the Book of Psalms. *The War of the Sons of Light* depicts the final apocalyptic struggle, involving God's angels as well as evil spirits led by Belial, and it ends with the triumph of God and his people. Possibly the author envisioned a real conflict with some nation, but because of many gaps in the fragmented manuscript it is not possible to identify the precise nation.

The Qumran community especially valued the *Thanksgiving Hymns,* which were a collection of psalms praising God and expressing the frustrations, hopes, fears, and joys of the just man. In style and content it is reminiscent of the Old Testament Book of Psalms. Many psalms begin with the phrase "I give Thee thanks, O Adonai." A. Dupont-Sommer thinks the author might have been the "Teacher of Righteousness," the sec-tarian leader who is prominent in the writings from Qumran.[15]

Fragment of the Isaiah Scroll found in Cave 1 at Qumran. The portion shown here contains Isaiah 51:13–52:12. Courtesy The Shrine of the Book, D. Samuel and Jeane H. Gottesman Center for Biblical Manuscripts, Israel Museum, Jerusalem.

Fragments of the Zadokite Document or Damascus Document were found in several caves at Qumran. This writing had been discovered in 1896 in a storage room of a Cairo synagogue and published in 1910. The work records the exodus of the men of the "new covenant" from Judah to dwell in the "land of Damascus." Probably "Damascus" is here a symbolic word, but scholars have not agreed on its meaning.

71

Some have conjectured it might mean any Essene settlement.[16] Since the Zadokite Document repeats many rules found in the *Manual of Discipline*, it is clear that the two works have a close relationship. The caves near Qumran have also yielded a recently studied *Temple Scroll*, which describes the Jewish temple in a manner that does not seem to fit the temple as known from other sources. Also found in the caves were a number of commentaries on Old Testament books. These commentaries have shed further light on the community's outlook. Of special interest are those on Nahum and Habakkuk.

Part of the Thanksgiving Scroll found in one of the caves at Qumran. The complete scroll contains about forty hymns.
Courtesy The Shrine of the Book, D. Samuel and Jeane H. Gottesman Center for Biblical Manuscripts, Israel Museum, Jerusalem.

It cannot be proved that members of the Qumran settlement were Essenes, though some evidence points in that direction. Pliny spoke of the Essenes as having a settlement "below" Engedi. If the term "below" is interpreted to mean "south" rather than a lower elevation, the description fits the location of Qumran. The time period of the occupation of Qumran fits the era of Essene activity (150 B.C.–A.D. 70). Josephus tells of the sect's interest in sacred books. He even mentions an Essene prohibition against spitting into the midst of the assembly. The same regulation appears in the Qumran *Manual of Discipline*. Other practices common to both Essenes and the Qumran sect include the initiation oath, strict asceticism, community of goods, the office of financial steward, strict sabbatarian rules, common meals, and the possibility of excommunication. But there were some practices at Qumran that do not jibe with the Josephus-Pliny-Philo traditional accounts. (1) That women had a place in the Qumran association is indicated by female remains in the cemetery, but this might be explained by the fact that Josephus speaks of "another order" of Essenes who married for the sake of posterity.[17] (2) The probationary period for initiates is another example of a divergence from Essene practice. At Qumran it lasted only two years instead of three. (3) Philo's assertion that the Essenes were pacifists does not fit the spirit of the Qumran book *The Sons of Light*, unless that work is to be interpreted in an allegorical manner. Such differences do not prove the Qumran group did not have some relationship to the Essene movement.

The Essenes probably displayed a variety of practices depending on their particular location or time period. The Qumran community, if not Essene, at least bears some resemblance to that sect.

The Dead Sea Scrolls are a valuable source for information on the Qumran community, and the sect itself is of importance for an understanding of the Jewish background at the time of the birth of Christianity. The once fashionable idea that Christianity is an outgrowth of Qumran or Essenism has been discredited. The "Teacher of Righteousness" was not a divine redeemer as was the Christian Messiah. Jesus mingled with publicans and harlots to bring them into his kingdom; he did not invite them to withdraw from established society. John the Baptist was an ascetic preacher of righteousness who offered cleansing to those who came to his desolate dwelling north of the Dead Sea, but he did not belong to a community as did the Qumran sect, nor did he challenge his converts to abandon their home cities to join a desert commune. Christianity cannot be explained simply as an outgrowth of Qumran. Jesus Christ was the author of Christianity.

The Oral Law

The oral law has occupied a significant place in the Jewish faith. The Jews of Jesus' day believed that the oral traditions went back to the age of the written law itself. According to the Mishnah, "Moses received the Law from Sinai and committed it to Joshua, and Joshua to the elders, and the elders to the Prophets; and the Prophets committed it to the men of

the Great Synagogue."[18] The "Great Synagogue" referred to those scribes who taught and administered the law after Ezra's day. It was understood that Moses had received the precepts of the oral law just as he had received the written law. The oral law in one sense was viewed as an aid to the written law. Yet it could be equal or superior to it in terms of application or authority for daily behavior. According to the Mishnah, "Greater stringency applies to (the observance of) these words of the (written) Law."[19] To add to the words of the scribes was worthy of greater condemnation than to add to the words of the Law itself.[20] Oral interpretation can be understood as a means of (1) guarding the intent or sanctity of the law, (2) explaining and interpreting it, and (3) determining its application to the innumerable practical situations of daily life. Through the development of oral tradition the written law's application to life could be conformed to a changing environment and thus would be workable for the contemporary scene. There would have been a need for interpretation at an early date. Deuteronomy 17:8–11 instructs God's people to bring the thorniest disputes before the appointed judge and the Levitical priests and to abide by their decision. A court system of itself creates precedents and traditions to guide in future decisions.

Although oral teachings must have developed at an early stage, the most important era of oral development came after the period of exile when Israel no longer had prophets to guide the nation. In the era from approximately 175 b.c. to a.d. 200, the scribes developed the traditions that were compiled in the Mishnah. The Mishnah (Hebrew, "repeated study") was compiled by Rabbi Judah ha-Nasi soon after A.D. 200. Later the Gemara, commentaries on the Mishnah, were placed with it to form what has been called the Talmud (Hebrew, "learning"). The Mishnah forms the core of the Talmud and is a complex and detailed set of laws, prescriptions, applications, and admonitions. It deals with such subjects as religious festivals, Sabbath observance, marriage customs, sacrificial offerings, leprosy, cleanness and uncleanness. One example of the Mishnah's meticulous concern with the details of observing the law is its concern with degrees of ceremonial uncleanness. Some actions or substances are more unclean than others. A dead body is so unclean that its shadow alone would render one unclean. As an example of the concern for covering every conceivable situation, the rabbis considered whether a raven with a piece of human flesh as large as an olive in its beak and flying so as to cast a shadow on a person would be enough to cause a person to be unclean. The answer is that if there is doubt on the issue, the person is considered unclean. But a vessel or implement in doubt in the same situation would be considered clean.[21] Although on one occasion Jesus commanded his followers to obey the Pharisees and teachers of the law in everything they told them (Matt. 23:3), he warned them not to emulate the behavior of these leaders. Matthew 23 contains a strong message charging the keepers of the oral tradition with hyprocrisy and pride. "You have a fine way,"

Jesus admonished them in Mark 7:9, "of setting aside the commands of God in order to observe your own traditions."

The Messianic Expectation

From the earliest days of Israel's history one finds examples of expectancy and hope for God's future blessing on the nation. Sometimes these hopes focused on a future golden age, one that would repeat the achievements of the eras of David and Solomon. Probably many people in Israel during dark days of foreign oppression looked for a better age more than for an individual messiah. But at times there are indications that God's people looked for an individual leader, a king who would usher in the age of blessing. It is often said that these hopes were nationalistic, aimed at an earthly independent kingdom free of foreign domination. The fervent nationalism of the Maccabean rebels is an example of the devotion of many Jews to the cause of making Israel free from Gentile control. But as T. W. Manson points out, it may be a mistake to speak of purely nationalistic and materialistic aspirations as opposed to spiritual motivations. After the exile, those who cherished the messianic hope would have made no separation between the two goals. Their aim was to preserve the life of Israel. This meant a struggle to free Jehovah's people and his land from Gentile rule and to restore not only political independence for its own sake but also the dominance of the Torah, the temple, and the faith in one God. Josephus' portrayal of the Jewish rebels of the first century as secular

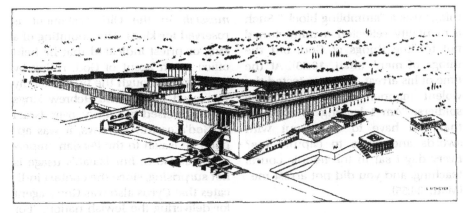

A reconstruction of the temple mount as it was in the time of Jesus, based on archaeological and historical evidence. Courtesy Carta, Jerusalem.

political agitators does not square with the tradition as seen in 1 Maccabees, in which devotion to God and the law is portrayed as the motivation for rebellion.[22]

By the time Jesus appeared on the scene, the messianic expectation probably was understood differently by various individuals. But Luke tells of two elderly Jews who, upon seeing the newborn child, recognized immediately his messianic role. They conceived of the Messiah as Israel's deliverer and redeemer, and as one whose message would go forth to the Gentiles. Simeon rejoiced, saying, "My eyes have seen your salvation, which you have prepared in the sight of all people, a light for revelation to the Gentiles and for glory to your people Israel" (Luke 2:30–32). Anna, the aged prophetess, "spoke about the child to all who were looking forward to the redemption of Jerusalem" (v. 38).

It would be a mistake to read too much of the postresurrection Christian conception of the Messiah back into the Old Testament era. Although in both canonical and noncanonical

writings there are references to Israel's hope, it was not possible for Jews of the pre-Christian era to have the more systematic and complete understanding of those who believed after the Messiah's coming. After the earthly ministry of Jesus, there was time to ponder more fully how all the diverse prophetic statements could be fit into a coherent scheme. Also it is clear that much of Israel's messianic expectation was not even consistent with Jesus' actual ministry. The excessive emphasis of some on the militaristic and nationalistic theme caused Jesus to shrink from being identified with an earthly independence movement. An illustration of the misunderstanding is apparent in an incident at Caesarea Philippi. After requesting the disciples not to tell others that he was the Messiah, Jesus warned them to expect his coming death. The idea that the hope of Israel would suffer defeat went counter to Jewish anticipation of the Messiah's leading Israel to victory and blessing. When Peter protested the thought of death, Jesus sternly informed him that his conception of things was a "stumbling block." Such a mentality reflected a mind tuned not to "the things of God, but the things of men" (Matt. 16:23). At the time of his arrest, Jesus protested the violent manner of his seizure by soldiers. "Am I leading a rebellion, that you have to come out with swords and clubs to capture me? Every day I sat in the temple courts teaching, and you did not arrest me" (Matt. 26:55).

The Concept of the Messiah in the Old Testament and Pseudepigrapha

The term *Messiah* comes from a Hebrew verb denoting "to anoint" and means "the Anointed One." The Greek form for the same title is *Christos* or Christ. This title is commonly added to the name of Jesus as though it were a part of his personal name. Eventually it came to refer to a divinely appointed ruler who would deliver Israel from oppression and bring an age of peace and blessing. While there are many important passages in the Old Testament that are considered to be messianic prophecies, the use of the term *Messiah* itself to describe the future royal deliverer is unknown except possibly for one passage: Daniel speaks of a time when "the Anointed One, the ruler" will come, and again of the Anointed One being "cut off" (9:25–26). It is only after the era of the prophets that *Messiah* becomes a designation of the promised unique Deliverer of Israel. More commonly the term is used of historical priests and kings. In the case of priests it is used as an adjective, as in Leviticus 4:3: "If the anointed priest sins. . . . "

The substantival use of the term *messiah* in the Old Testament is reserved for kings. The anointing of a king or priest indicated that he held office as an agent of God, ruling by his grace. Although the title generally was used only of the Hebrew kings who exercised authority over Israel as God's earthly viceroys, it was applied by Isaiah to the Persian emperor Cyrus (45:1). But Isaiah's usage is not surprising, since the context indicates that Cyrus also was God's agent for delivering the Jewish nation. "For the sake of Jacob my servant, of Israel my chosen, I summon you by name and bestow on you a title of honor, though you do not acknowledge me" (45:4). According to Ezra 1:1, it was Jehovah who "moved the heart of Cyrus king of Persia" to proclaim release for the exiles so that they might return to Jerusalem. The anointed Hebrew kings ruled with a special endowment of God's Spirit (1 Sam. 10:6; 11:6). Yet Israel's kings failed to live up to the ideal standard expected of one commissioned by Jehovah. Jeremiah called them "shepherds who are destroying and scattering the sheep," and he promised that in a future age God would "raise up to David a righteous Branch, a King who will reign wisely and do what is just and right in the land. . . . This is the name by which he will be called: The LORD Our Righteousness" (Jer. 23:1, 5–6).

The ideal future king had several notable characteristics. (1) He would be a righteous king who would rule in accord with the direction of God's Spirit. (2) He would be of the Davidic line. The prophet Nathan promised David, "Your house and your kingdom will endure forever before me; your throne will be established forever" (2 Sam. 7:16). Isaiah spoke of both concepts (the righteous king and the continuation of David's line). Speaking of the rebirth of the Davidic dynasty, he says, "A shoot will come up from the stump of Jesse; from his roots a Branch will bear fruit" (11:1). Just as the stump of a tree may appear lifeless for months and then suddenly send up a new stalk, so the seemingly powerless Davidic family would spring up again to national leadership. The chapter division obscures a poetic contrast. Isaiah 10 ends with a description of the fall of Lebanon as a cutting "down [of] the forest thickets with an ax." By contrast to the dead stumps in Lebanon, the apparent lifelessness also of the Davidic line is only a temporary dormancy. From the line of Jesse (David's father) there would suddenly appear a new royal deliverer. Especially significant is the statement that the Spirit of the Lord was to rest on him, an indication of this ruler's being anointed for a special task (11:2). He will bring justice to the poor, and rule with godly discernment (11:3–4). The promise of a coming ruler of David's line is also found in Jeremiah and Ezekiel (Jer. 33:15–16; Ezek. 34:23–24). (3) The ideal future king would also have a special relationship with the Father. "I the LORD will be their God," prophesied Ezekiel, "and my servant David will be prince among them" (34:24). Isaiah said a child would be born, a son, "and the government will be on his shoulders. And he will be called Wonderful Counselor, Mighty God, Everlasting Father, Prince of Peace" (9:6). Daniel's vision of "one like a son of man" also suggests the superhuman qualities of the coming ruler.

Daniel saw him "coming with the clouds of heaven. He approached the Ancient of Days and was led into his presence." Not only did he receive sovereign power, but all peoples "worshiped him," and he received a dominion that would be everlasting (7:13–14). Some scholars interpret the passage as a figure for the people of Israel, but it has been taken by many to be a reference to an individual king.

Controversy over the proper interpretation of passages taken as messianic has often obscured their meaning. The "servant passages" in the second half of Isaiah (42:1–9; 49:1–9; 50:4–11; 52:13–53:12) have often been taken to be a personification of the nation of Israel rather than an individual, but however one may interpret the prophet's own meaning, there is no doubt about the New Testament's application of those passages (see Matt. 8:17; 12:18–21; 26:67; John 12:41). Those who take the servant passages as predictive of an individual messiah find there an abundance of support for the concept that the messianic king would do more than usher in an age of peace and prosperity; he would also experience rejection and suffering. He would be "a man of sorrows, and familiar with suffering," would be "smitten," "afflicted," "pierced for our transgressions," and "crushed for our iniquities . . . " (Isa. 53:3–5). It should be admitted that there is clear biblical warrant for interpreting the "servant" as an image for the nation. Isaiah 41:8–9, where the term is first used, speaks of "Israel, my servant, Jacob, whom I have chosen, your descendants of Abraham my friend," whom God "took from the ends of the earth." It may be that while the servant represents Israel, the nation, the image can also be used of one individual from among the Jews who in himself is the supreme representative of that people.

The Old Testament Apocrypha (books accepted by Roman Catholics as part of the Old Testament canon) provide very little messianic information, but the Pseudepigrapha (Hebrew, Aramaic, and Jewish works that were not accepted as canonical) contain many indications of a messianic expectancy. The First Book of Enoch, composed sometime between 150 and 100 B.C., uses terms and concepts about the Messiah that appear later in the New Testament.[23] Enoch calls the coming king by the terms "Anointed One," "Righteous One," "Son of Man," and "Elect One." Enoch 62:5–7 speaks of the day when men will "see that Son of Man sitting on the throne of his glory. And the kings ... shall ... extol him who rules over all, who was hidden. For from the beginning the Son of Man was hidden, and the Most High preserved him in the presence of his might, and revealed him to the elect."[24] This passage might be understood to speak of a messianic figure who was preexistent. The book goes on to predict the destruction of all unrighteousness and the coming of a future era of triumphant righteousness. Especially interesting from a theological standpoint is the manner in which Jehovah speaks of his close tie with the Messiah at the close of the book: "For I and My Son will be united with them for ever in the paths of uprightness in their lives; and ye shall have peace: rejoice, ye children of uprightness."[25] These few illustrations from the Old Testament and the Pseudepigrapha can provide only a superficial survey of the character of the messianic hope. Much more could be done. But this survey will at least suggest something of the expectancy of the Jewish people by the first century A.D.

Chapter 4

Religion and Philosophy in the Roman Era

The Quest for Faith in the Roman World

The world into which Christianity came had no lack of philosophy or religion. When Paul came to Athens, the Epicurean and Stoic philosophers entered into intellectual dialogue with him and escorted him to Mars Hill so that he might give an account of his views. Many of the Athenians and foreigners who listened to him were accustomed to spending their days "doing nothing but talking about and listening to the latest ideas." But Paul experienced in Athens more than the confrontation of rationalistic speculation; he also saw an array of pagan shrines, and he declared the men of Athens to be "in every way ... very religious" (Acts 17:22). In the bewildering array of philosophies, superstitions, and deities the people of the Roman world found little satisfaction. Paul described paganism as an exchange of "the truth of God for a lie," and as the worship of "created things rather than the Creator" (Rom. 1:25). Such a perversion of truth inevitably led to the loss of ethical absolutes, a depraved mind, and indecent behavior. Yet ancient people, like people of all ages, wanted ethical guidance in their earthly life and assurance of a peaceful life beyond death. They desired reconciliation with the supernatural power behind nature, craved loving fellowship with a higher being, and sought some assurance that their creed or philosophy deserved intellectual acceptance. By the first century A.D. both the masses and the educated elite had the uneasy feeling that their religions and metaphysical inquiries had failed to meet these needs.

The Search for a System of Ethics

Three ethical systems of thought— Cynicism, Stoicism, and Epicureanism—gained acceptance in the Hellenistic age and won many adherents in Rome by the first century A.D. These philosophies displayed less concern with metaphysical speculations than had the earlier classical Greek philosophies. The Hellenistic philosophies were not primarily interested in determining the ultimate reality in nature but rather in discovering how one should behave and how one might live a virtuous and worthwhile life. The changing world that followed Alexander's conquests had brought renewed interest in ethics. The increased travel, trade, and cultural contacts resulting from the creation of Alexander's empire brought greater religious and philosophical tension. Old traditional local deities and time-honored ideas once held in relative isolation now met competing religious views, and in the resulting loss of security, people were seeking for new answers that could have a universal or cosmopolitan appeal instead of merely local acceptance. The Hellenistic age found a measure of comfort in Cynicism, Stoicism, and Epicureanism.

The Parthenon in Athens, built in the fifth century B.C. It was the chief temple of Athena on the Acropolis and is a superb example of Doric architecture. Courtesy Gerald Nowotny.

Three Hellenistic Ethical Systems

Cynicism

The Cynics traced their origin to Antisthenes, a philosopher who had been a disciple of Socrates. Their name may have come from the Greek word for dog (*kuon*). At any rate they took the dog as one of the symbols of their sect, and their chief aim was to "live like a dog"—i.e., without wants and pleasures in order to be free and independent individuals. Antisthenes sought to gain control over his own will by isolating himself from the influence of family, society, and politics. One of Antisthenes' students, Diogenes, who surpassed his teacher in popularity, is best known for his habit of toughening himself by residing in a tub. He thought people should live the simplest of lives, and after seeing a farm boy sipping water from his hands, he tossed his drinking cup aside as an unnecessary luxury. Diogenes and other itinerant ascetic teachers prized self-sufficiency. No tragedy or loss could ruffle the quietude of one who steeled himself against the vagaries of life by abandoning in advance any pleasure or comfort that might possibly be taken away. The Cynics gained many Roman adherents during the first century A.D.

Stoicism

A second Hellenistic philosophy that won many followers by the time of Christ was Stoicism. The founder of the movement, Zeno, was born about 336 B.C. on the island of Cyprus. His nickname, "the Phoenician," suggests he may have been partly Phoenician in his ancestry or heritage. At the beginning of the third century B.C. he moved to Athens to study. When news came, shortly after his arrival, that all his possessions had been lost in a shipwreck, he decided to dedicate his life totally to philosophy.[1] He gathered a band of followers in the *Stoa Poikile* (painted porch) and this colonnade gave Stoicism its name.

Zeno's teachings reflected the influence of earlier Greek thought. He studied under Crates, a leading Cynic philosopher, and from him Stoicism derived the concept of *autarkeia*, the independence of the individual from this world's cares and joys. From Socrates came an emphasis on self-control, and from Heraclitus the belief in a *logos* (reason) or fire-soul immanent in the universe. This belief in a world-soul ordering and guiding the material world tended toward pantheism and even bears a resemblance to Buddhism and Hinduism. Zeno taught that each man's individual *logos* or fiery spark was identified during life with the world-soul and at death merged with it. There was no real immortality for a Stoic since a vast conflagration periodically destroyed the universe. History repeated itself in an endless cycle, and after each universal holocaust the same forces and events were replayed.

Like Epicureanism, Stoicism chiefly concerned itself with ethics. It came into being at a time when the political system of ancient Greece, the city-state, was disintegrating, and when the ancient Greek mythologies began to lose their grip on the people. In such unsettled times men searched for some practical guide to live by. The virtuous life for a Stoic could be achieved only by willing acceptance of the order of nature, the pattern dictated by the *logos*. Inner tranquility and freedom from emotional reaction to life's events were the Stoic's highest goal. By accepting impassively the natural order, man's spirit could triumph over the vicissitudes of life. This ethic gained more disciples in Rome than it had earlier won in its Greek homeland. Among the most famous Roman Stoics were the philosopher Seneca (4 B.C.–A.D. 65), who was Nero's tutor as a boy and later his principal advisor, and the Emperor Marcus Aurelius (A.D. 121–180), a man of lofty ideals but a fierce opponent and persecutor of the church.

Paul's home city, Tarsus in Cilicia, became a center for Stoic teaching, and no doubt Paul knew well the tenets of this philosophy. Some Stoic concepts bear a rough similarity to Christian teaching, but the differences are substantial, and while many early Christian theologians were enamored of Greek philosophy, it is not accurate to portray New Testament theology itself as dependent on Stoic ideas. Two differences deserve emphasis: (1) Although the Stoics saw a pervasive force ordering and directing the cosmos, they were essentially materialists and semipantheists who did not sharply differentiate the creation from the creator. For Paul, God is external to the creation and transcendent above it. His hand providentially guides the course of the universe. He is immanent in but not identical to his creation. God the Holy Spirit comes into our lives to guide our own spirits, but Christianity does not identify or confuse our spirit with God's Spirit. In his message at Athens, Paul quoted a poet who expressed a pantheistic view: "For in him [God] we live and move and have our being" (Acts 17:28). But Paul's application of this phrase in his message makes it clear that he did not believe man to be part and parcel of God; his point in the Athens sermon is that since we are the work of God's creation we should not have a lowly view of God like those who fashion idols (Acts 17:29). (2) Stoicism also differed from Christianity in its tendency to recruit the upper classes. Although Stoicism viewed all people as equal, it drew its membership primarily from the elite few, the high and well-placed in Roman society, while Christianity appealed to people in all ranks of life. Paul told the Christians at Corinth that God had not called into their church many who "were wise by human standards ... influential ... of noble birth" (1 Cor. 1:26).

Epicureanism

The third ethical system, Epicureanism, first came to Rome early in the second century B.C. It was one of many elements of Greek life that the Romans found useful in their own society. Although the Romans adopted much of Greek thought and culture, they did not receive uncritically all that Greece had to offer. Rome "glorified power, organization, obedience, and discipline," while Greek culture valued philosophy, freedom, and beauty.[2] The fact that the Romans had a practical and utilitarian approach to life, helps explain their interest in Epicureanism. The upheavals of the first century B.C. drove many to ethical philosophy for consolation and encourage-

ment. The civil wars of Marius vs. Sulla, Caesar vs. Pompey, and the slave revolt led by Spartacus not only disrupted politics and society but also created a climate of mental and emotional tension. Epicureanism offered a way to withdraw from the annoyances of life to a placid and passive retreat. To the Romans, Epicureanism was not so much an abstract philosophy as a means for escape to a life of leisure and mental ease.[3]

Epicurus (341–270 B.C.), originally from Samos, came to Athens in 306 B.C. He taught that happiness was the greatest good and consisted of freedom from annoyance and fear. His philosophy has become in the popular mind a form of hedonism, but Epicurus was almost an ascetic, a gentle man who shunned sensual pleasures and sought peace of mind. Ataraxia (serenity) was his goal, and he knew it could not be attained through wanton abandon and dissipation. But Cicero recognized the ultimate tendency of a philosophy that made pleasure the chief virtue; he saw that Epicurean thought tended to encourage idleness, sloth, luxurious living, and withdrawal from the responsibilities of life.[4]

This ethical system was based on a materialistic conception of the universe. Epicurus derived his atomic theory in large part from the Greek philosopher Democritus. All matter including man's soul is physical and is composed of atoms that are eternally in motion. As atoms fall through space they automatically swerve and as they collide they form matter. Man's soul is simply an accidental collision of atoms that will eventually separate and terminate his existence.

There can be neither immortality for the soul nor resurrection of the body. For Epicurus, the knowledge that man is destined for physical annihilation was beneficial because it released him from the fear of death. Nor did he have to fear the gods because, although they do exist, they live in the void of space, unconcerned about man. They did not create the universe nor could they exercise any influence over it. Later, the Roman poet Lucretius (c. 98–55 B.C.) expressed the Epicurean view in his work *De Rerum Natura (On the Nature of Things)* when he passionately attacked religion and immortality as despicable superstitions that plagued man with unnecessary fears.

If Stoicism bears some faint resemblance to certain Christian attitudes, such as a concern for temperate living, Epicureanism is at many points a mirror opposite. The most basic teachings of the New Testament are at odds with Epicurus. For Christians the spiritual is as genuinely real as the created physical world. Knowledge of ultimate truth comes by God's revelation rather than through the physical senses. The highest good is to receive Jesus Christ as the deliverer from sin and punishment and then to live under his lordship awaiting a final resurrection and an eternal state of bliss. Christ did not tell his disciples to seclude themselves in a peaceful retreat; he ordered them to go into all the world and disciple people. Christianity is diametrically opposed to the major doctrines of Epicurean philosophy. Some scholars have attempted to demonstrate that the Pauline epistles reveal a dependence on certain Epicurean concepts and

terminology. Actually the vocabulary of the New Testament writers came from many varied sources and was adapted to the purposes of the author as led by the Holy Spirit. It is not surprising that Epicureanism and the New Testament should teach some concepts that bear a resemblance to each other, such as warnings to avoid the "deceitfulness of riches," the necessity of shunning all "injurious desires" (1 Tim. 6:9), and the importance of seeking peace. Such similarities do not, however, prove dependence.[5]

The Decline of the Ancient Roman Religion

Although Hellenistic philosophies gained popularity by the time of Christ, Roman religion had begun to lose its grip on both the educated and the masses. The faith of the earliest Romans had been animistic. Vast numbers of *numina* (powers or spirits) were thought to be at work in springs and streams, trees and hills. Even the home had its *numen* for the hearth and the doorway. Originally these "spirits" or "forces" lacked the anthropomorphic character of the Greek Olympian deities. While the Hellenic gods, portrayed in the colorful Greek mythology, possessed a very human character, the Roman *numina* appeared as vague and abstract powers representing some activity or locality. Eventually the attributes of many *numina* might be merged together to form a single anthropomorphic deity. Very early in the history of Rome the more picturesque gods of Greece began to influence the Roman concept of the gods. By the time of the Roman

Republic the Homeric gods had been merged with the Roman gods, but with the Greek conception remaining dominant. To the Romans, the Greek Zeus had become Jupiter; Aphrodite, Ares, and Hermes were identified respectively with the Roman Venus, Mars, and Mercury.[6] This syncretizing of Greek and Roman elements typified the Roman habit of freely blending their own religious and philosophic conceptions with those of the nations they subdued. Roman culture was eclectic, picking and choosing those elements of foreign custom that suited their utilitarian mood.

Remains of the altar of Zeus at Pergamum from the late third century B.C. Courtesy École Biblique et Archéologique Française, Jerusalem.

A variety of forces combined to weaken the grip of the ancient religion on the Roman people. The deities as described by Homer had not only been immoral in their behavior but were also of little aid to supplicants. Tales of gods involved in brawling, kidnapping, rape, murder, mutilation, and other atrocities shocked sensitive persons. Such deities could offer no model for ethical behavior. Nor could they be counted on to respond favorably to a call for aid. The Homeric gods could ignore, support, or spitefully vent their anger on supplicants. Although one might win favor with one divinity, he might incur the hostility of another. The deities had no responsibility to give account to anyone and could use their powers in an arbitrary fashion. In addition, their power had boundaries. They could not deliver man from the forces of fate; indeed, they were unable to wholly control their own destinies.

The inroads made by Stoicism and Epicureanism damaged faith in the ancient gods, and the latter philosophy especially was hostile to the formal religion of Rome. Somewhat like the eighteenth-century Voltaire, who stamped his letters with the slogan "Crush the infamous thing" (established religion), the Epicureans crusaded against religion as a decadent superstition. Another factor contributing to the decline of the ancient gods came from the rising influence of a philosophy known as "Skepticism." The Greek philosopher Pyrrho of Elis (c. 360–270 B.C.) founded this school of thought, which was based on the premise that it is impossible to arrive at truth. Since ultimate knowledge remains beyond reach, man should adopt an attitude of *ataraxia* (serenity) and retire from vain philosophizing and searching. Like Epicurus, Pyrrho took the path of withdrawal from the active life. Also contributing to the decline in faith was the work of the poet Ennius (c. 200 B.C.), who helped advance the teachings of the Greek philosopher Euhemerus (c. 300 B.C.). Both men portrayed the popular gods of Greece as originally mere men, heroic individuals whose exploits led to their deification in myth and legend.

One of the forces contributing to intellectual doubts about Roman religion arose from the unification of the varied peoples of the Mediterranean world into a single empire. The growth of travel, trade, and social contacts increased people's awareness of the welter of contending deities and notions. Rome took over, adapted, and harmonized as much as it could, but Roman religion was never able to rise above an "intellectual muddle" with such a jumble of opposing ideas.[7] Mobility led to a loss of faith in local gods. Individuals traveled easily across Roman roads that were no longer infested with bandit hordes and sailed seas relatively free of pirates. Leaving one's homeland often meant abandoning the locale of one's gods. Each small area had its own spirits and powers to be invoked. Even when the people of a region worshiped a well-known god, such as an Olympian deity, they were often using the more cosmopolitan name as a convenient symbol to be attached to their familiar and traditional local god, who had his own myths and associations.

The clash of gods and ideas created confusion and skepticism, but it would be too much to say that Roman religion had lost appeal for everyone by the time of Christ. Even as late as the time of Augustine (A.D. 354–430) many Romans thought the disasters befalling the empire resulted from the neglect of the ancient gods. Fourth-century Roman pagans feared that the barbarian invasions were the retribution of the ancient gods. They believed that when the people of Rome forsook the temple to acknowledge Christ as Lord, the spurned gods had retaliated by wreaking vengeance on Rome.

Attempts to Revive Roman Religion

Recognizing the decline of the ancient beliefs, Plutarch of Chaeronea (c. A.D. 46–120) in Greece, who earned fame as a prolific writer, historian, and biographer, championed a revival and reform of the Roman faith. He denied that the various nations actually worshiped different gods. Only one "Reason" governed the world, and all the different mythical powers served as representations of different aspects of this one god.[8] The tendency to syncretize a host of deities into one monotheistic force has a modern parallel in Hindu philosophy. Plutarch wanted to excise the barbarous and unethical behavior of the gods from ancient mythology and to set before the masses a deity who could inspire a morally upright life. His vision of a revitalized Roman faith never materialized. A century before his time, the poet Vergil (70–19 B.C.) sought to bolster Roman patriotism, the ancient virtues, and the traditional faith. In an epic poem, the *Aeneid*, he traced the odyssey of the heroic Trojan warrior Aeneas from Asia Minor to Italy, where he subdued all enemies and established the kingdom that gave birth to Rome. In these adventures Fate and the gods directed the steps of Aeneas and gave him aid. In the narrative the Roman gods emerge as being worthy of respect.

Vergil's nationalistic and moralistic outlook was shared by his friend and patron, Augustus. He set out in a purposeful way to strengthen the Roman religion. Augustus viewed the reform of the ancient faith as the avenue whereby the people might regain the moral strength, patriotism, and vitality of early Rome. He rebuilt fallen temples and established new ones. In a single year (28 B.C.) he refurbished 82 shrines. On the Capitoline Hill he erected a temple to the supreme Roman god, Jupiter, and on the Palatine Hill, one for Apollo. Under his guidance Rome also saw new shrines built for Mars, Magna Mater (the Great Mother), and Venus. Augustus restored and reorganized the priestly colleges that existed to serve particular deities. Some of these colleges had disappeared altogether, but now a new priesthood conducted the cultic ceremonies. The emperor also received the title of *Pontifex Maximus* (chief pontiff) and thereby assumed direction of the state religion. During the restive era after the Punic Wars, the Roman people had sought aid from the blind goddess "Fortune," from "Peace," and from Mercury. Roman religion tended to deify such abstractions as peace or fortune and to eventually grant them personality in addition to power. Augustus encouraged the veneration of these deities, but with his own name appended. Now the people gave honor to Pax Augusta, Mercurius Augustus, and Fortuna Augusta. He also permitted libations to be poured out before his own *genius*—i.e. the guardian spirit that hovered over and protected him. Worship of the *genius* was not quite the same thing as worship of the man Augustus. Scattered throughout the city of Rome were 256 shrines dedicated to the *genius* of Augustus.

Emperor Worship

Augustus cautiously avoided bringing to Italy itself any direct worship of himself as a deity. In the oriental world deification of rulers had been customary, but such honors for Augustus might have offended patricians who cherished the nonauthoritarian tradition of republican Rome. Worship of Augustus in the East would encourage patriotism, but in the West it might suggest monarchical pretensions. Augustus wanted the reality of power but was willing to sacrifice such titles as "King" or "Lord," which might be unsettling in Italy. In the Orient he could adopt a bolder policy. The Egyptians had for centuries deified their rulers. Antiochus Epiphanes, the Seleucid monarch, claimed by his title, "Epiphanes," to be the manifestation of a deity. In 29 B.C. at Pergamum in Asia Minor, Augustus permitted the erection of a temple to venerate the goddess Roma and himself. Roma, who personified the power of Rome, had been venerated by the Greeks since 197 B.C. Emperor worship had grown up on its own in the East. Now Augustus attached his own person to this cult and encouraged its spread as a means of strengthening his political control of Asia Minor. He also fostered the same imperial cult in Gaul, but not in Italy. This patriotic devotion to the state and its leader presented serious problems for the early Christians. As the custom gained acceptance it may have seemed like an innocuous ceremony, akin to saluting the flag in modern times, but for monotheistic Christians there could be only one *Dominus* (Lord): Jesus Christ. To pour out an offering of wine at the emperor's statue represented a denial of Christ as the only Master and God.[9]

Drawing of a statue of Tiberius Caesar.
Courtesy Carta, Jerusalem.

Generally, the Romans disapproved of conferring deity on living people. The Senate also believed it necessary to weigh the qualifications of a deceased leader before granting divine honors. Julius Caesar, great-uncle of Augustus, won the sacred office after his assassination, and his cult had many devotees during the time of Augustus. When Augustus died, the Senate gave their official stamp of approval to his deification.

The Roman historian Tacitus records that Tiberius, the successor of Augustus, followed the latter's example in allowing the worship of himself in conjunction with veneration of the city of Rome. But when a request came from Spain for permission to erect a shrine to Tiberius there, he responded with the statement, "I am mortal, . . . my functions are those of human beings."[10] Suetonius affirms that Tiberius would not allow the erection of even statues or busts without his prior consent and that when he did permit them, he would not allow them to be placed among the statuary of the gods. Suetonius also wrote that Tiberius refused to allow the renaming of the month of September in his honor.[11]

The next emperor, Caligula (or Gaius), took a wholly different approach. As a member of the Julian family he stressed his link with the deified Julius Caesar and Augustus. In the first year of his rule (A.D. 37) he dedicated a temple to the worship of Augustus. It is possible that Herod Agrippa I, king of Judea (A.D. 37–44), advised his friend Caligula to use divine honors as a means of establishing himself as an absolute monarch in the oriental mold. Near the end of his reign Caligula asserted his deity without restraint. He removed the heads from statues of Jupiter and replaced them with likenesses of himself. He became increasingly mentally ill, imagining himself discoursing with the gods. He erected a shrine to his own deity and appointed his horse to serve as a priest in his new temple. He ordered the erection in the Jerusalem temple of a statue of Jupiter bearing a resemblance to himself, but Herod Agrippa

I delayed the execution of this sacrilege for fear of a massive Jewish uprising. When a member of the Praetorian guard, weary of the emperor's disgusting and insane behavior, assassinated him, the Judean officials were free to ignore the provocative order and were able escape a disastrous upheaval.

Except for Nero and Domitian, the other emperors of the first century avoided Caligula's pattern of aggressively asserting deity. Claudius (A.D. 41–54) had restored Tiberius' policy of discouraging worship of the emperor, and Nero (A.D. 54–68) at least initially followed a similar policy, but the flattering honors offered to him eventually turned his head. He deified his infant daughter after her untimely death. In front of the Golden House, an ornate palace that he built as part of a slum-clearance project, he constructed a massive statue of the sun god, Phoebus Apollo. Significantly, the image bore his own features. He also issued new coins that portrayed him with a crown radiating beams of sunlight, suggesting an affinity with the sun deity.

Domitian (A.D. 81–96) determined to rule autocratically and was anxious to win the adulation and acclaim of the masses. He did not at first demand that his subjects address him as "*Dominus et Deus*" (Lord and God), but the title pleased him and he eventually adopted its use. Not surprisingly, the church has regarded Domitian as one of its leading first-century opponents. History has left little record of the persecution, but one can easily imagine the difficulty Christians must have experienced with an emperor who described himself in terms that could be worthily applied to Jesus Christ alone.

The Mystery Religions

Their Origin and Character

By the time of Christ the weaknesses of official Roman religion had become apparent, and the spiritual vacuum afforded an opportunity for a host of new cults. The traditional gods lacked personal appeal, and Rome's personified abstractions like Fortune or Chastity inspired little devotion. Rituals had become perfunctory and failed to evoke deep emotion or dedication on the part of the participants. Out of Greece and the Orient came a group of cults that sought to fill the void of Roman religion. These mystery religions appealed to those who longed for personal identification with a deity, wished for a blissful life beyond the grave, and sought emotional satisfaction in colorful pageantry and ritual. Their appeal was enhanced by their toleration of polytheism. The Eastern cults might elevate only one or two deities as the object of love and adoration, but they did not reject the existence of other gods. They were also universal rather than local faiths. The god of a mystery religion may have been derived from some locality or from an amalgam of a number of local mythical deities, but as a cult the religion offered its savior-god to all in the empire who accepted initiation into the faith.

The mystery religions differed in their origins and ritual, but most possessed certain common characteristics. None of them based their faith on an actual historical personality, like Jesus Christ, but drew instead on ancient mythology. In all of them, participants joined in celebrating certain major events in the life of their mythical gods. The ceremonies often included a dramatic reenactment of an event, or the viewing of sacred symbols. Sometimes the rituals involved wild music, frenzied dancing, or emotional processions in the streets. Not all of a cult's beliefs were secret, but a mystery religion, as its name implies, protected its most sacred rituals from the gaze of the uninitiated. The mystery was not necessarily esoteric or mysterious in the modern sense, but rather consisted of knowledge or experience acquired by participation in the rites. The Greek word *mysterion* means knowledge that has not yet been revealed. It does not, like the English term, imply something abstruse or elusive in meaning. The knowledge imparted to the new initiates might be quite simple, but it had not been experienced by them before. The elation and heightened perception achieved during the ceremony constituted the mystery revealed to the initiate. While outsiders might be well aware of the fact that secret rituals in a cult purported to bring immortality, the details of the ceremonies themselves were a carefully guarded secret. Only the *mystai* (those initiated) could have knowledge of the mysteries.

All of the mystery religions originated as nature cults with an emphasis on the seasons—on the death and rebirth of nature. A savior-god died, just as the plants and trees succumbed to the frosty blast of winter, but then his resurrection followed even as the tender spring vegetation followed the dark, bleak winter. Usually two deities, a male and a female, had the central place in the faith, and one of them had a role in restoring the other to life. The devotees of a cult, through the ceremonies, became personally identified with the redeemer-god and by their union with him participated in his immortality.

Magna Mater and Attis

One of the most popular of the oriental cults came from Phrygia in Asia Minor and centered on Magna Mater (the Great Mother) who was believed to be the mother of all gods. Although the Roman government had discouraged the introduction of foreign deities into Italy, the Senate itself promulgated the new faith in 205 B.C. Hannibal had dealt the Romans a setback at Cannae during the Second Punic War (218–201 B.C.). Consulting the Sybilline Books, the Romans learned of a prophecy promising deliverance to Rome if they would receive into her gates the Great Mother (sometimes called Cybele). The king of Pergamum welcomed a band of Romans to the temple at Pessinus where the black stone, the incarnation of the Great Mother, was housed. With the king's approval the Romans transported the stone to Italy and installed it in the Temple of Victory on the Palatine Hill in Rome. The wild pageantry and frenzied rituals of the new faith attracted many but repulsed the more educated Romans. Most shocking to Roman sensibilities was the self-emasculation of newly initiated priests. The Roman government prohibited any of its citizens from serving as a priest. But the sight of the eunuch priests lacerating themselves as they marched through the streets of Rome carrying their goddess and the sound of their shrieks and chants, horns, tambourines, and clashing cymbals stirred the passions of the Roman populace.

The Great Mother's consort, the young god Attis, may have been brought to Rome at the same time as the goddess. He was a youthful shepherd who had bled to death after emasculating himself under a pine tree. The Romans celebrated his death and resurrection in an annual spring festival. The rites evoked the memory of the Great Mother's grief and then the wild rejoicing at her revival of Attis. In the ritual, which lasted several days during March, the high priest drew blood from his arms and offered it to the goddess. In another ceremony the priests brought a sacred pine tree, symbol of Attis, from the woods and cutting themselves spilled their own blood on the tree. This mystery religion, like a nature or fertility cult, was closely linked with the cyclical dying and rising of vegetation in nature.[12]

Osiris and Isis

Another Eastern mystery religion that bore a strong resemblance to the fertility cults in its origin was the cult of Osiris, the god of the dead. Osiris and his consort Isis came to Rome from Egypt. Isis, like Cybele, was one of many feminine archetypes, a "great mother." She was the sister-lover of Osiris, by whose power the life-giving Nile flooded the land. The ancient Egyptians sometimes portrayed Isis with a column topped with stalks of wheat, a significant symbol because it demonstrates the vegetative aspect of the worship. The myths about the two gods vary greatly, some going back as early as the third millennium B.C. In the earliest tales a wicked brother, Set, killed Osiris and hid his body in a coffin. The grieving Isis recovered the corpse, only to have the angry Set dismember it and scatter the parts across Egypt. The faithful Isis patiently sought out the members of his body and restored him to life. When the legend was transformed into a Greek mystery religion, the initiate could by participating in the rituals gain the same resurrection and immortality that came to Osiris. The search for and reconstruction of the body became the central drama of this cult. Ptolemy Soter, one of the Hellenistic kings of Egypt, established the worship of the Greek god Serapis in Alexandria and identified him with Osiris, and from then on Osiris became known as Serapis.[13]

When the cult first arrived in Italy, in the first century B.C., it endured official persecution. But Caligula gave the devotees greater encouragement when he built a temple for Isis and Serapis in Rome. Because of its promise of victory over death, many people throughout the Mediterranean region found the cult attractive. It appealed especially to sailors and merchants, who swelled the ranks of worshipers in the port cities of the Empire. The cult included a festival to mark the beginning of spring, when the Mediterranean was no longer subject to the winter storms that threatened ships and commerce.

Osiris and Isis. In this drawing Isis is protecting Osiris with her wings.

The Eleusinian Mysteries

A third religion, the famed Eleusinian mysteries, had its beginning in Greece. Originally the rites of Demeter, a mother figure or fertility goddess, were not celebrated in Athens but only in the nearby town of Eleusis, about twelve miles from Athens. In the seventh century B.C., Athens absorbed the town of Eleusis and became involved in its cultic celebrations. Pilgrims from distant lands traveled in large numbers to participate in the rites. What came to be known as the "Great Mysteries" were celebrated in the fall, usually September, at the time of ploughing and of planting the new grain crop. The lesser mysteries, associated with the rebirth of nature, were celebrated in the spring. New candidates first attended the spring rites and immersed themselves in the purifying waters of the Ilissus River near Athens, but full induction into the mysteries could not be achieved until the initiate also participated in the autumn celebration. The latter festival lasted for eight days. It began with the carrying of sacred objects from Eleusis to Athens. The new candidates were again purified, this time by bathing in the sea. After offering sacrifices, the celebrants began a twelve-mile procession from Athens to Eleusis. Leading the march were priests carrying the image of Iacchus, eventually identified with the god of wine, Dionysus. By nightfall the joyful parade concluded its march at the Hall of Initiation in Eleusis with songs and dances.

Having reached Eleusis, the candidates were finally prepared for the secret mysteries. The reason for the celebration of these rites was no secret. Everyone knew that the goal was to gain a blessed life after death. But the actual rites were so well guarded that scholars can only guess at the nature of the ceremonies. Some of the early Christian writers have left us bits of information about the rituals, but since initiates who spoke too freely risked death, they revealed little about the ceremonies. Apparently the ritual included a fast, which was broken by partaking of sacred cakes and a drink made of meal and water. The central rite consisted of a drama, probably portraying Pluto, the god of the Underworld, abducting and raping Demeter's daughter, Persephone. This drama was based on a myth in which the grieving mother had deprived the earth of vegetation and life until Pluto restored Persephone to her care again. The seizure and restoration of Persephone symbolized the dying and rebirth of nature. Because Persephone had consumed food in the lower world, it was believed that she was required to return to Hades annually during the winter months. Her absence coincided with the withering of vegetation. But the worship of Demeter and Persephone during Hellenistic times came to signify more than the cyclical withering and rebirth of vegetation. Those who participated in the rites came to see the goddess Demeter as imparting immortality to themselves as individuals.

In a second dramatic portrayal the participants at Eleusis witnessed a priest, representing Zeus, leading a priestess, representing Demeter, away from the assembly into a darkened room. Later another priest announced to all that a sacred child had sprung from the union. After the drama, the priests led the initiates through dark underground caves dimly lighted by torches, and finally brought them out into a brilliant glare of light where they viewed the sacred objects of the faith. This strange pilgrimage pictured the soul's journey through the grim underworld and the winning of immortality.

Mithraism

A fourth major mystery religion, Mithraism, also appealed to the desire to gain immortality, but the fertility and vegetation characteristics were less apparent. The stalk of wheat that sometimes appears in the nature cults has indeed been found in the Mithraic pictorial representations, but the cult appears to have been free of the sexual frenzies and sensual excesses of the other religions. The Eleusinian mysteries seem to have had little or no effect on the ethical behavior of the initiated, but Mithraism, by contrast, inspired a disciplined and moral life. The teachings of Mithraism cannot be fully known or understood, for the initiated left no body of literature to guide modern researchers. The chapels and monuments serve as the primary evidence for Mithraic liturgy and doctrine. But scholars have not been able to agree on how to interpret the symbols carved on the stone walls of the sanctuaries.

A Mesopotamian cylinder seal and its impression, depicting the liberation of the sun-god from between two mountains. From the Akkadian period, c. 2360–2180 B.C.

The god Mithra (or Mithras) antedates the Persian religion of Zoroastrianism. To the Aryans who invaded India in antiquity he was a spirit of light or truth, and in Zoroastrianism he became a subordinate power to Ahura-Mazda, the god of light. Persian religion was essentially dualistic, picturing the universe as a battleground for the forces of light against the forces of darkness, good against evil, truth against falsehood. At some point Mithra must have been promoted from the position of captain in the struggle against darkness to the role of deity. The actual transition is shrouded in obscurity, but in some manner a new religion developed around this former angelic warrior. An early Persian myth tells of a rivalry between Mithra and the sun. Both were allied with Ahura-Mazda, but Mithra demonstrated his greater valor by capturing and slaying a bull. The blood of this bull gushed forth upon the earth to give it fertility and life. Ahriman, the god of darkness, tried but failed to stanch the life-producing flow. The unconquered Mithra in other tales defeated Ahriman's efforts to destroy man by flood and drought. In the early mythology Mithra and the sun first appear as separate powers, but sometimes they seem to coalesce into one deity.[14] Mithra's identification with the sun would eventually aid in winning favor for the cult in Rome, because sun worship had been practiced in varied forms there.

The worship of Mithra reached Rome via the pirates of Cilicia. In the first century before Christ, when Pompey purged the Mediterranean of the seafaring bandits, some of his captives introduced the faith into Roman territory. Mithraism had few adherents during the century of Christ and Paul, but in the next two centuries it grew more rapidly and reached the frontiers of the empire in Gaul and even Britain. Although the restriction of the cult to only males reduced the potential for growth, there was some association of the initiates with the women who worshiped Cybele. Roman soldiers especially admired the valorous exploits of their warrior deity Mithra, the strict discipline of the religion, and the hierarchical structure of the cult organization. They carried the faith to far-flung military posts. The small size of their chapels should not be taken as proof that converts were few in number. Worshipers met in a grotto that could seat only from fifty to one hundred people, but from excavations all across the empire archaeologists have discovered that there was a large number of these meeting places.

The initiates who met in these cavelike sanctuaries moved up in the cult's hierarchy through seven grades. During the rituals a participant wore the mask or costume of his degree. The lowest three grades were not considered communicants. In ascending order the degrees were identified as (1) Raven, (2) Hidden One or Bridegroom, and (3) Soldier. The highest grades that enjoyed fuller participation in the mysteries were (4) Lion, (5) Persian, (6) Courier of the Sun, (7) Father. Since no separate clergy existed in Mithraism, the two highest orders directed the ritual. The number seven, which is seen here in the number of orders, also predominated in the central mystery of the religion. According to this revelation the soul in its sojourn from space to earth passed by seven heavenly spheres or planets, each of which tainted the individual with some vice. Having arrived on earth, the Mithraic soldier had to discipline himself against these temptations that had attached themselves to him during his astral journey. In the battle to overcome vice he used the mysteries of Mithra as his chief ally. Those who gained victory over the darkness could traverse the same planetary path back to the place of the soul's origin. But before gaining the final destination and immortality, one still had to use his wits to defeat the grim guardians who blocked the pathway at each of the seven planets.[15]

The actual ceremonies in the Mithraeum (the chapel) included initiatory rites marking entrance into a new grade. Not totally unlike an old college hazing rite, they involved whippings, passing through fire, fasting, branding, and immersion in water to symbolize death. A sacred meal of bread and wine also served as a memorial to the last meal that Mithra celebrated with the sun. Another rite, the taurobolium, may have been borrowed from the Great Mother cult. The ceremony has been compared to baptism, but the crude and repulsive nature of the taurobolium is hardly analogous to Christian baptism. A bull was slain on a platform above the initiate who bathed in the falling gore. Actually the ceremony may not have been universally practiced, since most of the chapels were too small to accommodate the spectacle. Its introduction into Mithraism probably did not come until the second century A.D.

Mithraism became one of Christianity's chief rivals in the Roman era.

Part of the antagonism arose from the similarities between the two. In the view of the church fathers, Mithraism was a tool of Satan. The devil sought to delude mankind with his demonic travesty of genuine religion. Both Christianity and Mithraism differed from the philosophical sects in that they appealed to the masses instead of an intellectual elite. Other similarities included a kind of baptism, a Lord's Supper, an emphasis on abstinence and self-discipline, belief in a cosmic struggle between the forces of good and evil with good finally in the ascendancy, an early deluge, immortality, a resurrection, a final conflagration, a heaven, a hell, and a celebration on December 25th. But many of the similarities have been exaggerated and need not be taken as an explanation for the origin of Christianity. Unlike Christ, Mithra was not a historical person whose life and resurrection have been attested by historical documents. Some of the developments in Roman Mithraism can be explained as deriving from Christianity as easily as the opposite thesis that Mithraic elements penetrated Christianity. Any Mithraic contribution to the practice of early Christianity came after Christ's time and was not part of the original faith taught in the New Testament. For example, not until about A.D. 300 did Christians begin celebrating December 25th, the day of the sun's birth, as a convenient day for their own festival. This is not a case of Christianity in its original form displaying a dependence on a mystery religion.

When examined more carefully, Mithraism and Christianity are quite dissimilar. These examples must suffice here. (1) First, the Christian ordinance of baptism has little resemblance to the original taurobolium. This rite originated with the various mother-goddess cults of Asia Minor. In its primitive form the initiate who took his place in the pit below the sacrificial animal supposedly gained the vitality of the animal by being drenched in its blood. Only after the first century A.D. did Mithraism adapt this rite to its own use. By the second century the significance of the rite changed, since now the blood of the bull imparted, not strength, but a rebirth or renewal of the soul. (2) Second, Mithraism compromised with polytheism while Christianity stood firmly against idolatry. (3) Third, the Mithraic doctrine of the soul's journey was linked to erroneous views about the nature of the planets. Christianity's teaching on immortality was never chained to a pseudo-scientific astrology.[16]

The desire for a faith that satisfied the intellect, the yearning for a more personal and emotionally satisfying faith, and the quest for some assurance of a blissful future life all contributed to the preparation for the preaching of the gospel of Jesus Christ. The fantastic mythologies of the mystery religions and the debased ethics of the ancient Roman gods could not satisfy man's spiritual hunger. The Hellenistic ethical philosophies failed to offer a sense of certainty or emotional satisfaction. The spiritual wasteland of the early Roman Empire offered a potentially fertile field for the message about Jesus Christ. In Paul's words, the "fullness of time" had come and "God sent forth his Son."[17]

Roman ruins at Gerasa, showing the oval forum and the main thoroughfare. Jesus' ministry reached beyond the Jordan to Decapolis, "the region of the Gerasenes" (Luke 8:26). These ruins are identified with modern Jerash in Jordan. Courtesy Garo Nalbandian.

Chapter 5

Jesus and History

Jesus of Nazareth is a historical figure. He lived in Palestine about 5 B.C. to A.D. 30, and his birth, ministry, trial, crucifixion, resurrection, and ascension are well-authenticated events. Christianity is a historical faith that has at its core a historical person. While almost all scholars would not doubt that a man named Jesus lived, taught, and died in Palestine, not all would agree that the historical records found written in the New Testament should be accepted as trustworthy. It is not possible in a survey of the New Testament age to fully enter into the debate over the authenticity of the words and works of Jesus as found in the four Gospels. But Christians should not dismiss such questions out of hand. Rather, it is reasonable that intelligent believers should be aware of historical and critical issues.

The Value of the Historical Method of Criticism

Although the rise of the historical-critical method of evaluating sources has been a major contribution to man's understanding of his past, its use has also brought a decline of belief in the reliability of the New Testament witnesses. The historical method has been applied to New Testament studies for several centuries but primarily has gained currency in the nineteenth and twentieth centuries. One of the major assumptions of modern historical research is that one must not accept any primary source or witness as credible without first exposing it to critical analysis. The questioning spirit received special impetus during the eighteenth century when the French *philosophes* subjected many accepted "truths" to the scrutiny of man's reason. Some early Greek historians, such as Herodotus, had accepted without investigation and incorporated into their narratives, tales that would strain the credulity of the most simple-minded; but as early as Thucydides, who wrote a history of Athens' wars, historians began to question the veracity of witnesses before incorporating their testimony into the record. Objectivity and critical appraisal of sources gradually gained favor.

The critical method has demonstrated its value as a tool in evaluating sources. Scholars using historical methodology have frequently been able to demonstrate the fraudulent character of documents long accepted as reliable. Lorenzo Valla may serve as one example of the historian's craft. In A.D. 1440 he proved the famous Donation of Constantine to be a late forgery. This document had evidently been written by an unknown person in the eighth century A.D. to support papal claims to lands in central Italy. It granted the pope supremacy over all other patriarchs, a palace in Rome, the use of the imperial insignia, and sovereignty over lands in central Italy. Supposedly the grant had come from the Emperor Constantine in the early fourth century A.D. as a gift to Pope Silvester I in gratitude for his having healed the emperor of leprosy. Valla discovered anachronisms indicating the grant could not have come from Constantine's time. One such anachronism was a reference to Roman officials as *satraps,* a term used in the old Persian Empire but not in Constantine's time.[1] The Donation was clearly a fraud, but even when a document has been verified as authentic, it must still be subjected to questioning. Did the author have a propagandistic aim which led him to distort the truth? What biases or prejudices colored his thinking? Was he really in a position to give accurate information about his subject, or did he simply repeat hearsay? Did he record events of his own lifetime, or did he write long after the events when age and dimming of memory had weakened his ability to give an accurate witness? These are a few of the questions that must be posed before a historian can comfortably make use of a piece of evidence in his own narrative.

Limitations of the Historical Method

If the New Testament documents are to be accepted by the Christian as his standard for faith and life, certainly he should be willing to subject them to a valid historical method of analysis in order to determine their reliability as witnesses. The key word in the last sentence seems to be *valid.* The Christian does not fear truth but rather the error that might result from subjecting God's truth to the court of man's reason. The practitioner of the historical-critical method unavoidably comes to any document with a mind-set that includes many conscious and unconscious presuppositions. Generally he rejects out of hand the very concept that God could reveal his truth to mankind in written form by means of human instrumentalities so that there could exist a book that is without the frailties of human bias and imperfect understanding. He also presupposes that the divine cannot intervene in the natural order. Any account of the miraculous—a resurrection or healing—goes counter to normal human experience and is immediately suspect. Such a philosophy predetermines the outcome of any analysis of a book claiming divine inspiration. Such a book must be rejected.

Some Evangelicals have concluded that the historical-critical method as it has developed in the past century must be wholly abandoned. They view the method as an unneutral tool, one that cannot be separated from its antisupernatural bias. Harold Lindsell has asserted that "orthodoxy and the historical-critical method are deadly enemies that are antithetical and cannot be reconciled without the destruction of one or the other."[2] Many Evangelicals, however, would disagree with those who cast the historical method aside, believing that, if it is rightly used, it does have insights that are valuable for the believer. George Eldon Ladd has argued that only through the use of historical criticism can one uncover the cultural setting of the Jewish world out of which the New Testament came. A biblical phrase like "Son of Man" cannot be understood rightly without investigating its meaning in the Jewish historical context.[3] However, Ladd agrees that radical presuppositions on the part of scholars working from a secular approach prevent them from arriving at anything but a negative conclusion about accounts of the supernatural in Scripture. The theologian must not, he thinks, allow the naturalistic critic to set the bounds for inquiry into revelational or biblical history. He thinks that a proper method would deal with events in biblical history in a different way. They would be approached from the context of Christian faith and considered on a different dimension. He does not mean to imply that an event like the Resurrection did not occur in time and space, only that the event cannot be proved by historical method.[4]

Evangelicals readily admit that they have also adopted certain presuppositions and that their perceptions are colored by a world view. They cannot help but have a stake in the outcome of their investigation. They will not easily surrender faith in Jesus Christ, and so they come to Scripture with a prior commitment to its veracity. Yet Christians are no more liable to error than the critics who often falsely assume they have a greater degree of detachment. Christians must admit to bias and a commitment to a Christian philosophy, but having made this admission, they are able to entertain searching questions and even temporarily assume the role of doubter in the quest for certainty. Believers have a stake in the outcome; they also have an earnest desire to know the truth and to avoid delusion. Intelligent believers desire a faith that is worthy of belief and does not dodge the difficult questions.

The Synoptic Problem

It is especially important to know whether the four Gospels provide reliable information about the life and teaching of Jesus Christ. Are these records historically trustworthy, or are they simply collations of legend and myth? Did the authors of the Gospels compose original works, or did they copy various sources of dubious value? The question of the origin of the Gospels can only be sketched briefly here. The subject has had the concentrated attention of a host of scholars, especially in the last two centuries, and has given rise to a massive and complex body of literature. For a more thorough discussion of the subject one needs to consult standard works in New Testament introduction.

The last three verses of Luke and the first sixteen verses of John on a fragment of the Bodmer Papyrus XIV-XV, early third century. Courtesy Fondation Martin Bodmer.

In the past, some of the more radical critics dismissed the fourth Gospel out of hand as unhistorical and sought for the historical Jesus in the synoptic Gospels, which they believed to be closer to the earliest oral teachings about Jesus. The term *synoptic* is applied to Matthew, Mark, and Luke because they are so often parallel in their accounts and seem to view the life of Jesus from the same standpoint. Literally, the word *synoptic* means "to view together."

Even a casual examination of the first three Gospels reveals a surprising amount of parallelism in words, phrases, incidents, and stories and in the ordering or basic structure of the material. Most of Mark can be found in Matthew, and a high proportion is also repeated in Luke. Of the 661 verses in Mark, 606 are essentially in Matthew, and 308 in Luke. But there are also striking divergences in the Synoptics. Luke is the most distinctive, with 520 verses peculiar to itself, and Matthew has 300 verses found nowhere else.[5] Mark is the least distinctive, with about 93 percent of its material duplicated in the other two. These facts bring to mind questions about the origin and relationship of the Gospels to each other. Some of the questions involved in the so-called "synoptic problem" are: (1) If the three Gospels were the works of three men working independently, why are there so many similarities? (2) On the other hand if they used each other's works, how can one account for the differences?

Attempts to Resolve the Synoptic Problem

The Oral-Tradition Theory

The earliest attempt to explain the relationship of the synoptic Gospels was the oral-tradition theory. There is some very early support for this theory from the early church fathers. Papias (c. A.D. 120), whose writings are extant only in the quotations found in Eusebius' *Ecclesiastical History* of the early fourth century, wrote that the second Gospel represents Mark's recollection of the preaching of Peter. He also claimed that the first Gospel was written in Hebrew (evidently meaning Aramaic) by Matthew and consisted of the *logia* of Jesus. By *logia* Papias may have been referring simply to sayings (oral teaching) or to oracles in the sense of divine revelation (1 Peter 4:11). Usually it is assumed that he used the term in the sense of oral teaching. The oral-tradition theory gained prominence at the close of the eighteenth century and began to lose ground by the fourth decade of the next century. According to this view, the oral teaching and preaching of the apostles, after frequent repetition, assumed a stereotyped form as Christian leaders fixed it in their memory. Possibly Jesus himself had repeated some of his messages to help imprint his teaching on the minds of the hearers. Although this theory might not provide a complete and final solution to the synoptic problem, it probably contains an element of truth. It is clear that the good news was communicated orally for several decades before the Gospels were written. As long as most of the apostles were still alive the need for a written record seemed less pressing, and attention would have been given to preserving an accurate oral account. Several Scripture passages suggest this. Speaking of the content of the gospel message that he preached, Paul said he had received it from others and passed it on to the Corinthians (1 Cor. 15:1–3). He also asserted that there was only one authoritative gospel message (Gal. 1:8).

But the oral-tradition theory alone cannot answer all the questions posed by the synoptic problem. One wonders how a fixed and stable tradition could allow for so many verbal divergences in the Synoptics. It is also difficult to believe that the oral gospel could have been maintained in a fixed form as it spread beyond Judea to Syria, Asia Minor, and Greece.

The Interdependence Theory

The theory of interdependence is another very early attempt to resolve the synoptic problem. Simply stated, it is the view that the earliest Gospel written became a source for the second one, and the third writer depended on both predecessors. Augustine (A.D. 354–430) thought Matthew wrote the earliest Gospel, and he believed Mark wrote an abridgment of Matthew. Luke then was able to utilize both Matthew and Mark. This traditional view was also held by two scholars of German heritage, Johann Jacob Griesbach (1745–1812) and Theodore von Zahn (1838–1933), and it is still the common view of Roman Catholic students. Griesbach believed that Mark was the last of the Synoptics to be written and depended on the other two and that Matthew may have been the first Gospel. But most biblical scholars of the past century have rejected Griesbach's order, preferring instead Marcan priority. Within the last decade, however, a few scholars within the liberal tradition have rejected Marcan priority and have attempted a revival of the Griesbach hypothesis. Among these rebels are a retired German school administrator, Hans-Herbert Stoldt, and an American critic of the Bible, William R. Farmer.[6]

Theodore von Zahn's version of the interdependence theory is somewhat more complex than Augustine's. He believed an Aramaic form of Matthew appeared first and became the basis for Mark's Greek Gospel. The Aramaic Matthew was then rewritten in Greek with the aid of Mark's Greek account. The two Greek versions were then available for Luke's narrative.

The theory of interdependence has also been developed in many other varied forms. All the three Gospels have been placed first by one or another scholar, and the various possible ties have been explored at great length. There exist only six basic usage patterns that are theoretically possible—i.e., six different temporal sequence orders.[7] They can be graphically portrayed thus:

Order of Writing	1	2	3	4	5	6
FIRST	Mt	Mt	Mk	Mk	Lk	Lk
SECOND	Mk	Lk	Mt	Lk	Mt	Mk
THIRD	Lk	Mk	Lk	Mt	Mk	Mt

The interdependence theory could offer a practical solution to the synoptic problem, but it poses several problems of its own. Some view it as portraying two of the Gospel authors as copyists who relied on others for a large portion of their work. Ancient authors had no scruples about plagiarism; so the theory does not suggest the writers did anything unethical, but it does reduce the originality of the later writers. The theory also fails to account for many of the phenomena in the Synoptics, especially the differences. Even those sections that are thought to be parallel exhibit many variations in vocabu-

lary, word order, and material omitted or included.[8] The theory of interdependence does help to explain similarities but by itself does not answer all the questions.

Source Criticism

A third approach to the synoptic problem is "source criticism." Early in the nineteenth century source criticism began to supplant the oral-tradition theory, which was losing favor with Bible scholars, although a few, such as Brooke Foss Westcott, continued to support it. The new discipline attempted to identify written documents that were hypothesized as lying behind the known three synoptic Gospels. One of the earliest documentary hypotheses argued that a single ur-gospel (original gospel), written in Aramaic and lost in the haze of antiquity, must have served as the basis for the three known Synoptics, but this theory quickly fell by the wayside because it failed to account for differences in the writings and because no manuscript of this hypothetical document had ever surfaced.

Much more influential, and continuing as the most common view today, is the two-document theory. Usually the two-document theory argues that Mark was the earliest of the canonical Gospels and became for Matthew and Luke one of their two sources. This assumption of Marcan priority has set aside the testimony of the early church fathers that Matthew wrote his Gospel first. According to at least one modern literary critic, the choice of Mark as the earliest also reflected a theological bias. Stoldt argues that the initial reason for interest in the Marcan priority theory was the belief that Mark would provide a more historical basis for theology than Matthew and Luke, whose accounts were "encumbered by mythological and legendary birth narratives or resurrection stories. . . ." He also believes that Marcan priority has managed to maintain a strong following over a long period of time because influential scholars like Martin Dibelius and Rudolf Bultmann have accepted the view and lent their prestige to it.[9] Despite such recent attacks most literary critics still place Mark first, and the majority of Evangelical scholars also continue to accept Marcan priority. Critics also hold that Matthew and Luke made use of a second hypothetical document, which they label Q. The symbol Q is probably derived from the German word for source, *Quelle*. This supposed work contained primarily sayings or teachings of Christ. Matthew and Luke utilized Mark for much of their narrative material, and Q for their discourses or sayings. No Q document has even been found, although *logia*, or collections of Jesus' sayings, were not uncommon in the early Christian era.

What evidence has been offered to support the two-document theory? First, the order of events in the three Synoptics is surprisingly similar. Since the narratives often do not give a chronological or geographical setting for a particular story, it is odd to find such agreement as to order. Sometimes Matthew and Luke do not follow the same sequence of events as Mark, but in such cases they also do not usually agree with each other's sequence. In other words, while Matthew often agrees with

Mark against Luke as to sequence of events, and Luke sometimes agrees with Mark against Matthew, Matthew and Luke seldom ever agree with each other against Mark. This situation has been used to support the theory that Matthew and Luke used Mark as a source. Second, the actual phraseology and words of the text follow a similar pattern. Often we find similar phrases in all three Gospels. A striking example is in Mark 2:20, "But the time will come when the bridegroom will be taken from them, and on that day they will fast." The parallel passages in Matthew 9:15 and Luke 5:35 are almost identical. The Greek word for "taken away" is the same term in all three, although it is not used elsewhere in the New Testament. This suggests the possibility of some kind of literary relationship. Again, we discover that when Matthew and Luke diverge from Mark, they do not seem to be so similar to each other in phraseology.

One of the chief difficulties of the two-source theory is its inability to account for unique material in Matthew and Luke. Westcott found 42 percent of Matthew and 59 percent of Luke to consist of distinctive material. How could those who sought explanations through literary dependence account for this evidence for originality? In the 1920s B. H. Streeter sought to resolve the problem by assuming the existence of four sources instead of two. He used M to designate Matthew's distinctive material, which he thought originated in Jerusalem and had a strong Jewish cast as seen in the frequent quotations from the Hebrew Scriptures. Luke's peculiar material came from L, a document that supposedly originated at Caesarea. A major defect of Streeter's view is that it appears to be an attempt to bolster up the old two-source theory against objections that have been raised by positing more sources to explain the problems. A more complex set of hypotheses is set forth to allow for the confusing phenomena, but in so complicating the solution one also reduces the credibility of the explanation.

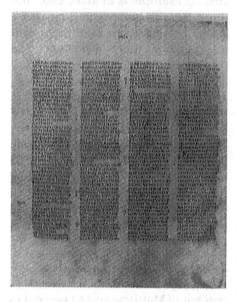

A page of the Gospel of Matthew from the Codex Sinaiticus, written in uncial letters on vellum, fourth century. Courtesy the British Library.

Most Evangelical scholars have accepted the current view that Matthew and Luke used Mark and Q. Some conservatives would still reject this view. But their objection is not based on the idea that the biblical authors could not have been divinely inspired if they utilized sources of information. It is obvious that biblical books did sometimes use sources: the Book of Ezra begins with a decree of Cyrus; Luke's prologue (1:1–4) speaks of other accounts of Christ's work as having preceded his own and asserts that he "carefully investigated everything from the beginning." Certainly the authors of the Gospels could have used a variety of oral and written sources. The only issue should be whether the evidence is sufficient to accept the two-document theory.

Could the Gospel writers be viewed as writing primarily without the aid of written sources? Some conservatives have viewed this as possible. The Gospel authors had personal access to a great deal of information beyond that obtainable only from written sources. Matthew had firsthand knowledge of his Master's teaching and was not dependent solely on other sources. His five great discourses were messages he himself had heard from the lips of Christ. We do not know if Mark knew Jesus personally, but the Scripture indicates that his mother's home was a gathering place for the first believers (Acts 12:12). Clement of Rome, a first-century Christian leader in Rome, says Mark aided in the ministry of Peter in Rome. Mark must have had numerous opportunities to secure information from those who knew Jesus intimately, including his own relatives. Luke, the Gentile physician, was not part of the early Jewish inner circle; yet he traveled with Paul and also had opportunity to speak with those who had direct knowledge about Christ's life. While Paul was imprisoned at Caesarea (A.D. 57–59), Luke would have had time for personal investigation. All three writers could have had personal contact with one another. Because all three had occasion to visit cities such as Antioch, they could have heard some of the traditionally fixed preaching and teaching on Christ's life. Familiar with some of the same bodies of teaching in early church centers, they could have sometimes accommodated their own accounts to the typical preaching of the day. Certainly the authors could have done more than copy one another's work. But the question remains whether the scenario of personal contact that is presented here is sufficient to explain the level of dependence that appears to be required by the striking similarities of many sections of the Synoptics.

The Rise of Form Criticism

By the close of World War I, source criticism seemed to have gone as far as its proponents could carry it. Interest began moving in a new direction: toward analysis and criticism of the oral tradition that preceded written sources. The German approach was called *Formgeschichte* (form history), but in the English-speaking world it became known as form criticism. Martin Dibelius and Rudolf Bultmann were among the early proponents of the method. Some of their conclusions were quite radical, and I am not suggesting that those Evangelicals who use their methodological tools are to be identified as "destructive critics." Bultmann believed that the stories and sayings in the Gospels circulated first as a large number of independent and unconnected units, which could be classified as fitting into several literary forms. Some of the forms identified have been pronouncement stories (or paradigms), miracle stories, myths, and sayings (including parables, "I" sayings, and other categories).

The different types of oral tradition, according to form criticism, were a product of the Christian community. According to the more radical brand of form criticism, as the church told and retold the stories and sayings, it modified them and even created new elements to help resolve then-current problems and theological controversies. In other words, the church did not preserve a pure and uncorrupted tradition, but rather adapted and even invented material to meet the needs of the time. The units then become for the scholar a primary source for the history of the first-century church, but a secondary source, and an unreliable one, for the life and teachings of Jesus. In order to ascertain how a unit might have developed, form critics attempt to reconstruct the background situation that gave rise to that unit's preservation or creation. By understanding the *Sitz im Leben* (life setting) of a story, one can discover the particular controversy or interest that shaped the unit until it assumed its final form.

Bultmann can serve as an example of the manner in which the most radical brand of form criticism operates. One of his categories is the apophthegm (called a paradigm by Dibelius), which is a narrative attached to a brief wise saying of Jesus. One kind of apophthegm is the "controversy dialogue." The Palestinian church experienced various theological debates, such as whether the Jewish Sabbath was to be strictly observed, or whether the church had the power to confer forgiveness for sin; and with this given *Sitz im Leben* it ascribed to Jesus a saying that provided an authoritative statement on the topic. To provide an occasion for the saying, he thinks, the church would also have constructed an imaginary situation involving a debate between Jesus and his critics. In the story of the healing of the paralytic (Mark 2:1–12), Bultmann believes that both the statement to the man seeking healing, "Son, your sins are forgiven," and the ensuing debate were imaginary creations intended to lend weight to the claim that the church could forgive sin. Bultmann does not think Jesus actually claimed the power to forgive sins. The debate in the church prompted the fabrication of the controversy episode. For Bultmann, any dialogue in controversy is an imaginary scene used to ascribe some concept to Jesus.[10]

The more destructive criticism of Bultmann may obscure the fact that form criticism need not be a radical methodology. The idea that the church preserved and shaped an oral tradition seems reasonable. No one doubts that the gospel had an oral form before it assumed a written form. If the church did develop recollections of the sayings and stories about Christ, it does not seem surprising that scholars today could try to categorize these stories according to their form. It is also likely that the church would have emphasized those aspects, words, and deeds that seemed most relevant to the situations and crises in the church. These remembrances could have been utilized by the Gospel authors. In other words, there is no reason to view the methodology in itself as totally baseless or destructive. It should be possible to examine the Gospels with form-critical tools without necessarily accepting the idea that the Gospels contain inventions of the church. Some of the form critics have avoided the extremes of Bultmann.[11]

Because the form-critical method as used by the more radical critics has raised questions about the authenticity of the material in the Gospels, conservatives have sometimes raised objections to the method. Some of these objections can be briefly stated. (1) The brief period of several decades between the Crucifixion and the writing of the Gospels did not afford sufficient time for the creation of oral folk tales. (2) The presence of a number of apostles and other eyewitnesses of Christ (Luke 1:2) during this era of an oral gospel would have prevented invention and imagination from running rampant. Not only the friends of the gospel but also its enemies could testify against fabrications. (3) It is hard to conceive of the early church risking life and limb for a gospel they knew to be their own creation. (4) The early church had a high degree of interest in preserving the authentic sayings of Jesus with accuracy. Paul takes special care to distinguish between his own words and those of the Lord (1 Cor. 7:10–12). Add to this interest in accuracy the fact that the Jews in their teaching and learning emphasized memorization. A rabbi like Jesus would have frequently repeated his sayings, and the disciples would have stored them carefully in the mind. Jesus also promised to grant the Holy Spirit to the apostles to bring to remembrance his sayings (John 14:26). (5) If the Gospels reflect the preaching (*kerygma*) of the apostolic church more than the original sayings of Jesus, and given Christ's heavy reliance in the Gospels on parables, it becomes difficult to explain why in the messages recorded in Acts and the epistles there are no parables. The use of the parable must have been a distinctive of Christ's own teaching method, and the recorded parables must have come from his own lips. (6) The method results unnecessarily in classifying the oral tradition as secondary rather than primary material, and the Gospel authors become mere copyists who assembled these numerous bits of unreliable information into an even less authoritative written record. (7) As F. F. Bruce once noted, form criticism does not succeed in its attempt to pare away myth and accretions to arrive at a human Jesus "who simply taught the Fatherhood of God and the brotherhood of man."[12] It is the Messiah and divine Savior who emerges even if one accepts the "demythologizing" method. The supernatural and divine are too interwoven in the accounts to be easily dismissed. (8) The church did not create Christ and the Resurrection, but the reverse. Without Christ's historical existence and teaching there would have been no church and no gospel tradition. (9) The failure of form critics to find agreement among themselves on the classifications of the oral tradition and on the *Sitz im Leben* of a particular saying does not lend credence to their system. Not all Evangelicals believe such objections would prove the method invalid. Also, some of the arguments seem to be aimed more at the most radical brand of form criticism than at its more moderate use.

The Rise of Redaction Criticism

After World War II, a new critical method, redaction criticism, emerged from *Formgeschichte*. The new criticism built on the former, but it also reacted against some of the earlier emphases. Instead of focusing attention on individual units, redaction criticism began analyzing the works of the three synoptic authors as unified literary compositions. Rather than viewing the writers as mere copyists whose editorial connections and additions needed to be excised in order to get back to an original oral tradition, the new approach saw the diversity of the accounts as an indication of creativity. The contribution of each author consisted primarily of a distinctive theological emphasis. Matthew is portrayed as writing in order to defend the Gentile Christian concept of Christ and the church against an opposing Jewish Christian view. In representing the Gentile view, he described Jesus as a teacher not of Mosaic law but of the true spirit of the law (Matt. 5:17–48), and he saw the church as a replacement for the synagogue. Mark was more eschatological in his emphasis, viewing Christ's return as immediately over the horizon. Luke writing after Mark and Matthew's day (about A.D. 90) supposedly no longer held to the imminence of Christ's return and directed attention instead to the work of the Holy Spirit among believers. This new approach has merit in that it sees the writers as genuine literary figures who made a distinctive contribution. Undoubtedly the authors of the Gospels had theological aims and their writings reflect unifying themes. While there is a positive aspect to this trend in criticism, there is also a danger that the assumption may be made that the authors invented material to bolster their viewpoint.[13]

Evangelicals have disagreed among themselves on whether redaction criticism (along with its predecessor, form criticism) is a legitimate tool for the orthodox. Some scholars believe that the utilization of this method inevitably leads to the acceptance of presuppositions destructive to faith. Others have argued that if the methodology is applied carefully and kept subject to a high view of Scripture, it can yield useful insights. Grant R. Osborne has suggested that the method not only helps scholars determine the theological emphasis of each Gospel but also is useful in resolving differences in the synoptic material. Some of the difficulties created by variations in the parallel accounts (see, for instance, Matt. 10:10; Mark 6:8–9; Luke 10:4) could be more easily explained if one allowed more flexibility for the evangelists. If the authors sought to preserve the true intent of Jesus' original words by use of summarization and paraphrase rather than simply trying to restate the oral tradition in a wooden fashion, the apparent difference in detail might be explained. Osborne would accept "coloring" of the *logia Jesu* (sayings of Jesus) but not creation or distortion. This is admittedly not the kind of redaction criticism used by the more radical practitioners of the method.[14] Another scholar has differentiated between the use of form criticism by the Evangelical as compared to that of the radical practitioners of the method. The naturalistic critic views the

oral tradition behind the Gospels as a merely human production, while an Evangelical views the orally transmitted words of Jesus as the inspired Word of God. Like the words of the ancient prophets, they were inspired in their oral form long before they were put into writing.[15]

A Conservative Approach to the Origins of the Gospels

It is not possible to discover the precise circumstances surrounding the origin and date of composition of the Gospels. The major theories have not received universal acceptance. Without presuming to have a final solution to the synoptic problem, I will make a few basic suggestions. These suggestions represent a viewpoint that would not be acceptable to all Christians, but they do reflect the views of many conservatives. These statements are offered without any attempt to provide detailed argument. One needs to go to works on New Testament introduction for such discussions. (1) The Gospels are divinely inspired and constitute an authoritative record for both historical fact and Christian doctrine. Yet this inspiration included not only a divine hand guiding the authors but also a human mind that was alert and operative, not in a trancelike state. It is difficult to come to an understanding of the exact human processes through which God brought His revelation before it reached the final written form of the Gospels that we possess. We do not understand very well the manner in which God used Matthew, Mark, and Luke in the production of the Synoptics. (2) Matthew, who personally knew Christ and could testify as an eyewitness, wrote his work sometime before A.D. 70. Critics have argued that this Gospel belongs to the decades after 70, because of the reference in Matthew 24:15 to the fall of Jerusalem. Such a view assumes that Jesus could not have made a prediction before the event. (3) Mark, an associate of Peter and one who was acquainted with many other eyewitnesses, wrote his gospel before 70. He relied especially on the preaching of Peter. Mark might have preceded Matthew, as most modern scholars believe, but such a view rejects the uniform persuasion of the early fathers. (4) Luke, who was a companion of Paul and met many eyewitnesses of Christ and who admittedly researched written documents for his own account, wrote after Matthew and Mark, possibly about A.D. 60. Since Luke wrote Acts as a second volume of a two-part work and refers to his first volume in Acts 1:1, his Gospel must have a date earlier than Acts. The Book of Acts must then be dated about A.D. 60 and the third Gospel about 59 or 60.

The Uniqueness of the Fourth Gospel

Is the Gospel of John a reliable record of historical teachings and events in the life of Christ? Some scholars have too easily dismissed the fourth Gospel as unhistorical and have relegated it to a place far below that of the Synoptics. This disparaging view arose in part because of the strikingly unique character of John's Gospel.

Six of the differences may be considered here. (1) John's account seems to demand a three-year ministry of Jesus because of the references to at least three Passovers (2:23; 6:4; 13:1), while the Synoptics mention only one. By way of answer it may be noted that while the Synoptics may be viewed as requiring only one year, it is possible to fit their events into a three-year framework. (2) The fourth Gospel omits a surprising amount of synoptic material. John does not record Christ's birth, baptism, temptation, transfiguration, and many smaller details that the other Gospel writers include. But these omissions do not prove that John was careless with facts. His omissions may simply be a result of his own distinctive purpose (20:30–31) and his familiarity with the synoptic version. He may have intentionally bypassed much well-known information, not, as some suggest, in order to present a view of Christ that represented his own mystical imagination, but to provide new information and a different perspective. (3) There is also much material that has no parallel in the Synoptics: the prologue (1:1–18); the early Judean ministry, which includes Christ's first miracle; the interviews with Nicodemus and the Samaritan woman; the healings of the lame man and the man who was blind from birth; the raising of Lazarus; the washing of the disciples' feet; the lengthy upper-room discourse; the intercessory prayer; and the miraculous catch of fish. None of these has any place in the synoptic record. These events may have been included in John's Gospel to fulfill his purpose of persuading people to believe and also simply because they were in his own memory of Christ's deeds. John may have intentionally omitted much that he knew had already been recorded in the gospel tradition. (4) The fourth Gospel places the cleansing of the temple at the outset of Christ's ministry (2:14–16), whereas the Synoptics picture it as an event just preceding and also precipitating Christ's trial and judgment. The most likely solution is that Christ twice saw the need for cleansing the temple of those who made the sacred grounds a place for commerce. (5) John pictures Jesus as the announced Messiah in the first chapter of his Gospel, but the Synoptics indicate the disciples only gradually came to perceive Jesus as the Messiah. But this need not be a discrepancy. The disciples may have only later fully apprehended and received a truth that had been taught earlier. (6) The style of Christ's teaching is very different in the fourth Gospel. John does not present the parables or short aphorisms of Jesus as the Synoptics do. Here Jesus seems to adopt a more intellectual tone and a very special vocabulary with emphasis on words like love, light, darkness, and the world. John omits teachings about the kingdom, which is a central theme in the Synoptics. These differences should not be dismissed lightly, but perhaps a solution can be found in two ways: (a) Jesus may have adapted his teaching style to the particular audience and (b) most of the discourses in John took place in Jerusalem where Jesus would have had a more knowledgeable audience than in Galilee.

The above list of differences should not be taken as complete. To set forth the extent of John's distinctiveness would require a much more detailed analysis of content and style. Nor could the space limitations of this work make a detailed study of the problems possible. The solutions proposed are suggestive, and other works should be consulted for more detailed discussion.

A papyrus fragment of John 18:31–33, dated c. 150. Courtesy John Rylands Library.

The Authorship and Date of the Fourth Gospel

Questions of the authorship and date of the fourth Gospel are also quite technical and can be only briefly explained. Irenaeus (c. A.D. 180) attributed the work to John the disciple. Another important witness to the authorship of the fourth Gospel is Papias, who was bishop of Hierapolis near Laodicea in Asia Minor. Papias wrote about A.D. 125, but his works are known only through surviving quotations. Eusebius of Caesarea in the fourth century provided the following significant statement by Papias:

> And whenever anyone came who had been a follower of the presbyters, I inquired into the words of the presbyters, what Andrew or Peter had said, or Philip or Thomas or James or John or Matthew, or any other disciple of the Lord, and what Aristion and the presbyter John, disciples of the Lord, were still saying. For I did not imagine that things out of books would help me as much as the utterances of a living and abiding voice.[16]

Eusebius argued that this statement should be understood to mean that there were two Christian leaders in Ephesus named John, one the apostle and the other a presbyter.[17] He believed that John the apostle wrote the fourth Gospel and that John the presbyter wrote the Book of Revelation. In modern times some scholars have taken the opposite view and suggest that John the presbyter wrote the Gospel and that John the apostle wrote the Book of Revelation. This is possibly based on a misunderstanding of what Papias meant. John the presbyter and John the apostle could well be the same person. Internal evidence in the Gospel also suggests that the "beloved disciple" or "other disciple," who penned the work, was one of the inner circle of three disciples: he was either James, John, or Peter. The fourth Gospel makes it clear that Peter is not the "other disciple" (John 21:20–21). Since James' death came early (Acts 12) in the history of the

church, it seems likely that John was the author.[18]

In the mid-nineteenth century, radical critic F. C. Baur of Tübingen dated the Gospel of John as late as A.D. 170. The discovery of a papyrus fragment of John (18:31–33, 37–38) in Egypt dated about A.D. 130 has shattered this theory. This little scrap, the so-called *Ryland's John,* is the oldest extant text of any part of the New Testament. The significance of this papyrus is that it requires a date for John before A.D. 100, or 110 at the least, in order for a copy to have been circulating in Egypt by A.D. 130. Most liberals and conservatives have now agreed on a date near A.D. 90 for the authorship of the fourth Gospel.

A surprising new theory has recently gained a hearing, if not acceptance. John A. T. Robinson, a British scholar, has proposed a drastic revision of the dating scheme not only for the fourth Gospel but also for all of the New Testament documents. Although he accepts and utilizes to some extent the critical method, he is essentially a maverick in concluding that all of the New Testament had been completed before the fall of Jerusalem in A.D. 70. The basis for his theory is his belief that there is no mention of this dramatic and life-changing event from a post-A.D. 70 perspective in any of the writings. He disagrees with the view that the preciseness of the predictive material in the Synoptics indicates that the writers had prior knowledge of the fall of Jerusalem. In his scheme the fourth Gospel is dated A.D. 40–65. Robinson disagrees with those form critics who do not see the Johannine material as having historical content. He also thinks the fourth Gospel does not reflect the Hellenistic or later phase of church doctrinal development as much as it does the thought patterns and vocabulary of the Dead Sea Scrolls. His ideas may not reflect the standard views of New Testament scholarship, but his call to reexamine the evidence without the weight of a century's "orthodox criticism" prejudging the results may provoke new inquiry.[19]

The Question of Bias

A common objection to taking the four Gospels as historical witnesses is that the record has been produced by Christians who would be predisposed to present a biased view. It must be admitted that our evidence for Christ's life comes almost entirely from Christian sources, but this should not automatically lead to their dismissal as reliable witnesses. Their passionate commitment to Christ does not necessarily rule out a concern for accuracy and truth. Historians often have no testimony for a particular event except that of an individual who was involved in the circumstances. A scholar should be alert for any indication of distortion because of bias, but he should not automatically assume that an interested witness could not have spoken without prejudice.

In addition to the Gospels, the witness of Acts, the Revelation, and the epistles provide some information on Jesus' life. Acts provides examples of early preaching about Christ and includes a saying not found in the Gospels. In Acts 20:35 Paul's message to the Ephesian elders closes with an admonition to remember Christ's injunction, "It is more blessed to give than to receive." One of the earliest witnesses to the Resurrection is 1 Corinthians. Although Paul was not an eyewitness of the actual event, he did meet the resurrected Christ three times.

Noncanonical Christian Witnesses to the Life of Christ

A large volume of noncanonical Christian material also speaks of Jesus but is of much less value than the New Testament evidence. Some of the papyrus texts are mere fragments that contain no real historical material. The best example is the Oxyrhynchus fragment designated as P. Oxy 840; it consists of a single paragraph describing a verbal clash between Jesus and a temple priest. The church fathers mention three Jewish-Christian Gospels: the Gospel of the Hebrews, the Gospel of the Nazarenes, and the Gospel of the Ebionites. These exist only in brief quotations, and it is not even clear whether the names given represent a single book going under three designations or whether there are two or three books. F. F. Bruce thinks there might have been two such works. He sees the Gospel of the Hebrews and the Gospel of the Nazarenes as two names for the same book, which he thinks paraphrased and modified the Gospel of Matthew. The Ebionites also formed their Gospel from the text of Matthew. Since this Jewish-Christian sect apparently rejected the Virgin Birth, they deleted the whole birth narrative from Matthew.[20] In 1945 at Nag Hammadi in Egypt archaeologists discovered three gnostic gospels: the Gospel of Thomas, the Gospel of Truth, and the Gospel of

Philip. The original Greek text of the Gospel of Thomas belongs to the second century, but the extant version is in Coptic and belongs to the fourth century. It contains 114 *logia* (sayings). Many of the sayings are variations on known canonical sayings of Jesus, and others are often based on phrases in the canonical epistles.[21]

A second type of noncanonical Christian source is the "Infancy Narratives." These consist of fanciful stories constructed to fill in the gaps in the life of Christ—gaps left by the canonical Gospels. It is natural that early Christians wondered about the early life of Jesus, and these stories appealed to that curiosity. The Infancy Story of Thomas illustrates the character of these accounts. The five-year-old boy Jesus molded twelve sparrows from clay, evidently impressing his playmates. Because Joseph scolded Jesus for violating the Sabbath rules, he clapped his hands, and the birds came to life and flew away. When another child frustrated him, Jesus made a withering verbal attack and then caused the boy to shrivel like a dead plant.

The Witness of Gentile, Non-Christian Writers

Very few scholars have ever doubted that Jesus was a historical person who actually lived in Palestine, even though they have often been skeptical of the reliability of the Gospels on matters of detail. Nevertheless, many Christians would like to know if there is some information about Christ in the pagan Roman records of the era. As F. F. Bruce has ably pointed out, the paucity of references to Jesus by Roman writers during the first century after the Crucifixion should not be at all surprising. One would have to understand the Roman citizen's outlook to see why there would have naturally been little reference to Jesus. The Romans thought of Judea as a remote and troublesome province that had more than its share of bandits, rebels, and dissidents. The execution of a rabbi whose followers were so few as to cause little stir would not be mentioned in the contemporary historical accounts. A Roman historian would not be prone to mention Jesus until his movement gained sufficient numbers to provoke some kind of crisis. Trouble makes news, and only when the Christian movement came into serious conflict with the government would an incident involving Christianity be likely to be included in the historical records.[22]

The Roman historical references are valuable as a confirmation of the actual existence of Jesus but do not offer any information not found in the New Testament. It is also clear that the Roman writers received their information from the Christians or enemies of the Christians. The pagan authors did not have direct knowledge. Still, their testimony does indicate that information about Jesus did reach Rome in the middle of the first century. Suetonius (A.D. 70–150), who served Emperor Hadrian as secretary, mentioned the Christians in a book written about A.D. 120—*The Lives of the Caesars*. In this work he collected twelve biographies running from Julius Caesar to Domitian. In a list of the events of the reign of Claudius (A.D. 41–54) he says, "Since the Jews constantly made disturbances at the instigation of Chrestus, he expelled them from Rome."[23] Luke also records the expulsion of the Jews by Claudius in Acts 18:2, where he tells of Paul's association in Corinth with the tentmakers Priscilla and Aquila, who were among the refugees. Although the name should be spelled in Latin *Christus*, the misspelling with an *e* probably reflects a common spelling error of the time. Suetonius also seems to have thought "Chrestus" was personally in Rome leading some kind of tumult. He also, like many Romans during the first century of Christianity, did not clearly distinguish between Judaism and Christianity. Christianity often appeared to be only a branch of Judaism to the uninformed. Probably Suetonius' information was very sketchy, but the incident behind his report is not difficult to imagine. Believers were preaching to unreceptive Jews that Jesus was the Christ (Messiah), and, as so often happened in the Acts accounts, the message provoked hostility. The resulting flare-up in A.D. 49 caught the attention of the authorities who were ever alert for threats to the order and stability of their rule. The resulting ban on Jews living in Rome was not enforced by the time of Claudius' death (A.D. 54), and many Jewish Christians had returned to revive their fellowship there by the time of Nero's reign. In Suetonius there is another brief reference to Christianity in the context of a discussion of abuses and corrupt practices ended by Nero. In his list of reforms, Suetonius notes that "punishment was inflicted on the Christians, a class of men given to a new and mischievous superstition."[24]

Another Roman historian, Tacitus

(A.D. 60–120), describes Nero's persecution of the Christians in greater detail. Nero had, he says, accused the Christians of burning a section of Rome in order to divert attention from the rumor that the emperor himself had been guilty of arson. About A.D. 120, Tacitus wrote his description of the persecution in the *Annals*, a work that traced the imperial administrations from Tiberius through Nero. Tacitus confirms both

Nero, Roman emperor from A.D. 54 to 68.
Courtesy Carta, Jerusalem.

the execution of Christ and its occurrence under the administration of Tiberius and Pontius Pilate:

> Christus, from whom the name [Christian] had its origin, suffered the extreme penalty during the reign of Tiberius at the hands of one of our procurators, Pontius Pilatus, and a most mischievous superstition thus checked for the moment, again broke out not only in Judaea, the first source

of the evil, but even in Rome, where all things hideous and shameful from every part of the world find their centre and become popular.[25]

Another Roman author, Pliny the Younger (A.D. 61–113), described Christianity in some detail. This Pliny is to be distinguished from the well-known Pliny the Elder, a naturalist who met his death in a volcanic eruption when his observations brought him too close to Mount Vesuvius. The younger man was his nephew and later an adopted son. About A.D. 110, while serving as governor of the province of Bithynia in northwest Asia Minor, Pliny the Younger wrote a letter to the Emperor Trajan (A.D. 98–117) requesting advice on how to deal with the "contagion" of Christianity. His letter indicates that Christians sang hymns "to Christ as to a god," and that Christianity was spreading so rapidly that the pagan temples seemed nearly deserted. In his lengthy epistle he wrote in part:

A drawing of Trajan, emperor of Rome from A.D. 98 to 117. Courtesy Carta, Jerusalem.

Presently the mere handling of the matter produced the usual result of spreading the crime, and more varieties occurred. There was published an anonymous pamphlet containing many names. Those who denied that they were Christians or ever had been, when, after me, they invoked the gods and worshiped with incense and wine your statue which I had ordered to be brought for that purpose along with the images of the gods, and, further, reviled Christ—things which it is said that no real Christian will do under any compulsion—I considered should be dismissed. Others who were named by the informer admitted that they were Christians and presently denied it, admitting that they had been, but saying that they had ceased to be, some several years before, some even twenty. All these likewise did homage to your statue and to the images of the gods and reviled Christ. They affirmed moreover that the sum of their crime or error was that they had been wont to meet together on a fixed day before daybreak and to repeat among themselves in turn a hymn to Christ as to a god and to bind themselves by an oath, not for some wickedness, not to commit theft, not to commit robbery, not to commit adultery, not to break their word, not to deny a deposit when demanded; these things duly done, it had been their custom to disperse and to meet again to take food—of an ordinary and harmless kind. Even this they had ceased to do after my edict by which, in accordance with your instructions, I had forbidden the existence of societies. For these reasons I deemed it all the more necessary to find out the truth by examination—even with torture—of two maids who were called deaconnesses. I found nothing but a perverse and extravagant superstition.[26]

Trajan's reply was much more succinct and indicated approval of his subordinate's policy:

No formula capable of universal application can be laid down. The Christians are not to be sought out; if reported and convicted they must be punished, with this reservation that any person who denies that he is a Christian and confirms his testimony by overt act, that is, by worshipping our gods, however suspect he may have been in the past, shall obtain pardon by penitence. Anonymous publications ought to have no place in a criminal charge. It is a thing of the worst example and unworthy of our age.[27]

Jewish Sources

In addition to the writings of Christians and the pagan historians, the extant records include the witness to Christ of Jewish non-Christians. The most significant Jewish testimony is that of the historian Josephus. He records that the high priest Annas "assembled the sanhedrin of the judges, and brought before them the brother of Jesus, who was called Christ, whose name was James" and delivered him to be stoned.[28] A more detailed statement appears in connection with a description of the procuratorship of Pilate. Josephus says:

Now, there was about this time, Jesus, a wise man, if it be lawful to call him a man, for he was a doer of wonderful works,—a teacher of such men as receive the truth with pleasure. He drew over to him both many of the Jews, and many of the Gentiles. He was the Christ; and when Pilate, at the suggestion of the principal men amongst us, had condemned him to the cross, those that loved him at the

first did not forsake him, for he appeared to them alive again the third day, as the divine prophets had foretold these and ten thousand other wonderful things concerning him; and the tribe of Christians, so named from him, are not extinct at this day.[29]

It is surprising to find in the writings of Josephus such a positive description of Jesus and especially the affirmation that "He was the Christ." According to Origen, an early Christian scholar who lived in the third century A.D., Josephus was not a Christian. Many scholars, including Evangelicals, believe the passage reflects interpolations by Christians sometime shortly after Origen's era. Nevertheless, despite the possibility that some insertions were made in the text, it seems likely that there is still an important body of confirmatory evidence in Josephus' writings. There should be no doubt that Josephus did indeed write about the life of a wise teacher named Jesus who did unusual works and was crucified in the time when Pontius Pilate was procurator in Palestine. The passage on James makes it clear that Josephus knew that believers claimed Jesus was the Messiah. Perhaps the second passage also included a reference to the belief in Jesus as the Messiah instead of the known text's bold assertion, "He was the Christ."

Another Jewish source dealing with Christ is the Talmud, a collection of the traditions and teachings of Jewish rabbis. The references to Jesus provide very little useful information, but seem to be aimed at portraying him as a false teacher who led Jews into error. The Talmud mentions his attacks on the Pharisees, his supposed use of sorcery, and his execution on the eve of Passover.

The testimony of many sources confirms that Jesus lived, but to construct an account of Christ's deeds and words one must rely on the canonical Gospels.

An aerial view of Bethlehem, facing north. Courtesy Israel Government Press Office.

Chapter 6

Jesus: The Early Years and the Roman Environment

It is not possible to produce a biography of Jesus. The Gospel writers did not intend to provide the materials for a detailed study of Jesus' family life, his feelings and thoughts as he grew to manhood, the formative influences that affected his development, or how he might have spent his leisure time. We do not even have a description of his physical appearance in the Gospels, and artists over the centuries have allowed free rein to their imagination in depicting the Savior. The Gospels focus rather on his mission and message. They proclaim the good news about Jesus but do not make it their aim to satisfy our curiosity about the variety of his experiences on earth. We have birth narratives, a story about the twelve-year-old lad Jesus at the temple, and then we are plunged directly into an account of his public ministry. The last week before the Crucifixion, the Passion Week, receives much more space in the Gospels than any other brief period of Jesus' life. Clearly the em-

phasis of modern-day Christians should also be to proclaim his message, his death for all people, and his resurrection. But we also need to discover what we can about the birth and early life of the most important figure in human history.

The Birth of John the Baptist

About six months (Luke 1:26, 36) before Jesus' birth at Bethlehem of Judea, another child was born in the Judean hill country. All four Gospels stress the importance of John the Baptist's preparatory ministry. Mark introduces his Gospel with a quotation from the prophet Isaiah: "I will send my messenger ahead of you, who will prepare your way—a voice of one calling in the desert, 'Prepare the way for the Lord, make straight paths for him' " (Mark 1:2–3). He then briefly describes John's ministry as a crusade to bring people to a baptism of repentance and to prepare the way for "one more powerful than" John. Luke's narrative begins with the an-

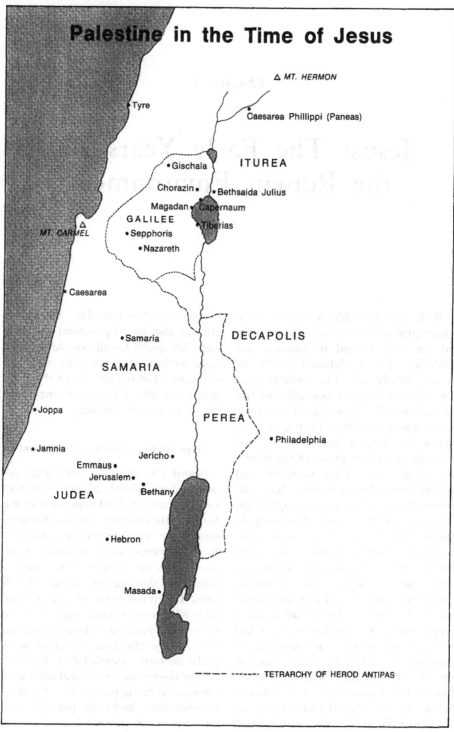

Palestine in the Time of Jesus

△ MT. HERMON

Tyre

Caesarea Phillippi (Paneas)

ITUREA

Gischala

Chorazin
Bethsaida Julius

Magadan   Capernaum

△
MT. CARMEL

GALILEE
Sepphoris   Tiberias

Nazareth

Caesarea

Samaria

DECAPOLIS

SAMARIA

Joppa

PEREA

Jamnia

Philadelphia

Jericho
Emmaus
Jerusalem
Bethany

JUDEA

Hebron

Masada

- - - - - - - - - - - TETRARCHY OF HEROD ANTIPAS

nouncement of John's birth by the angel Gabriel to Zechariah and his wife Elizabeth. John's parents lived in a village near Jerusalem, were both descended from a priestly line, and were "upright" servants of God. Zechariah held membership in one of the twenty-four divisions of priests (1 Chron. 24) who ministered in the temple. There were too many priests to permit serving in the Holy Place more than once during a whole lifetime. Zechariah's opportunity to burn the incense on the altar was thus a momentous occasion for him. During this reverent moment, he was perhaps as much surprised by the angel Gabriel's appearance as by the information that despite advancing age he would have a son. The angelic declaration that this son would never drink wine has been interpreted to mean that John was a Nazirite (Num. 6:1–8). But another requirement, that a Nazirite never cut his hair, was not mentioned by the angel. John can better be viewed as a prophet with an especially important commission: the heralding of the Messiah.

The Birth of Jesus

Six months after his appearance to Zechariah, Gabriel appeared to Mary in Nazareth and revealed to her the startling news that she would give birth to One who would be called "the Son of the Most High" and would reign on the throne of David (Luke 1:31–33). Mary obediently accepted the role of a virgin mother although it easily led later to rumor and whispering in her village. Matthew notes that Joseph at first considered her pregnancy cause for divorce. Engagement for Jewish couples was considered binding, and to end such a betrothal required a formal break. But an angel of the Lord appeared to Joseph and assured him that Mary's conception was of the Holy Spirit and that the Child would not only be known as Immanuel (God with us) but would also "save his people from their sins" (Matt. 1:20–23). Mary made a hurried journey from Nazareth to Judea and spent "about three months" with Elizabeth, leaving evidently just before the birth of John.

Luke records that Augustus decreed a census for the whole Roman world. To comply with the requirement that family heads return to their original home for the enrollment, Joseph journeyed to Bethlehem in Judea, which was the city of his ancestor David. There Mary gave birth to the boy Jesus in the quarters where animals found shelter. The shepherds who tended their sheep on the barren hills of Judea that night also received an angelic visitation, and so by heavenly arrangement humble shepherds instead of Galilean kinsmen would visit the newborn Child.

The Date of Jesus' Birth

Luke and Matthew provide information that gives us an approximate date for Jesus' birth. Luke places the nativity within the reign of Augustus, from 27 B.C. to A.D. 14 (Luke 2:1). Luke also dates Gabriel's announcement to Zechariah within the reign of Herod the Great (Luke 1:5). This forces one to place Jesus' birth either within Herod's reign or less than a year afterward. But Matthew settles the matter by stating flatly that Jesus was born "during the time of King Herod" (Matt. 2:1). Herod's reign began either in 40 B.C., when the Roman Senate proclaimed his kingship, or in 37 B.C., when he actually subdued his opponents and possessed his throne. Since we know at least the approximate time when Jesus reached the age of thirty, we also realize he could not have been born as early as the beginning or middle years of Herod's reign. Luke 3:1 tells us that John the Baptist's ministry began in the fifteenth year of Tiberius Caesar's reign, and in the same chapter Luke states that John baptized Jesus when He was "about" thirty years old. The use of the term "about" indicates Luke had only an approximate age in mind. Also the fifteenth year of Tiberius is not as unambiguous as it appears, since some scholars believe Luke might have been reckoning the beginning of Tiberius' reign from the date of his co-regency with Augustus (A.D. 11 or 12) instead of from the death of Augustus (A.D. 14). Thus Jesus' thirtieth year must have occurred no later than the time between A.D. 24 and A.D. 30 (see chapter seven for a discussion of chronology). The point to be made here is simply that Jesus' birth must have occurred late in Herod's reign.[1]

The date for Herod's death is well established. Josephus states that the king died just before a lunar eclipse and preceding the Passover. Such an eclipse occurred in March, 4 B.C., and Jesus' birth then occurred before the spring of 4 B.C. Herod must have died by March or no later than the Passover of April 11 (Nisan 14) of 4 B.C., and Christ's birth then occurred before the spring of 4 B.C. It seems impossible that Jesus' birth could be dated much before 6 or 5 B.C., since this begins to be too early for Luke's statement that Jesus was about thirty in Tiberius' fifteenth year.[2]

The present calendar used by Western civilization is based on a miscalculation of the year of Jesus' birth. In the early sixth century A.D., Pope John I commissioned a revision of the calendar that would use Jesus' birth as the fixed point for counting years. Unfortunately the monk Dionysius who established the new calendar calculated that A.D. 1, the year of Jesus' birth, should be the 754th year after the founding of the city of Rome. Although his reckoning of Jesus' birth was at least four years too late, it has not been practical to make changes in our present calendar.[3] It is not possible to determine the date of Jesus' birth. Eastern traditions suggest January 6, and in the Western church December 25. Some Bible scholars, noting that the shepherds would not be in the fields during the winter nights, have suggested a springtime birth. However, Palestinian weather does not always prevent sheep from grazing in winter, and it is not really known whether or not sheep were kept enclosed on winter nights. A date for Jesus' birth sometime during winter is a possibility.[4]

The Problem of Quirinius

The most perplexing problem in connection with the chronology of Jesus' birth is the statement by Luke that the census ordered by Augustus took place "while Quirinius was governor of Syria" (2:2). Luke also specifically dates John's birth in the days of Herod the Great (1:5), while Matthew is even more specific in locating

Jesus' birth in Herod's reign (2:1, 19). Remember also that Herod died in 4 B.C. According to Josephus, Augustus sent Quirinius to be governor of Syria at the same time he sent Coponius (the first prefect of Judea) to rule the Jewish nation (A.D. 6). The Jewish historian in the same narrative records the census as provoking a popular uprising against foreign tribute. This uprising and the census associated with it is a well-known event of Jewish history. Judas the Gaulonite and Sadduc, a Pharisee, led the freedom fighters in a struggle reminiscent of the Maccabean zeal.[5] In Acts 5:37 Gamaliel in a speech to the Sanhedrin describes Judas' rebellion as occurring at the time of the census. Quirinius' accession to the governorship of Syria clearly came in A.D. 6. Equally clear is the fact that Quintilius Varus, not Quirinius, held the post from 7–4 B.C., when Jesus' birth and the enrollment occurred.

Sir William Ramsay, a professor of classical art and archaeology at Oxford and later at Aberdeen, an authority on the life of Paul, ably defended Luke's accuracy in his writings at the close of the nineteenth century. By Ramsay's view Quirinius ruled Syria on two different occasions, the first time coinciding with Jesus' birth. A fragmentary inscription found in central Italy at Tibur in 1764 appears to be a description of Quirinius, though the name is missing from the marble monument. The unnamed official lived during and after Augustus' reign, held the office of proconsul of Asia, had won significant military victories for which he received two supplications (thanksgivings to the gods for victory), and twice ruled Syria as Augustus'

legatus. These statements fit only Quirinius and indicate that he could have ruled Syria for a time previous to his A.D. 6 accession. Luke's terminology does not require that Quirinius be the sole governor. Ramsay argues that the Greek term *hegemoneuontos,* as used by Luke, might be applied to "any Roman official holding a leading and authoritative position in the province of Syria." He believed the term was used not only of a governor but also for one sent on a "special mission of a high and authoritative nature."[6] Quirinius would have been a logical choice to accompany Varus to Syria in 7 B.C. Varus had no military experience, and Augustus probably appointed him to lead the internal administration and Quirinius to direct foreign affairs.

If we accept the earlier rule of Quirinius as probable, one still wonders why Luke did not simply name the acknowledged governor, Varus. Two suggestions may be offered. First, Quirinius was not so obscure a figure when Luke wrote his Gospel. His original readers probably understood the time period indicated by the mention of Quirinius' name. The difficulty arises after the mists of centuries have obscured the career of this official. Second, as Ramsay suggested, Quirinius ruled for a shorter period than Varus, and thus his term as "Lieutenant of Augustus" in Syria would be a more specific point of reference for Luke's readers.[7]

Ramsay's argument has been questioned by some scholars. Since Quirinius' task in the East involved subduing the hill country warriors (the Homonadensians) of Cilicia, there would have been little opportunity to serve in the Syrian capital at Antioch. The argument is also weakened by the fact that censuses were taken on a fourteen-year cycle, and since the census recorded by Josephus took place in A.D. 6, an earlier unrecorded census in Syria would have to be dated about 8–7 B.C. Ramsay answered this objection by suggesting that the census in Herod's kingdom might have been delayed a few years, until 6 B.C., because of the unsettled situation in Palestine. A. N. Sherwin-White questions whether the use of a nameless and ambiguous inscription can lend credence to Ramsay's solution. Quirinius' career is summarized by Tacitus, and the details found there do not match up very well with those of the inscription.[8] In the view of Harold Hoehner, Ramsay's theory needs too many props to support it. Like F. F. Bruce and others, he prefers a grammatical solution. In Luke 2:2 he would translate the term "first" in the sense of "before." Instead of "This was the first census that took place while Quirinius was governor of Syria" (NIV), he suggests "This census took place before Quirinius was governor of Syria." According to this view, Luke meant that the enrollment and Jesus' birth occurred before Quirinius took office. Hoehner does think Quirinius might have held office earlier, perhaps in 3–2 B.C., as well as in A.D. 6, but he does not see the earlier governorship as the solution to the difficulty.[9] The grammatical solution is appealing because of its simplicity, but since such a translation is not universally accepted, there remains some doubt as to which resolution of the problem is best.

Although Luke's reference to Quiri-nius has created some uncertainty among Bible scholars, one should not dismiss the matter by assuming an error in Luke's narrative. The problems are admittedly complex, but the biblical writer deserves at least as much credence as is given to Josephus. Our difficulty in reconciling Luke's statement with other known facts may simply be a result of our lack of information. For example, some critics have assumed that since Josephus recorded an enrollment under Quirinius in A.D. 6, there could not have been an earlier enrollment as described by Luke, and that Luke must have confused the time of Quirinius' census. This is an argument based on the silence of Josephus or other witnesses as to an earlier enrollment, but silence cannot be used as a testimony against Luke's witness.

As new information becomes available, problems often disappear. It has been denied that the Romans would ever have required Joseph to return to Bethlehem for the census as Luke 2:3 asserts. But it is now clear that the practice of returning to one's home district for a census was not unknown to the Romans. While there is not any independent corroboration of such a practice in the region of Judea for the time of Augustus, there is an indication that the Roman governors of Egypt did require such a return early in the second century A.D. The following is an edict from the Egyptian governor who held office in A.D. 104:

> Gaius Vibius Maximus, Praefect of Egypt, says: The enrollment by household being at hand, it is necessary to notify all who for any cause soever are outside their nomes to return to their domestic hearths, that they may also

A view of modern Bethlehem. The Church of the Nativity is at top center. Courtesy Israel Government Press Office.

accomplish the customary dispensation of the enrollment and continue steadfastly in the husbandry that belongs to them.[10]

This kind of evidence suggests that Luke's explanation for Joseph and Mary's being in Judea instead of Nazareth at the time of Jesus' birth is not inconsistent with what is known about Roman enrollment procedures.

The Infancy of Jesus

The circumcision of Jesus eight days after his birth indicated that he would be raised according to Jewish religious tradition. This ceremony, like his baptism later, would serve "to fulfill all righteousness" (Matt. 3:15). In both ceremonies he identified himself with his people. The name "Jesus," given at his circumcision, revealed his mission as Savior of his people. Mary and Joseph were faithful to the Torah and educated their son in its precepts. Several weeks after the circumcision, they traveled with the Child to the Jerusalem temple to meet the requirements of the law that an offering be given for a male child (Num. 8:15–16), and a pair of doves be sacrificed for the purification of the mother (Lev. 12:1–4, 6). Luke seems to have a special interest in individuals, and he alone tells of the aged Simeon and the elderly prophetess Anna who met the child Jesus in the temple. Their testimonies reflect Israel's expectation of a messianic Deliverer. Simeon's song also recognized that the Child's mission went beyond the confines of Israel for he would be "a light for revelation to the Gentiles" (Luke 2:32).

Gateway to the Church of the Nativity in Bethlehem. The arch of the original opening can be seen around the present opening. The gateway was made smaller in the Middle Ages to prevent riders from entering the church on horseback.
Photograph by Richard L. Niswonger.

Exactly when the Magi appeared cannot be determined. The fact that Herod had all male infants slain up to two years of age may indicate that the visit came a year or more after Jesus' birth, or it may simply be another confirmation of Herod's thoroughness when it came to brutal repression of any possible threat to his dynastic ambitions. The Greek term *magoi* suggests wise men or priests who had expertise in cultic arts such as astrology or interpretation of dreams.[11]

Luke does not speak of the trip to Egypt. He simply tells of the return to Nazareth. Matthew, on the other hand, does not mention Nazareth as the home of Mary and Joseph until after the story of the escape to Egypt. The accounts are not contradictory but supplemental. Matthew and Luke had different pieces of information and so constructed their narratives with certain omissions. The sojourn in Egypt lasted until death removed Herod from the throne. The holy family then journeyed to Palestine but bypassed Judea and returned to Nazareth. Archelaus, as ethnarch, had inherited his father's Judean, Samaritan, and Idumean provinces; he also quickly gained the same reputation for cruelty as his father. But at Nazareth in Galilee the young Child would be in a more stable environment. Herod Antipas established in Galilee a "strong centralized system of government," which was capable of keeping order in the region.[12]

Jesus as a Youth

Very little information is available about the childhood and youth of Jesus. Yet it is clear that he lived in an upright Jewish home. His parents journeyed to the religious festivals in Jerusalem. The boy Jesus in his human consciousness must have gradually realized his distinctiveness and his unusual mission. Perhaps his family mistook the dedication to his heavenly Father as arrogance or misguided zeal. They seem to have misunderstood him. On one occasion, after Jesus had begun his preaching ministry, his mother and brothers came to Capernaum to restrain him, thinking he was beside himself. When Jesus taught in the Nazareth synagogue, the hometown acquaintances "took offense at Him." Jesus reminded them that a prophet is usually honored, but not "in his home town and in his own house" (Matt. 13:57); his neighbors responded by trying to edge him over a cliff. When told on another occasion that his family waited outside for him, Jesus replied, "My mother and brothers are those who hear God's word and put it into practice" (Luke 8:21), perhaps implying that his own family had not yet fully received the message he proclaimed. Jesus also warned his followers that the gospel would be a divisive force in their families. Such statements may reflect a division in Jesus' own household. When Jesus chose his earliest disciples, they came not from his own family and neighbors but from among John's disciples. Later, his brothers may have become believers. At least James, after personally seeing the resurrected Jesus, joined those of "the Way" and became a leader in the Jerusalem church.

The Scripture provides a small amount of information about the family of Jesus. Because there is no mention of Joseph after Jesus' twelfth birthday, it seems likely that he died sometime before the period of Jesus' ministry. Jesus had four brothers: James, Joseph, Simon, and Judas. There were also sisters, but their names are not recorded. The belief that Mary remained a virgin after Jesus' birth and that the brothers were actually cousins or children of a previous marriage of Joseph has no

foundation. Mary, at the cross, was placed by her loving Son in the care of the beloved disciple, John, and she must have lived on as a witness to her Son's message.

A veil of darkness covers Jesus' life after his infancy and up until the time of his ministry. Luke provides the one brief glimpse behind this curtain in his account of the journey to the Passover celebration. The twelve-year-old Jesus amazed the learned scribes at the temple with his understanding of the law. The narrative tells us several things about the boy Jesus: (1) He was interested in learning the traditions and laws of Judaism, since he not only displayed knowledge but respectfully asked questions of the scholars and listened to their answers. (2) He was "obedient" to his parents. (3) He had some sense of his mission and his special relationship to the Father. Luke adds to the story the comment that "Jesus grew in wisdom and stature, and in favor with God and men" (Luke 2:52).

Jesus must have been thoroughly educated in the Law, the Prophets, and the Writings (the three Jewish divisions of their Scriptures). Frequently he was able to quote or allude to the Old Testament in his teaching. During the temptation period, Jesus repulsed Satan with quotations from Deuteronomy and the Psalms. He could expound in detail on the messianic prophecies from all the Jewish Scriptures, as he demonstrated to the two disciples on the road to Emmaus after the Resurrection (Luke 24:27). As a child, Jesus must have learned the oral traditions of Judaism, since Pharisaic influences pervaded Galilee at that time. He also probably learned to read Hebrew at a young age. The readers of the Law in the synagogue services at Nazareth, as elsewhere, read the scrolls first in Hebrew and then gave an Aramaic translation for the masses. Since Aramaic had become the spoken language by Jesus' time, this was his native tongue. The Targums, Aramaic translations of Scripture, had not yet been written and preserved, but Jesus no doubt was able to carefully follow the Hebrew reading and then the translation. This may have been the manner in which the intelligent youth began to learn Hebrew. After his ministry began, Jesus surprised those who knew him at Nazareth by reading a messianic prophecy concerning himself from the Hebrew scroll of Isaiah. The discovery of the Isaiah scroll in 1947 suggests how the scroll at Nazareth might have looked. It would have had no stick or rollers as modern Jewish rolls of the Law do. The writing would have been on one side only. To find chapter sixty-one Jesus would have had to unravel about twenty feet of the scroll; since there were no chapter breaks, he could have found it only if he were very familiar with the Hebrew text of Isaiah.[13]

Jesus and Galilee

Nazareth was the hometown of Jesus for most of his lifetime on earth. When he went out to meet John to be baptized, he "came from Nazareth in Galilee" (Mark 1:9). He was called the "one from Nazareth" and "the Nazarene." Nazareth lay in a valley enclosed by hills on all sides except the south. It possessed only one good spring, now identified as *Ain Maryam*, or Mary's Well. Nazareth was not a major town and is mentioned neither in Josephus nor in the Old Testament. Although no trade routes passed through the village, they were not far distant, and Jesus did not grow up in isolation from the commercial activities of his day. The more populous coast of the Sea of Galilee was only twelve miles to the east. Jesus must have stood many times on the hillsides around Nazareth, which were sixteen hundred feet above the sea, and gazed at the beautiful landscape that could be viewed in all directions. To the northeast Mount Hermon raised its snow-clad peak toward the clouds. Looking to the west, he would have seen Mount Carmel and the Mediterranean coast, to the south the Plain of Esdraelon, and to the east the hills of Gilead.

Jesus did not only grow to manhood in Galilee, but here he also did most of his preaching. The Synoptics give special emphasis to the Galilean ministry. This pleasant country afforded a relief from the barren, unproductive, and forbidding landscapes of Judea. It had green valleys, rivers, and springs; there were trees of all kinds including olive, fig, and almond; and along the lake were bustling fishing villages. The New Testament mentions one of the most important cities on the lake, Tiberias, only once (John 6:23). Herod Antipas built the city in the style of a Greek *polis* (city) and named it for the Emperor Tiberius, but strict Jews avoided the town after workers who labored at the site dug into a forgotten burial site. Antipas established it as his capital city, and 170 years after Christ's death it would also have a synagogue and a community of Jewish scholars. Josephus describes the location as "the best part of Galilee, at the lake of Gennesareth."[14] Since Jesus ministered primarily to those of the house of Israel, he bypassed this Hellenistic city. He chose instead to make Capernaum, on the northwest shore, his base for ministering to Galilee. He possibly lived for a time in Peter's home during his Capernaum stay (Matt. 8:14). Capernaum had sufficient population to have a customs booth (Matthew's post) and a Roman military force of at least one hundred men. The ancient synagogue at Capernaum uncovered by archaeologists belongs to the second or third century A.D.

A drawing of Jesus and his mother studying the Torah. From Wallace, "The Boyhood of Christ," Harpers Magazine, 74/439 (December 1886): 11.

Three Herodian Rulers

Herod Antipas

The land of Jesus' birth remained under the rule of Herod the Great for no more than a few years at the very most after Jesus' birth. By the time the Egyptian sojourn ended, the kingdom had been divided among three sons: Herod Antipas, Philip, and Archelaus. Herod Antipas received the prosperous little Galilee region and the more arid land called Perea, a long narrow strip extending along half of the eastern coast of the Dead Sea and reaching northward along the eastern side of the Jordan almost to the Sea of Galilee. But the two lands did not touch each other, being separated by the territory of Decapolis. Augustus may have thought Herod Antipas would pose less of a problem if his territories were not united. A more powerful Antipas might wrest territory from Archelaus or even defy Roman authority.[15] Herod Antipas received the title of tetrarch, as did Philip, a less prestigious office than that of a king. He rebuilt the city of Sepphoris after it had been destroyed by the Syrian governor Varus in putting down a rebellion there. After he strengthened the walls, it became his capital city until he completed the new city of Tiberias about A.D. 23. Sepphoris had the largest population of any city in Galilee. Since Nazareth lay just four miles away to the south, Jesus as a boy could have often walked to this center of Roman power. Perhaps he very early formed a negative opinion of the nearby tetrarch whom he later called "that fox." Hoehner's study of the term *fox* suggests that it depicted "an insignificant or base person" who

The city of Nazareth. Courtesy École Biblique et Archéologique Française, Jerusalem.

did not possess "real power" but used "cunning deceit" to accomplish his will.[16]

Despite rebellions, Antipas generally managed to keep his subjects pacified. To avoid offending Jews he would not allow images to be placed on the coinage. He even attended Jewish festivals in Jerusalem to win favor.[17] But when he imprisoned and then executed John the Baptist, he outraged the followers of the desert preacher. Antipas had regretfully agreed to have John beheaded. The story of Herodias' exploitation of the wiles of her daughter to entice the tetrarch into carrying out the execution is a familiar one (Matt. 14:6–10). John had angered her by his condemnation of her marriage to Antipas. Both Antipas and Herodias had been married previously. Herodias had been the wife of Herod Philip, a lesser son of Herod the Great. She

had abandoned him to marry Antipas but insisted that her new mate also divorce his spouse. The abandoned wife was the daughter of Aretas IV, king of Nabatea, and this Arab monarch did not passively accept the ouster of his daughter. The divorce brought war with the Nabateans, and the Syrian legate Vitellius had to come to defend Antipas' realm against the attacking Arab King Aretas. Herodias eventually brought Antipas' administration down because of her envy and quest for power. When she heard that Emperor Caligula intended to exalt her brother Agrippa to the kingship, she prodded her husband to seek the same title. Annoyed by such aggressiveness, Agrippa complained to the emperor, who then banished Antipas and his cunning wife to Lugdunum (modern Lyons), Gaul, in A.D. 39.

Philip the Tetrarch

Josephus described Tetrarch Philip as a man of "moderation and quietness" who fairly and efficiently ruled his subjects.[18] He governed Iturea and Trachonitis, territories located east of the western source of the Jordan River and to the north of Galilee. He enlarged the town of Bethsaida, east of the Jordan and a mile north of the Sea of Galilee, and he named it Julius in honor of Augustus' daughter Julia. He also built a new city at the old town of Pan, where a broad, clear stream pours out of a mountainside just south of Mount Hermon. In honor of Augustus he named the city Caesarea Philippi. The addition of his own name helped distinguish the town from the Caesarea that Herod had built and which was Judea's administrative capital as well as a seaport. Since fewer Jews lived in Philip's region than in the other areas of Palestine, coinage could bear the emperor's image without provoking the population. Philip married Salome, daughter of Herodias, but he died without an heir in A.D. 33 or 34, and his tetrarchy then was placed under the direct rule of the province of Syria.

Archelaus

Archelaus, the third ruler of Palestine, had requested the title of king, but Augustus installed him as ethnarch with the possibility that after proving himself he might receive the more elevated title. But Archelaus inherited the brutal character of his father without his father's administrative ability. He also shared his father's interest in architecture. He restored Herod's palace at Jericho, for it had been damaged in the rebellion of 4 B.C., and he built aqueducts to water the palm groves north of the city. Near Jericho he also built a new town, which he named Archelaus in honor of himself. His rule lasted only nine years before he was banished to Gaul (A.D. 6). His territory included Samaria and Idumea as well as Judea. At the outset of his rule a demonstration against him occurred in the temple area during the Passover festival. Archelaus' response to the riot set the tone for his brief regime. He suddenly surprised the Jews at the shrine with an assault by cavalry and foot soldiers. Josephus claims that three thousand Jews were slain, many while they were bringing their sacrifices to the altar.[19] Shortly afterward, while the three brothers were at Rome seeking Augustus' ratification of Herod's will, rebellions broke out across Palestine. In Archelaus' region a shepherd named Athronges led the rebels. The Pharisees backed Simon, a former slave, in a Perean revolt. Judas, son of the earlier freedom-fighter Hezekiah, rallied the discontented Galileans and attacked the Roman stronghold of Sepphoris. The Maccabean dream of an earthly independent Jewish state was still alive. Varus, the Syrian governor, temporarily dimmed these nationalistic hopes by crushing the rebel forces with two Roman legions. He destroyed the city of Sepphoris, which Antipas later restored. The same kinds of disturbances occurred again in A.D. 6, after Archelaus' deposition, when Judas led a protest against Quirinius' taxation.

Judea as a Roman Province

After the removal of Archelaus, Augustus made Judea a Roman imperial province. While the larger and more important possessions were senatorial provinces and had governors from the senatorial class, men from the equestrian class ruled minor areas. Equestrians, originally members of the cavalry, had in later centuries become a class of businessmen and tax collectors; thus they belonged to the upper middle class. Augustus utilized this ambitious class to offset the power of the senatorial class. The equestrian governors ruled over districts that had been recently added to the empire or had a record of rebellion. Egypt, Sardinia, and some of the Alpine regions were imperial provinces similar to Judea in government.[20] The prefects of an imperial province had light-armed auxiliary cohorts of six hundred men each instead of legions under their command. The soldiers for the cohorts were recruited from the province where they served. There were five cohorts in Judea, each one headed by a tribune who had six centurions serving under him. Besides keeping order and security, a prefect's chief responsibility was to supervise the financial administration of the province. Governors of imperial provinces were directly responsible to the emperor. Augustus used such an official to rule Egypt because he wished to keep the grain trade, which was vital to keep the masses in Rome pacified, in his control. The Judean prefect was not, therefore, directly under the control of the Syrian governor, but since Syria was a larger province with a large military force, its governor did have some voice in Judean affairs and could send his troops into the region to prevent disorder. Usually the Judean prefect remained at his palace in Caesarea, the administrative capital, but at festival times when pilgrims filled the streets of Jerusalem, he would often be on hand with beefed-up forces there to prevent riots. This explains why Pilate was present in Jerusalem for Jesus' trial at Passover time. During normal periods a single cohort remained in Jerusalem to keep the peace.

Remains of storehouses at Beersheba dating to the Israelite period. Beersheba was the sourthernmost town in the province of Judah. Courtesy Zev Radovan.

The prefects governed Judea from A.D. 6 until A.D. 41, when Emperor Claudius established Herod Agrippa I as king of Judea. Agrippa's rule lasted only until A.D. 44, when the procurators again took over the administration. The early prefects under Augustus held office for only a brief term of about three or four years, but with the accession of Tiberius (A.D. 14) they were allowed to hold office for much longer periods. Tiberius appointed only two prefects during his twenty-three years, the second one being Pontius Pilate. According to Josephus, Tiberius believed that if the rapacious prefects were allowed to hold office only briefly, they would "more severely hurry themselves to fleece the people," whereas those who continued in office would eventually be satiated. Tiberius illustrated his policy by telling a story of an injured man who lay on the ground with a mass of flies covering his wounds. A passer-by pitied the suffering man and, thinking he was unable to disperse the flies, offered aid; but the wounded man refused and offered the following explanation:

> If you drive these flies away, you will hurt me worse; for as these are already full of my blood, they do not crowd about me, nor pain me so much as before, but are sometimes more remiss, while the fresh ones that come, almost famished, and finding me quite tired already, will be my destruction.[21]

The story illustrates the well-known truth that the prefects often misgoverned and preyed on the peoples they ruled. Actually Augustus had already reformed the financial administration of the eastern regions. No longer would men like Brutus, Cassius, and Antony drain the resources of the East with their fratricidal wars. Augustus' use of the census helped apportion taxes more realistically. He also sought to choose prefects for the imperial provinces who had ability, and he gave them a fixed salary to relieve the need for exploiting their subjects. Despite such improvements, it was not possible to maintain a just administration when the individual's only avenue for se-

curing redress of grievances against an unjust prefect was the cumbersome process of appealing to Caesar himself.

The Reign of Augustus

At the summit of Roman political authority, during the era of Jesus' infancy and youth, stood Augustus. As Rome's first emperor, he not only brought stability to the troubled empire during Jesus' early years, but the era of peace was to continue through at least the first century and a half of the early church's ministry. Providentially, the gospel message could be carried from city to city on roads relatively free from bandits and to distant regions no longer menaced by the clashing of rival Roman generals and their armies. This period of order and peace, called the *Pax Romana*, ended finally in A.D. 192 when Emperor Commodus was assassinated. The Prince of Peace entered the world in a relatively calm period of history. Frontier wars continued as Rome consolidated her territory and enlarged her boundaries, but the internecine strife of a century's duration no longer disrupted the life of the average inhabitant.

Augustus' success in maintaining himself in power for nearly a half century primarily depended on his creation of a new political system. Under the guise of restoring the old Republic, he managed to establish himself as a virtual autocrat or dictator. The Republic with its powerful senate and constitutional traditions had failed to establish order during the civil wars. Only as strong leaders emerged had the Republic experienced brief periods of peace. Bold

The Roman Empire Under Augustus

------- AREA CONTROLLED BY ROMAN EMPIRE IN TIME OF AUGUSTUS

generals like Julius Caesar who sought the appearance of power as well as the reality of authority aroused too much resentment to keep powerful senators in line. Augustus contented himself with holding the reality of power without the trappings of an oriental monarchy. He achieved dominance despite his refusal to use the title *dominus*. Rome's powerful generals had enjoyed this title, but Augustus recognized that the term *dominus* ("lord") was also used by slaves to address their masters.

Over a period of time Augustus did accept many titles and offices, which collectively placed central authority in his hands. (1) In 28 B.C. he became *princeps senatus*, which gave him the right to speak first in the senate debates. The title enabled him to dominate the senate, a body that had proved intractable to other would-be dictators. From this title came the name historians use to designate Augustus' form of government, the principate. (2) As the princeps, Augustus proclaimed himself alone to be *primus inter pares*, "first among equals," a description that seems self-contradictory. (3) In 27 B.C. the senate appointed him proconsul of Spain, Gaul, and Syria for a period of ten years. The senate from time to time renewed this proconsular authority for varying terms of office. Through the title of proconsul Augustus secured control over most of Rome's legions. (4) As explained earlier, the emperor's personal name was Octavian and the title Augustus was conferred on him by the senate in 27 B.C. The title meant "revered," and although it was in a sense only an honorific title, it reflected the reality that the masses did revere Augustus as a popular deliverer. (5) His control over all armies was vital for the maintenance of order, and in 23 B.C. he gained the *imperium* which in effect made him commander-in-chief. (6) In the same year the senate granted him the power of a tribune, an officer whose major responsibility was to defend the people's interests in government. Augustus held the authority without the office itself. Since Rome had more than one tribune at a time, to actually take the office would have meant sharing the honor. (7) Augustus held other offices also—such as the consulship, which early in his quest for power gave him authority over Italy and the city of Rome itself. It was an office he held intermittently. (8) In 13 B.C. Augustus assumed the leadership of Roman religion by taking the office of *pontifex maximus*, high priest. In his rapid climb to authority, Augustus would have found it inconceivable that in the latter half of his reign there should arise in Judea a Jewish lad who would eventually be hailed as the eternal High Priest (Heb. 7:23–26) and "King of Kings" (Rev. 19:16).

Modern Cana. It was at Cana that Jesus performed his first miracle—turning water into wine at a wedding feast—and it was here that he announced to the nobleman from Capernaum that his son was healed. Courtesy John Frye.

Chapter 7

The Ministry of Jesus

Roman Rulers During the Ministry of Jesus

Tiberius (A.D. 14–37)

Jesus conducted his public ministry during the reign of Tiberius, Rome's second emperor. Luke says it was "in the fifteenth year of the reign of Tiberius Caesar—when Pontius Pilate was governor of Judea . . . [that] the word of God came to John [the Baptist]" (Luke 3:1–2). The ministry of John led quickly into that of Jesus, probably within the same year. Tiberius came to the imperial throne by way of adoption. His mother, Livia, had married Augustus in 39 B.C. when Tiberius was three years old. Tiberius spent much of his life, before becoming emperor, in military camps where he proved himself to be a dutiful and able commanding officer. Despite his abilities, he lacked confidence, was shy and reserved, and viewed his colleagues with a suspicious eye.

Personal tragedies in Tiberius' life engendered a morose and sour disposition. He had been deeply devoted to his wife Vipsania but was compelled by Augustus to divorce her (11 B.C.) and marry the twice-widowed, notoriously immoral Julia, daughter of Augustus. After he became emperor, a second experience shattered and embittered Tiberius: his son by his first marriage, Drusus, suddenly died. Only later did he discover that his most trusted friend and confidant, Sejanus, whom he had appointed prefect of the Praetorean Guard, had been involved in the plot to poison Drusus.

Augustus officially designated Tiberius one of his potential heirs when he adopted him in A.D. 4. Tiberius was not one of Augustus' favorite candidates, but the other contenders died before the long Augustan reign ended. Two or three years before Augustus died, he in effect made Tiberius co-regent (A.D. 11 or 12). Before Augustus died, Tacitus described Tiberius' position as one of a "colleague in the empire."[1] Tiberius finally became sole ruler in A.D. 14, when he was well into his fifties.

The modern city of Tiberias on the western shore of the Sea of Galilee. Courtesy A. Strajmayster.

Historians generally give Tiberius high marks for his handling of the administration of government in his early years. He tried to cooperate with the senate, granting it freedom of debate, attending its meetings frequently, and allowing it to exercise a broad judicial power. But the Roman historian Tacitus condemned Tiberius for his brutal administration of justice and especially his misuse of treason trials. He sometimes used the law to rid himself of those he suspected of disloyalty or to acquire the wealth of those executed. One victim whom Tacitus described as "the richest man in Spain" was charged with incest and thrown from a high rock to his death. "To remove any doubt that the vastness of his wealth had proved the man's ruin, Tiberius,"

according to Tacitus, "kept his gold mines for himself." The same historian asserted that "the force of terror had utterly extinguished the sense of human fellowship, and, with the growth of cruelty, pity was thrust aside."[2] In modern times historians have concluded that Tacitus' obvious prejudice against Tiberius led him to exaggerate the latter's brutality. Tacitus lived through Domitian's era of repression when many leaders were executed for treason. He probably saw the origins of such excess in Tiberius' use of the treason charge during the latter years of his reign. Actually Tiberius held to a relatively moderate policy up to at least A.D. 26.[3]

It was about the time of Jesus' ministry that Emperor Tiberius entered a period of mental deterioration and increasing cruelty. Sejanus, one of his few trusted friends, began to plant seeds of suspicion in his mind. He tried to convince Tiberius that Agrippina, the widow of the emperor's popular nephew, sought power for her children. At the same time (A.D. 26) he even persuaded Tiberius to retire to the island of Capri. The move left the ambitious Sejanus with even greater power. As the prefect wished, Tiberius secured the banishment of Agrippina by the senate in A.D. 29. Sejanus' plot to seize control came to an ignoble end two years later when the emperor sent a message to the senate denouncing the sly rebel. By order of the senate Sejanus was imprisoned and strangled, and a reign of terror followed for his friends. When the embittered old emperor died in A.D. 37, the Roman populace jubilantly shouted "To the Tiber with Tiberius!"[4] The senate often granted divinity to emperors after their death as a mark of honor, but it withheld this distinction from Tiberius.

Pontius Pilate (A.D. 26–36)

Shortly before John the Baptist's ministry began, another important Roman leader took office. Sejanus appointed Pontius Pilate as prefect of Judea and Samaria in A.D. 26, and he ruled there until A.D. 36, just a year before the emperor's death. Pilate was the fifth of the prefects to govern the region. The rule of the Roman prefects or governors began in A.D. 6 with the banishment of Archelaus. Very little is known of the first four governors beyond their names. Outside of the New Testament, Philo and Josephus provide information on Pi-

late. Philo's brief testimony is given less credence because of his strong prejudice against Pilate. He portrayed Pilate as cruel, corrupt, and conceited. Most of our information must be derived from Josephus and the New Testament. Pilate brought his wife with him and established his residence in Caesarea, the Roman administrative capital, but he made frequent trips to Jerusalem. In the Gospel of John, Pilate displayed a cynical character when he responded to Jesus' claim to testify of truth, with the sardonic question, "What is truth?" (18:38). His lack of compassion was apparent in his willingness to allow Jesus to be tortured, humiliated, and crucified. Yet, it would be a mistake to think of Pilate as one of Rome's more barbaric governors. His conduct was consistent with the standards of his time.

Josephus provides several examples of Pilate's troubled relations with the Jews. One of his first acts as prefect was to dispatch soldiers from Caesarea to take up winter quarters in Jerusalem. Josephus viewed their arrival as a move "to abolish the Jewish laws." The imperial banners carried by the soldiers bore the image of Tiberius, and to the Jews such a representation was idolatrous. No one had ever dared before to disregard Jewish scruples by bringing the ensigns into the sacred city of Jerusalem. A huge delegation descended on Pilate at Caesarea and for five days implored the obdurate governor to remove the banners. On the sixth day Pilate surrounded the protestors with soldiers and threatened them with death. But he withdrew the troops when he saw that force would serve no purpose against Jews who would quite willingly die before surrendering their principles. On another occasion Pilate displeased his subjects by improper use of the temple treasury to finance the building of a twenty-five-mile aqueduct for carrying water into Jerusalem. When an angry mob responded by hurling insults at the governor, he used soldiers in civilian clothes with hidden weapons to suddenly attack and scatter them. The incident may be the same one that is briefly mentioned in Luke 13:1. According to Luke a contingent of Jesus' hearers told him "about the Galileans whose blood Pilate had mixed with their sacrifices."

A final violent act was the undoing of Pilate. A false prophet had deceived some of the Samaritans into believing that he had knowledge of the location of sacred vessels left by Moses at Mount Gerizim. Since the Pentateuch clearly states that Moses never crossed the Jordan, the movement fed itself on ignorance as well as superstition. A group of followers took arms and, joining with their prophet at the base of Gerizim, searched for the golden vessels. Apparently Pilate viewed the armed contingent as an insurrectionary force; he sent an armed band to slay the "conspirators." The Samaritans lodged a complaint with Vitellius, governor of Syria and Pilate's superior. Vitellius removed Pilate from office and sent him to Rome for trial, bringing his ten-year reign to an end.[5] The events of Pilate's later life are lost in the haze of time, but various legends developed about him, including the unsubstantiated story that he was converted to Christianity.

The Ministry of John the Baptist

While Tiberius and Pilate held the reins of secular power in Rome and Caesarea, John the Baptist preached in the Judean desert the dawning of a messianic kingdom. The ascetic prophet came clothed in a leather loin cloth and camel's hair and subsisting on an austere diet of locusts and wild honey. He sternly admonished the masses in Jerusalem and Judea to confess their sins, repent, and be baptized in the Jordan. John's importance as the forerunner of the Messiah is indicated by the fact that all four Gospels describe his ministry as initiatory to that of Jesus. Jesus himself asserted, "Among those born of women there is no one greater than John" (Luke 7:28).

Frequent references to John's words in the Book of Acts make it clear that his followers were widespread and that early preaching about Jesus included narratives of John's ministry as an essential part of the gospel story. Amos had prophesied that there would be a "famine of hearing the words of the Lord" (8:11), but the long drought ended when John appeared like an Old Testament prophet warning his hearers about the coming judgment. John's style harked back to an earlier age, but as the herald of the Messiah he became a part of the New Testament era. As the forerunner he was "more than a prophet" (Luke 7:26); he was the messenger prophesied by Malachi who would prepare the way for the Messiah (3:1).

The date for the beginning of John's ministry could be set as early as A.D. 26 or as late as A.D. 28 or 29, depending on whether one considers

Luke's reference to the fifteenth year of Tiberius (Luke 3:1) to have been reckoned from the co-regency of Tiberius and Augustus in A.D. 11/12, or from the time when Tiberius became the sole ruler in A.D. 14. Since Herod Antipas executed John during Jesus' public ministry, John's period of activity could not have covered many years. He might have preached as little as four to six months before Jesus' baptism. Although John preached in a desert region, his work was not carried out in isolation. He baptized and preached at the crossing of the Jordan north of the Dead Sea where many people traveled between Judea and Perea. The Gospel of John indicates that people came continually to John for baptism at "Aenon near Salim" (3:23).

Some scholars have seen a link between John and the Qumran community. Both John and the Qumran inhabitants claimed a priestly lineage, followed an ascetic regimen, and ministered in the Judean desert near the Dead Sea. Both placed special emphasis on Isaiah's challenge: "In the desert prepare the way for the LORD; make straight in the wilderness a highway for our God" (40:3). Baptism or a cleansing ceremony was also common to both. Luke 1:80 states concerning John, "the child grew and became strong in spirit, and he lived in the desert until he appeared publicly to Israel." This does not prove that John might have visited or even lived among the Qumran people during his days in the wilderness, but it raises the possibility that he did so. However, the similarities may be more superficial than substantial. John's baptism was a once-for-all symbol of repentance rather than an oft-repeated ceremonial washing. He offered baptism, not to initiates who would enter an isolated and regulated commune, but to those who would practice the fruits of repentance and ethical living in the towns and villages of Palestine. His exhortation to soldiers who came to ask his advice was not to join him in his desert habitation but to stop extorting money and to deal justly with the people (Luke 3:14). His message of repentance was not intended for a select few who would become initiates in a new community but a message for all who would respond in sincere repentance. Although the Qumran people looked for an era of blessing in the future, John indicated to his disciples that they were already at the dawning of the kingdom.[6]

When Jesus came to be baptized of John, the forerunner insisted that he had need rather to be baptized of Jesus (Matt. 3:13), thus indicating that Jesus was One greater than himself, One who would usher in the kingdom of heaven. Although there is no firm basis for asserting dogmatically that John had been an Essene or a member of the Qumran group, he certainly could have come into contact with the inhabitants or viewpoints of some such desert community. John's perceptions may have been affected by many strands of Judaism, but his message came to him, as it did to the prophets of old, from God. John the Baptist is described in Josephus simply as "a good man, [who] commanded the Jews to exercise virtue, both as to righteousness towards one another, and piety towards God, and so to come to baptism. . . ." He interpreted

John's baptism as the physical washing that symbolized an earlier spiritual purification.[7]

The Jordan River, looking downstream; this is the traditional site of John the Baptist's ministry. Courtesy Duby Tal.

Josephus gives an account of John's death, but his account is not parallel to that recorded in Matthew 14 and Mark 6. The two Gospel writers cite revenge by Herodias as the motive behind the beheading of the prophet. Herodias wished to rid herself of the man who had scolded Herod Antipas for taking her as a wife. Herodias was already married to Antipas' brother Philip (not the tetrarch but a lesser known brother, Herod Philip), and John had the gall to call attention to the situation. But in Josephus' account the motive given for the execution was not anger over an indiscreet remark but rather Herod's fear that John's hold over the masses might make this desert prophet the focal point for an insurrection. The two motivations are not necessarily contradictory. Both fear and hatred led to John's death. Evidently Herod had a certain admiration for John, yet he thought his tetrarchy would be more secure if the disturber were held in prison. Antipas' fascination for the powerful man of God made it difficult for him to agree to a death verdict, but Herodias' hatred of the prophet, Antipas' promise to her, and the safety of his tetrarchy led him to decree execution.

Harold Hoehner sees the divergence between Josephus and the Gospel accounts as arising mainly from the different perspectives of the writers. The New Testament authors primarily were interested in the immediate precipitating cause of John's death, the actions of personalities. But Josephus, being concerned with political factors, ignored the personal causes. The Jewish historian was more interested in John as a potential rebel leader than as a prophetic voice. In fact, as Hoehner notes, John's denunciation of Antipas' liaison with Herodias as recorded in the Gospels no doubt had political overtones. If a religious renewal had stirred Galilee, the people might have risen up in moral indignation against Antipas. When a people are filled with religious zeal and are expecting a prophesied kingdom to arrive, they will exhibit stronger moral sensitivity. Such fervent morality would bode ill for a ruler perceived to be immoral and godless. The two accounts of the motivations behind John's execution appear in this light to be complementary rather than contradictory.[8]

The Baptism and Temptation

The baptism of Jesus marks his dedication to the ministry given to him by the Father. Mark states that Jesus came from Nazareth in Galilee to be baptized in the Jordan by John (1:9). Matthew adds that John at first resisted the request (3:14). Some scholars see Matthew's version as an invention to explain the problem of a sinless Savior undergoing a rite associated with repentance. But Matthew is not alone in viewing the baptism of Jesus as unique. The other Gospels also portray this baptism as distinctive in that it was accompanied by a heavenly voice and the descent of the Holy Spirit on the Messiah (Mark 1:10–11; Luke 3:22). Jesus explained to John that the rite was a proper action in order "to fulfill all righteousness" (Matt. 3:15). John probably failed to comprehend the full meaning of Jesus' words of explanation, but he may have realized at least that Jesus wished all to know that he stood with those whom John had baptized and who were preparing themselves for the kingdom that was being established. Perhaps the Lord intended also to identify himself with all people in order that he might better serve as the mediator and the sacrifice for sin. Luke may have implied such a purpose when he recorded that it was when "all the people were being baptized" that Jesus was also baptized (3:21). He who would be the sin bearer and high priest for the people would first follow them in the baptism ritual. Later in his ministry Jesus linked baptism with the Cross. He spoke of the impending crucifixion as a baptism, as an ordeal that oppressed or distressed him whenever he contemplated it (Luke 12:50).[9] In this statement Jesus portrayed not only his death but also his baptism as events associated with the work of redemption and sin-bearing.

The Mount of Temptation with a Greek Orthodox monastery built into its rock face. According to tradition, it is the site where Jesus was tempted. Courtesy Israel Government Press Office.

A second episode, the Temptation, was also a preparation for ministry. The Synoptics place the Temptation immediately after the baptism of Jesus. According to Luke 4:1, Jesus "returned from the Jordan and was led by the Spirit in the desert." Exactly where the testing of Jesus occurred is not made clear. The term "desert" has usually been taken to mean the Judean desert, but some scholars think Jesus might have "returned from the Jordan" to lower

Galilee.[10] It is more likely that Jesus was led into some part of the forbidding wastelands of Judea that lay between Jerusalem and the Jordan. The region had had even less habitation than the Negev (the southern desert of Palestine near Egypt), and its bleak, rocky setting was well adapted to test the fitness of the Son of Man to embark on his arduous mission. This barren region is only about ten miles wide and is easily accessible from inhabited areas. An old tradition specifically locating the Temptation at Mount Quarantania, west of Jericho, has very little support to it. Part of the temptation experience included a viewing of the world's kingdoms from a very high mountain, but there is not convincing evidence to locate the site.

Satan tried three times to trap Jesus into committing a disobedient act. The order of the temptations is different in the parallel accounts (Matt. 4:1–11; Luke 4:1–13). Since Matthew uses the designation *then* (4:5), his order is probably to be considered the chronological one. It must be remembered that the Gospels do not always follow a strictly chronological order of events. All three temptations involved the question of obedience to God's purpose. As John's Gospel emphasizes, the Son came to carry out the will of the Father. There was an intentional subordination, the acceptance of the role of servant in order to fulfill the divine mission. In the words of Paul, Jesus "made himself nothing, taking the very nature of a servant, being made in human likeness . . . " (Phil. 2:7). For the Son to seize the power he rightfully possessed and, without the Father's direction, to use it to supply his own physical or psychological wants would be an indication of inability at the outset to carry out the role of a servant. His obedience during testing would give him strength later to face the Cross itself. His final victory over temptation was evident later, during the Passion Week, when he spoke of his approaching death: "Now my heart is troubled, and what shall I say? Father, save me from this hour? No, it was for this very reason I came to this hour. Father, glorify your name!" (John 12:27–28).

The same taunt Jesus would hear at his death, "Come down from the cross, if you are the Son of God!" (Matt. 27:40), was used by Satan as the first temptation: "If you are the Son of God, tell these stones to become bread" (Matt. 4:3). Satan's design was to lure him into displaying his power to overcome a difficult circumstance. But Jesus knew that he had surrendered the independent exercise of his authority. The hunger pangs were all the stronger because Jesus had not been accustomed to fasting. His critics commented on his love of feasting. He came "eating and drinking." Forty days without food left Jesus vulnerable to the temptation of hunger.[11] The rocks strewn about the arid landscape could have been transformed into fresh bread to satiate his appetite. The second temptation, the suggestion that Jesus throw himself down from a high point of the temple, was an appeal to mistrust the Father's will and use his miraculous powers in an inappropriate manner. The third temptation, and last in Matthew's chronology, offered a way to gain universal dominion by worshiping Satan. Rather than win his kingdom through the role of a suffering servant, he could take a short cut. The end was justifiable, but the means used to attain the goal would have destroyed the integrity of the Messiah's kingdom. The means could not be separated from the end. Luke states that "when the devil had finished all this tempting, he left him until an opportune time" (4:13). The verse implies that testing would not be limited only to this one period in the life of Jesus. Satan continually sought to entice the Messiah to deviate from the Father's path. Jesus recognized one such diabolical suggestion in Peter's words when the big fisherman tried to persuade Jesus that he must not consider death as a part of his mission.[12]

The Call of the Twelve

Jesus chose his earliest disciples from among the followers of John the Baptist. Two of John's disciples, Andrew and possibly John "the Beloved," were early impressed by the Baptizer's teaching about the Coming One. On two succeeding days they heard him describe Jesus as "The Lamb of God" (John 1:29, 35). They may have only vaguely perceived the role of Jesus as the Paschal lamb, but they understood enough of his preeminence that they forsook the Baptist to follow him. In rapid succession Peter, Philip, Nathaniel, and probably James became members of the group. Later in Galilee when Peter, Andrew, James, and John had returned to the fishing business, Jesus called them to follow and become fishers of men, and they left their co-workers, who were mending nets, and followed Jesus (Matt. 4:18–22; Mark 1:16–20).

Luke 5:1–11 appears to record another call to the Galilean fishermen after Jesus had used one of the boats as a preaching platform. On this occasion Jesus graphically demonstrated the harvest of people that his disciples would lead into the kingdom. He ordered Simon and his helpers to let down the nets despite a long night of unsuccessful fishing. The astonished fishermen took in such a large number of fish that they had to signal a second boat to come from shore to help carry the catch. "From now on you will catch men" (Luke 5:10), Jesus said. The words were similar to those used on an earlier occasion (Matt. 4:19; Mark 1:17).

Jesus did not immediately begin his ministry with a clearly recognizable band of twelve official followers. It was only after he had gone "through all the towns and villages, teaching in their synagogues, preaching the good news of the kingdom," that he finally designated from among his disciples an inner group of twelve specially commissioned apostles (Matt. 9:35). Matthew specifically lists the twelve and records at length the commissioning message of Jesus. He also tells of a particular mission that arose out of Jesus' recognition that the crowds were "harassed and helpless, like sheep without a shepherd" (Matt. 9:37). Because of this need, Jesus sent his twelve workers out into the harvest field, but for the immediate task he restricted their ministry to Israel and forbade entry into Samaria or Gentile regions (Matt. 10:5–6). But his commissioning message also anticipated a time in the future when the apostles would be "brought before governors and kings as witnesses to them and to the Gentiles" (Matt. 10:18). The many sayings in the discourse recorded in Matthew 10 should probably be regarded as a single original message, though some scholars think they are diverse sayings that Matthew assembled and recorded as one sermon.

Characteristics of Jesus' Teaching

A major aspect of Jesus' ministry involved preaching and teaching. The term *disciple* (Greek, *mathētēs*) literally means a "learner" or "pupil." When Jesus chose twelve men, he had in mind a group that would follow him and heed his instruction. Mark says that Jesus came "proclaiming the good news of God" (1:14). He spent many months, days, and hours preparing and training his disciples, who would then be able to continue bearing the good news. The disciples often addressed Jesus as "Rabbi," a term of respect usually reserved for persons highly trained in the law. It is used once in the New Testament of John the Baptist (John 3:26), but in every other case only of Jesus. The term came from the Hebrew word *rabi*, meaning "master," and in the form *rabbi*, "my lord." Another expression used in addressing Jesus, *Didaskale*, was a Greek word that meant "teacher." But it would be a mistake to think of Jesus as simply another rabbi whose main aim was to impart information to a group of disciples. Jesus came to do more than teach. He came "to give his life as a ransom for many" (Mark 10:45). His teaching called for a decision, repentance, and preparation for the kingdom of God. Jesus wanted his hearers to do more than accumulate knowledge: He wished to impel them to come to him as Master and Lord, to enter into eternal life, and to follow his ethic. He wanted his followers to learn more than a new set of ethical principles: He taught them about himself, his person and work. John records more of the teaching of Jesus than any other Gospel writer. In the discourses in John, Jesus portrayed himself as the Son of God sent by the Father to bring eternal life to all who would believe in him. The miracles in the fourth Gospel are signs selected primarily to direct people to Jesus. Each of these signs teaches some truth about the person of Jesus Christ and typically serves as the occasion for a discourse.

Jesus spoke with authority and independence. Ordinarily a Jewish scribe avoided any deviation from the fixed oral interpretations of the law. The goal was not novelty or individuality but conformity to the accepted traditions. But Jesus said that a teacher of the law would be like a homeowner "who brings out of his storeroom new treasures as well as old" (Matt. 13:52). The new treasures would be the teaching of the Messiah about the kingdom. The disciples should draw from the Old Testament Scriptures and even from valid traditions when they taught, but they should also accept as authoritative the new teaching of Jesus. Because he did not hesitate to teach his views emphatically without relying on traditional views, Jesus astounded many of his hearers and exasperated others. "The people were amazed at his teaching," exclaimed Mark, "because he taught them as one who had authority, not as the teachers of the law" (1:22). Jesus did not hesitate, on his own authority, to challenge those scribal interpretations that he saw as in effect nullifying or weakening the force of the Old Testament law. The antithetic clauses "You have heard that it was said to the people long ago . . . but I tell you . . . ." occur frequently in the Sermon on the Mount (Matt. 5–7). Jesus' purpose was not "to abolish the Law or the Prophets" (5:17, i.e., to attack the Old Testament Scripture), but actually to return to a more perfect and pure form of the law. "For I tell you," Jesus said, "that unless your righteousness surpasses that of the Pharisees and the teachers of the law, you will certainly not enter the kingdom of heaven" (5:20). It is not surprising that such bold assertions from one who had not sat at the feet of the scribes antagonized the established religious authorities.

The Form of Jesus' Teaching

One of the forms used most often by Jesus in his teaching was the parable. A parable is an extended metaphor, a simple story based on everyday kinds of events. These narratives or comparisons could be easily understood by those who heard them because they fit into the experience of the common folk of Judea and Galilee. Most had seen a sower casting seed, a fisherman throwing out his net, or a woman mixing leaven in dough. Our term "parable" is a transliteration of the Greek word *parabolē*, which means a "comparison." The Greek word is used in the New Testament to describe a brief saying or proverb as well as a longer story, but the English term is usually used in a narrower sense to denote one of Jesus' illustrative stories. Although Jesus used parables frequently, the fourth Gospel does not record any of them. The term "parable" found in the King James Version in John 10:6 is not a translation of *parabolē* but of another word, *paroimia*, which means "a figure of speech." The figure of the Good Shepherd is more likely an allegory than a typical parable. Since John contains more discourse in proportion to narrative than the Synoptics, his omission of parables is puzzling. Perhaps John knew the recorded parables of the kingdom well, but saw the importance of recording instead those sections of the teaching of Jesus that dealt with his own person and work.

The most important purpose of the parable was to simplify, clarify, and illuminate a spiritual truth. The parables also made Jesus' message vivid and dramatic. But parables apparently were also a device for concealing truth, to make it less obvious, so that only by careful attention could one elicit the meaning. Thus a parable may be either a "dark saying" or an enigmatic story, understood only by those who sincerely sought the meaning of the images. Scripture seems to suggest that Jesus did sometimes intend to veil his meaning from unworthy eyes or the insincere. Jesus told the Twelve that "the secret of the kingdom of God" had been given to them. But to those on the outside everything was said in parables so that, "they may be ever seeing but never perceiving, and ever hearing but never understanding; otherwise they might turn and be forgiven" (Mark 4:11–12). Some Bible scholars have found the concept of

147

Jesus obscuring truth offensive. But a consideration of the attitude of Jesus' hearers may help to explain the statement. Those who came to hear the parables with receptive hearts would certainly not have been included with those who would have the truth veiled from their eyes. But there were some who came with hardened hearts and unwilling ears. Scornful scribes and disdainful Pharisees dogged Jesus' footsteps to find some basis for criticism and accusation. When Jesus spoke even to a small group, he could probably have expected to find a coterie of critics present. Such impatient hearers might fail to apprehend a parable, and Jesus probably would not have favored them with a detailed explanation such as he gave the disciples for the parable of the weeds and wheat (Matt. 13:36–43). The disciples had heard that parable along with the crowds by Lake Galilee. The story had whetted their interest, and coming with eager hearts they sought more understanding. Jesus wished to communicate truth, but his parables would seem like meaningless stories to those who had hardened their hearts against him. After interpreting the parable of the weeds to the disciples, he admonished them, "He who has ears, let him hear" (Matt. 13:43).

More often Jesus did intend for his antagonists to clearly understand his message, and he often seemed in fact to be condemning them in the parables. The parable of the prodigal son, sometimes called the parable of the elder brother, is a good example of an attack on Pharisaic hypocrisy. In it Jesus pictured his enemies as being like an older brother who was callously unconcerned about the salvation of his lost and ungodly brother while eager to receive plaudits for his own righteousness. Many parables stress the danger of rejecting the Son or his kingdom. The critics probably clearly understood such warnings, but most of them refused to come in a spirit of repentance to seek further truth from Jesus.

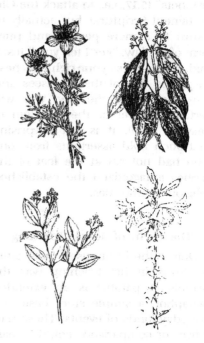

Plants of Palestine. "Why do you worry about clothes?" Jesus asked. "See how the lilies of the field grow" (Matt. 6:28). Courtesy Carta, Jerusalem.

Other teaching devices included similes, proverbs, and paradoxes. Jesus also used provocative questions to induce his listeners to think carefully about serious matters: "What good will it be for a man," he queried, "if he gains the whole world, yet forfeits his soul? Or what can a man give in exchange for his soul?" (Matt.

THE MINISTRY OF JESUS

16:26). Sometimes Jesus made brief dramatic statements to capture attention: "If your right eye causes you to sin, gouge it out and throw it away" (5:29). Such injunctions were not intended to be followed literally but to arouse laggard hearers to the seriousness of godless behavior.

The Content of Jesus' Teaching

Matthew recorded six major discourses of Jesus. They include (1) the Sermon on the Mount (5:1–7:29), (2) the commission to the Twelve (10:1–42), (3) the parables of the kingdom (13:1–52), (4) the message on humility and forgiveness (18:1–35), (5) the seven woes against hypocritical scribes and Pharisees (23:1–39), and (6) the Olivet Discourse (24:1–25:46). Five of the six sermons end with words such as "When Jesus had finished saying all these things ... " (7:28; 11:1; 13:53; 19:1; 26:1). (1) The first message emphasized the importance of a faith that is characterized by a genuine desire to serve God and fellow man rather than giving lip service to a shallow legalism. (2) The second provided directions for the Twelve in conducting a special preaching tour. (3) The third message is one of the greatest collections of parables in the Synoptics. All of these parables deal with some aspect of the kingdom, such as the reception of the message of the kingdom (the sower), the judgment that results from rejecting the kingdom (the parable of the weeds, parable of the net), the growth of the kingdom (mustard seed, leaven), and the exceeding value of the kingdom (hidden treasure, pearl). (4) The fourth sermon admonishes would-be disciples to

come humbly as little children into the kingdom and to forgive a brother graciously without any reservation. (5) In the fifth message Jesus warns his hearers to respect the rulings of the scribes and Pharisees but not to fall victim to the same spirit of religious display (23:2–3). (6) In the final discourse in Matthew Jesus answered the disciples' question, "When will this happen, and what will be the sign of your coming and of the end of the age?" (24:3). In his eschatological message Jesus discussed some of the events and trends that would manifest themselves before the consummation of the age.

Mark gives less space to the sayings of Jesus, though he frequently refers to the Lord's preaching and teaching ministry. Luke provides at least seventeen parables not found elsewhere. Some of these distinctive parables are the good Samaritan (10:25–37), the rich fool (12:16–21), the rash builder (14:28–30), the prodigal son (15:11–32), the shrewd steward (16:1–13), the persistent widow (18:1–8), and the Pharisee and the publican (18:9–14). The Gospel of John contains more teaching than any of the Synoptics. The longest message is the Upper Room Discourse (13:1–16:33), in which Jesus gave final instructions and comfort to his disciples before his departure. John also records messages about Christ's authority and deity (5:19–47), his role as the Bread of Life (6:26–59), and his work as the Good Shepherd (10:1–30). The teaching of John is more concerned with the person and work of Christ, especially his deity and his close relationship with the Father, than with the ethics of the kingdom as in the Synoptics.

Much of the content of Jesus' teaching in the Synoptics can be summarized in a study of the "Disciples' Prayer," usually called "The Lord's Prayer" (Matt. 6:9–13). "Our Father" suggests Jesus' teaching that God is One who is compassionate and concerned about every detail of life's needs, such as "daily bread." Jesus never included himself in the pronoun "our" when addressing God because he had a unique relationship with his Father. "Our Father" is a designation for the use of the disciples, to whom Jesus taught the prayer. The Father is the sovereign ruler of the universe who intends that his "will be done on earth as it is in heaven." "Your kingdom come" suggests Jesus' teaching that the kingdom was at hand. His teachings included the concept of a spiritual kingdom of his own disciples who would live by the ethical demands of the Father in an age of wickedness, but they also predicted a coming future kingdom in which justice and godliness would triumph and judgment would come to the wicked.[13] Jesus did not align himself with those who sought an immediate earthly political kingdom, but he certainly taught that in the final day God's rule would be complete. He spoke of the Son of Man's coming "on the clouds of the sky, with power and great glory," and of the mourning of the nations when they saw his appearance (Matt. 24:30). When Jesus first began his ministry, he called on people to repent (literally, to change their minds) because the kingdom was near (Mark 1:15). He intended that people should join in the brotherhood of the kingdom, a group that included those who were not simply physical descendants of Abraham, but rather those who would turn from the hypocrisy and wickedness about them to live on the higher plane of kingdom teaching. Although Jesus often spoke of the kingdom, he did not usually use the term *church* (*ekklesia*, Greek), but in Matthew 16:18 he does promise, "I will build my church," and in his message on humility and forgiveness he provided a formula for an aggrieved brother to seek reconciliation by appealing "to the church" (Matt. 18:17).

The Chronology of Jesus' Ministry

Attempts to outline the chronology of Jesus' ministry have failed to produce a clear consensus. The precise years when Jesus began his ministry and the date of his crucifixion cannot be stated with certainty. The outer limits are A.D. 25 and 33, and there can be no reasonable doubt that Jesus ministered and died within that period. But the length of Jesus' ministry within this time span cannot be fixed precisely. The Synoptics require at least a one-year ministry, and in modern times the outer limit for the length of Jesus' ministry has generally been agreed to be four and a half years. The Gospel of John cannot be interpreted, without serious questioning of the text, to allow for less than a two-year ministry. Thus one can say with assurance that Jesus' ministry covered a two- to four-and-a-half-year span within the period A.D. 25–33.

Several statements in the Scripture help to establish fixed points for determining the chronology of Jesus' ministry. Under close examination these do not provide unambiguous information but rather allow for conflicting interpretations. Luke states that Jesus "was about thirty years old when he began his ministry" (3:23). Although his quotation uses the term *about*, it could be taken to express a time that is more precise than appears in translation. William Ramsay argued that Luke was indicating a fairly narrow space of time. He attributes this apparent inexactness to the Greek preference for avoiding definite or "harsh forms of statement." Ramsay believed the only point in question would be whether Jesus was in his thirtieth year or had recently passed the thirtieth anniversary of his birth. According to this interpretation, Luke, as a careful researcher, did not wish to imply a wide range of ages such as twenty-eight to thirty-two.[14] But most scholars have rejected Ramsay's view and prefer to take Luke's term "about" (*hosei*) to be indefinite and to be capable of including the range of twenty-eight to thirty-two years. Since Jewish teachers did not usually begin active leadership before thirty, Jesus' age was more likely somewhere between thirty and thirty-two. The participle translated "began" (*archomenos*) in Luke 3:23 also presents a grammatical difficulty. The King James Version takes it to mean that Jesus "began to be about thirty . . . ." Modern versions that interpret "began" as a reference to the outset of Christ's ministry, rather than to the time when he began to be thirty, are probably correct. Since Jesus' birth must have been in 6 or 5 B.C., it is easy to calculate that he was between twenty-eight and thirty-two sometime within the span of years from A.D. 23 to 29.

Luke also gave a chronological clue in his statement that John came preaching the Word of God in the fifteenth year of the reign of Tiberius Caesar (3:1). Since Jesus was among the crowds who came to be baptized by John, the ministry of Jesus began shortly after the outset of John's work. Thus the dating of John's ministry aids in estimating the commencement of Jesus' ministry. Ramsay argued that Luke was counting the fifteen years from the beginning of Tiberius' co-regency with Augustus in A.D. 11. This would make A.D. 25 or 26 the date for the beginning of John's ministry. Ramsay thought Jesus' baptism occurred just a month or two before the Passover (March 21) of A.D. 26. For the purpose of this study, the view of Ramsay has been adopted. Luke's reckoning of the reign of Tiberius is assumed to begin with the year A.D. 11. Thus we assume that Jesus' ministry began in A.D. 26 or possibly A.D. 27. But since one cannot be dogmatic on this point, it is worthwhile to consider an alternative approach.

Harold Hoehner presents another view. He has disputed the use of the A.D. 11 date because there is no evidence from coins or documents to support the idea that Tiberius counted his reign from the date of his co-regency. Ramsay bases his argument on the witness of Tiberius' close associate Velleius that the senate conferred on Tiberius authority over the provinces and armies equal to the power of Augustus, not long before the celebration of his military triumph in January, A.D. 12. Hoehner thinks Luke would more likely have "used the normal Roman method of reckoning," because he addressed his

Gospel to a government leader, Theophilus. A Roman official would not have had difficulty in counting in terms of dynastic years. The beginning of the reign of Tiberius as sole ruler is a well-known date: August 19, A.D. 14. By this manner of reckoning Hoehner arrives at the conclusion that John's ministry began early in A.D. 29 and that Jesus' ministry followed in the summer or autumn of the same year. Since he believes Jesus' ministry lasted at least three years he fixes on A.D. 33 as the crucifixion year.[15]

The method of determining Luke's meaning is more complicated than can be indicated here and can be understood fully only by further reading on the subject of New Testament chronology. In addition to the co-regency theory held by Ramsay and the Roman dynastic method favored by Hoehner, three other methods of interpreting the "fifteenth year" deserve at least mention:

1. Some scholars think Luke used the Jewish calendar and thus believe that the first year of Tiberius ran from August 19, A.D. 14, to Nisan 1, 15. This would make the fifteenth year run from April A.D. 28 to April A.D. 29.

2. Others, using a Syrian method of reckoning, think the fifteenth year could have fallen in the period from September A.D. 27 to September A.D. 28. If Luke, as many believe, spent a great deal of time in Antioch, he may have used this system. This view would allow no more than a two-year ministry of Christ if the Crucifixion occurred in A.D. 30.

3. If Luke was following the Julian calendar, the first year would run from August through December of A.D. 14, and the fifteenth year would

be A.D. 28. But there is a variation of this approach. Tacitus and Suetonius followed an accession-year system by which the first partial year was called an accession year (in this case August 19 to December 31, A.D. 14) and the next full year (January 1, A.D. 15, to December 31, A.D. 15) was designated as year one. Thus the accession-year system would move the commencement of Jesus' ministry to a later date, A.D. 29. Hoehner thinks this method was one of the two most likely used by Luke.[16] As has been stated, the working assumption of this book is more in line with Ramsay's calculations, putting the beginning of the ministry about A.D. 26 or soon thereafter. But one cannot decisively settle the issue to everyone's satisfaction.

The Length of Jesus' Ministry

The duration of Jesus' ministry has usually been estimated to have been about three or three-and-a-half years. But arguments have also been put forth for a one-, two-, or four-year ministry. The Synoptics do not give much attention to indicating the passage of time. They are much more concerned with the words and works of Jesus than with sequence of events or fixed points of time. Because the Synoptics mention only one Passover, that which came at the death of Jesus (Matt. 26:17; Mark 14:12; Luke 22:7), some scholars have posited a ministry of a single year. Valentinus, the Alexandrian Gnostic, who taught at Rome in the middle of the second centuryA.D. , is the earliest person known to have held to a one-year ministry. Irenaeus, bishop of Lyons in Gaul near the end of the second century, denounced this viewpoint and offered instead his own implausible theory that Jesus had a ten- or even twenty-year ministry.

Actually the Synoptics do not require a ministry limited to a one-year time period. The lack of mention of more than one Passover cannot be taken as conclusive evidence that the era of Jesus' activity could not have included several Passover feasts. Those who hold to a one-year ministry take Mark 2:23 as implying an initial Passover not long after Jesus' baptism. Mark speaks in this passage of the disciples plucking ripened heads of grain on the Sabbath. This would have been at the time of the spring harvest, the same time of the year as the celebration of the Passover. But the one-year view has a serious flaw. If Mark omitted mentioning the Passover by name on this occasion, he could have left other Passovers unrecorded.[17] One cannot assume the passage of only one year with any certainty. In fact, Mark might be understood to require at least a two-year ministry because at the occasion of the feeding of the five thousand Jesus had the people sit down on the "green grass." All four Gospels recount the story of the feeding of the multitude in a grassy area, but only Mark adds the adjective "green," which implies another springtime. By itself Mark's testimony might be explained as only a reference to grass that had been greened by a nearby spring and not by the rains of the springtime. But if one leaves the Synoptics and takes into account the parallel story in the fourth Gospel any ambiguity ends, because John asserts that "the Jewish Passover Feast was near" (6:4).

The most important evidence for a ministry longer than one year is found in the Gospel of John. Those who accept the historicity of John's record cannot reconcile it with a one-year ministry without serious textual emendation or locating passages in another sequence. John mentions three different Passovers by using the specific term (2:13; 6:4; 11:55) and also mentions an unnamed feast (5:1), which is usually taken to indicate a fourth Passover. These four Passovers indicate a ministry of slightly over three years. A two-year ministry might be conceivable on this evidence alone if the unnamed feast was not a Passover, but a one-year ministry is not possible.

The four Passovers in the fourth Gospel can be identified as follows: (1) John's first Passover is mentioned in 2:13 and 2:23 and occurred after the baptism, the wedding at Cana, and a stay with Jesus' disciples and family in Capernaum. "When it was almost time for the Jewish Passover," says John, "Jesus went up to Jerusalem" (2:13). There he purged the temple of the money-changers and then remained in Jerusalem during the Passover (2:23). Some scholars believe there was only one cleansing of the temple, that which occurred during the Passion Week, and thus the fourth Gospel has the story out of sequence. If one accepts this kind of analysis, John's Gospel could be brought into conformity with the one-year-ministry theory. (2) It may be that the unnamed "feast of the Jews" mentioned in John 5:1 should be considered a second Passover and that a little over a year of ministry ended with this feast. (3) The Passover mentioned in connection with the feeding of the five thousand (6:4) would then end a second year. (4) The Passover of the Passion Week (mentioned by name in 11:55; 12:1; 18:28; 19:14) ended a little more than three years of activity. Most scholars believe the three-year ministry accords best with the biblical data.

A recent harmony of the four Gospels edited by Robert L. Thomas and Stanley N. Gundry argues for the traditional view of a three-and-a-half-year ministry. Another recent work by Evangelical scholars attempts to weave the four accounts into a single continuous narrative like the ancient *Diatessaron* by Tatian in the second century. This narrative does not adopt the usual pattern of the harmonies, which place parallel accounts in parallel columns. The latter work, by Johnston M. Cheney and Stanley A. Ellisen, presents a four-year chronology based in part on the argument (1) that harmonizers who use the traditional three-year chronology must crowd the final six months of Jesus' life with too many events and (2) that John should not be assumed to have given a complete list of the Passovers for chronological purposes. This is supported by the fact that John omitted mention of important feasts like Pentecost. John did not intend to provide a chronological outline. Thus if other evidence in the fourth Gospel seems to require more time, there is no need to assume that John's silence about one or two more Passovers makes them improbable.[18] One problem with Cheney's view is that it requires nearly a full year between chapters 10 and 11 of John's Gospel. Cheney uses this gap of a year primarily for the events of Luke 9:51–18:17, a lengthy

section that contains mostly material distinctive to Luke. Because in this section Luke says that Jesus set his face toward Jerusalem and his death, it is sometimes labeled "Luke's Travel Account" or "The Perean Ministry." It may not be inappropriate to locate Luke's distinctive section between John 10 and 11, but it may be questioned whether this section required a year. It could also be questioned whether John would have omitted reference to a full year of activity. Despite these difficulties, the argument for a four-year ministry is certainly possible from a biblical standpoint.

An Outline of Jesus' Ministry

The ministry of Jesus may be divided into seven periods: (1) The Early Judean and Samaritan Ministry, (2) The Great Galilean Ministry, (3) The Withdrawal From Galilee, (4) The Later Judean Ministry, (5) The Perean Ministry, (6) The Passion Week, and (7) The Resurrection Ministry. Such an outline is really an oversimplification. Although the Gospels do give an overall chronological sequence, they do not provide a simple geographical outline nor a detailed sequential order of events. Sometimes the writers do indicate a time pattern, but often they seem to be more interested in a topical approach. An example of the topical approach can be seen in Mark 2:1–3:5, where the unifying theme seems to be controversy between Jesus and his critics. Questions are raised about authority to forgive sins, eating with sinners, fasting, and observance of the Sabbath. The section begins with a time designation, "a few days later

... " (2:1), but the stories that follow begin with phrases like: "Once again" (2:13), "One Sabbath" (2:23), "Another time" (3:1). Thus while it is possible to provide an accurate general outline or broad overview of the ministry, one cannot be certain of every detail of itinerary or the location in time of every event. Again, the writers were interested in presenting the words and works of Jesus and were less concerned with chronological precision.

The modern village of Cana. Courtesy Zev Radovan.

1. The Early Judean Ministry began with the baptism and temptation of Jesus as found in the Synoptics, but the other events of the period are recorded only in John's Gospel (2:1–4:42). The teaching activity of Jesus began while John the Baptist was still ministering in the desert. Despite the title given to this period, Jesus' work was not confined to Judea alone. The fourth Gospel records a quick trip to Cana of Galilee where the first miracle occurred (2:1–12). Then the scene returns to Judea where Jesus drove the money changers from the temple and held a private interview with

Nicodemus. During the early Judean ministry, Jesus' fame had not yet spread, and he primarily spent his time teaching individuals, especially the small group of disciples that gathered about him. The Judean ministry ends as Jesus travels through Samaria, reveals to the Samaritan woman his messianic role, and journeys on to Galilee.

2. Opposition to Jesus had not yet intensified when he began his Great Galilean Ministry. John pictures Jesus' Galilean effort as opening with good will on the part of the native people. "When he arrived in Galilee, the Galileans welcomed him" (4:45). But John also hints of trouble to come in verse 42 when he reminds his readers of Jesus' own statement that "a prophet has no honor in his own country" (v. 44). Luke describes Jesus' rejection at his home town of Nazareth after he had read from the Isaiah scroll to the synagogue worshipers (Luke 4:16–30). Still, most of the Galilee region heard the news about Jesus' miracles and preaching and were filled with excitement and anticipation. Matthew says that "news about him spread all over Syria," and "large crowds from Galilee, the Decapolis, Jerusalem, Judea and the region across the Jordan followed him" (4:24–25). The religious leaders were the first to oppose Jesus, but as their rejection hardened and became more public, the masses also began to entertain doubts about the claims and authority of Jesus. The Lord condemned the cities of Galilee, Korazin, Bethsaida, and Capernaum, which witnessed his miracles yet rejected the light (Matt. 11:20–24).

After Jesus presented himself in

Capernaum as the Bread of Life without whom there can be no eternal life, many of the earlier disciples turned away saying, according to John, "This is a hard teaching. Who can accept it?" (6:60). Many parables reflect this rejection theme. Because of the resistance to Jesus, some interpreters have viewed his Galilee mission as a disastrous failure.[19] But such a view (1) fails to recognize that a major aspect of Jesus' work involved the training of a core of devoted followers and (2) fails to emphasize that Jesus did not come primarily to teach but to offer himself as an atonement for sin. It is true that in the parable of the sower, in which reception of the message is the main theme, most of the seed (the message of Jesus) did not bear fruit, but the seed that did fall on good ground (receptive hearers) produced a crop that yielded "a hundred, sixty or thirty times what was sown" (Matt. 13:23). Who could, for instance, measure the success of Jesus' teaching as reflected in the life and work of a man like Peter?

The Sabbath controversies (Mark 2:23–3:6) led directly to a sinister alliance between the Pharisees and the Herodians. Ordinarily these two groups had little in common, but opposition to Jesus brought them together. Very little is known about the meaning of the term *Herodian*, but it apparently refers to a body of political leaders loyal to Herod Antipas. This influential political group joined hands with the religious leaders to plot "how they might kill Jesus" (Mark 3:6). Eventually Herod Antipas himself must have become uneasy about the potential danger from such a popular leader in Galilee.

The tetrarch feared that the miracle worker might be John the Baptist, resurrected, and he sought an opportunity to see Jesus (Luke 9:7–9).

An aerial view of the remains of the synagogue at Capernaum. The Sea of Galilee is in the foreground. Courtesy Israel Government Press Office.

3. At this point the Great Galilean Ministry ends and we come to the third period of Jesus' ministry—Withdrawal From Galilee. The growing menace of hostile forces suggested the propriety of leaving the territory of Herod Antipas for the region ruled by the more moderate Philip. Mark adds another reason for the withdrawal, a need for rest and solitude (6:31). But despite increased hostility, crowds still sought after him, and Jesus found little respite. In the region of Bethsaida a multitude of five thousand thronged about him.

Even then, the compassionate Jesus gave spiritual as well as physical food to the hungry crowd. This period brought Jesus into more contact with Gentile populations to the north in Tyre and Sidon and to the southeast in Decapolis.

Toward the end of the tour around the perimeter of Galilee, Jesus came to the countryside near Caesarea Philippi, a town named for the ruler of the area, and located near Mount Hermon. There Jesus questioned his disciples about their perception of him. Peter testified, "Thou art the Christ [Messiah or Anointed One], the Son of the living God" (Matt. 16:16). The expression of a faith like Peter's was the foundation on which Jesus would build his church. Before Jesus left the northern region he spoke of his coming death, and Peter showed his lack of perception by questioning the path to humiliation and death. Perhaps the perplexed disciple gained a little more confidence in the authority of his Lord when Jesus took him along with James and John up into a high mountain where he was transfigured so that his face and clothing shone brightly. The mountain is unnamed but was possibly Mount Hermon, the same lofty peak that towered above the Caesarea-Philippi area.

4. John's Gospel (chaps. 7–10) records a fourth period, the Later Judean Ministry, when Jesus taught at Jerusalem during festival seasons. At the Feast of Dedication, the Jews celebrated the restoration of the temple in the Maccabean era from the Syrian desecration. The Jews remembered the story of the miraculous lighting of the temple for eight days by one flagon of oil, normally enough for only one day. Jesus shocked the Jews by proclaiming himself the light of the world, the source of spiritual illumination. The healing of the blind man gave greater credence to his bold assertion that he could give light to those in darkness.

5. A fifth period, the Perean Ministry, is primarily found in Luke's Gospel (chaps. 13–19). Much of the material recorded by Luke in this section is distinctive to his Gospel. It is a section that includes many parables not found elsewhere, such as the parable of the good Samaritan. The designation for this part of the ministry is not entirely accurate, for Jesus did not limit his activity to Perea but also spent some time in other regions. Luke 17:11 speaks of traveling "along the border between Samaria and Galilee." It was during this time that Jesus made his final trip to Jerusalem.

6, 7. The sixth and seventh periods of Christ's ministry, the Passion Week and the Resurrection, receive special emphasis in the Gospels and are the subject of the next chapter.

Bethany, the home of Mary, Martha, and Lazarus. Courtesy École Biblique et Archéologique Française, Jerusalem.

Chapter 8

The Passion Week and the Resurrection

The Road to Jerusalem

Jesus' death was not the martyrdom of an unwilling or unsuspecting victim. He predicted his crucifixion and steeled himself for it with steadfast purpose. Luke describes his determination: "As the time approached for him to be taken up to heaven, Jesus resolutely set out for Jerusalem" (9:51). The word *resolutely* literally means "to fix or set one's face toward a thing" and is a Hebrew term that suggests firmness of purpose (see Ezek. 6:2). Speaking of surrendering his life, Jesus said, "No one takes it from me, but I lay it down of my own accord. I have authority to lay it down and authority to take it up again" (John 10:18). But the agony of the coming death also troubled the thoughts of the Lord. In the context of a warning about the future struggles and trials of his disciples, Jesus gave some insight into his own ordeal: "I have a baptism to undergo, and how distressed I am until it is completed!" (Luke 12:50). The Greek term for "distressed" (*synecho*) connotes vexation and torment. Although the prospect of the Cross cast its shadow over Jesus' life, he never wavered from his purpose of offering himself for the redemption of humanity.

A large part of Luke's narrative covers the events and teachings during the final journey to Jerusalem. The precise itinerary to Jerusalem and the sequence of events during that journey are not fully clear. The teaching ministry recorded in Luke 13:22–19:28, as well as the healing of Lazarus at Bethany (John 11:1–43) belong to the travel period. During the time of this so-called Perean Ministry the opposition forces led by the chief priests and Pharisees became better organized, especially after they heard reports of the healing of Lazarus. A meeting of the Sanhedrin discussed a looming danger: the popularity of this miracle worker might make him the focal point for insurrection against the governing authority, and this in turn might provoke the Romans to drastic military measures against the Jewish nation. The Sanhedrin meeting determined to lay specific plans for the execution of the trouble-maker. During this dangerous period (probably in the early months of A.D. 30) Jesus avoided entering Jerusalem. He would not offer up his life until the Passover season.

Jesus spent most of the Perean Ministry not only in the area of Perea (Transjordan) but also along the borders of Galilee, in Samaria, and in northern Judea. Within these regions he visited the towns of Jericho, Ephraim (a village in the rugged hill country about fifteen miles northeast of Jerusalem), and Bethany. Bethany was the home base for Christ's ministry during his final week. At this same small village, he had often had fellowship with Mary, Martha, and Lazarus. The town was only about two miles southwest of Jerusalem and lay along the last lap of the steep road that ran from the Jordan valley at Jericho up to Jerusalem. The hamlet of Bethany was "perched on a broken rocky plateau on the other side of Olivet."[1] John 12:1 states that Jesus arrived at Bethany six days before the Passover. It is likely that the Passover came this year on a Friday, and Jesus must have arrived in Bethany on a Saturday. Since his arrival came on a Sabbath, he probably had been close to Bethany when he stopped for a night's rest on Friday evening. He would then have had only a very short trip into the village. It is not likely that Jesus would have ignored the rabbinical requirement limiting travel on a Sabbath day. According to the oral tradition one was not permitted to journey more than two thousand cubits (a little more than one-half mile) on the seventh day. On that Sabbath at Bethany, Mary anointed the feet of Jesus with an expensive fragrance, and Judas condemned the act as wasteful. John's Gospel notes that thievery as well as the intent to betray Jesus had already marred Judas' character (12:4–6).

At night after the events of Sunday and Monday, Jesus returned to Bethany to the home of either Lazarus or Simon the Leper. Luke says that during the last week Jesus taught in the temple daily, "and each evening he went out to spend the night on the hill called the Mount of Olives" (21:37). Since Bethany was situated on this mountain, it is possible that Luke also was referring to the stay at Bethany.

The Gospels devote a great deal of space to the last week of Jesus' ministry. John's Gospel arrives at the Passion Week by chapter 12, only a little over half-way through the book, and the Synoptics give about one-fourth of their chapters to the topic. Statements in the four Gospels provide some information on the schedule of events running from the Triumphal Entry on Sunday to the Crucifixion on Friday. Wednesday is one day that does not appear to be discussed in the Gospels. Perhaps Jesus withdrew to Bethany during a part of that day to seek the comfort of friends and to find rest from the hurried pace that he followed during that week. The order of events for each day of the week cannot be stated with absolute certainty, but a commonly accepted scenario for the week can be presented here. This outline is not to be taken as a settled matter. Scholars debate the chronology of the week.

A Daily Schedule of the Passion Week

Sunday, a Day of Presentation

The major event on Sunday, the first day of the Passion Week, has been traditionally called the Triumphal Entry. The term is not inappropriate. Jesus deliberately chose to present himself on that day as Israel's promised Messiah and King. The choice of a donkey's colt for the two-mile ride from Bethany to Jerusalem was intended as a fulfillment of Zechariah's prophecy, "Rejoice greatly, O Daughter of Zion! Shout, Daughter of Jerusalem! See, your king comes to you, righteous and having salvation, gentle and riding on a donkey, on a colt, the foal of a donkey" (9:9). Both Matthew (21:4–5) and John (12:14–15) indicate that the event fulfilled Old Testament prophecy.

The crowd perceived it as a royal procession. Mark says they cried, "Blessed is the coming kingdom of our father David!" (11:10), and Luke records the shout, "Blessed is the king who comes in the name of the Lord!" (19:38). Probably some in the crowd expected an immediate earthly kingdom with freedom from the Roman yoke. The old Maccabean fervor seemed to fire the pilgrims along the roadway into Jerusalem. But Jesus did not enter the city like a conquering general. The triumph of this day was to be marked by meekness and gentleness. Some Pharisees called on Jesus to silence those who shouted acclamation, but Jesus refused and asserted that if the crowds had remained quiet, the rocks on the hillsides of Olivet would have proclaimed his glory (Luke 19:39–40). Jesus had on most other occasions avoided direct public assertions of his messiahship. When he fed the five thousand, he had refused the crowd's attempts to declare him a king, but now Jesus set aside such restraint and deliberately welcomed public acclaim.

The shouting crowds who lined Jesus' pathway on the Bethany-to-Jerusalem road had assembled there from opposite directions. Some were pilgrims who had earlier arrived in Jerusalem to purify themselves in preparation for the coming Passover. They had been questioning among themselves whether the Galilean Prophet would appear in Jerusalem for the feast. Now they came out to the Bethany road to watch his arrival. Another group came from Bethany and included some who had been anxious to see for themselves the resurrected Lazarus (John 12:9). The two groups filled the roadway along the hillside into Jerusalem and prepared the road for the King by spreading palm branches and garments in the path.

The crowds could scarcely have perceived the significance of the occasion. For them it was a time of exultation and excitement. For Jesus the event had serious and even somber meaning. When the roadway brought him into view of the city, he wept, not this time because of the prospect of the agony of death for himself but because of the prospect of destruction of the beloved city that lay before him. He envisioned the besieging armies and the leveling of the magnificent buildings. Jesus recognized that in this final week, the rejection of himself as Messiah and King by the nation would bring God's judgment. The nation had failed to perceive the season of God's "visitation" among them. The term *visitation* is used in the King James Version in Luke 19:44 to translate the Greek word *episkopē*, which may mean a benevolent or gracious appearance of God's power, or it may signify God's coming to man in judgment. God had come to Jerusalem in his Son, a gracious visitation, but the rejection of that advent would bring a demonstration of God's wrath through the instrumentality of Titus' army in A.D. 70.

When Jesus finally reached Jerusalem, he began ministering in the temple area to the sick, but since the hour was late already, he soon returned to Bethany.

Monday, a Day of Purging

Mark explicitly states that it was "the next day" that Jesus cursed a fig tree and cleansed the temple (Mark 11:12). Fig trees could not have been expected to bear their main crop of fruit in the spring, but they could have had a few early ripe figs. The real intent of Jesus was to take the occasion to graphically illustrate the fruitlessness of God's chosen people. The fig tree, like the vine, was a common Old Testament figure for the Jewish nation. As R. A. Cole suggests, the fruitless fig tree and the purging of the temple were both acted out as parables with a similar meaning.[2] God's Son came to his people (represented by the fig tree) and to his temple and found them

wanting. The fig tree withered within the day, and the temple would be similarly devastated in A.D. 70. A fig tree might be expected to give figs, and a temple to give the fruit of worship and glory to God, but Jesus saw a tree without fruit and a temple overrun with money changers and dove sellers. Jesus demonstrated his authority and his righteous indignation by driving out those who made his temple a place of commerce instead of prayer. The overturning of tables and disruption of business angered the religious leaders for more than religious reasons. The priesthood undoubtedly had a financial stake in the temple trafficking. The chief priests and scribes now began actively seeking for an opportunity to kill the Galilean teacher (Mark 11:18).

Tuesday, a Day of Confrontation

Tuesday was a very busy day of discussion, teaching, and confrontation for Jesus. Again he taught publicly in the temple most of the day, but he also privately instructed his disciples on the Mount of Olives in the evening (Luke 21:37). On Tuesday the chief priests, scribes, and elders questioned his authority and tried to ensnare him with well-planned questions. "By what authority are you doing these things?" they queried (Matt. 21:23). This was a pertinent question for one trained in the Jewish faith to ask. The scribes believed that teaching should be based on long-standing tradition rather than on novelty. The phrase "these things" refers to the events of the previous days. Certainly the overturning of tables in the temple on Monday and the messianic triumphal procession the day before had aroused indignation. Possibly the enemies of Jesus had carefully prepared their challenge and thought they were ready for a confrontation that would leave Jesus discredited, abandoned, and ineffective.

Jesus so deftly answered his questioners and so cleverly made use of parables that he left his opponents speechless. To the first question of the day Jesus responded with a question of his own. He asked, "John's baptism, where did it come from? Was it from heaven—or from men?" (Matt. 21:25). John's ministry had been closely tied to that of Jesus. If the inquisitors should admit that it was a divinely authenticated ministry, Jesus could have inquired why they had then rejected John. If they said that John's ministry was not of God, they would antagonize the large group that respected the Baptizer and thus weaken their own position of leadership. The questioners refused to give any answer at all.

Jesus took the silence of his questioners as an opportunity to present three parables dealing with rejection and disobedience. In all three the Pharisees and scribes must have clearly seen that Jesus was portraying them in a bad light. (1) In the parable of the two sons, the son who promised his father he would work in the field and then did not fulfill his duty was like a pious religionist who professed much but did not demonstrate faith and repentance when God's messenger arrived. The son who at first balked from toil but then went into the vineyard was like the tax collector or prostitute who repented at John's message (Matt.

21:32). (2) A second story is known as the parable of the tenants. It graphically portrayed the rejection of the Messiah, his crucifixion, and God's turning to the Gentiles. In the story a son came to collect the fruit produced by his father's vineyard, but the wicked tenants wishing to keep the profits to themselves murdered the son.

Explaining the meaning of his story, Jesus quoted Psalm 118:22: "The stone the builders rejected has become the capstone" (Matt. 21:42). Matthew states that on this occasion the chief priests and Pharisees knew that Jesus had spoken of them (Matt. 21:45). They knew that they had been likened to the ungrateful tenants who had beaten and slain the vineyard owner's servants and then killed his son. They would have gladly arrested Jesus at that moment, but they did not dare seize him publicly in the temple. (3) In the third parable, that of the wedding banquet, Jesus compared his opponents to guests, who, upon being invited by a king to a wedding dinner, ignored and ill treated those who bore the message of invitation (Matt. 22:1–14).

The Herodians and Pharisees entered into an unlikely combination for the purpose of snaring the Galilean. After flattering Jesus as a "man of integrity," they proposed a "yes or no" question: "Is it right to pay taxes to Caesar or not?" (Matt. 22:17). Mark's account adds a further question, "Should we pay or shouldn't we?" (12:15). The latter question moved from the realm of ethics or the hypothetical to the real-life issue that the average citizen could not dodge, whether or not to pay tribute to Rome. It was not a serious request for information. The Herodians had long ago decided to opt for accommodation to Rome and favored paying taxes. But the Pharisees were uneasy about seeming to acquiesce to the rule of their homeland by Gentiles. Jesus did not allow these opponents to force him to a simple yes or no answer. He asked for a coin, but not just any coin. Many kinds of coins circulated in Palestine. Jesus asked for a denarius, a small silver Roman coin used throughout the empire to pay taxes. On the denarius were inscribed in Latin abbreviation the words "TIBERIUS CAESAR DIVI AUGUSTI FILIUS AUGUSTUS" (Tiberius Caesar Augustus, Son of the Divine Augustus); the coin bore also the image of Tiberius. A contemporary Syrian coin with a similar inscription in Greek further illuminates the meaning of the Latin inscription. The Syrian imprint read, "TIBERIOS KAISER THEOU SEBASTOU HUIOS SEBASTOS" (Tiberius Caesar, August Son of the August God), and the reverse side portrayed the emperor's mother, Livia, as the incarnation of the deity *Pax* (peace).

A silver shekel, minted in A.D. 68. The obverse (right) depicts the omer cup of the temple and the inscriptions "Shekel of Israel" and, above the cup, "Year 3." The reverse has three pomegranates and the inscription "Jerusalem the Holy." Courtesy Reuben and Edith Hecht Museum, University of Haifa.

The denarius symbolized Roman power and the Roman cult. It represented Roman power because it was the official coin for paying taxes to the Roman government. Its possession and use meant submission to Roman authority. But the images on coins in Rome also had a cultic significance. One of Julius Caesar's last provocations had been a plan to claim divinity and to issue coins with his image. While the Latins were reluctant to accept the concept of an emperor's deity, the Jews were adamant in rejecting this blasphemous notion. The second commandment warned, "You shall not make for yourself an idol in the form of anything in heaven above or on the earth beneath or in the waters below" (Exod. 20:4). While a devout Jew might bring himself to give grudging acknowledgment to Roman rule, he would consider the possession of Caesar's image to be morally repugnant and akin to idolatry. It must have embarrassed the critics of Jesus that they could so easily produce the coin he requested. Jesus did not have a denarius in his possession, but he had probably seen denarii falling from the tables when he drove out the money changers. These hated coins were even found in the holy sanctuary. "Whose portrait is this?" and "Whose inscription?" were also embarrassing questions. The logical answer would have been "the divine emperor's," but this reply would have been an admission of Rome's power and an acceptance of the cultic role of the emperor. The respondents answered with the less offensive term "Caesar's."

Jesus finally returned to the original question, "Is it right to pay taxes to Caesar or not?" His answer: "Give to Caesar what is Caesar's, and to God what is God's" (Matt. 22:21). This reply avoided (1) an open-ended approval of the ultranationalistic movement for restoring an earthly Jewish kingdom. Jesus would not rule as a literal king until the appointed time for his kingdom, and he would not sanction a Maccabean type of revolt. The Herodians could not then have a basis, as they had hoped, for reporting him to the Roman authorities as a dangerous insurrectionist. But the reply avoided also (2) any implication that the Roman authority superseded that of Israel's God or Messiah. There are two differing spheres of authority, one earthly and one heavenly. The teaching looks forward to Paul's statement that "the authorities that exist have been established by God" (Rom. 13:1). Caesar had a legitimate realm of authority, but it extended only so far as God allowed. Paul's later explanations make it clear that man's duties to the magistrate or civil authority constitute one aspect of his broader obligation to obey God. If Jesus had simply given a yes answer to the tribute question, the Pharisees could have used his accommodationist position as evidence of compromise with the hated Roman autocracy. But instead of gaining ammunition to destroy Jesus' popularity with the Passover pilgrims, the Pharisees stood silent in amazement at his skillful answers. Jesus was not to be manipulated by cunning questioners, but rather he would control the discussions.[3]

Jesus ended the period of interrogation by initiating a question of his own, a question that led to an assertion of his deity: "What do you think about the Christ? Whose son is he?"

(Matt. 22:42). The critics standing around Jesus would have hesitated to ascribe deity to the Messiah, but Jesus demonstrated to them from Psalm 110 that the Messiah was Lord. The Jews commonly acknowledged that the Messiah would come from David's line, and in the 110th Psalm David addressed this coming one as "Lord." A descendant would normally be considered of lesser rank than his ancestral fathers, yet David spoke of his distant offspring in terms of deference. Jesus then delivered a message of stinging rebuke to those scribes and Pharisees who had proven themselves insincere in their pious professions (Matt. 23).

The final teaching on Tuesday was restricted to the apostolic band. The disciples came to Jesus that evening, as he sat on the Mount of Olives, with questions of their own. In answer to inquiries about the timing of the end of the age and of his own return Jesus gave an eschatological lesson to the disciples, including a series of parables to warn them to be alert and faithful.

Wednesday, a Day of Silence?

The events of Wednesday do not appear to be recorded, and in most scholarly accounts it is considered a silent day. But some writers suggest a different schedule of events for the Passion Week. By one view, Monday instead of Sunday was the day of the Triumphal Entry. This view accords with typology in that the lamb for the Passover would be selected on this same day that Jesus presented himself to Israel. The cleansing of the temple would occur on a Tuesday, and the day of controversy and teaching would be placed on Wednesday instead of Tuesday.[4] This scheme is one possible way of interpreting the biblical data, but it has not become the commonly accepted view. In the schedule presented here, Wednesday is a day of silence, perhaps given to rest and prayer.

Thursday, a Day of Passover Celebration

The next major event recorded in the Gospels, after Tuesday's controversies, was the occasion of the Last Supper. This meal, which the disciples and their Lord ate on Thursday evening, was their Passover observance. Matthew 26:2 and Mark 14:1, which follow the description of Tuesday's activities, indicate that the Passover was coming in two days. All three Synoptics speak of this Thursday as the Passover day when the Paschal lambs were sacrificed and also as the time when Jesus and his disciples ate the Last Supper. It is abundantly clear that the first three Gospels consider the meal a Passover meal (see Matt. 26:19; Mark 14:16; Luke 22:13). At the table Jesus told the gathered disciples, "I have eagerly desired to eat this Passover with you before I suffer" (Luke 22:15). But John is equally clear in stating that the Passover would be celebrated the next day and not at the time of the Last Supper. He precedes his description of the meal with the statement "It was just before the Passover Feast" (13:1). John 18:28 asserts that the Jews who led Jesus from Caiaphas to the palace of the Roman prefect refused to enter the building because to do so would make them ceremonially unclean, and "they

wanted to be able to eat the Passover." John is clearly also describing the Lord's Supper, the same meal as the Synoptics. He states that the day of the Crucifixion was "the day of Preparation of Passover Week" (19:14). Thus John pictures the Jews as not yet having celebrated their Passover when they tried and crucified Jesus on a Friday.

Some scholars have simply concluded that either the Johannine account or the Synoptic version must be in error. But there is no need to conclude that the records are irreconcilable. A variety of solutions have been proposed to harmonize the accounts. One possible resolution of the apparent discrepancy lies in the existence of two different methods for reckoning the time for Passover, the Galilean method followed by the Synoptics and the Judean system used by John. (1) The Galilean, or older Jewish, system thought of the day as beginning at sunrise and running up to the next sunrise. It may be that the Jews in Galilee followed this older custom, and this would explain why the Synoptics have an earlier Passover meal than John. (2) The officially recognized system in Jerusalem, followed by the priesthood and evidently by John as well, reckoned a day as running from sunset to sunset. (1) By the older method of reckoning, the Synoptic version is understandable. The Passover, which was to fall on Nisan 14, began at sunset on Thursday and the lambs were slain on that afternoon. After sunset it was still Thursday (Nisan 14), and the Passover meal would then be eaten on Thursday night. (2) But John's perspective is equally accurate. From the official calendar followed by the priesthood, the Passover day did not begin until sunset Thursday, and the lambs would not be slain until the next afternoon on Friday. On Friday as the lambs were prepared, Jesus offered his life on the cross. John thus is accurate in portraying the Jews at the trial of Jesus as having not yet eaten the Passover (18:28). They would eat it at sundown on Friday.[5]

But the idea of two different calendars for Passover celebrations has not been accepted by a large number of Bible scholars. One other possible method of reconciling John and the Synoptics suggests that the Lord's Supper was a Passover meal for the disciples but that it was eaten early and without the Paschal lamb. Thus the designation of the meal as a Passover meal by the Synoptics was correct, and John's assertion that Passover would not be eaten until Friday is also accurate.[6]

The chronology of events in the Passion Week involves many complex problems and a thorough discussion belongs to specialized works on the subject. The brief outline sketched here can only be considered suggestive and is not presented dogmatically as the only possible way of dating events. Since the Gospel authors did not primarily aim at communicating chronological data, those who seek to construct a dated sequence of events are operating in an area of uncertainty. Their work is valuable and necessary but cannot always provide final answers. Conservative scholars have at least been able to show that the Gospel accounts can be harmonized and are credible in their chronological references. While one is anxious to come as close as possible to an understanding of the timing of events in Jesus' life, it is necessary also to remember that from the biblical perspective there is a much more important message to be communicated, the good news about Jesus' sacrifice for sin and the invitation to repent and receive him.

Friday, the Day of Crucifixion

Before making an attempt to determine the possible year of Jesus' death, it is necessary to know first the day of the week and the date of his crucifixion. All four Gospels indicate that Jesus was crucified on the day of "Preparation" (Greek, *paraskeuē*), which meant Friday, the day before the Sabbath. But some Bible students have argued that Jesus' crucifixion was on a Thursday or even Wednesday. They cite Matthew 12:40: "For as Jonah was three days and three nights in the belly of a huge fish, so the Son of Man will be three days and three nights in the heart of the earth." Several answers can be given to this view. (1) This single verse is the major reason for rejecting a Friday crucifixion, and this one verse is interpreted in an excessively literal manner. It has been well established that the Jews counted any portion of a day as a whole day, and Jesus was in the tomb for one whole day and parts of two other days. But a Friday crucifixion allows for his being in the tomb only two nights. (2) Matthew's statement seems to be an idiomatic expression rather than an indication that seventy-two hours were spent in the grave. (3) Frequent references to a third-day resurrection make three literal nights unnecessary. Jesus said that his resurrection would be "on the third day" (Matt. 16:21). There are other numerous references in the Gospels to the third day (Matt. 17:23; 20:19; 27:64; Luke 9:22; 18:33; 24:7, 21, 46). Paul also said that the gospel he received included the belief that Jesus was "raised the third day according to the Scriptures"(1 Cor. 15:4).

Another argument used to support a Thursday crucifixion is a special definition of the term "day of preparation." It is claimed that this term may mean a preparation day for the Passover festival rather than specifically Friday, the day before the Sabbath. But there is substantial proof that the term refers to Friday, and there is no evidence that it ever had any other meaning.[7] Josephus used the Greek term meaning "preparation" to refer to the day before the Sabbath. He cited a decree that was given by Augustus granting that the Jews need not appear "before any judge on the Sabbath day, nor on the day of preparation to it, after the ninth hour. . . . "[8]

The Year of Jesus' Death

Jesus was crucified on Friday, Nisan 14. At sundown, Nisan 15 officially began, and the Judeans ate the Passover. Astronomical observations indicate that Nisan 14 and 15 occurred on our Friday during the year A.D. 30 and again in 33. These dates all come within the administration of Pontius Pilate, A.D. 26–36, and years earlier or later than his governorship would be out of the question. Harold Hoehner has ably presented the argument for A.D. 33.[9] The chief problem with the later date is the difficulty of reconciling chronological

information in the apostolic era with it. A late date for the Crucifixion crowds the events of Paul's early activity into a narrow time span.

The A.D. 30 date for the Crucifixion seems to fit the biblical data fairly well. If one is correct in taking Luke's reference to John's ministry beginning in the fifteenth year of Tiberius as the fifteenth year of the co-regency (A.D. 11), then John the Baptist may have begun his ministry early in A.D. 26, and Jesus could have been baptized in the fall of that year. A three-and-a-half-year ministry would then terminate in A.D. 30. To place the beginning of Jesus' ministry much later than 27 or 28 would be difficult to reconcile with Luke's statement that Jesus was about thirty years old at the outset of his ministry since his birth at the latest would be 4 B.C. Another piece of chronological information is available in these words spoken to Jesus: "It has taken forty-six years to build this temple. . ." (John 2:20). Herod began the project in 19 or 20 B.C., and it continued in process until A.D. 64. Forty-six years after 19 or 20 B.C. brings one to A.D. 26 or 27, the first year of Jesus' ministry. An A.D. 30 date is then a good possibility, but one must remember that the chronological issues are exceedingly complex and any scheme of dating is based on interpretation of a few pieces of evidence that are not unambiguous.

The Arrest of Jesus

After an evening of teaching and feasting with his disciples, Jesus led them to one of his favorite retreats, Gethsemane, a grove of olive trees along the Mount of Olives. There he

A view of the Mount of Olives, showing the Basilica of the Agony at the center. Courtesy Israel Government Press Office.

agonized in prayer as his final hour approached. After finishing his prayers, Jesus saw Judas approaching with the temple guard sent by the chief priests. John's Gospel adds the information that Judas came with a Roman cohort. It has been questioned whether such a large force as a Roman cohort of 760 infantry and 240 cavalry would have been sent against Jesus and his small band of disciples in the garden, and that the Roman force would have responded on the basis of the priesthood's dissatisfaction with Jesus. Perhaps John did not mean that the cohort's full numerical strength appeared on the hill. Probably a much smaller detachment was dispatched. Also, the Romans would have wanted to cooperate with the elders and chief priests

in keeping order during the turbulent festival seasons. Passover saw many pilgrims pouring into Jerusalem, some of whom might be easily provoked to insurrection by a popular leader.

The Trial Before the High Priests and the Sanhedrin

The trial of Jesus included three Jewish phases followed by three Roman phases. (1) In the first phase Jesus appeared before Annas, who had served in the office of the high priest on an earlier occasion. Annas questioned Jesus about his disciples and his teaching, possibly to determine if Jesus might reveal himself to be an ultra-nationalist. But Jesus, in effect, denied any secretive or seditious plots when he responded that he had "spoken openly to the world," and had "taught in synagogues or at the temple," and not secretly (John 18:20). (2) Jesus appeared next before Caiaphas at his house where some of the members of the Sanhedrin had also gathered. Caiaphas at that time held the office of high priest and was Annas' son-in-law. The meeting was not a legal session of the Sanhedrin because that body could not officially meet at night. The hastily gathered group was holding a preliminary meeting, in expectation of ratification of their work at dawn by the full Sanhedrin. Witnesses brought charges against Jesus that would have convicted him of blasphemy if the accusers had been able to agree in their testimony. Because of the inconsistency of their testimony, Caiaphas tried another line of attack. He charged Jesus to testify under oath whether he was "the Christ, the son of God." "Yes, it is as you say" was the reply (Matt. 26:64). The high priest in a display of righteous indignation tore his garments and charged Jesus with public blasphemy. The whole group agreed that witnesses were now unnecessary, for Jesus had convicted himself of blasphemy by his own mouth. The Old Testament punishment for such a crime was death.

The opponents of Jesus knew that they could not induce the Romans to execute Jesus on the basis of Jewish law. The Romans would not be impressed by a charge of blasphemy. But Jesus claimed to be the Messiah, and this could be the basis for a charge of sedition. Jesus' answer to Caiaphas had included the assertion that he was the Son of Man who

would sit at his Father's right hand and return again in a heavenly cloud (Matt. 26:64). The reference was clearly to Daniel 7:13–14, a prophecy that portrayed one called the Son of Man, "coming with the clouds of heaven" and receiving "authority, glory and sovereign power," as well as a kingdom that would be everlasting. By applying Daniel's prophecy to himself, Jesus claimed to be the Messiah and to have a special relationship with the Father. C. H. Dodd believes that the real reason the Sadducees sought to condemn Jesus was not because of a specific instance of blasphemy but because of his claim to special authority. They were reacting against various words and deeds that had implied a special tie to God. The question of authority, Dodd thinks, lay behind the blasphemy charge. The teaching of Jesus had called into question the whole oral tradition so honored by the Pharisees; it was a tradition that provided a guide for every possible situation in life. The priestly hierarchy had determined that Jesus was too dangerous and must be removed from the scene. The blasphemy charge was primarily a device used by the Sadducees to elicit Pharisaic and public support, while Jesus' claims of authority were the real reason for a Saducean plot.[10]

(3) At dawn Jesus appeared before the full Sanhedrin, which confirmed the preliminary verdict of those who had pronounced him worthy of death. The account of Jesus' trial has been attacked at many points as lacking in credibility. Critics have questioned whether a trial before the Sanhedrin even took place, as such a trial would have violated Sanhedrin

procedure at so many points. But it is very well possible that an angry and nervous leadership violated their own rules in their haste to execute Jesus. The mere existence of a law or custom cannot be taken as certain evidence of its enforcement or practice. It is also not fully clear what the rules might have been in A.D. 30. The charge of inaccuracy against the Gospels is based on the Sanhedrin tractate in the Mishnah. But these oral laws had not been collected until the end of the second century A.D. The procedures described in the Mishnah may not have represented the actual practices of A.D. 30.[11]

The Question of Capital Punishment

When Pilate told Jesus' accusers to hold their own religious trial, they objected, "But we have no right to execute anyone . . . " (John 18:31). Critics have questioned the historicity of John's statement that the Sanhedrin did not have the authority to exercise capital punishment. A. N. Sherwin-White has presented an effective rebuttal to this objection. Capital jurisdiction was, he asserts, "the most jealously guarded of all the attributes of government."[12] Only a few highly privileged communities were allowed by Rome to have unlimited authority over their own citizens. Such areas received their status as a reward for loyal services. But Jerusalem would have been the last area to be named a "free city." One would need to produce strong evidence to prove that the Romans would have allowed such privileges in a turbulent province like Judea. It is true that a few executions did occur in Jerusa-

lem at the hands of the Jewish leaders, and it is well established that the Sanhedrin did have the right to execute any Gentile including even a Roman citizen, if he trespassed the sacred shrine of the temple. But the temple authority involved a special grant of power. If the Jews had possessed a general authority to administer capital punishment, then the special provision of power would have been unnecessary. The killing of the apostle Stephen has sometimes been cited as evidence that the Sanhedrin did have broad powers of capital punishment. But the stoning of Stephen sounds more like the action of a lynch mob than of a council exercising its prerogative through a trial proceeding. Some elements of a regular or formal hearing were apparent: Stephen appeared before the Sanhedrin, the high priest was presiding, and witnesses were present. But the execution scene sounds less official. The men who stoned Stephen were "furious and gnashed their teeth" (Acts 7:54) and after hearing Stephen's prayer, "yelling at the top of their voices, . . . rushed at him, dragged him out of the city and began to stone him" (Acts 7:58). Although the Sanhedrin had no absolute power of capital punishment, it might have dared to practice vigilante justice in exceptional cases when popular feelings were at a fever pitch.[13]

The Trial Before the Roman Authorities

Before Pilate

In Luke's account the charges against Jesus before Pilate are specific: "We have found this man subverting our nation. He opposes payment of taxes to Caesar and claims to be Christ, a king" (23:2). This was primarily a political charge, an attempt to arouse in Pilate a fear of sedition and insurrection. All four Gospels record that when Pilate questioned him, Jesus admitted his claim to kingship.

A reconstruction of the Tower of Antonia, at the northwest corner of the temple area. Courtesy Zev Radovan.

Before Herod Antipas

Hearing that Jesus was a Galilean, Pilate decided to send him to the ruler of that region, Herod Antipas, who had come to Jerusalem for the festival. It was perhaps Pilate's way of ridding himself for a time of the troublesome issue, and it might have been interpreted by Herod as a generous act of respect for his jurisdiction. Luke says the incident created a friendship between the tetrarch and the prefect, who had formerly been at odds (23:12). The earlier enmity might have been a result of Pilate's having slaughtered some of Herod's subjects. Pilate had slain them in the temple and had mingled their blood with their sacrifices (Luke 13:1). He had also offended Herod Antipas and the Jews by placing votive shields in the temple area. Tiberius himself had ordered the removal of the shields.[14]

After his meeting with Jesus, Herod made no formal decision, deferring instead to Pilate's authority. Herod made the hearing a scene of mockery and irreverent buffoonery. He ordered that Jesus be attired in an elegant robe as though he were a king and sent back to Pilate. The use of a purple robe was Herod's way of demonstrating to Pilate that he shared his view of Jesus' innocence.[15] Both rulers considered the charges against Jesus to be lacking serious substance.

Before Pilate Again

The third and final Roman phase of the trial took place before the reluctant and uneasy Pilate. Although the prefect could find no sound basis for a capital offense, he grudgingly agreed to the demands, "Crucify him." But Pilate made a last effort to release Jesus by appealing to a Passover custom whereby one prisoner would be given his liberty at festival time. The exact character of this tradition is obscure since it is mentioned only in the Gospels. Pilate's gambit failed because the crowds refused to request the release of Jesus and asked instead for the bandit leader Barabbas. Luke says that Barabbas had led a rebellion in Jerusalem and was guilty of murder (23:19). It is ironic that Pilate would have held in custody for execution the Prince of Peace while releasing a rebel leader who had actively sought to subvert Rome's temporal power.

The Jews found a way to give Pilate a none-too-subtle warning when they said, "If you let this man go, you are no friend of Caesar. Anyone who claims to be a king opposes Caesar" (John 19:12). Some scholars think the term "friend of Caesar" was an official title given to certain individuals and that Pilate must have possessed this special distinction.[16] Perhaps the term is not used in a technical sense here and simply indicates that Pilate was in danger of putting himself in a position of enmity toward Tiberius. The point of the warning was that if Pilate released Jesus, the Jews could then report to the ultra-suspicious Tiberius that he had released an insurgent with pretensions to kingship. Pilate certainly would fear that such an accusation would be sufficient to cost him his office or worse. If one accepts A.D. 33 as the date for the Crucifixion, the warning would seem even more ominous. By that date Sejanus, the leader of the palace guard who had evidently been instrumental in Pilate's receiving his office, had been discovered to be involved in the poisoning of the emperor's son as well as plotting against Tiberius himself. After Sejanus' death in A.D. 31, Tiberius reversed Sejanus' policy of antisemitism. Pilate must have been more cautious about giving offense to the Jews after Tiberius' change of course. Pilate had on earlier occasions deeply offended the Jews. Now, after A.D. 31, he would be a much more compliant governor.[17] But even assuming the A.D. 30 crucifixion date, even though Sejanus' exposure had not yet put Pilate in extreme danger, the sour and suspicious mentality of Tiberius would have provoked caution in Pilate. The

veiled threat of blackmail by the Jewish leaders succeeded, and Pilate finally surrendered Jesus to be crucified.

The Hour of the Crucifixion

It appears that the hour of Jesus' crucifixion cannot be precisely set. Although the Gospels have time indications, they probably should be understood as approximations. Mark says that Jesus was crucified at the "third hour" (15:25), while John says it was "about the sixth hour" that Pilate turned Jesus over to the chief priests for execution (19:14). If Mark and John were using the same time system, it would appear that John has Jesus being tried three hours after Mark says he was crucified. Some commentators have assumed a contradiction.[18] Others, seeking a way to harmonize the two accounts, suggest that John used Roman time, counting from midnight to 6:00 A.M. to arrive at the sixth hour when Jesus appeared before Pilate. Assuming that Mark used Semitic time, counting the hours from sunrise, his statement would mean that Jesus was crucified by 9:00 A.M. The three hours between 6:00 A.M. and 9:00 A.M. would easily allow sufficient time for the movement from the final trial to the execution scene.[19] But this explanation has serious difficulties. There is no convincing historical evidence to show that the Romans did make use of midnight as the beginning point for counting the hours of the day. Johnny V. Miller has presented a more acceptable method for harmonizing the accounts. He has argued that time notations among ancient peoples were never intended to be more than approximations. The sundial did not provide precise timekeeping, and the ancients did not concern themselves with the kind of exactitude that modern man with his easily available clocks and watches could attain. Days were thought of as having four divisions, each containing a three-hour period. Mark's reference to a "third hour" was intended to mean nothing more than that the second quarter of the day (9:00 A.M. to 12:00 P.M.) was approaching. John's reference to the sixth hour refers simply to the period before noon or about the middle of the day. The time references thus are not contradictions but are inexact time notations that fulfilled the intent of the writers.[20]

The Via Dolorosa ("Road of Sorrow"), on the way from Pilate's judgment hall to Golgotha. Courtesy Zev Radovan.

The Resurrection

All four Gospels indicate that Jesus was physically raised from the dead on the first day of the week, Sunday. While it is true that no one actually saw the Resurrection itself as it occurred, there certainly were witnesses to the empty tomb and to the reality of a living Christ ministering among his disciples. Luke states that during a forty-day period up to the Ascension Jesus "showed himself to these men and gave many convincing proofs that he was alive" (Acts 1:3). In the Jerusalem area Jesus appeared to (1) Mary Magdalene, (2) a group of other women, (3) Peter, (4) two disciples on the Emmaus road, (5) ten apostles, (6) eleven apostles with Thomas present, (7) a group of disciples at the Mount of Olives at the time of the Ascension. Jesus also made a series of Galilean appearances. He appeared there to (8) seven disciples beside the lake and (9) a group of about five hundred that met on a mountain (Matt. 28:16; 1 Cor. 15:6). He also manifested himself to (10) his brother James, an event that might have been the turning point that brought James from doubt to faith. At any rate we find James numbered among the believers in the earliest account of the church (Acts 1:14). In Paul's list in 1 Corinthians 15 he includes his own encounter with the Christ on the Damascus road as the last of six specific appearances.

The earliest preaching of the church emphasized the importance of the resurrection of Jesus. In his first recorded message in the Book of Acts, Peter asserted that God had raised Jesus from the dead (2:24). The resurrection theme recurs frequently in the apostolic preaching as found in Acts. Paul's testimony in 1 Corinthians 15:4 that Jesus "was raised on the third day" may have been written before any of the Gospel accounts; there are also repeated references to the event in the other epistles. Many modern writers have taken in hand to assess the evidence for the Resurrection from every possible standpoint, but the multitude of arguments cannot be surveyed here. A few scholars, such as Bultmann consider a physical resurrection an absurdity. But others have argued that the historical evidences are sufficient to bring one to conclude that a bodily resurrection of Jesus is the only rational explanation for the origins of Christianity. Some would argue that the evidence is adequate if one is free from presupposed notions that a resurrection is *per se* impossible.[21] The importance of the Resurrection as a crucial element in the faith of the early church is indisputable. For Paul it was more than a mystical event in the realm of faith; it was an objective fact without which one's whole faith would be useless (1 Cor. 15:14).

Evidence for the Resurrection

The early Christians did not preach the Resurrection as an invitation to put faith in an utterly irrational event. The idea that Jesus should rise from the dead is not presented by the Gospels as something the disciples accepted easily. The apostles' attitude was rather one of doubt and fear, of resignation to the fact that their dream of a messianic kingdom had been shattered. Thus the Gospels present evidences to substantiate the rationality of accepting the Resurrection. While these evidences may not, in the view of many, compel faith, they do provide a rational basis for giving credence to the gospel.[22] Several lines of evidence may be suggested:

1. *The Fact That Jesus Died.* Because some have argued that Jesus was not raised because he did not die, it is necessary to show that he actually died and did not merely enter a state of suspended animation. The four Gospels clearly testify that Jesus died. Mark and Luke say he "breathed his last" (15:37; 23:46), and Matthew and John say "he gave up his spirit" (27:50; 19:30). John tells the story of the piercing of Jesus' side with a sword. Since a victim of crucifixion might survive for days despite brutal suffering, it was the Roman practice to eventually break the legs of those condemned. John says this was done to the two men who were hanging beside Jesus but not to Jesus himself, since the soldiers "found that he was already dead" (John 19:33). The Roman soldiers charged with carrying out the execution certainly had enough experience to know when one of their victims had died. John adds that they also pierced Jesus' side with a spear, "bringing a sudden flow of blood and water" (John 19:34). The separation of the serum from the red corpuscles was a clear evidence that death had occurred. Joseph of Arimathea and Nicodemus, who took charge of the burial of Jesus with Pilate's approval and who wrapped the body with spices and linen, were substantial men, members of the Sanhedrin, who had sufficient intelligence and skill to discern death (John 19:38–40; cf. Matt. 27:57–60; Mark 15:43–46; Luke

23:50–53). Pilate specifically requested and received confirmation of Jesus' death from the centurion (Mark 15:44–45).[23]

2. *The Removal of the Stone.* Mark records that the women who came to the tomb at sunrise on the first day of the week asked one another, "Who will roll the stone away from the entrance of the tomb?" While they pondered this, they suddenly "saw that the stone, which was very large, had been rolled away" (16:3–4). The tomb has usually been understood to have been closed by means of rolling a large flat rock, shaped like a millstone, down a grooved incline. This stone could be kept from shutting off the tomb by placing a small obstruction to prevent its rolling until the time of the tomb's use. Once the small block was removed, gravity would move the stone into the closed position, and only extraordinary effort by several people would be able to roll it back up the grooved track. The women could not have displaced the stone. If the disciples had gathered a large enough group to move it, their activity would have alerted the guards placed there by Pilate. Since the sealing of the tomb had been authorized by the Roman governor (Matt. 27:65–66), it would have been extremely dangerous for anyone to attempt to open the grave and remove the body.

3. *The Witness of the Empty Tomb.* All the Gospels agree that on the third day the grave was no longer occupied (Matt. 28:5–6; Mark 16:6; Luke 24:3; John 20:2, 7). The disciples, full of doubt, anxiety, and fear (John 20:9), were not in a mood to raid the guarded grave. The opponents of Jesus had nothing to gain by stealing

his body and secreting it away. It was to their advantage to have the corpse's existence and location well known so that any attempt to renew the movement could be squelched outright.

4. *The Graveclothes.* The presence of the graveclothes also suggests that the body was not removed in a normal manner. The Gospel of John makes a special point of Peter's examination of the linen burial cloths (20:5–7). There appears to be an implication in John's statement that the strips of cloth that had been wound around the body of Jesus and had, with the aid of the gummy burial spices, assumed the shape of his body now lay somewhat limp but still displaying the contours of a human form. No one could have removed graveclothes in such a manner. The removal of the body so as to scarcely affect the shape of the linen clothing is an indication of a miraculous removal of the physical body.

5. *The Development of the Early Church.* The disciples were transformed by the Resurrection. From doubt and despair they suddenly moved to certainty and boldness as they gave testimony to the raising of their Messiah. Peter at Pentecost, preaching in the power of the Spirit, is a dramatic contrast to the man who with cursing denied knowledge of the Galilean. There can be no doubt that the apostles accepted the truth of the Resurrection and that their preaching of this message led to the growth of the Christian church.

6. *The Evidence of the Gospel Records.* The Gospels tell of numerous appearances of the risen Christ. Luke sums up the record: "After his suffering, he showed himself to these men

and gave many convincing proofs that he was alive. He appeared to them over a period of forty days" (Acts 1:3). Although the four accounts of the resurrection events and appearances contain many differences in detail, the four Gospels agree on the essential elements of the story. The most important of these can be briefly summarized: (1) Jesus was crucified and died; he was buried by Joseph of Arimathea, who had asked Pilate for permission to take the body. (2) He wrapped the body in linen cloth. (3) The women came on Sunday morning and found the tomb empty. (4) The risen Christ manifested himself to his followers by appearing to them after his resurrection.

Difficulties in the Resurrection Narratives

Anyone who objectively studies the accounts of the Resurrection must admit that there are many differences between the four narratives. But difference in detail need not destroy the credibility of the witnesses. Differing accounts of the same event are to be expected because witnesses will see different aspects of the same episode or because their later testimony will be directed toward emphasizing some parts of their experience while omitting others. The narratives of the appearances were never presented with the intention that they be the object of precise literary analysis. They are simply the record of the witness of artless and guileless men who honestly reported the information available to them.

Because the accounts seem to diverge at so many points, it is important to be aware of some of the more significant discrepancies:

1. John records that Nicodemus brought spices to anoint Jesus' body at the time of burial (19:39–40). But Luke 24:1 and Mark 16:1 agree that the women's visit early on Sunday morning was for the purpose of bringing spices to anoint the body. John Wenham has attempted to establish a possible chronology and reconstruction of events to demonstrate that the various seemingly contradictory statements in the Gospels can be harmonized. In this instance, he suggests that Nicodemus, Joseph of Arimathea, and the women planned the burial rites and that they took into account the need for haste in their work. They had to finish the rites before sunset and the beginning of the Sabbath. There was not time for the usual washing of the body and a careful anointing with oils. Wenham believes they then decided to pack the body in dry spices as a "temporary measure" until the women could return to the tomb to perform a more complete anointing.[24]

2. The Synoptics (Matt. 28:1; Mark 16:1; Luke 24:1, 10) report that Mary Magdalene and one or more other Galilean women came to the tomb early on Sunday morning. But John reports only the visit by Mary Magdalene (John 20:1–2). The resolution of this conflict in the accounts illustrates how such matters can be understood. John's purpose seems to be to supplement the Synoptic accounts. Perhaps he displayed a special interest in Mary Magdalene's own part of the drama because he saw in her an example of Jesus' power to transform a sin-sick soul

into a trophy of grace. By such a view John does not contradict; he simply focuses in more narrowly on the aspect of the story that suits his aim. John himself seems to imply the presence of the other women at the tomb when he quotes Mary as saying that the Lord's body had been taken and "we don't know where they put him!" (John 20:2; italics supplied).

3. In some versions of the New Testament it appears that Jesus told Mary Magdalene not to "touch" him because he had not yet ascended (John 20:17 KJV). Yet when the other women saw him, according to Matthew 28:9, they "clasped his feet and worshiped him." Similarly, Jesus invited doubting Thomas to reach out and put his hand in Jesus' side (John 20:27). The problem is resolved by more careful attention to the verb translated "touch" by the KJV in John 20:17. The present tense of the Greek verb (*haptou*) in the imperative mood coming with a negative suggests the prohibition of an act being carried out. It was not that Jesus did not want her to approach him, but rather that he wanted her to cease clinging to him. Mary Magdalene in her mingled sorrow and sudden joy feared that she might lose her Lord again. Jesus' words to Mary, "Do not hold on to me, for I have not yet returned to the Father" (John 20:17), are a compassionate explanation that she must learn to accept the reality that the Master must again be taken from her presence on earth.

4. Luke describes the resurrection appearances in Jerusalem and Judea without even a mention of Jesus' command to the disciples to meet him in Galilee (Matt. 28:7, 10; Mark 16:7). In Acts 1:4 Luke records that the resurrected Jesus commanded his disciples, "Do not leave Jerusalem. . . ." Thus Luke-Acts portrays only Judean appearances. Matthew and John describe appearances in both Jerusalem and Galilee. Most scholars would not bring Mark's Gospel into the discussion of this question because that Gospel presents a problem of its own. The earliest manuscript evidence supports an ending for this Gospel at 16:8, omitting the appearances recorded in verses 9 to 20. This is one of the most significant textual problems in the New Testament and is too complex to resolve here. Simply stated, some would end the Gospel at this point. Others opt for another shorter ending found in some manuscripts. A small number of scholars favor the long ending. More likely Mark had an ending that has been lost. It seems impossible that he intended to conclude his story with the women being silent and afraid (Mark 16:8). He had already proclaimed the resurrection hope by quoting the words of the young man in white (evidently an angelic being), who said, "He has risen! He is not here" (16:6). The issue of the locale of the resurrection appearances is then not to be conclusively settled by the text in Mark 16:9ff. since it has probably been irretrievably lost. Mark 16:7 notes that an angel told the women, "[Jesus] is going ahead of you into Galilee. There you will see him." This might imply later Galilean appearances in a lost ending. But when considering the known endings of Mark, one would have to say that whether one accepts the longer or shorter ending, Mark would, like Luke, restrict its narrative to Jerusalem appearances.

Although from the command to go to Galilee (Matt. 28:10), a command that came from Jesus himself and also from the angel (Mark 16:7), one might assume that the disciples left almost immediately for Galilee, it is clear in John's account that they waited at least eight days in Jerusalem (John 20:26). It appears that the disciples left for Galilee on the Monday after the Resurrection. The delay would have been natural, as it was a festival time in Jerusalem. The Feast of Unleavened Bread occupied a period of six days after the Passover, and the disciples probably did not interpret Jesus' command to require a departure to Galilee before that time.[25] There need be no contradiction in the varying accounts. One need not assume that Galilean appearances preclude the possibility of Jerusalem appearances. Luke's lack of discussion of Galilee may have been a natural effect of his purpose. He set out in Luke-Acts to show how, first in Jerusalem and then in Rome, the Jews rejected the gospel preached by Paul, while many of the Gentiles in the Roman world received Paul's message.[26] Galilee did not fit in with this emphasis on the Jewish capital.

The preceding list of difficulties does not begin to catalog all the questions raised by those who question the possibility of harmonizing the four Gospels. But it does suggest that while some problems may seem baffling, it is probably a result of lack of information on our part. The differences in detail in the narratives do not diminish their witness to the basic message of the gospel: that Jesus died, was buried, and rose from the grave.

A panoramic view of Jerusalem, looking northeast. Courtesy Israel Government Press Office.

Chapter 9

The Jerusalem Church

Biblical Sources for Early Church History

The most important source of information for the history of the church from A.D. 30 to 60/61 is the Book of Acts. While the epistles provide only a small amount of historical narrative, letters like 1 Corinthians can provide insight into church behavior and practice in this period. Galatians 1:11–2:14 is one of the more important narrative sections in the epistles. This passage provides some information on the chronology of Paul's ministry. But the primary value of the epistles lies in their emphasis on the practical application of Christianity to living rather than in their being used as sources of early church history. For the beginnings of church history Luke's second volume, the Acts, is the indispensable work. However, it does not provide an exhaustive history of the church over the three decades covered. Luke loses sight of most of the apostles midway through the story and focuses almost exclusively on Paul in the latter half of his book.

Luke and Acts are the only New Testament books authored by a non-Jew. William Ramsay found many evidences in Luke's writing that indicated Greek nationality, such as (1) the author's love for the sea as seen in detailed descriptions of sea travel with less attention given to overland journeys, (2) his knowledge of the character of the city of Athens, and (3) his facility in the Greek language of the postclassical era (after Alexander's death in 323 B.C.). Although there is a tradition that Luke came from Antioch, Ramsay thinks it more likely that he was a Macedonian.[1] The so-called we passages, in which the author of Acts includes himself as a part of Paul's company, indicate not only that the writer was a traveling companion of Paul but also that he might have come from Macedonia (Acts 16:10–17; 20:5–21:18; 27:1–28:16). The shift from the third person to the first person plural (we) first begins when Paul sets sail s on his second missionary go to Macedonia. The use ﾭ ddenly halts at Philippi (a city of Macedonia) in Acts 16:17. The we passages begin again when Paul sails from Philippi on his third journey (Acts 20:5–6).

It is also evident from the introductions of Luke and Acts that the same author wrote both. In Acts 1:1 Luke speaks of his "former book" as an account of "all that Jesus began to do and to teach." Both books mention the name of Theophilus. In Luke 1:3 the dedication is to the "most excellent Theophilus," a title of respect that suggests the recipient of Luke's two volumes might have been a Roman government official. By implication the second volume would be an account of all that Jesus continued "to do and to teach" through the church and his apostles.

It is not possible to present a detailed defense here for using Acts as a historically reliable source. Other works have considered the question at length and may be consulted. But a few of the Bible scholars who have adopted a positive stance toward Acts may be mentioned. Near the end of the last century William Ramsay began research into Luke's writings. He approached his study convinced that Acts was simply a second-century "imaginative description of the early church" that showed very little regard for geographical or historical accuracy. But Ramsay's research revealed a precision in detailed matters that convinced him the writings of Luke should be considered generally trustworthy first-century works.[2] Despite Ramsay's scholarly contribution, objections are still raised against the acceptance of Acts as a depend-

able source. Recently I. Howard Marshall has carefully examined the question of Luke's reliability. Although he does not lightly dismiss the objections of critics, he concludes that Ramsay's basic viewpoint is still defensible. He also found that while Paul's letters and Acts are different portrayals of events, they do not need to be considered irreconcilably opposed in their general outline of Paul's missionary journeys and activities.[3] Another scholar, who is an expert on Roman law and history, A. N. Sherwin-White, states that Luke-Acts also can be considered generally reliable when it deals with Roman law and provincial administration. "Any attempt to reject its basic historicity even in matters of detail," he asserts, "must now appear absurd."[4]

The Church in Galilee

Although the Book of Acts, in its early chapters, focuses attention almost exclusively on the church at Jerusalem, there must also have been a substantial band of believers in Galilee who remained faithful to the message of Jesus. Galilee had been the scene of much of Christ's ministry. It was probably on a Galilean mountain that the risen Christ appeared to over five hundred brethren at one time (1 Cor. 15:6; cf. Matt. 28:16). Yet Acts does not mention the church at Galilee until after the account of Paul's conversion. At that point in the narrative, Luke says only that "the church throughout Judea, Galilee and Samaria enjoyed a time of peace" (Acts 9:31). In the preceding chapter (8:1) there is an account of the missionary activity that began with Stephen's death. There we are told of the spread of the message to Judea and Samaria, without any reference to Galilee.

Some critics have questioned Luke's accuracy and have posited a beginning for the church in Galilee instead of Jerusalem. But such a reversal of the traditional account lacks documentation. Although the disciples had gone to Galilee and the risen Christ had revealed himself there, as recorded in Matthew and Mark, it is not necessary to assume that Luke is mistaken in placing them back in Jerusalem.[5] Luke did not try to provide a complete or exhaustive account of the work of the early believers. This explains why he suddenly mentions people of "the Way" at Damascus (9:2). Possibly the Damascus disciples heard the message of the risen Christ from the Galilean church. It seems natural for Luke to have focused his attention on Judea. Jerusalem had been the site for the climactic events of the Passion Week as well as for most of the resurrection appearances. As the traditional center for Jewish worship, Jerusalem would inevitably become the focal point for Jewish-Christian activity also.

The Prominence
of the Jerusalem Church

The Jerusalem church maintained its importance even after other populous cities like Antioch had a flourishing church. It exerted leadership and guidance over these daughter assemblies. When word of Philip's revival in Samaria came to Jerusalem, the church sent Peter and John to oversee the new work. Although Paul expressly stated that he did not re-

ceive his message of grace for the Gentiles and Jews from the apostolic leaders in Jerusalem but from God himself (Gal. 1:16–17), he clearly recognized the importance of the Jerusalem church. Along with Barnabas, he was chosen by the saints at Antioch to journey to Jerusalem and represent them to the leaders. There he sought the support of the elders and apostles for the policy of accepting Gentiles into the fellowship without the prerequisite of circumcision (Acts 15). Once the Jerusalem Council had made its decision to accept the Antioch proposal, the pronouncement was considered authoritative, at least for Syria and Cilicia.

One reason for the Jerusalem church's special leadership position was the presence there of the apostles, a group with a special commission from Jesus Christ. In Matthew 10:1 Jesus appointed the apostles and gave them authority to heal the sick and to overcome evil spirits. The term *apostle* literally means "one sent out," and just before his ascension Jesus sent the Eleven forth to be "witnesses in Jerusalem, and in all Judea and Samaria, and to the ends of the earth" (Acts 1:8). Not long before, on a Galilean mountain, Jesus in the "Great Commission" commanded the Eleven (1) to make disciples of all nations, (2) to baptize, and (3) to teach obedience to Christ's commands (Matt. 28:19–20). After the Ascension the Eleven chose a twelfth member to replace Judas, who had committed suicide. They established two criteria for selection: (1) an apostle would be one who had been in the company of Jesus since the time of John the Baptist's ministry, and (2) an apostle must also have been a f the resurrected Christ -22). One of the most im- ontinuing functions of an apostle was to serve as an official witness of the Resurrection. Matthias was the choice of the believers in the Upper Room to fill the place vacated by Judas.

Paul fulfilled one of the major requirements of an apostle because of his personal encounter with the risen Christ on the Damascus road. But since Paul had not been with Jesus during his earthly ministry, the validity of his claim to apostleship was questioned by his opponents. For Paul, his apostleship rested on a definite call of God (Rom. 1:1; Gal. 1:1). Although the term *apostle* applies primarily to the Twelve plus Paul, Scripture also uses it in a broader sense to include other early leaders such as Barnabas (Acts 14:4, 14) and James the Lord's brother (Gal. 1:19; 2:9).

It is a debatable point whether the apostolic band should be looked on as a formal governing board for the church. The leadership role and the respect for the apostles are evident in Acts, but the organization of the church at its earliest stage seems to have been simple and spontaneous rather than formalized. The apostles might best be thought of as men who had received a special call from Jesus himself to go forth as official witnesses. Their brethren were also bearers of the message.

The Upper-Room Believers

The early believers met continually for prayer in a private home in Jerusalem (Acts 1:14). In addition to the apostles this group included Mary the mother of Jesus as well as other unnamed women. Luke, in his Gospel, often referred to the work of women in connection with the ministry of Christ. He cited Mary Magdalene as an example of one of the many who had been healed of demon possession or disease and had then joined with the band that was with Jesus on his journeys (Luke 8:2). He also tells of Joanna, the wife of the manager of Herod Antipas' household; she was one of the more prominent members of a group of women "who were helping to support" Jesus and his disciples "out of their own means" (Luke 8:3). Mary Magdalene and Joanna had been with the women who took spices to the tomb of Jesus early Sunday morning and found the stone rolled away (Luke 24:10). They would very likely have been among the unnamed company of women in the Upper Room. The earliest disciples probably included Susanna, Salome, and Mary the mother of James (Mark 16:1; Luke 8:3; 24:10). Perhaps it was the generosity of these unselfish women that provided the example for the experiment with the sharing of goods in the Jerusalem church. The first band of disciples also included the brothers of Jesus, who had previously doubted their brother's call. The whole assembly numbered one hundred twenty. Many of these believers were Galileans who had remained in Jerusalem in response to Jesus' command to await the gift of the Holy Spirit, whom He had promised to send (Acts 1:4).

Pentecost and the Descent of the Spirit

The descent of the promised Holy Spirit on the company of believers inaugurated the Christian church. The one hundred twenty had gathered in an "upper room," possibly in a home near the temple area (although some scholars think the room might have been located in one of the buildings on the temple grounds). The occasion was the Jewish festival of Pentecost, which came seven weeks after Passover and celebrated the first harvesting of the wheat crop. Jews of the Dispersion would join local inhabitants to swell the crowds celebrating the joyous festival. Although the believers had anticipated the gift of the Spirit, the dramatic event caught them by surprise. The external phenomena consisted of a visual appearance of fire above each head and the sound of a gale blowing through the room. Accompanying these manifestations to the senses was a filling by the Holy Spirit—a filling that would empower the believers and unite them for the task of the church.

The coming of the Spirit had been promised by the prophets of old and by Jesus himself. Ezekiel had used the imagery of four winds blowing the breath of life into the dry bones of the valley (Ezek. 37:9), and Jesus had likened being born of the Spirit to a blowing wind (John 3:8). In both Hebrew (ruah) and Greek (pneuma) the word for "spirit" means also "breath" or "wind." John the Baptist had predicted a baptism "with the Holy Spirit and with fire" (Luke 3:16). In the Old Testament, fire sometimes symbolized God's presence; God had revealed his presence to Moses in a visual way in a flaming bush (Exod. 3:2). Both wind and fire were among the physical symbols evident at the fulfillment of the promise of the

Spirit's outpouring. Just seven weeks before Pentecost, when the disciples celebrated the Passover, possibly in the same Upper Room, Jesus had instructed them about the coming Spirit. He promised that in his absence He would send another Paraklete (counselor, comforter, or advocate) (John 14:16). This Spirit, Jesus said, would bear testimony of him, "and you also must testify, for you have been with me from the beginning" (John 15:27). The grant of the Spirit at Pentecost would enable the disciples to carry out the command to be witnesses.

The descent of the Spirit was authenticated to the pilgrims in Jerusalem through the miracle of tongues. The believers had apparently moved from the Upper Room down to the street below where they began to preach the gospel in languages they had never learned. This phenomenon occurred subsequently in the Book of Acts only when a new group of believers were ushered into the church. At the home of Cornelius in Joppa, Gentiles converted through Peter's preaching received the Holy Spirit and spoke in tongues (Acts 10:45–46). This "Gentile Pentecost" demonstrated that non-Jews should be welcomed into the church on the same basis as Jews. When Paul found a group of disciples at Ephesus who had been baptized after hearing only of the teaching of John the Baptist, he preached Jesus to them and baptized them in Christ's name. This new group of converts then received the Spirit and "spoke in tongues" (Acts 19:6).

Only in the miraculous event of Pentecost is it fully clear that those who received the gift actually spoke in known foreign languages for the purpose of evangelization. Luke does not specify whether the Joppa and Ephesus converts spoke in known languages or in unintelligible utterances. The gift as described by Paul in 1 Corinthians, although not all would agree on this interpretation, might have involved ecstatic utterances for the purpose of individual worship of God rather than foreign languages to reach people of other nations. When Paul wrote his first letter to the Corinthians, he commanded that the exercise of the gift of tongues be accompanied with interpretation so that the assembled believers might understand and be edified by what was said. Without an interpreter the "angelic" speech (1 Cor. 13:1) instead of making a message clearer would actually obscure the thoughts of the speaker. Paul insisted that the gift be restricted in use, and he counseled the greater exercise of the more significant gift of prophecy (preaching), since it would edify all who heard (1 Cor. 14:1–5).

The character of the gift of tongues had apparently changed over the course of time. In fact the Corinthian church had somehow managed to use a gift granted by the Holy Spirit in a fleshly manner. In 1 Corinthians 12:14 Paul implies that some of those who had received the gift were displaying it ostentatiously and were so anxious to be heard that they created disorder and confusion in the assembly (14:27). They had disdained other gifts and displayed an arrogant rather than a loving attitude (12:21; 13:1, 4). Although Paul established limitations on the exercise of tongues, he did not proscribe the exercise of the gift

altogether. He expressly warned the Corinthians to "not forbid speaking in tongues" (14:39) and testified that he himself had the gift (14:18). Just how the gift developed from its Pentecostal form to that described in 1 Corinthians is not explained in Scripture.

Ruins of the forum at Corinth, with pillars of the temple of Apollo in the background. Courtesy Gerald Nowotny.

Peter's bold sermon at Pentecost, like the gift of tongues, was a demonstration of the newly given power of the Spirit. In his message he explained that the phenomenon of unlettered Galileans speaking in foreign languages was a fulfillment of Joel's prophecy: "In the last days, God says, I will pour out my Spirit on all people. Your sons and daughters will prophesy, your young men will see visions, your old men will dream dreams" (Acts 2:17). Peter proclaimed that Jesus was the Christ (Messiah), that He was the Lord (Greek kurios, a term often used of a deity), and that God had raised him from the dead. The church increased its number dramatically as three thousand heeded the call to repent and be baptized. Many of those who came into the fold were Hellenistic Jews from distant lands. Luke mentions fifteen different groups or areas in the empire that were represented among the pilgrims at the Passover. Some of these converts must have remained in Jerusalem beyond the festival season in order to receive further instruction about Jesus. Perhaps the church at Rome had its beginning at Pentecost. Nothing definite is known concerning the founding of that non—Pauline church, but Luke records that among the pilgrims were a group of "visitors from Rome" (Acts 2:10). Perhaps some of these converted "visitors" returned to their home and established a fellowship in Rome.

Early Christian Teaching

The church at its inception did not need a complex or developed theology. The first Christians, in Luke's terminology, "devoted themselves to the apostles' teaching" (Acts 2:42). It is evident that the Jerusalem church possessed a body of oral teaching that had been received originally from Christ by the apostles and then had been transmitted to other believers. Yet in its infancy the church had no New Testament writing, and only during the course of the century did the apostles provide more detailed doctrinal and ethical instruction. Theological development was a gradual process. Creedal statements and detailed doctrinal formulations ordinarily arise when conflicting views and the rise of heretical sects make more precise definition neces-

sary to protect the faith from error. There is very little evidence of anything approaching creedal formulation in the New Testament itself except perhaps in the pastoral epistles (e.g., 1 Tim. 3:16).

Peter's first sermon contained the essential elements of the early theology. He offered forgiveness of sins to his hearers through Jesus Christ and proclaimed that Jesus was the Messiah and that He had been raised from the dead. Resurrection was the major theme of Peter's preaching. Some of the Hellenists present at the Pentecost festival might have already heard some of the resurrection stories told by adherents of the mystery religions. Strange myths about the restoration of life to Attis, Adonis, and Osiris had become the basis of these Oriental faiths. Clearly the story of the raising of Jesus did not derive from such influences. The cult legends differed radically in tone from the faith of the early Christians, and Arthur Darby Nock has suggested one major difference. In the pagan stories death meant defeat, and the worshipers mourned the passing of a god who suffered as a victim of misfortune. Christians did not grieve so much at the thought of death for their Savior as for the unjust betrayal of those who crucified the Righteous One. Jesus did not arise from defeat; He both died victoriously and rose triumphantly.[6] Peter in his first sermon explained to the Jews that Jesus was "handed over to [them] by God's set purpose and foreknowledge" (Acts 2:23).

Although Peter's sermons provide some information on the teaching of the early church, it would be a mistake to think that an analysis of his messages would provide a complete overview of the beliefs of early Christians. The sermons, reported only in summary form by Luke, were intended to persuade people to believe and must have omitted much of the content of early instruction. The church rooted its instruction in the whole of the Old Testament and in the teaching of Jesus. Jesus told his disciples in the Upper Room that He had much more to teach them, but since they were unable then to receive it all, the Holy Spirit would later "guide them into all truth" (John 16:13). The Spirit, He said, "will teach you all things and will remind you of everything I have said to you" (John 14:26). In his sermons Peter touched on some of the major Christian concepts. These sermons speak of Christ's remaining in heaven and returning to earth a second time (Acts 3:20–21). Peter declared him to be holy and righteous (3:14), the author of life (3:15), the judge of people (3:23), and the savior not only of the Jews but also of all who will heed his call (2:21, 39).

Certainly the church also, despite the simplicity of its doctrine, must have believed much that could not be extracted from the sermons in Acts. One cannot find the doctrine of the atonement developed in the sermons or for that matter in any part of Luke's two volumes. According to students of redaction criticism, Luke had no "theology of the cross." But I. Howard Marshall, in his study of Luke's works, asserts that Luke did see the necessity for Christ's sufferings even if he did not develop a theology to explain how Christ's death atoned for sin.[7] For a more fully developed theology one needs to look beyond the sermons and the Book of Acts itself to the epistles.

Early Christian Practice

The striking degree of unity and brotherhood within the Christian community is especially manifested by the interest in fellowship, the eating of common meals, and the practice of selling one's possessions in order to share the proceeds with poorer brethren. The believers met in private homes where they "broke bread . . . and ate together" (Acts 2:46). The breaking of bread was a real dinner, not simply a religious ritual. A participant would break pieces from a loaf for the purpose of sharing his or her food with the larger group. The meal also included commemoration of the Lord's Supper. Apparently there is no difference in the New Testament between references to the "breaking of bread" and the "Lord's Supper." Eventually this fellowship meal became a part of the observance of the Lord's Day services (Acts 20:7–11).[8]

One practice of the early believers, the sharing of property, failed as an economic experiment but was apparently motivated by worthy ideals. It must have been an initial success, since Luke records that because of it "there were no needy persons among [the believers]" (Acts 4:34). But in the long run the Jerusalem church did not find its program adequate to meet the needs of the poor and widows. It was necessary later for Paul and Barnabas to bring a famine relief offering from the Antioch church to Jerusalem (about A.D. 46). Paul also makes references in his letters to systematic collections of money in Macedonia and Achaia (Greece) for the Jerusalem church; these were collections he had organized during his third missionary journey (Rom. 15:25; 1 Cor. 16:1–3). During a visit to Jerusalem with Titus and Barnabas, Paul received a request from the apostles that he "should continue to remember the poor" (Gal. 2:10).

What motivated the communal sharing project? One motive may have been the belief that the return of Christ and the end of the age would occur almost immediately. But more important was the impact of the teaching and example of Jesus and his apostles. When they followed Jesus, the disciples forsook their means of living, whether fishing nets or a tax-collecting booth. Jesus had emphasized that discipleship would cost the sacrifice of self and material possessions. "Any of you who does not give up everything he has," Jesus admonished the crowds that traveled with him, "cannot be my disciple" (Luke 14:33). Jesus informed the rich young man who asked the way to eternal life that he must sell all his possessions and give the proceeds to the poor before he could be a disciple (Mark 10:17–21). Concern for those in poverty and the importance of alms-giving are recurring themes in Jesus' ministry. It is not surprising, then, that the Jerusalem believers, motivated by altruism and love, should have given up their possessions to aid the destitute.

Problems surfaced early in the sharing venture. Barnabas' sacrifice of a field had been a beautiful example of generosity, but the practical difficulty of systematizing such a practice became evident in the case of Ananias and Sapphira's hypocritical gift. Probably motivated by a desire for the esteem given to Barnabas, rather than by genuine concern for the needy, they pretended to have given all that they had received from the sale of their property, when in reality they had given only a portion. Another type of difficulty arose in connection with the distribution of the alms. The Hellenistic believers in Jerusalem criticized the apostles for overlooking their widows in favor of the needs of Hebraic Christians (native Aramaic-speaking believers). One reason for the ineffectiveness of the venture may have been the difficulty of handling administrative problems as the brotherhood increased in size. The communitarian lifestyle worked better when practiced by a small cohesive group.

Although, as Luke states, no one claimed his property as a private possession (Acts 4:32), it is also clear that actual surrender of property was a voluntary and individual decision. Peter told Ananias that his property was his own before the sale and the disposal of the proceeds a matter of his own choice (Acts 5:4). The lack of coercion in the Christian communal experiment contrasts with the Qumran communitarian rules. The Qumran sect compelled all members to divest themselves of belongings when they were admitted to the order. The Christian model displayed more spontaneity and freedom than the highly organized and disciplined Qumran example. The use of the term *communism* to describe the Christian practice is misleading because the modern world identifies the term with Marxism-Leninism, which obviously has nothing to do with the so-called primitive Christian communism. Marxism holds to enforced state ownership and control of property rather than the right of individuals to choose whether they will voluntarily contribute privately owned property to a religious community. The Jerusalem church probably realized, after experiencing difficulties with its experiment, that individuals might do better to retain some of their capital rather than distributing all of it.

The Relationship With Judaism

The early believers maintained a close tie with Judaism, and to most observers Christianity would have appeared to be just one more sect within Judaism. One evidence of the close relationship appears in the continued Christian attachment to the temple. Daily the Christians met in the outer precincts of the temple (Acts 2:46). When Peter and John healed the lame man at the temple gate, they had evidently gone to the sanctuary to participate in praying at the time of prayer. After healing the lame man, Peter preached his second recorded sermon at Solomon's Colonnade, a roofed area of the temple that faced the Kidron Valley to the east. Luke states that the believers met frequently at the colonnade (Acts 5:12). The connection of Christianity with Judaism was also made more apparent by the presence of converted priests and Pharisees in the Christian brotherhood. Some of the latter continued to insist on circumcision and law-keeping as essential even for Gentile converts (Acts 15:5). The close relationship with Judaism is apparent as late as Paul's visit to

Jerusalem after his third missionary journey, when he sought to conciliate his more traditional Jewish brethren by observing the prescribed purification rites in the temple (Acts 21:26).

The believers continued to attend synagogue services after conversion. It has been suggested, though no documentary evidence is available to support the theory, that the Christians might have formed their own synagogues. Various nationalities in Jerusalem did establish synagogues (Acts 6:9), and the Mishnah permitted as few as ten Jews to form one.[9] Even if the Christians did not form a synagogue of their own, it is at least clear that early believers commonly attended the synagogues.

The Hellenistic Jewish believers mentioned in Acts 6:1 also retained close ties with Judaism. Although they had lived in foreign lands and many might not have understood Aramaic well enough to be comfortable in synagogues where Aramaic was spoken, the Hellenists had retained allegiance to the temple and the law. Greek-speaking Jews from abroad would have a breadth and tolerance lacking in Palestinian Judaism, yet the very fact that the Hellenists in Jerusalem had made the choice to return to the site of their holy shrine indicates that they had maintained an allegiance, a zeal, and an emotional attachment to Judaism that may have gone beyond that of many Hebraic Jews.

In a later period the addition of Gentiles to the Christian community would diminish the ties that the churches outside Judea had to Judaism. Yet as late as mid-century, Christianity still seemed to such outsiders as the Roman official Gallio to be only another sect of the Jews. When hearing the complaint of local Jews against Paul, he dismissed the matter as a question of Jewish laws and traditions (Acts 18:15). In A.D. 70 the dispersal of Jerusalem's Jewish believers and the destruction of the temple further weakened the link with Judaism. Certainly those who preached the resurrection of Jesus the Messiah were a distinct group with a new message and mission, even though they, like others, did not always understand the full significance of this fact. But the distinctiveness of Christianity did not remain obscured. As large numbers of Hellenistic Jews and Gentiles entered the fold, the independence of the new movement became increasingly apparent.

Growth and Persecution

Peter's sermon in the temple after the healing of the lame man led to the first persecution of the believers. His message condemned the "men of Israel" who had handed Jesus over to be killed. That the leaders had acted in rebellion against God himself was evident, Peter asserted, since the Father had resurrected the crucified Savior. This "servant Jesus" was none other than the Messiah promised by Moses and the prophets. Peter's sermon antagonized the Sadducees and especially those who were of the high priestly clan because it denounced them for the murder of Jesus. The message also aroused the Sadducees because it proclaimed the Resurrection, a doctrine they denied. It was not only the teaching about the Resurrection that disturbed the Jewish

leaders, but also the claim that through it God had vindicated Jesus and had condemned their villainy. Another cause of the persecution was the growth in the company of the believers. Three thousand had joined the movement at Pentecost, and now the ranks swelled to five thousand men (Acts 4:4). The Christians must have been a significant minority, and from the Sadducean viewpoint they seemed to be a potential threat to stability and the established religious leadership. According to one scholarly estimate, the city of Jerusalem did not likely exceed 44,000 in the first century, except for festive times when thousands of pilgrims would drastically swell the numbers. Thus the Christian element was not simply a tiny fraction of the inhabitants. The much larger population figures for Jerusalem given by Josephus probably included the multitudes of pilgrims who camped about the environs of Jerusalem at the times of feasts.[10] The conversions included not only Pentecost pilgrims and local citizens but also priests and Pharisees. This increase must have made the Sadducees increasingly nervous. It is understandable, then, that they ordered the captain of the temple guard to incarcerate Peter and John.

The Jewish leaders were unable to repress the bold preachers. After a night in prison, Peter and John were brought before the Sanhedrin, were warned to stop spreading their message, and then were released (Acts 4:1–18). But the apostles continued to preach and to heal the multitudes of sick folk that were brought to them. Again a group of apostles were imprisoned (Acts 5:18), but an angel intervened to release them, and they resumed their ministry. The report came to the authorities that the former prisoners were "standing in the temple courts teaching the people" (Acts 5:25). After a second Sanhedrin hearing, the leaders flogged them, warned them "not to speak in the name of Jesus," and released them again (Acts 5:40).

At the second hearing the respected scholar Gamaliel advised the Sadducees to end the crusade against the apostles. If the new sect was of human origin, it would fall of its own weight, but if it was of God, then it could not be successfully defeated anyway. Gamaliel had been Paul's teacher. He was a Pharisee and a member of the moderate school of Hillel. Gamaliel's interpretation of the law tended to be pragmatic and liberal. His views were in contrast to the stricter application of the law by the school of Shammai. Gamaliel's wise counsel, as recorded in Acts, fits with his reputation for reason and moderation. It is not likely that a man like Gamaliel would have harbored a spirit of generous toleration toward Christianity. His attitude was probably closer to indifference than benevolence.

The reference in Gamaliel's statement to the rebel leader Theudas is sometimes considered a historical blunder chargeable to Luke's having constructed a speech to put in Gamaliel's mouth. According to the speech, Theudas led a doomed insurrection with four hundred men. Then came a second rebellion led by Judas the Galilean. Judas' rising came in reaction to the census (referring apparently to the census undertaken by Quirinius). According to Gamaliel's address, Theudas would belong to a period before A.D. 6. But Josephus places Theudas in the time of the Procurator Cuspius Fadus (A.D. 44). Gamaliel could not have spoken about the insurrection recorded by Josephus, since it occurred more than a decade after he made his address. On the surface it appears that Luke made an error, but this is not the only possible explanation. There were frequent uprisings in Palestine, and Theudas was a very common name. Perhaps there were two rebel leaders named Theudas. If this was in fact so, then both Josephus and Luke would have reported accurately.

Stephen and the Hellenist Christians

The growing number of Hellenistic Christians in Jerusalem registered a complaint against the administration of alms for widows. Jerusalem had large numbers of Hellenists because many came from the Diaspora to attend the festivals and then stayed on in the city. The converted Hellenists may have had separate house-churches. Many of them knew little or no Aramaic and would have felt more comfortable worshiping in Greek. Differences in culture and language would naturally set apart the two Christian groups as distinct entities.[11] But this does not mean that the two groups held to a drastically different theology or that they were seriously divided. Acts emphasizes the unity and brotherhood of the early community of believers despite the differences (4:32).

There is evidence that some of the Hellenists in other lands adopted a liberal brand of Judaism. But it is inaccurate to stereotype Palestinian Jews as legalistic and Diaspora Jews as having a broader outlook. Some of the Diaspora Jews remained devoted to the literal application of the law. Although Philo, the Alexandrian Jewish philosopher, found allegorical meanings in the law himself, he condemned those Jews who thought that the symbolic significance of a rite could negate the necessity for a physical ceremony. He agreed with those Jews who said that circumcision was a symbolic act signifying the removal "of pleasure and all passions, and the putting away of impious conceit." But then he warned, "Let us not on this account repeal the law laid down for circumcising. Why we shall be ignoring the sanctity of the temple and a thousand other things, if we are going to pay heed to nothing except what is shown us by the inner meaning of things."[12] Perhaps some of the Hellenists who came to Jerusalem had imbibed the kind of Greek spirit that Philo condemned. Foakes-Jackson and Kirsopp Lake think the persecution that developed on the occasion of Stephen's martyrdom may have been directed specifically against Hellenists, whether Christian or not, and that this explains why the Twelve did not need to flee Jerusalem with their Hellenistic brethren. Their reconstruction of events predicates a sharp distinction between Hellenists and native Jews. But this division may not have been as consistent as their analysis implies.[13]

The Twelve delegated the task of administering the distribution of alms to a group of seven chosen by the brethren. All of the seven had Greek names. Although Hebraic Jews also sometimes used Greek names, it is probable that the church chose Hellenist Christians to be overseers of the distribution. There would be no grounds for charging prejudice if the seven were chosen from among the aggrieved community itself. One of the seven, Nicolas from Antioch, is called a "proselyte." The term refers to a Gentile who has been circumcised and has accepted the regulations of the Old Testament law. Other Gentiles, like Cornelius (Acts 10:2), are described as "God-fearing," a designation that seems to apply to Gentiles who worshiped and prayed to the God of the Jews, Jehovah, but had not been circumcised. The Jerusalem church in the time of Stephen was a Jewish church and had very few proselytes and no Gentiles. Thus the dispute over alms was a disagreement within the Jewish Christian community.

The task of the seven may not have been restricted to serving. The only qualification mentioned—"full of the Spirit and wisdom" (Acts 6:3)—suggest a spiritual ministry as well. The preaching activity of two of the Hellenist leaders, Stephen and Philip, indicates that their administrative duties did not exclude the possibility of ministry of the Word and the performing of miracles (Acts 6:8; 8:6). Stephen preached so persuasively in the Hellenistic synagogues that he aroused the bitter opposition of the men from Cyrene, Alexandria, Cilicia, and proconsular Asia. It is not clear whether the Hellenistic synagogue mentioned in Acts 6:9 should be interpreted to mean one or several assemblies. Some writers have understood Luke to mean that there were up to as many as five synagogues.

The Hellenists brought false witnesses before the Sanhedrin to accuse Stephen. The charge that he spoke against the temple and the law probably contained some germ of truth, though the simplistic accusations as stated were erroneous. Stephen has sometimes been portrayed by modern scholars as a proponent of such advanced concepts that he offended both Jews and Christians. But it is not likely that Stephen called for the immediate abandonment of the temple worship and the law. His message in Acts 7 echoes themes in the teaching of Jesus himself, and the intent of Stephen's sermon might best be understood in the light of Christ's statements about the temple. Jesus told the Samaritan woman, "A time is coming when you will worship the Father neither on this mountain nor in Jerusalem," and added that genuine worship would be "in spirit and in truth" (John 4:21, 23). Stephen's message coincides with the essential teaching of Jesus in the Sermon on the Mount in that he stressed the greater importance of the inner and spiritual experience over against the outward and legal forms of religion. The charge that Stephen spoke against the law, blasphemed Moses, and wanted to change the customs handed down by Moses probably could be understood to mean that Stephen had attacked the oral tradition of the Pharisees. Like Jesus before him, he may have seen that in effect the traditions were nullifying the intent and spirit of the law.

Stephen's view of the temple and the law may have anticipated in germ form the teachings of Paul and the author of Hebrews, but it is not really clear that he had advanced as far as either. There is no definite indication that Stephen could have envisioned accepting uncircumcised Gentiles into the church as Paul and even Peter did later. Stephen's sermon does not suggest either, as the Book of Hebrews does, that the Old Testament ritual was primarily a symbol that had its fulfillment in Christ. It is even less likely that Stephen held a view as radical as that found in the Epistle of Barnabas (c. A.D. 130), which views the building of the temple by the Jews as contrary to God's will and a mistake from the very beginning. Barnabas described those who built the original temple as "wretched men (who) went astray and set their hope on a building, as being the house of God, instead of a God who made them." Those who offered sacrifices there performed "almost like the heathen." The only true temple in Barnabas' view is the presence of God in the regenerated individual.[14] F. F. Bruce holds to a contrary opinion. He maintains that Stephen did condemn the building of the temple as a mistake at the outset. He sees the speech as a manifesto of the Hellenistic community, which held to such a radical stance on both the law and the temple that they were sharply differentiated from other believers both theologically and culturally. According to Bruce's view, the teaching of the Epistle of Barnabas flowed naturally from the tradition of Stephen.[15]

Stephen's speech to the Sanhedrin consists of a lengthy historical narrative touching on varied incidents in Israel's past. Modern interpreters have often debated the actual intent of the address, but two themes seem to stand out: (1) The Jews have repeatedly rejected God's law and his messengers and (2) God cannot be limited geographically to a single shrine.[16] Stephen develops his first theme in his retelling of the familiar story of Joseph. His brothers, the Jewish patriarchs, rejected him by selling him as a slave (Acts 7:9). The Israelites misunderstood Moses' attempt to rescue them from slavery (7:25), and they questioned his authority to be "ruler and judge" (7:35). Moses had promised, "God will send you a prophet like me from your own people" (7:37), yet the pattern of rejection had now reached its ultimate stage in the murder of the promised Righteous One. Stephen summed up his first theme in a dramatic accusation that he made before the Jewish council: "You are just like your fathers: You always resist the Holy Spirit! Was there ever a prophet your fathers did not persecute?" (7:51–52).

In his second major theme, Stephen attacked the superstitious reverence the Jews held for the Jerusalem temple. The "God of Glory" had revealed himself to Abraham, not in Canaan or on Mount Zion, but while Abraham was still in Mesopotamia (7:2), and God had blessed Joseph as Israel's deliverer while he was in Egypt (7:9–10). It was near Mount Sinai that God revealed himself to Moses in the flaming bush (7:30–32), and it was on that mountain that God gave him the Law (7:38). God directed Moses to build a tabernacle that could be moved from place to place (7:44). The implication seems to be that a mobile place of worship suited a universal deity better than a fixed place.[17] God permitted Solomon to build the temple that David had requested (7:45–46), but "the Most High does not live in houses made by men" (7:48). Stephen apparently believed that the emphasis of the contemporary Jewish leadership on the impressive Herodian temple did not accord with the earliest pattern of Jewish worship.

The speech so enraged the men of the council that they reacted with moblike passion and stoned Stephen in a hasty and illegal manner. The Sanhedrin lacked authority to exercise capital punishment. Possibly in Stephen's case they were acting more like a lynch mob than a legally constituted body. Pilate may not have wished to make an issue of this breach of procedure because of fear of antagonizing the Jewish authorities. Perhaps Pilate accepted a *fait accompli* because his relationship with the Emperor Tiberius was becoming increasingly uneasy. Some scholars have given a different explanation for what appears to be an illegal execution. Instead of dating Stephen's martyrdom in A.D. 33 (the chronology followed here), they have suggested A.D. 37. In the latter year Pilate left Judea for Rome, and it is possible that Caiaphas could have seized the moment to vent his fury on the Hellenist Christians before a new prefect arrived. But a date as late as 37 poses problems in establishing a chronology for Paul's life.

The Expansion of the Church

The martyrdom of Stephen initiated an organized persecution of the church. Saul, with official priestly endorsement, sought "to destroy the church" (Acts 8:3). The term "destroy" (Greek, *elumaineto*) suggests that Saul was ravaging or spoiling the church. It is a word used to describe the ravages of a wild animal or the intemperance of a glutton; Luke does not try to gloss over the vehemence of the persecutor.[18] Despite his training under the moderate Gamaliel, Saul must have viewed Stephen's preaching on the law and temple as dangerous and blasphemous heresy. The earliest opposition to the faith had come from the Sadducees, who viewed the proclamation of Jesus as Messiah and Savior as a threat to stability and to their authority. The Pharisees, as illustrated by Gamaliel's attitude, probably viewed the movement as less threatening. There had been no frontal assault on the law, the traditions, and the temple. But many Pharisees must have mistakenly viewed Stephen's message as such an attack. Because of their new perception of the believers, Saul and other Pharisees began to make common cause with the Sadducees against the Christian community.

A Roman four-wheeled chariot. Courtesy Carta, Jerusalem.

Among those who fled Jerusalem was Philip "the evangelist," who had been one of the seven chosen to minister to the widows. This Hellenist leader should not be confused with the disciple Philip, who is never mentioned by name in Acts. Philip the evangelist brought the message that Jesus is Messiah to the Samaritans. Luke speaks only of the region of Samaria and does not specify the city that Philip visited. After healing the sick, casting out evil spirits, and preaching to joyous crowds, Philip was suddenly led southward to a desert road running between Gaza and Jerusalem. There he evangelized and baptized the first known African convert. The Ethiopian eunuch was a member of the court of his queen and minister of the treasury. "Candace" apparently signified a title rather than the personal name of the ruler. Nothing is recorded of the early centuries of Christendom in Ethiopia, but it is possible that Philip's convert formed the beginning of a small band of believing Blacks. Since Ethiopia lay south of the borders of Rome, Luke's report of this conversion indicates that Christianity reached distant regions very quickly. The Ethiopia of the Bible lay just south of Aswan, Egypt, and included a region that today is located in southern Egypt and the northern part of Sudan. The modern state of Ethiopia occupies an area known in ancient times as Abyssinia.

One of Philip's Samaritan converts, Simon Magus, became for the early Christian church the fountainhead of many destructive heresies. Simon, according to Acts 8:13, believed Philip's message and received baptism. But his later behavior and subsequent reputation as reflected in the writings of the church fathers raise doubts as to the genuineness of his conversion. Simon had been a magician and had claimed to possess divine power. In fact, Luke's phrase describing the accolade given to Simon by the Samaritan people might indicate that he had even claimed to be some kind of incarnation of deity (Acts 8:10).[19] When the Jerusalem church had dispatched Peter and John to Samaria, and they had laid their hands on the believers there, Simon witnessed the outpouring of the Holy Spirit. Immediately Simon saw the demonstration as an example of magical power that could be exploited for personal advantage. In the foolish belief that he could purchase the power of granting the Holy Spirit, he offered money to Peter. Acts does not specify whether the believers on this occasion received the gift of tongues, but Simon apparently witnessed some kind of external phenomenon that impressed him. Peter delivered a stinging rebuke but did not entirely close the door to the possibility of repentance. But Simon probably did not alter his course, at least this is the only conclusion possible if the tradition preserved by the early church fathers has even a kernel of truth. The early Christian writers pictured him as the founder of Gnosticism, a heresy that became influential in the second century. While Simon did not actually develop the full-blown heretical philosophy that plagued the church in the next century, it is possible that he did found a cult that persisted after his death and merged with Gnosticism. Justin Martyr, an apologist who wrote in the second half of the second century, stated that Simon eventually went to Rome and was

reputed by his followers to be a god.[20]

Philip led the way in introducing the gospel to non-Jewish areas. After ministering to the Samaritans, he preached in the towns along the Mediterranean coastal plain, beginning at Azotus (Ashdod) and continuing northward to the Roman administrative capital of Caesarea. Perhaps Philip's travels ended at this point since Paul found him still at Caesarea after completing the third missionary journey (Acts 21:8–9).

The Conversion of Saul

One of the most dramatic events in the life of the early apostolic church was the conversion of the organizer of the persecution that arose with Stephen's death. Saul was to become the apostle to the Gentiles, one specially commissioned by Christ to bear the gospel to those who had been outside the pale of Judaism. He had been born in the Diaspora and could understand the Greek way of thinking. Paul described his birthplace, Tarsus in Cilicia (a Roman province in southeastern Asia Minor), as "no ordinary city" (Acts 21:39). Located on a river and only about ten miles from the sea, Tarsus served as a seaport. Trade came to Tarsus not only by sea but also via the Cilician Gates, a much-used nearby pass through the Taurus Mountains. The city had a reputation for scholarship. A school of Stoic philosophers taught there, and the city also prided itself on being the hometown of Athenodorus, the teacher of Augustus. If it is correct to assume that Paul lived in Tarsus for a number of years, his early surroundings must have helped to forge in him a cosmopolitan outlook. He would have learned the basics of Greek language, literature, and philosophy, which would arm him later for his ministry among Gentiles. But Saul should not be thought of as a typical liberal Hellenist. Not every Jew of the Diaspora allowed himself to be molded by Greek ways of thinking. Some, like Saul, remained Hebraic in their temperament and convictions. He described himself as "a Hebrew of Hebrews; in regard to the law, a Pharisee . . . " (Phil. 3:5). Writing to the Galatians, he characterized his position thus: "I was advancing in Judaism beyond many Jews of my own age and was extremely zealous for the traditions of my fathers" (1:14).

Perhaps the influence of Saul's parents led him to seek further training under the famous Gamaliel in Jerusalem. He may have lived in Tarsus until he was thirteen, the age at which boys were expected to make a stronger commitment to the law and the traditions of their faith. Some scholars have interpreted Acts 22:3 to mean Saul was brought up in Jerusalem from a very early age—i.e., that Tarsus had been his birthplace but not the scene of his early education.[21] This view depends on a modification of the punctuation found in the KJV and RSV. The suggested punctuation change is reflected in the NIV: "I am a Jew, born in Tarsus of Cilicia, but brought up in this city." Whichever view is adopted, Saul still had roots in the Diaspora as well as a definite commitment to the Hebraic tradition. He could use the Aramaic, Hebrew, and Greek languages skillfully. His Greek style, while not as artful as that of the

writer of Hebrews, reflected the competence of one educated in the language.

Above, a general view of Damascus. Below, a narrow street of the city. Courtesy École Biblique et Archéologique Française, Jerusalem.

Saul did not restrict his vendetta against the Christians to Jerusalem. He obtained letters from the high priest ordering the extradition of those of "the Way" from Damascus. How the high priest could have claimed such authority over Jews of the Diaspora is not entirely clear. He might have retained some religious authority over all Jews in the empire that had been given to Archelaus as "ethnarch." Perhaps this claim to such power rested on a less formal basis. Jews of all lands generally respected the leadership of the high priest. A specific grant of power had been made to Simon the high priest in Maccabean times. According to 1 Maccabees 15:21, a Roman consul sent a letter to Ptolemy VIII (Euergetes II Physcon) of Egypt (145–116 B.C.) stating: "If therefore any traitors have escaped from their country [Judea] to you, hand them over to Simon the high priest to be punished by him according to the law of the Jews." It is not conceivable that such a broad grant of political power remained in effect more than a century later. But the incident does demonstrate that the Romans did invest the high priests with certain powers, and it may be that by the time of Saul the high priest held some authority to use extradition in religious cases.

When Saul encountered Jesus Christ on the road to Damascus, he experienced something more than a mere vision or inward impression, yet his fellow travelers failed to understand what had happened. Paul implied that the incident was more than an ecstatic experience when he asked the Corinthians "Am I not an apostle? Have I not seen Jesus our Lord?" (1 Cor. 9:1). Barnabas would later tell the apostles in Jerusalem that "Saul on his journey had seen the Lord and that the Lord had

spoken to him" (Acts 9:27). Paul also ranked his own witness of the risen Christ along with the other major resurrection appearances of Jesus. After mentioning the appearances to Peter, the Twelve, James, and others, he adds, "And last of all he appeared to me also" (1 Cor. 15:8). Those who were with Saul heard an indistinguishable sound rather than recognizable Aramaic words spoken by Jesus. They also saw the blinding light yet saw no visible person. Perhaps the bewilderment caused by the sudden flash of light and the unexplained sound left them shocked and confused. The manifestation was not for their particular benefit but was directed to Paul specifically.

Luke records three different accounts of the conversion experience, each account having a different setting and serving a different purpose in Luke's narrative. The first one, found in Acts 9:1–7, is Luke's own version, which he introduces as part of the story of the persecution and spread of the faith. The other two accounts are found later in speeches of Paul. In the first of these speeches Paul stood on the steps leading to the Antonia fortress in the temple area, and while he was in the custody of guards he testified to a riotous crowd that had finally been calmed (Acts 22:1–21). Paul's second message was an *apologia* (a reasoned defense) before King Herod Agrippa II in Caesarea. Since the setting and purpose of these accounts vary greatly, it is not surprising that some details are also different. Paul was probably selective and more interpretive in his accounts, but his speeches do not actually contradict Luke's first story.

The most striking variation is in the

description of the voice. In Acts 9:7 it is said that Paul's companions "heard the sound," whereas Acts 22:9 says they did not hear the voice and in Acts 26:14 Paul states simply that he heard the voice. The statement in Acts 22:9 probably means that the companions did not "understand" the sound, rather than that they did not "hear" it. This explanation is based on the grammatical solution proposed by the famous grammarian A. T. Robertson. He notes that the verb *akouō* (Greek, "hear") in 9:7 is followed by the word for voice in the genitive case, while in 22:9 it is followed by the accusative, which is the usual case for a direct object. The genitive "calls attention to the sound of the voice without accenting the sense," while the accusative (in 22:9) emphasizes the "intellectual apprehension of the sound."[22] Even apart from questions of case usage, it is possible to see an explanation for the apparent problem simply in the wide range of meanings for *akouō*. It can mean "hear," "understand," and "obey." In addition it is possible that different members of Paul's group saw or heard different things. The truth about any event may be complex if one seeks for technical accuracy, and accounts about an event are often brief and selective. Numerous separate events are telescoped into general statements that are in reality oversimplifications. Thus variations then can be expected in the telling of an episode, but this does not automatically imply historical inaccuracy.

Paul at Damascus

The appearance of the risen Christ left Paul prostrate on the ground. He lost his vision as well as his appetite for food or drink for three days. He did not know when he set out for Damascus if he would find any Christians in that area (9:2), but there was in the city a company of disciples and among them was a man named Ananias. Ordered in a vision to go to the house of a certain Judas on Straight Street, the reluctant and fearful Ananias found Paul praying. With the laying on of hands, Paul received both his physical eyesight and the inward illumination of the Holy Spirit's presence.

Luke does not offer much detail about the chronology of events in Paul's life from his conversion (A.D. 33/34) until the first missionary journey (A.D. 47/48). In his description of the Damascus period, Luke mentions time spans of "several days" (9:19) and "after many days" (9:23). In Galatians 1:17–18 Paul speaks of going "immediately into Arabia," then of returning to Damascus, and finally of a trip to Jerusalem that came three years after the conversion experience. Possibly the period spent in the desert region of northern Arabia did not involve a large block of time. The text does not say that all of Paul's three years in the Damascus area were spent in the desert. But it was only after he had found time in the wilderness to consider his new commitment and the call of God that Paul came to the city of Damascus and began a more prolonged ministry. By this time he had searched the Scriptures and was able to preach the messiahship of Jesus with convincing biblical proof (Acts 9:22).

Paul fled from Damascus to escape a plot on his life by the aroused Jews. Coming to Jerusalem, he found the disciples fearful of him until Barnabas took him under his wing and brought him into the fellowship. After Paul had boldly preached to the Hellenistic Jews after the pattern of Stephen, another plot forced the brethren to take him to Caesarea, where he began a journey to his home in Tarsus. Paul's activities in Tarsus are shrouded in obscurity. However, we know that during these silent years (A.D. 35–43) he spent time in both Syria and Cilicia (Gal. 1:21). Perhaps Paul was referring to this period of time when he spoke of being "in danger from [his] own countrymen" (2 Cor. 11:26). Eventually Barnabas went to Tarsus and recruited Paul for the ministry in Antioch in Syria (Acts 11:25–26).

An ancient wall of Damascus, thought to be the place where Paul escaped from the city. Courtesy Studium Biblicum Franciscanum, Jerusalem.

The story of Paul's escape from Damascus raises some questions. According to 2 Corinthians 11:32, an ethnarch under King Aretas (IV) ruled over Damascus during Paul's stay there. It appears that Damascus was part of the Roman province of Syria rather than a city ruled by the Nabatean Arab king. Although no clear documentation has been found to prove that Aretas IV did rule over Damascus, several possible explanations can be offered to account for the apparent discrepancy. Archaeologists have found a surprising lack of Roman coinage in Damascus for the period A.D. 34–62. Possibly Aretas' representative (the ethnarch) was allowed by Rome to dominate a section of the city inhabited by Nabateans. The Romans often found it useful to give authority to native leaders. Another possibility is that Aretas, who had long wished to conquer Damascus, seized the city briefly. It is known that when Vitellius (A.D. 35–37) ruled Syria, he had a great deal of trouble subduing the Parthians on his northeastern border.[23] Possibly Aretas took advantage of some such distraction to assert greater influence in the Damascus area. Part of the problem in understanding the statement in 2 Corinthians may be our lack of information on the actual political and military situation in Damascus during the time of Paul's ministry there.

Peter's Ministry to the Gentiles

Peter became one of the first leaders of the Jerusalem church to recognize that the Gentiles should be brought into full fellowship without circumcision being considered a prerequisite. His ministry in Samaria with John demonstrated his early breadth. After that ministry he traveled to the coastal plain (as Philip had done earlier), where he healed the sick and even raised the dead.

But the most momentous event was the conversion of the centurion Cornelius at Caesarea. This leader of the "Italian Regiment" had not become a proselyte before his conversion, as had Nicolas, who was one of "the seven" (Acts 6:5). Cornelius represents that group of Gentiles who had come to worship the one God of the Jews, Jehovah, but who had not accepted the requirements of Jewish law and ritual. Such Gentiles are described by the term "devout" or "God-fearing" (10:2).

With God's help Peter overcame his reluctance to associate with Gentiles. Yet his behavior was not always consistent. It appears that it was after the lesson at Caesarea that Peter succumbed to the pressures of stricter Jewish brethren and withdrew from table fellowship with Gentile believers. The incident occurred at Antioch. Peter had been fellowshiping with the Gentiles until Jewish brethren from Jerusalem arrived. Apparently Peter feared offending James and the other Jerusalem church leaders, for he immediately withdrew from eating with the Gentiles. Paul sharply condemned Peter's act as hypocritical (Gal. 2:11-14). The incident also is further biblical evidence for the new leadership role of James the brother of Jesus. James had become the leading spokesman for the Jerusalem church.

The Antioch episode probably occurred before Peter's address to the Jerusalem Council. In his message he argued (1) that God made no distinction between Jew and Gentile and (2) that Gentiles should not be put under the yoke of the law (Acts 15:9-11). It is difficult to imagine Peter acting as he did at Antioch after having delivered such a ringing message for acceptance of the Gentiles. If one accepts an early date for Galatians, before the Council of Jerusalem, then Peter's relapse at Antioch obviously had to precede the Council. Those who hold to the early date for Galatians (A.D. 48/49) also accept a view known as the "South Galatian Theory" (a fuller discussion of this view belongs in a later chapter). Peter's movement toward a position of liberality toward Gentile brothers did not come easily. He must have felt moments of uncertainty and hesitation. His lack of complete consistency is understandable when one considers the pressures applied by the stricter Jews, such as the converted Pharisees who continued to insist that Gentiles must be circumcised and obey the law of Moses (Acts 15:1, 5).

The Persecution Under Herod Agrippa I

In A.D. 44 King Herod Agrippa I initiated a persecution against the Jerusalem church. The policy may have been a deliberate attempt to curry favor with the Jewish leadership and priesthood. Agrippa seems to have dreamed of creating a great empire for himself. By cunning and good fortune he had gathered all of Palestine under his sway. His rise to power began when Gaius Caligula succeeded to the emperorship in A.D. 37. Agrippa had spent much of his early life in Rome, receiving an education there and squandering his wealth. Josephus records that Agrippa developed a friendship with Caligula and happened one day to be sitting in a chariot with the future emperor. He commented to Caligula that he prayed "that Tiberius might soon go off the stage and leave the government to Gaius who was in every respect more worthy of it."[24] The remark, overheard by one of Tiberius' servants, was passed on to the emperor. Agrippa spent the next six months in prison, but when Tiberius died and Caligula (A.D. 37–41) took the throne, he was released and given the lands that had belonged to Philip the Tetrarch. He also received the title of king. In A.D. 39 Caligula exiled Herod Antipas to Gaul and gave the tetrarch's possessions to Agrippa. Antipas lost power partly through the connivance of Agrippa but also in part because his wife Herodias pressured him to aggressively lobby Caligula to grant him the title of king. When Claudius (A.D. 41–54) became emperor, he gave Judea and Samaria to Agrippa. From 41–44 no Roman procurator ruled Judea. All of Palestine was once more under the rule of a king as in the time of Herod the Great. But when Agrippa died, Claudius placed Judea under Roman procurators who were subordinate to the governor of Syria. The procurators, called prefects before the time of Claudius, now ruled from the Roman administrative capital of Caesarea.

Herod Agrippa's life came to a dramatic end in A.D. 44, not long after he had executed James the son of Zebedee and had imprisoned Peter (Acts 12). Josephus tells a story about his death that is in many respects similar to the one found in Acts. According to Josephus, Agrippa celebrated a festival at Caesarea and on the second day wore a resplendent garment of silver. When the people saw the reflected rays of the sun flashing from the king's robe, they shouted to the king that he was a god. Immediately a violent pain seized Agrippa in the stomach, and he predicted his own death, which came five days later.[25] The biblical account states that an "angel of the Lord struck him down, and he was eaten by worms and died" (Acts 12:23). Luke records at this point that the "word of God continued to increase and spread" (Acts 12:24). Undoubtedly the shocking death of the monarch who had executed a disciple of Jesus created greater curiosity about the message of the people of "the Way."

A bronze coin of Agrippa I. Courtesy Carta, Jerusalem.

A view of the Acropolis in Athens, looking west from the Areopagus. Courtesy Gerald Nowotny.

Chapter 10

Paul the Missionary

The Church Planters

Paul holds the honor of being the preeminent missionary of the apostolic age. But his prominence in our thinking should not obscure the fact that there were many other messengers of the gospel who had a significant role in spreading the faith beyond Judea. Some of them are mentioned by name in the New Testament; Philip the evangelist, Peter, Barnabas, Silas, Timothy, Titus, and Luke are among the more familiar pioneering missionaries. But there must have been many whose careers were not recorded. We do not know the names of the "men from Cyprus and Cyrene" who journeyed to Antioch to tell the Gentiles there "the good news about the Lord Jesus" (Acts 11:20). We also have very little information about the ministry of the eleven disciples of Jesus, but some of them did travel beyond Palestine. Clement of Rome tells of Peter's martyrdom in his own city ("among us"), and Irenaeus asserts that John re-

sided in Ephesus.[1] Although traditions about the other disciples' travels may be less reliable, some of them probably did journey beyond Palestine. But it is necessary for any history of missionary expansion to place the greatest emphasis on the work of Paul since this is the focus of the New Testament itself. The Book of Acts, beginning at chapter 13, almost exclusively concentrates on his activity.

Paul's missionary work was not a series of hasty visits by an itinerant preacher who spent the greater part of his time on the road. He often remained with a church for an extended period of ministry. On his second journey he stayed in Corinth for two years, and on this third journey he remained at Ephesus for three years. Frequently he retraced his steps because of his concern for strengthening the churches already planted. Although it had always been his desire to preach Christ in regions where the message had not yet gone, he also wished to remain in communication with those who had already received the gospel (Rom. 15:20). His letters reveal how passionate was his devotion to the task of building up these established churches.

The Home Base: Antioch

Antioch of Syria served as the home base for Paul's missionary endeavors. Even before his three journeys from Antioch, the city had been a major Christian center. It continued to be a powerful voice in Christendom until the time of the Muslim invasions of the seventh century A.D. It is not surprising that Antioch would have had a major role in the spread of the gospel. It was the third largest city in the Roman Empire, exceeded only by Rome and Alexandria. Located about three hundred miles north of Jerusalem, it was much closer to that city than the great churches that would be founded at Ephesus, Thessalonica, and Corinth. Antioch's geographical position made it the logical jumping-off place for the evangelization of the provinces of Galatia, Asia, Macedonia, and Achaia.

Seleucus had founded the city in 300 B.C., and it later became the capital of the Seleucid Empire. Greeks and Macedonians were the first settlers, but Jewish inhabitants were also present at an early date and by the time of Paul occupied three separate ghetto areas. They comprised about one-seventh of a total population of something over a half million. Under Roman rule the city became the capital of the province of Syria, and it continued to be the focus for much of the commercial activity of the East. The greater wealth of the Christians at Antioch made it possible for them to send Paul and Barnabas with a gift for the Jerusalem poor during a time of famine (Acts 11:29–30). Antioch must have been an impressive sight in the New Testament era. The four-and-a-half-mile-long granite paved street that ran through the heart of the metropolis was flanked by roofed, colonnaded walkways. One could walk the length of the city shaded from the sun. Every four years Antioch became the setting for one of the empire's major Olympic festivals. For a month the city hosted boxers, wrestlers, chariot racers, and other athletes.[2] The Christians at Antioch lived in a culturally, religiously, and ethnically diverse society.

Antioch on the Orontes River in Syria, looking west from Mount Silpius. Courtesy École Biblique et Archéologique Française, Jerusalem.

It was at Antioch that the believers received the name "Christian" (Acts 11:26). They had earlier been known as "disciples," "brethren," "believers," or people of "the Way." The new designation did not originate with the believers themselves and just as clearly did not derive from the Jewish community. The Jews would never have used the Greek term *Christos* (meaning "anointed one") as part of a designation for the followers of Jesus, since the word was the equivalent of the Hebrew word for Messiah. To have used the name "Christian" would imply acquiescence to the claim that Jesus was the Christ promised by the prophets of old. The term "Christian" is found only three times in the New Testament, and in each passage it is a designation used by those outside the fellowship. King Agrippa II used it in speaking to Paul (Acts 26:28), and in 1 Peter 4:16 the reproach implicit in the name is clear in the phrase, "if you suffer as a Christian, do not be ashamed . . . ."

According to Acts 11:19, some of those who suffered persecution at the time of Stephen's martyrdom (A.D. 32/33) traveled to "Phoenicia, Cyprus, and Antioch." They established a Jewish-Christian church. But some of them, "men of Cyprus and Cyrene," began preaching to the Gentiles. This might be taken to mean that Antioch had a large Gentile Christian community at the outset. But some scholars believe that the church at Antioch had been almost exclusively Jewish for several years before the evangelization of Gentiles began. It is not possible to clearly establish the chronology from the text of Acts.[3] Whatever the actual timing, it is clear that at some point the large influx of Gentile believers did evoke real concern in the Jerusalem fellowship. The mother church sent Barnabas to investigate. Probably the Jerusalem leadership feared a breakdown of

respect for
drastic c
cultural
Barnabas
rejoiced w
God among
(Acts 11:22–2
of the Antioch
after his account o.
Cornelius, apparently to.
of emphasizing the awak
Jewish Christians in Judea to need for accepting with grace the new Gentile Christian community into the fold of believers.

The city of Tarsus, birthplace of the apostle Paul. In the foreground is the "Gate of St. Paul." Courtesy École Biblique et Archéologique Française, Jerusalem.

The date for the founding of the church at Antioch is not clearly indicated by the Book of Acts. It might have been established as much as a decade before Paul's arrival there in A.D. 43 or 44. The most cautious statement would simply place its establishment between 32 and 44. Luke says only that the church was founded by those who left Jerusalem

the persecution con-
~~h~~ Stephen's martyrdom
~~ts~~ 11:19). According to his
, the church did not precede
~~ry~~ long period the investigative
~~of~~ Barnabas, and that visit could
have occurred until sometime
~~ter~~ Barnabas had introduced Paul
~~to~~ the Jerusalem church. Paul's first
visit to Jerusalem and his introduction by Barnabas probably dates
about A.D. 35/36. It does not seem
likely, then, that the church would
have been founded before 36. One
reason for placing the date no later
than 44 is the fact that Acts records
the death of Herod Agrippa I (which
is well established as occurring in
that year) immediately after its description of the Antioch church. But
Luke does not use precise terminology here. He uses the phrase "It was
about this time" to begin his record
of the death of James and Herod
(Acts 12:1). Before giving the description of Herod's death, Acts records
Barnabas' visit to Antioch, his search
for Paul in Cilicia, his return with
Paul to Antioch to minister for a year
together, and his famine-relief mission with Paul to Jerusalem (Acts
11:25–30). It seems probable that
these events at Antioch, except for
the famine-relief trip, did occur before A.D. 44, and so would require
some years before that date for the
founding of the church. It may be
possible to narrow the field down to
the period between 36 and 39.

When did Paul arrive in Antioch
from Tarsus with Barnabas? According to Acts 11:27, the ministry of the
two men coincided with the arrival of
prophets from Jerusalem. One of
these prophets, a man named Agabus, predicted a famine. Luke's statement about the prophecy can be
interpreted to imply that it was given
before the accession of Claudius (in
41, Acts 11:28). On this basis the
arrival of Paul could be estimated to
have been about 39/40. It is not
possible to pinpoint the date when
the predicted famine occurred, although it clearly belongs to the reign
of Claudius (Acts 11:29). It was not
rare to find a shortage of food in the
Roman Empire, but there is no record to confirm Agabus' prophecy that
it would "spread over the entire
Roman world" (v. 28). But Josephus
does tell of a famine in Jerusalem
that led to large-scale starvation
there. A devoted friend of the Jews,
Queen Helen of Adiabene, sent servants to buy grain in Alexandria and
figs in Cyprus to distribute to the
Judeans. According to Josephus, this
famine occurred during the procura-
torships of Cuspius Fadus (A.D. 44–46)
and Tiberius Alexander (46–48).[4] Kirsopp Lake's careful analysis of Josephus concludes that the latter did
not really make clear whether the
famine began in the time of Fadus or
Alexander. Lake thinks a date of 46 is
probable if the famine began in Alexander's procuratorship, but he would
date it in 45 if Josephus intended
Fadus' period of rule.[5]

The First Journey

When Paul and Barnabas returned
from the famine-relief trip to Antioch,
they brought with them John Mark, a
cousin of Barnabas (Col. 4:10). Mark
was a younger man, but he had
possibly witnessed much of the early
activity of the Jerusalem leadership
because the home of his mother,
Mary, served as a gathering place for

believers (Acts 12:12). He probably had an early association with Peter, for it was to Mary's house that Peter fled when freed from prison (Acts 12:12). Mark's later service alongside Peter is attested to by 1 Peter 5:13 and by the writings of the early church fathers.[6] When he served with Barnabas and Paul, he ministered as a *hyperetes*, a Greek term used of an assistant who served under a superior.[7] Mark seems to be viewed as a helper or intern, and when Luke describes the commissioning of Barnabas and Paul by the church at Antioch, he omits Mark's name. The names of Barnabas and Paul appear in Luke's list of the "prophets and teachers" at Antioch, but the absence of Mark's name indicates he had not yet attained such a status (Acts 13:1). Before they set out on the "first missionary journey," Barnabas had been the recognized leader of the team. He had been in good standing with the Jerusalem church, and his name is placed by Luke before Paul's until we come to the description of the trip from Cyprus to Pamphylia (Acts 13:13). At that point Paul's name is given priority of order. Paul seems to have been the spokesman almost at the outset of the journey. He took charge during the confrontation with the sorcerer Elymas at Paphos on Cyprus (Acts 13:9). It is also at this point in Luke's narrative that he drops the designation "Paul" and begins uniformly to refer to the apostle by his Graeco-Roman name, "Paul." The first journey of Paul is probably best dated in the years A.D. 47 and 48. This chronology is based primarily on the assumption that the famine-relief visit belongs to the year 46, and also on the better established date of Paul's first visit to Corinth (in 50–51).

Paul established a pattern during his first trip that he would follow throughout his ministry. It was his habit to preach first to the Jews and proselytes who attended the synagogue and then, after opposition mounted, to turn to the Gentile community. At Pisidian Antioch, Paul announced, "We now turn to the Gentiles" (Acts 13:46). This does not indicate an end to his ministry to Jews. As late as his third journey, he wrote from Corinth to the Romans that the gospel was "first for the Jew, then for the Gentile" (Rom. 1:16). He continued to preach in any synagogue that would open its doors to him. His turning to the Gentiles was a recurring event, not a once-for-all decision (see Acts 18:6). The rejection of his message by so many of his Jewish brethren brought him "unceasing anguish" (Rom. 9:2), and his "heart's desire" was their ultimate salvation (10:1).

The first journey covered a smaller area than later travels. Paul and Barnabas confined their work to Cyprus and to the south central section of Asia Minor, which included the province of Pamphylia and the southern part of the province of Galatia. On later trips Paul journeyed farther westward to the provinces of Asia, Macedonia, and Achaia. On the first expedition the missionaries began their travels with a sixteen-mile trip from Antioch to the seaport of Seleucia. From this port they sailed to Cyprus, which had received missionaries about the same time as Antioch (Acts 11:19). Cyprus had also been the homeland of some of those missionaries who had left Jerusalem to

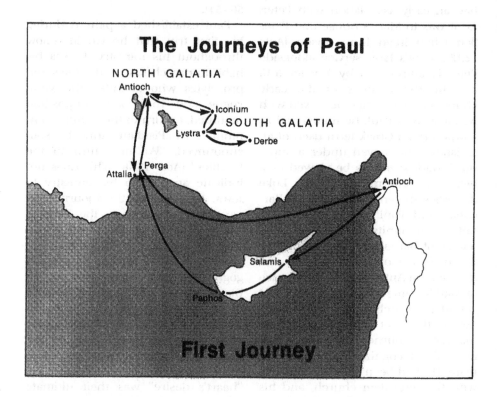

The Journeys of Paul

NORTH GALATIA

Antioch

Iconium

SOUTH GALATIA

Lystra

Derbe

Perga

Attalia

Antioch

Salamis

Paphos

First Journey

preach to the Gentiles at Antioch. Barnabas himself had originally come from Cyprus, and he was thus well-prepared for a ministry on his home turf. Cyprus had served as a major source of copper and tin for the Phoenicians. It became a senatorial province by Paul's time. Such a province would be ruled, as Luke correctly states, by a proconsul (Acts 13:7).

The ministry to Cyprus began with Paul's message at a Jewish synagogue in Salamis. Luke does not provide many details of the Cyprus trip. He simply states that they "traveled through the whole island until they came to Paphos" (Acts 13:6). Con-

cerning the events at Paphos, the capital city, he provides more information. There Paul struck the sorcerer Elymas with blindness after this evil magician had tried to subvert the new-found faith of the proconsul, Sergius Paulus. The procurator has usually been identified with Lucius Sergius Paulus, the curator of the Tiber, but recently he has been identified as Q. Sergius (Paulus) whose name appears on an inscription found in Cyprus.[8] The mission to Cyprus probably required very little time. Paul's first journey would not include the extended stays at specific towns that characterized his later ministry. Thus Paul's first trip may be more properly labeled a journey than those that followed.

Remains of the city and colonnaded street at Perga. Courtesy Studium Biblicum Franciscanum, Jerusalem.

The walls of Perga, behind which is the theater. The visible remains belong mostly to the Roman period. Courtesy Dan Bahat.

After landing at Perga in Pamphylia, on the southern coast of Asia Minor, John Mark suddenly abandoned the work and returned to Jerusalem. Luke does not explain the reasons for Mark's departure, but he does make it clear that Paul considered the abandonment an irresponsible act that would disqualify Mark

from serving on another expedition. Barnabas, whose name means the "son of consolation" or "son of exhortation," was more compassionate and forgiving toward his kinsman and would later take him on a second journey (Acts 15:37–38). The episode eventually led to a "sharp disagreement" and a parting of the ways for Paul and Barnabas (Acts 15:39). It is unwise to view Paul as unfailing in judgment. Despite his eminence and his apostolic office, he was a human being capable of egotism and perhaps even spitefulness. At the same time Barnabas may have been too hasty in overlooking the failings of a young relative. Both Paul and Barnabas erred in allowing the issue to become divisive. Fortunately, Paul's anger did not prevent him from eventually establishing a good relationship with both men. He would commend Barnabas as an example of one who, like himself, would willingly work for a living rather than demand remuneration in the ministry (1 Cor. 9:6). That a young man who falters should have another chance to prove himself useful is the lesson of 2 Timothy 4:11. There Paul advises Timothy, "Get Mark and bring him with you, because he is helpful to me in my ministry."

Leaving Perga without Mark, Paul and Barnabas began a preaching ministry in Antioch of Pisidia, Iconium, Lystra, and Derbe. This particular Antioch was one of many cities with the same name. Although located on the eastern fringes of Phrygia, it was commonly called "Antioch of Pisidia" because of its proximity to Pisidia and to distinguish it from another Phrygian town named Antioch. Two of the cities Paul visited,

Antioch and Lystra, had the special status of Roman colonies. A "colony" was actually a little Rome. Although the Romans allowed exercise of local laws and customs in most areas they controlled, colonies were ruled more strictly according to Roman law and were somewhat independent of the provincial administration. They used Latin instead of local languages on their coinage and usually had larger Latin populations.

Antioch, Iconium, Lystra, and Derbe lay within the southern part of the Roman province of Galatia. Some of the details of Galatian history are of significance because of an important controversy to be discussed later. The term *Galatia* originally referred to a kingdom established by Gauls, one of the Celtic peoples who also had spread over large areas of western Europe and the British Isles. Those who settled in Asia Minor were a group of warriors who had broken away from the Celtic tribes of Greece. They established control over a plateau region in Asia Minor south of Bithynia and Pontus, and northeast of Phrygia. Through a Roman alliance the Galatians successfully enlarged their kingdom to include non-Celtic areas. After Galatian King Amyntas died in 25 B.C. in a struggle to subdue the troublesome Homonades tribes in the highlands to the south, Augustus created from the kingdom the Roman province of Galatia. The kingdom had previously added to its territory regions that included Phrygians, Lycaonians, and other ethnic groups besides the dominant Celtic people. Now Augustus added part of Pisidia and other territory to the Roman province of Galatia. This gradual accretion of diverse areas meant

that the term *Galatia* could be used either in a narrow sense to describe the ethnic Gaulic region in the north or in a broader way to include also the Hellenized Phrygian, Lycaonian, and Pisidian cities of the south. Southern Galatia also had a significant Jewish population. This part of the Diaspora dated back to the time of Antiochus the Great.[9] It was to this racially diverse southern region that Paul and Barnabas preached on Paul's first journey. In fact it cannot be clearly proved that Paul ever visited northern Galatia, although some scholars think the references to a Phrygio-Galatic region in Acts 16:6 and 18:23 indicate such a visit. But the references to Galatia in the latter passages are cast in such general and vague language as to make it impossible on this basis to settle the issue whether Paul ever visited ethnic Galatia. The view presented here is that Paul probably visited only southern Galatia, but it is impossible on the grounds of biblical evidence to state dogmatically that Paul never visited ethnic Galatia. The issue cannot be settled with finality.

Paul delivered his first message at Antioch of Pisidia to a group of Jews and proselytes who had gathered at the synagogue for Sabbath services. After the synagogue had rejected his ministry, he spoke to a largely pagan audience on the next Sabbath (Acts 13:45). The first message in the synagogue is the first of Paul's sermons recorded in Acts. The sermon is primarily a historical summary, reminiscent of Stephen's address. Paul's emphasis was twofold: (1) Jesus fulfills the scriptural prophecies of a coming messianic king from David's line, and (2) Jesus was raised from the dead. There is also an early foregleam of Paul's doctrine of justification by faith: "Through him everyone who believes is justified from everything you could not be justified from by the law of Moses" (Acts 13:39).

Modern Konya, site of Iconium, in Asia Minor. Courtesy Dan Bahat.

At Iconium Paul followed the same pattern as at Antioch: he spoke first to the Jews at the synagogue. When resistance came, he moved on to another city, Lystra. There the healing of a lame man led excited crowds to proclaim the two missionaries to be gods "come down ... in human form" (Acts 14:11). Barnabas seemed to temporarily regain the preeminence over Paul, but in a manner he could not have appreciated. The crowds proclaimed him to be Zeus, the father of the gods, and they identified Paul as Hermes, the spokesman of the gods. Hermes was a Greek god who had often been portrayed as a shepherd or herald. The choice of Paul as Hermes (the Roman god Mercury) might be an indication that Paul was short of stature compared to Barnabas. The image of the helmeted Mercury as

the diminutive messenger with winged boots is a familiar symbol even in the twentieth century. Since Paul became the principal speaker for the evangelistic team, it is logical that he should have been identified with the god of oratory. The Latin poet Ovid recorded the legend that Zeus and Hermes had visited the region of the Lycaonians but had not been recognized by the people. Not wishing to be thus embarrassed again, the people of Lystra discussed a plan to offer sacrifice to the two missionaries. One might wonder why the act of worship caught Paul and Barnabas by surprise. This is probably explained by the fact that the local people would have been speaking to each other about their plans for worship in their own native dialect, which the missionaries would not have understood.[10]

Paul's brief message to the pagans at Lystra is somewhat similar to his message at Mars Hill in Athens. Instead of appealing to the Jewish Scriptures as he did at the synagogue in Antioch, he spoke of the natural revelation that God gives to all people. He cried out to those who wanted to worship mere men that they should reverence instead the God "who made heaven and earth," who testified of himself by giving "rain from heaven and crops in their season" (Acts 14:15, 17). Soon afterward Jews from Antioch stirred up the Lycaonians, who then stoned Paul and dragged his body outside the city. Luke does not seem to be indicating that Paul was dead after the stoning but only that the crowd thought him to be dead, though there are some interpreters who believe that Paul had literally expired and risen from the dead. Perhaps Paul referred to this event when he reminded the Galatian church that he bore on his "body the marks of Jesus" (Gal. 6:17).

After ministering in Derbe, the missionary team retraced its steps through the cities of Galatia, appointed elders, then turned southward again to Pamphylia and set sail from Attalia for Antioch of Syria. The official report Paul and Barnabas gave to the sending church at Antioch implies that the work of the missionaries was more than the ministry of several individuals—it was a team effort, commissioned and supported by the church.

The Epistle to the Galatians

A great deal of controversy has focused on the question of the identity of the Galatians to whom Paul wrote his epistle. The question is intertwined with many other unresolved issues; it is related to the chronological problems in the life of Paul, to the harmonization of Galatians 1 and 2 with Acts, and to the date of the writing of the Galatian epistle. There are basically two viewpoints about the destination of the letter, and they are known as (1) the north Galatian theory and (2) the south Galatian theory. It would be unwise to be dogmatic in defending one or the other view since the ablest scholars have failed to reach unanimity. Generally speaking there is a tendency recently for those who accept the historical accuracy of Acts to lean toward the south Galatian theory and for those who have less regard for Luke as an accurate reporter to identify with the north Galatian

theory. But this is not always the case, and there is no essential reason why the line should be drawn in this manner. The issue should not be viewed as a liberal vs. conservative debate.

The north Galatian theory has the weight of tradition behind it. The earliest church fathers assumed that Paul addressed his letter to ethnic Galatia (north Galatia) rather than to the cities of south Galatia that he visited on his first missionary journey. The early writers believed that after traveling through Derbe, Lystra, and Iconium on his second journey, Paul had visited ethnic Galatia, possibly the cities of Ancyra, Pessinus, and Tavium, even though Acts never mentions these cities. The view of the early church fathers hinged on two very brief and imprecise references to Galatia in Acts. Acts 16:6 states simply that Paul "traveled throughout the region of Phrygia and Galatia" without specifying what precise part of the broad areas was intended. Acts 18:23 speaks of Paul's traversing again through "Galatia" a second time while on his third missionary journey. Perhaps the early church fathers erred. By the time of Jerome the southern region had been detached from the province of Galatia, and so early scholars would naturally have thought of Galatia as the region where the Gauls lived.

Some of the more important arguments usually put forward to defend the north Galatian theory may be briefly summarized as follows:

1. It had the support of all the earliest Christian writers as already described above.

2. The characteristics of the people designated Galatians by Paul in his

letter fit those traits ascribed by ancient writers to the Celts or Gauls of north Galatia. These qualities include fickleness, drunkenness, impulsiveness, belligerence, and superstitiousness.[11] This argument rests on such a subjective foundation that it cannot stand up to close analysis. It could be argued just as easily, as F. F. Bruce points out, that the Lycaonians at Lystra, who at first worshiped Paul as a god and then shortly after stoned him, were displaying both fickleness and superstitiousness and therefore fit the characterization made by Paul's epistle.[12]

3. The Book of Acts does not designate the churches in the southern part of the province as "Galatian" but as "Phrygian" or "Lycaonian," ethnic terms, and it would seem natural for Paul to use the term similarly in his epistle, because he is denoting not a political division but a people, the Galatians.

4. The circumstances of Paul's visit alluded to in the epistle do not fit the events of the first journey as recorded in Acts 14. For example, in Galatians 4:13–15 Paul attributes the decision to visit Galatia to a sudden illness, one that apparently affected his eyes and his appearance. But Acts 14 does not mention any such motivation for preaching in the Phrygian and Lycaonian areas.

One of the ablest defenders of the north Galatian theory was J. B. Lightfoot. But his research on the topic in the 1860s came three decades before William M. Ramsay's massive investigative efforts, which were carried out on the scene in central Asia Minor. The latter's careful study of geographical and cultural conditions in the Asia Minor of Paul's day led him

to abandon the traditional viewpoint in favor of the south Galatian theory. He defended his theory in *The Church in the Roman Empire* (1st edition, 1893) and in *A Historical Commentary on St. Paul's Epistle to the Galatians* (1st edition, 1899).[13]

Ramsay was not the first to argue for the south Galatian theory. Others had written in support of the view during the century preceding his time, but Ramsay discarded many of the earlier arguments used to prop up the theory and advanced what he believed to be more impressive evidences. His studies demonstrated that south Galatia lay astride the most "familiar and important road" in Asia Minor and that this region was far more important in the early empire than northern Galatia. The presence of the Judaizers in Paul's Galatia, disturbing the church with legalistic preaching, is presupposed in Paul's letter, and Ramsay thought their presence in the area so soon after Paul's ministry must indicate that a church was located on a route frequented by travelers from Syria.[14] Ramsay also argued that it would be hard to imagine that Paul did not write a letter to so important a body of believers as his converts in south Galatia. Yet with the north Galatian theory we are left without a letter to that group. None of Paul's other letters contains even a passing reference to the people of Antioch of Pisidia, Iconium, Lystra, and Derbe. That the people of these cities were among the earliest and most cherished of Paul's converts is evident in the Acts account. Paul's deep concern for the churches he had established is evident in all his writings, and it is difficult to imagine on the one hand that he should write a letter to the people of north Galatia, whom we are not even able to prove clearly that he even visited, and on the other hand that he should not write a letter to the churches he had established in south Galatia or even make a reference to them. On the basis of the north Galatian theory it would appear that Paul retained no "kindly recollection" of or interest in the southern area.[15]

Some of the other arguments that have been used to defend the south Galatian theory may be listed briefly:

1. Paul tended to use Roman provincial names in his letters and so could easily have used the broad designation in his letter (Gal. 1:2; 3:1). Within the same chapter in 1 Corinthians Paul spoke of the Galatians, the Macedonians, the Achaians, and the Asians—all of which are Roman provincial designations (1 Cor. 16:1, 5, 15, 19). It is difficult to imagine what other single term he could have used to describe the variety of peoples living in south Galatia.

2. Paul speaks of Barnabas by name in Galatians 2. Since Barnabas had traveled with Paul to south Galatia, he would be well known to the churches there, yet there is no evidence that he ever visited north Galatia. This is not one of the better arguments for the south Galatian theory. Paul also mentioned Barnabas in his letter to the Corinthians, who, as far as we know, had not seen his face (1 Cor. 9:6).

3. In Acts 20:4 there is a list of companions who traveled with Paul to Jerusalem to deliver the collection for the poor. Luke here mentions delegates from various regions, including Timothy (from Lystra) and

"Gaius from Derbe," but he does not mention anyone from north Galatia. In 1 Corinthians 16:1 it is said that Paul had collected gifts from "the Galatian churches." As part of the cumulative evidence for the theory, this might have some value, but it is not one of the better arguments, since it is based on silence.

Chronological Problems in Acts and Galatians

Another issue that has drawn much ink from scholarly pens is the question of how the events in Paul's life as recorded by him in Galatians 1–2 are to be harmonized with the story as told by Luke in Acts 11:29–30; 12:23–25; 15:1–29. Two major historical questions arise from a comparison of these passages: (1) How are we to reconstruct a chronology of Paul's life from these two accounts? (2) How are we to reconcile the narrative in Acts with the historical references in Galatians? In pursuing these questions, we discover many specific problems and questions of interpretation along the way. Bible scholars have not been able to find universally acceptable solutions to these many thorny issues. How one puts together the whole story of these chapters depends on how one might choose to resolve the many interpretive problems along the way. In other words there are many related issues or variables that need to be resolved before one could present a final scheme of events. In fact it is unwise to argue dogmatically for any particular arrangement of events as the final or definitive answer. One must be content to admit that Scripture gives us only fragments of the story, and it is the task of the biblical student to reconstruct a more detailed account as best he can.

The central problem of harmonization involves the attempt to choose, from among the five visits of Paul to Jerusalem recorded in Acts, those two that are described in Galatians. It is not so difficult to identify the first Acts visit (9:26–30) with the first visit mentioned in Galatians (1:18–24). In both Acts and Galatians the first visit occurred not long after Paul's conversion and his sojourn in Damascus. According to Galatians 1:18 the visit came three years after the conversion experience. But the identification of the second visit in Galatians is much more difficult. As recorded in Acts the second visit could be properly labeled the famine visit. Luke tells that Paul and Barnabas carried a gift to Judea for the relief of the brethren there. He does not speak of a church council or even of an informal discussion between Paul and the apostles on this trip. The third visit in Acts involved a public discussion by the apostles and elders with Paul and Barnabas present. The conference dealt with the assertion of converted Pharisees that Gentile Christians "must be circumcised and required to obey the law of Moses" (Acts 15:5). The second visit as described in Galatians 2:1–10 tells of Paul, Barnabas, and Titus meeting privately with James, Peter, and John. The three Jerusalem leaders acknowledged the ministry to the Gentiles as legitimate and signified their approval by giving the "right hand of fellowship" to Paul and Barnabas (2:9). Most scholars identify the second Galatians visit (Gal. 2:1–10) with either (1) the second Acts visit (11:30; 12:25) or (2) the

third Acts visit (15:1–29). These two views may be schematically represented as follows:

FIRST VIEWPOINT

| Acts visit #1 (9:26–30) | = | Galatians visit #1 (1:18–24) |
| Acts visit #2 (11:30; 12:25) | = | Galatians visit #2 (2:1–10) |

SECOND VIEWPOINT

| Acts visit #1 (9:26–30) | = | Galatians visit #1 (1:18–24) |
| Acts visit #3 (15:1–29) | = | Galatians visit #2 (2:1–10) |

Several arguments may be presented in defense of the first view (that the two visits of Galatians are the first two in Acts):

1. Paul's line of reasoning in Galatians 1–2 seems to require that he mention every Jerusalem visit up to the time of the composition of the letter. For him to omit the second visit of Acts and leap to a discussion of the visit of Acts 15 would seem to be dishonest, for the whole point of the first chapters is to demonstrate the lack of contact with the apostles in Jerusalem. Paul's intent is to use this lack of association with the Jerusalem community as evidence that his gospel did not come from any human agency. His message came by revelation, directly from God. When he received God's call, he "did not consult any man" (Gal. 1:16). Paul states that on his first visit he saw only Peter and James, the brother of the Lord. On his second visit he met privately (2:2) with the apostolic leadership. Paul, in other words, aims to document his independence from the Jerusalem church. In such a rehearsal of events it would seem to

be a distortion to omit one of his visits with the apostles.

2. The conference described in Galatians is private, but the Acts 15 Council is a public meeting.

3. Titus is mentioned as being present at the Galatian visit but not in Acts 15.

4. The reputation of Acts for historical accuracy, which is acknowledged by many biblical scholars, might be and indeed sometimes has been called into question by those who hold to the second view. Some of those who have identified Galatians 2 with Acts 15 see the famine visit of Acts as an error or invention.

5. If Paul wrote his Galatian letter after the Acts 15 Council, he would likely have mentioned the decision of that body since it confirmed his own argument in the epistle that the Galatians need not be bound by circumcision and the law. The lack of any reference to the outcome of the Council suggests both that the Epistle to the Galatians refers to the first two visits recorded in Acts and that it should be dated early.

The five above arguments are not ironclad. They are answered by those holding to the second viewpoint in the following way:

1. It could be argued that Paul's line of reasoning in Galatians does not demand mention of every visit, but only those that were relevant to the issue of Gentile conversion and law keeping. The famine came at a time of persecution under Herod Agrippa I when the apostles were in hiding or, as in the case of Peter, in prison (Acts 12:1–5). There would have been little opportunity for discussions about Gentile matters. Thus Paul would be under no obligation to mention this visit in the context of Galatians. This solution involves some chronological issues. Herod Agrippa I died in A.D. 44, and by the best estimate the famine occurred two years later. However, it must be admitted that the placement of the famine account at the beginning and end of the story of Herod's death could suggest an earlier famine visit (see Acts 11:29–30; 12:1, 25).

2. The dissimilarities of the two conferences described in Acts 15 and Galatians 2 are offset by the striking similarities. Paul and Barnabas both travel from Antioch to Jerusalem to answer Jewish Christian opponents before a gathering of the apostles. The discussion involves Gentile conversion and behavior. The Jerusalem church gives its blessing to the work of Paul and Barnabas among the Gentiles.

3. The omission of Titus' name in Acts 15 is not a valid argument against the second view because Acts does not limit the delegation from Antioch to Paul and Barnabas. Luke says they "were appointed, along with some other believers, to go up to Jerusalem" (Acts 15:2).

4. It is not an essential part of the second viewpoint to assume that Acts is inaccurate in recording a separate famine visit. Paul's failure to mention the visit in Galatians (as explained earlier) may be understood as a natural omission because of the character of the visit. The famine visit if conceived of as not involving discussion with the apostles could easily have been considered by Paul to be irrelevant to his argument. There are, of course, Bible scholars who not only think the Acts record has confused the chronology of the Jerusa-

lem council but also believe that the defenders of Luke's historical trustworthiness have not fully established their case.

5. Paul may have omitted reference to the decision of the Jerusalem council because it did not completely vindicate his contentions. The council of Acts 15 did not specifically acknowledge his apostleship, and it did insist on certain legalistic restrictions on Gentile eating habits. Paul's later discussion of Christian liberty rejects a single hard-and-fast rule that would outlaw, regardless of the situation, partaking of meat that has been offered to idols (1 Cor. 10:23–30).

In addition to these attempts to refute the first viewpoint, those who hold the second view offer other arguments:

1. It seems unlikely that there should be two conferences dealing with the same problem and arriving at a similar solution without any mention in Acts 15 of the problem having arisen before.

2. No one reading about the famine visit in Acts would think of identifying it with Galatians 2 if it were not for the concern for harmonizing Galatians and Acts.

3. The identification of the famine visit with Galatians 2 creates a difficult chronological problem. Paul says he did not arrive in Jerusalem the first time until three years after his conversion (Gal. 1:18) and that he went up to Jerusalem again fourteen years later (2:1). The addition of these two figures would make seventeen years, too long a time period to squeeze into the period between Paul's conversion and the famine

visit. The famine visit cannot be dated later than A.D. 46. Paul's conversion can hardly be placed earlier than two or three years after the Crucifixion.

It will be assumed here that the first viewpoint, which identifies the first two visits of Acts with those in Galatians, is the preferable solution. The knotty chronological problem is not insuperable. Paul does not clearly make the fourteen-year period begin subsequent to the three-year period. The two periods of time mentioned in Galatians may run concurrently, beginning with Paul's conversion. Also it is generally agreed that ancient writers often counted any part of one calendar year as a full year. If Paul's conversion came about A.D. 32, there is room for the "fourteen years" to be completed before 46, the date of the famine visit. The Epistle to the Galatians may have been written on the eve of the Jerusalem council in 48/49. This would make the letter the earliest of Paul's extant epistles. J. Gresham Machen suggests a resolution for the problem of having two conferences dealing with the same issue. The famine-visit conference was probably a private one, with Paul and a few apostles present. Since the outcome of this discussion was not a matter of public knowledge or understanding, there would have been the possibility of further attacks on Paul and his work. The advocates of freedom for Gentile Christians had no official charter to which they might appeal. There was still need for a larger public gathering to deal not only with Gentile freedom but also with the problem of Gentiles and Jews fellowshiping together in mixed communities.[16]

Ein Karem, now a part of modern Jerusalem. From Jerusalem the gospel spread throughout the world: "Repentance and forgiveness of sins will be preached in his name to all nations, beginning at Jerusalem" (Luke 24:47). Courtesy Duby Tal.

Chapter 11

The Outreach to the Gentiles

The Decision of the Jerusalem Council

As recorded in Acts 15 the apostles and elders of the Jerusalem church rejected the contention of the converted Pharisees that the Gentiles should be required to be circumcised and obey the Mosaic law. Before the assembled brethren Peter raised the question whether anyone would seriously wish to place "on the necks of the disciples a yoke that neither we nor our fathers have been able to bear." Salvation, he insisted, was "through the grace of our Lord Jesus" (15:10–11). James, who by this time had become the leading spokesman for the church, warned against making it "difficult for the Gentiles who are turning to God" (15:19). But he did suggest several restrictions on Gentile freedom for the sake of avoiding offense to those who attended the synagogues in the many cities around the empire. Basically, James aligned himself with those who wished to avoid legalistic require-

ments for Gentile believers. He specifically omitted circumcision from his list of "burdens." His moderate counsel prevailed, and the official letter addressed to the churches in Antioch, Syria, and Cilicia called on Gentiles "to abstain from food sacrificed to idols, from blood, from the meat of strangled animals and from sexual immorality" (15:29). The Council commissioned Silas and Judas to join with Paul and Barnabas in delivering these instructions to the churches.

The delivery of the Jerusalem decision to the churches in Asia Minor must have helped to satisfy Gentile Christians there who had been disturbed by the unwillingness of some to welcome them into the full fellowship of the Christian community. Paul's work among the Gentiles now had the recognition and blessing of the mother church. After ministering for a time at Antioch, Paul proposed to Barnabas a visit to the churches they had established. The trip is commonly called "the second mis-

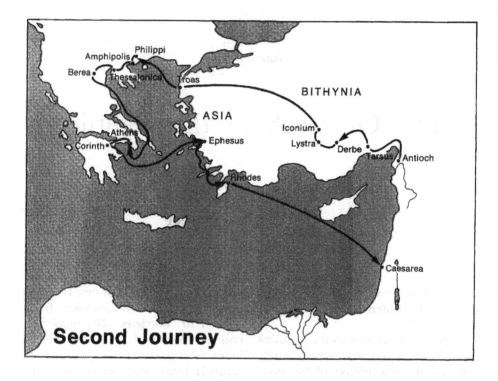

Second Journey

sionary journey." Now controversy severed the relationship between Paul and Barnabas. They separated over the question of whether to take with them John Mark, who had earlier deserted the work. The sharp contention might have arisen in part from a weakness in Paul's own character, a tendency to be overbearing, or perhaps it could be equally attributed to Barnabas' overprotectiveness of a younger relative. Perhaps Barnabas' earlier hypocritical withdrawal from table fellowship with Gentile Christians, following Peter's example (Gal. 2:13), may have continued to sour Paul's attitude toward his colleague. Whatever the underlying causes, the two men found it best to chart separate courses, Barnabas taking Mark along to minister in Cyprus,

and Paul teaming up with Silas to return to Asia Minor. Silas was a logical choice. Like Barnabas, he had good rapport with the Jerusalem church. Also, like Paul, he probably held Roman citizenship (Acts 16:37), and as a team these men could appeal to certain legal privileges and rights, as they did in fact at Philippi. Silas is probably the Silvanus mentioned in Paul's letters (2 Cor. 1:19; 1 Thess. 1:1; 2 Thess. 1:1) and may also be the Silvanus who apparently served as an amanuensis for Peter (1 Peter 5:12).

Paul's second journey covered some of the same ground as the first, but this time he began his trip over land. After a visit to the brethren in Syria and Cilicia, he came to the south Galatian churches. At Lystra

Timothy joined the evangelistic tour. Paul's decision to circumcise Timothy indicated his willingness to be flexible in gray areas—that is, in peripheral matters—for the sake of conciliating Jewish Christians. Paul had never opposed the rite of circumcision for Jews; he opposed it only as a requirement for Gentiles. Timothy was a special case, as his father was a Greek and his mother a Jew. If Timothy had joined the preaching company without the rite, his presence could have jeopardized the ministry of Paul in the synagogues, which so often, at least initially, opened their doors to hear his message. Paul made a somewhat similar gesture just before being taken into custody in Jerusalem. At that time in order to dispel the rumor that he disdained the Jewish law, and at the suggestion of James, he took part in a purification rite in the temple (Acts 21:20–26). These concessions did not violate Paul's basic conviction that Gentiles should not be forced to undergo circumcision and give obedience to the law as a prerequisite for acceptance into the fellowship of believers.

The precise course of Paul's journey after leaving south Galatia is not known. Acts 16:6 indicates that he had intended to move westward into the Roman province of Asia. That area had a large Jewish population and a populous city, Ephesus. This was exactly the kind of mission field Paul normally sought out, but somehow he sensed that the Holy Spirit had closed that door to him. Luke then records that Paul traveled in the Galatia-Phrygia region. This could mean that he visited the land of the Gauls in north Galatia, but the language could also suggest that he merely skirted that area on the way toward the more northerly province of Bithynia. Since there is no discussion of a ministry to north Galatia in Acts, it appears that Paul passed by that region. Divine guidance came to Paul again and directed his path away from Bithynia and toward Troas (Acts 16:7–8).

Walking through the streets of Troas, Paul no doubt saw many Macedonians who had come to do business at the thriving port. Perhaps Luke himself was one of the Macedonians whom Paul met in the city. In the night Paul saw a vision of a man in Macedonian garb imploring him to bring the message to his country. In response to the vision Paul set sail for the continent of Europe. Such a move would not have seemed so dramatic in Paul's time since his voyage would be seen as only a move to a neighboring province within the Roman Empire. Besides, it was not the first time that Europeans heard the gospel. Some of those present for Peter's Pentecost sermon were pilgrims from Rome, and it is possible that some of them were converted and had carried the message to Rome.

There appears to be a hint in Acts that the author of that book had now joined the missionary group. The shift from third person (they) to first person (we) begins at Troas (16:10) and continues until the group reached Philippi. The "we passages" begin again when Paul returns the second time to Philippi. These sections may be taken to imply that Luke, a companion of Paul, was a Macedonian (16:10–17; 20:5–15; 21:1–18; 27:1–28:16). It is also possible that

Luke might have come originally from Antioch or some other city.

Ministry in Macedonia

Paul sailed from Troas to the coast of Macedonia, landing at Neapolis, the port city of nearby Philippi. Luke's comment that Philippi was "the leading city" of the area may be an example of a native son's justifiable pride in his hometown. Philippi had some claim to fame: it could boast an outstanding school for physicians, and the city had originally been named for Philip II of Macedon. Philippi lay along a major military and commercial route called the Via Egnatia, which linked the Aegean and Adriatic seas. After Octavian had defeated his opponents near Philippi in 42 B.C., he made the city a Roman colony and sent civil-war veterans who had supported Mark Antony to retire there. The Romans found such colonies useful places for retiring old soldiers and also for planting little islands of Latin influence in scattered locations around the non-Latin areas of the empire. Because it was a colony, Philippi had its own coinage and its own Roman political institutions. Luke designates the two chief magistrates of the colonial city as *stratēgoi*, a term that was popularly used to describe the praetors or rulers of Philippi. Even though this was not the official title, inscriptions from the city demonstrate that it was in common use.[1]

Evidently Philippi did not have the necessary minimum of ten Jewish males to establish a synagogue. On the Sabbath Day, Paul and Silas set out to find a "place of prayer" outside the city gate along the river. Just outside Philippi there is a gushing narrow stream of water known as the Gangites River. Here, devout women gathered to worship each Sabbath. Among them was Lydia, a proselyte, who was a woman of some wealth. She had come from the land of Lydia (whence her name was derived) and from the city of Thyatira in particular, where she had been a dealer in purple dye. The city of her origin had a guild of dyers, as attested by ancient inscriptions.[2] After Paul's message at the river bank, Lydia and her household received baptism and then extended the hospitality of her home to Paul.

At Philippi Paul came into direct conflict with the demonic power of paganism. The influence of Judaism was far weaker in the region he now ministered in than in those areas he had left behind.[3] This conflict is dramatically illustrated by Paul's confrontation with the female soothsayer. Luke says literally that she had the "spirit of a python" (Greek, *pythōna*). According to tradition, a python had guarded the Delphic oracle. Later the term came to be used of one with a "spirit of divination" or of a ventriloquist (believed to have a spirit inhabiting the abdomen).[4] The slave girl in Luke's story not only could foretell future events but also could cast her voice about her to produce a dramatic effect. For days this wretched woman dogged the heels of Paul and Silas, shrieking at them. But when Paul commanded the python spirit to leave her, those men who had exploited her powers, seeing their livelihood gone, dragged the preachers before the rulers.

The accusation made by the slave owners seems to be confused and irrelevant. Their charge that these men were teaching Judaism was insubstantial, since the Jewish faith had long been recognized and tolerated by Roman law. Despite the lack of adequate grounds, the authorities had Paul and Silas beaten and imprisoned. After the conversion of the jailer, and another baptism service, Paul and Silas surprised the local authorities with the belated announcement that they possessed Roman citizenship. One wonders why the missionaries did not appeal to their rights at the outset. Luke does not mention it, but Paul might have tried to appeal to his rights as a citizen earlier, at the trial before the *stratēgoi*. The whole trial scene had something of the atmosphere of a riot, and possibly Paul's words were lost among the outcries of the mob.[5] After one final meeting with the church at Lydia's home, Paul and Silas continued their journey. The church they left behind proved later to be supportive of Paul both spiritually and financially (Phil. 1:4–5; 4:10–19) at a time when other believers were less sensitive to his needs.

Traveling westerly on the main highway, the Via Egnatia, Paul came to the most populous city of Macedonia, Thessalonica. It was both a busy seaport and the capital of the province. The city was ruled by five or six magistrates called "politarchs," a term used only in Macedonian cities. The discovery of this title on inscriptions found in the city testifies to the accuracy of Luke's account.[6] At the synagogue in Thessalonica Paul preached Christ on three consecutive Sabbaths. Converts included Gentiles who worshiped Jehovah (these were God-fearing Gentiles who had not

become proselytes), some Jews, and some of the leading Gentile women of the city. Paul asserted that his work in Thessalonica "was not a failure" (1 Thess. 2:1): despite efforts to prevent his "speaking to the Gentiles" (2:16), there were many who "turned to God from idols" (1:9). Thessalonica became a center for the spread of the message throughout Macedonia and Achaia (1:8). Violent opposition forced Paul to retire to the smaller town of Berea, where he found a Jewish population more amenable to his messianic preaching. The Bereans faithfully examined the Scriptures every day during Paul's preaching ministry in order to determine the validity of his expositions. When Thessalonican Jews descended on Berea with the purpose of creating another disturbance, the missionary-evangelist quickly departed for Athens. But he left Silas and Timothy behind to further instruct the Macedonians.

Ministry in Achaia

Before Paul even touched land, the grandeur and the idolatry of Athens must have impressed him. In ancient times one could stand on the deck of a ship making its way to Piraeus (the port of Athens) and view the gleaming bronze statue of Athena adorning the acropolis. After Paul had disembarked and traveled the five miles from the Piraeus to Athens, he would have seen in the six-acre agora (market place) an even more impressive array of monuments and statues. The evangelist "was greatly distressed to see that the city was full of idols" (Acts 17:16). The glory of Athens as an intellectual center had already lost some of its luster to Alexandria. But

Paul could still speak with the Epicurean and Stoic philosophers of Athens who were among those who, as Luke says, "spent their time doing nothing but talking about and listening to the latest ideas" (Acts 17:21). Apparently, Timothy arrived in Athens not long after Paul, but because of deep concern for the Christians of Macedonia, Paul sent him again to Thessalonica "to strengthen and encourage" the believers (1 Thess. 3:2).

Paul ministered in both the synagogue and the agora. We are not told of the Jewish reaction, but Acts does speak of the pagan philosophers debating with Paul in the agora. Paul delivered a sermon in the Areopagus, located on a hill overlooking the agora. Known as Mars or Ares Hill after the name of the God of War, the hilltop site was the meeting place for a council of judges who had jurisdiction over the agora. Whether Paul's appearance and speech constituted a formal hearing or simply an informal discussion is uncertain. But it is clear that the pagan Athenians raised questions about Paul's God and the doctrine of the resurrection. The altar to the one unknown God (Acts 17:23) mentioned in Paul's speech has never been located, but ancient writers (Pausanius, about A.D. 150) did mention an Athenian monument to unknown gods (plural).

When Paul left Athens for Corinth, he approached his new endeavor with anxiety and discouragement. Opposition from either Jews, Gentiles, or both had arisen at every city in Macedonia and Achaia. Imprisonment in Philippi, a riot in Thessalonica, disruption of the work at Berea, and a meager response to his message at Athens gave him scant reason to expect dramatic results in the cosmopolitan city of Corinth. Having once already squared off with the intellectual leadership of Athens, he now determined not to approach the Corinthians with "eloquence or superior wisdom" but to preach with the Spirit's power the message of "Jesus Christ and him crucified" (1 Cor. 2:1–4). Paul evidently traveled to Corinth without the encouraging presence of Timothy and Silas, but despite obstacles, he began a work that established a large church (Acts 18:10). When the inevitable opposition arose at the synagogue, Paul boldly moved next door to preach at the home of a God-fearing Gentile, Titius Justus. Confrontation did not lead to a sudden departure as at Thessalonica. In a night vision Christ appeared to Paul and challenged him not to "be afraid," to "keep on speaking," and promising him protection from any harm at Corinth (Acts 18:9).

Whether one be a merchant, missionary, or marching soldier, one could hardly move southward into Achaia without a stopover at Corinth. The city lay at the southern end of a narrow neck of land, the Isthmus of Corinth, which connects northern Greece with the Peloponnesus. The city's location on high ground made it nearly impregnable to attack and also gave it control over the land route that armies had to traverse when moving northward out of the Peloponnesus or southward into it. Commerce not only moved by land north and south, but also by waterborne traffic it moved east or west across the isthmus. Because passage around the southern peninsulas of Greece was dangerous for shipping, many sea-farers preferred to use the

Gulf of Corinth on the west of the isthmus and the Saronic Gulf on the east. For large vessels this involved unloading goods, carting them four miles across the isthmus and reloading them into another ship. But for smaller boats the Greeks had constructed a wooden tramway with a system of log rollers. This made possible a land crossing without removal and reloading of cargoes. Nero began constructing a canal to connect the two gulfs but left the task uncompleted. These gulfs were not to be joined by a canal until the late nineteenth century.

Before Roman control Corinth had been a major rival of Athens as a colonial and military power. When the Romans conquered Greece, they proclaimed Corinth a free city (196 B.C.), but when it became the focus of an uprising against Roman authority in 146 B.C., the Romans razed the city and left it abandoned and unpopulated for exactly one century. In Julius Caesar's time the city was rebuilt and became a Roman colony. With the coming of Latin settlers the newly revived city had few native Greeks, but it rapidly attracted large numbers of Greeks, Jews, Syrians, and Egyptians. Along with its cosmopolitan population, the new Corinth possessed a welter of religions and cults. The temple of Aphrodite stood at the very peak of the two-thousand-foot plateau called the acrocorinthus. It once had a thousand priestesses, who provided revenue for the priests by serving in ritual prostitution. In fact much of the wealth of old Corinth had come from prostitution. The city's reputation gave rise to the Greek term *korinthiazesthai*, which meant to behave immorally like the people of Corinth. It is somewhat easier to understand the troubled character of the Corinthian church when one considers that most of Paul's converts in that city were Gentiles who had been part of a culture that placed a high value on idolatrous festivals, luxury, self-indulgence, and sensuality. In this context Paul's call for purity becomes more meaningful: "Come out from them and be separate. . . . Touch no unclean thing, and I will receive you" (2 Cor. 6:17), and "Flee from sexual immorality" (1 Cor. 6:18).

Ten miles from Corinth athletes gathered every three years to participate in the Isthmian Games. These contests ranked just below the Olympic games in importance. Perhaps Paul himself witnessed some of the athletic competition during his eighteen months at Corinth. In his first letter to the Corinthians he used the "strict training" of a runner as an example of the kind of self-discipline required of a believer who would surrender some of his Christian freedom for the sake of not offending a weaker brother. The runners at Corinth sought "a crown that will not last," actually a pine wreath (1 Cor. 9:25). Picturing himself as a boxer, Paul says, "I beat my body and make it my slave" (1 Cor. 9:27). The first verb in the latter phrase is the Greek term *hypopiazō*, which literally means to "strike under the eye, give a black eye to."[7] While the Corinthian church needed to shun the self—indulgence of the local culture, it could well emulate on a spiritual level the self-abnegation that brought a disciplined athlete to his moment of temporal glory.

Amid the cultural and ethnic diversity of Corinth a church developed—a church that has come to be known through Paul's two epistles as a community of Christians plagued with immoral behavior and aberrations in church practice and doctrine. Egotism, arrogance, and strife severed the unity of the congregation. A sectarian spirit divided the church into four factions that fancied themselves as the disciples of one or another church leader. (1) One splinter group set up Apollos as the object of admiration. Perhaps this group was captivated by the human wisdom and the eloquence of a Bible scholar educated at Alexandria. (2) Paul's own followers may have appreciated his role as church planter and defender of Gentile liberty. (3) The party of Peter might have identified with those who favored a higher regard for Jewish law and tradition. (4) There was even a party of Christ, a faction that one might think should have included all the believers. Yet their spirit is apparently condemned also—perhaps because of a spiritual arrogance or a misguided belief that they alone were genuinely of Christ. Actually, Paul never explicitly describes the nature of the factions, but he clearly condemns the divisive spirit. Paul's final word on sectarianism was "All things are yours, whether Paul or Apollos or Cephas . . . and you are of Christ . . . " (1 Cor. 3:21–23).

In addition to boasting of human leaders there were those who reveled in their liberty, ignoring the tender consciences of others who could not yet simply dismiss idols as "nothing at all in the world" (1 Cor. 8:4), nor think of food that had been offered to idols as wholesome and untainted.

Even the Lord's Supper observance became a source of sin for the church. Instead of being a time for sharing (koinonia), it had become a drunken and gluttonous festival for some, while poorer saints sat watching hungrily. Believers claiming the gift of tongues used their power for dramatic effect rather than for the edification of the body of Christ. Many ostentatious saints disrupted the congregational services by trying to prophesy, speak in tongues, or interpret—all at the same time (1 Cor. 14:26–27). Worship became disorderly and chaotic instead of edifying. Doctrinal error also crept into the church; some individuals had raised doubts about the resurrection of the believer. Yet, even with such a record of abysmal failures, the Corinthians were not a hopeless or totally degenerate lot. Paul was sincere in commending them for having been "enriched in every way" and for not lacking "any spiritual gift" (1 Cor. 1:5–7). The problems were the birth pangs of a new church, born in the midst of a corrupt city.

Paul did not attempt to induce the new church to support him financially. He returned to his tentmaking trade in collaboration with Priscilla and Aquila, who practiced the same craft. Later Silas and Timothy brought gifts from Macedonia, and these enabled him to devote full time to preaching Christ (1 Cor. 9:11–12, 15; Phil. 4:14–16). Aquila and Priscilla, who had opened their home to Paul, had lived in Rome until Claudius expelled the Jews from the city (Acts 18:2). Luke does not specify whether they had been converted in Rome or under Paul's ministry.

Paul Before Gallio

While Paul was at Corinth, the Jews brought him before the proconsul's judicial bench (Greek, *bema*) and accused him of "persuading the people to worship God in ways contrary to the law" (Acts 18:13). Gallio, who served as governor of the senatorial province of Achaia, threw the case out of court on the grounds that he had no jurisdiction over matters of Jewish religion and law. Gallio viewed the messianic preaching of Paul as nothing more than one interpretation of Jewish faith and not as a new religion. Christianity had not yet gained sufficient notice from the Roman authorities to be recognized as a distinct faith. If it had been so perceived, it would have been illegal, since freedom to practice a particular religion could only be granted after the senate had given it official recognition. Gallio's benevolent or apathetic attitude indicates a policy or lack of policy that would allow Christianity to continue its growth with only sporadic repressive actions by Roman officers during most of the first century.

The mention of Gallio provides a significant point of contact with Roman history as well as a chronological clue to aid in dating Paul's travels. Gallio was born in Cordova, Spain. His father, the elder Seneca, was a rhetorician. His brother, Lucius Annaeus Seneca, was a Stoic philosopher and a tutor of Nero. Gallio was adopted by another family and took the name of his patron. He then became known as Junius Annaeus Gallio. The younger Seneca described him as a man of common sense, a beloved brother, and one whose unaffectedly pleasant personality charmed all who met him.[8] Nero's vile wrath eventually brought the younger Seneca down, and immediately Gallio's fortunes began to decline also. Because of suspicions of treasonous plotting, eventually both men either were forced to commit suicide or were executed.

The date for Gallio's proconsulship can be fairly accurately established from information found on an inscription at Delphi. Although only four fragments remain, there is sufficient information to fix Gallio's rule within narrow limits. The inscription consists of a letter from Claudius to Gallio. According to the text, Gallio was a friend of Caesar, a proconsul of Asia, and had reported to Claudius about troubles among the citizens of Delphi. The message contains a reference to the occasion of Claudius' being acclaimed Imperator (Emperor) for the twenty-sixth time. Acclamations came after irregular intervals, but Kirsopp Lake reckoned that the twenty-sixth acclamation, which fell in the twelfth year of Claudius' tribunician power, belonged to the year running from January 25, A.D. 52, to January 24, 53. Several questions remain unanswered: (1) How long was Gallio proconsul? The normal length of service was one year, but sometimes the office might be held for two years. Without an answer to this question the possible time span runs between A.D. 50 to 54. The date of Gallio's accession was probably early within this time span, but it probably should not be pushed earlier than A.D. 51 since time must be allowed for Gallio to consider the issue at Delphi, write a letter, and then get the response as recorded by the inscription.[9] (2) Did Paul's trial come at the beginning or at the end of Gallio's proconsulship? From the account in Acts it appears that the episode occurred near the end of Paul's eighteen months in Corinth. Thus Paul could have arrived in Corinth as early as A.D. 50, and his departure to Ephesus could be dated 52.

The Thessalonian Letters

Paul wrote his two epistles to Thessalonica from Corinth about A.D. 51, probably within a few weeks of each other. Timothy had come to Paul in Athens, but Paul sent him back to Macedonia. He finally joined Paul again at Corinth and brought him encouraging news about the steadfast faith and love of the Thessalonians despite persecution (1 Thess. 3:1–6). In a joyful spirit Paul wrote his first of two letters to commend and encourage the young church. He also sought to correct a misconception that the living saints at the *parousia* (a Greek term referring to the second coming) would somehow obtain a glory denied to those who had fallen asleep. Paul asserted that the dead would be raised before the living saints were caught up to be with Christ (1 Thess. 4:13–18). The second letter also contains a strong eschatological element. Paul had heard reports that some of the same problems remained at Thessalonica. Idleness on the part of those anticipating the second coming needed still to be corrected. In addition, some of the believers had wrongfully assumed that the "day of the Lord" had already begun, and Paul wrote to squelch this error.

Concluding his ministry at Corinth, Paul took Priscilla and Aquila with him to Ephesus. After a brief visit to the synagogue and a promise to return, he took ship for Caesarea, visited the Jerusalem church, and returned to his home base, Antioch.

The Third Journey

Paul and Silas' third journey from Antioch followed many of the same paths traversed on the second journey. The trip began with a visit to the south Galatian churches ("the region of Galatia and Phrygia," Acts 18:23). But this time, instead of avoiding the province of Asia, the evangelists headed directly to one of the leading cities of that province—Ephesus. The third journey may have covered the years 52 to the early months of 56 (before the Passover, which Paul hoped to celebrate in Jerusalem, Acts 20:16). Paul spent the greatest part of this period at Ephesus, where he stayed at least for two years and three months. The first three months were given to preaching at the synagogue, and then two years were spent teaching at the "lecture hall of Tyrannus" (Acts 19:8–10). Paul's statement to the Ephesian elders at Miletus that he had warned them night and day for three years may be interpreted to mean one full year and parts of two other years (Acts 20:31). As has been seen, ancient practice permitted the designation of any portion of a calendar year as a year.

Ephesus was one of Asia's leading cities. Because the Roman governor resided at Ephesus, it could claim to be a political center. Religiously, it was significant because of the location there of the great temple of

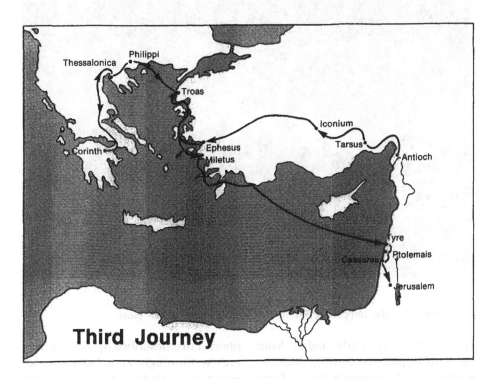

Third Journey

Artemis or Diana. Commercially, its claim to leadership rested on the trade routes leading up the Lycus and Maeander valleys and on its position near the mouth of the Cayster River, which flowed into the Aegean Sea. By the time Paul visited the city, its seaport was beginning to feel the effects of centuries of deforestation and the consequent erosion, which in turn led to the silting of the Cayster River. Larger vessels could no longer enter the port. Still, Ephesus remained an important trade center and was able to make up for any lost trade by attracting tourists who would visit the temple of Diana and spend their drachmas on the images hawked by local silversmiths. The temple of Paul's day had been built in the time of Alexander the Great to replace one destroyed by fire on the night of the conqueror's birth. This colossal structure was four times larger than the Parthenon; it measured 370 feet by 180 feet and was located on an enormous platform. Huge columns, six feet in diameter and rising sixty feet high, supported the roof. The greatest sculptors and artisans of the ancient world applied their skills to this temple, which became one of the seven wonders of the world.

The cult of Diana focused its worship on a stone figure believed to have fallen from heaven. The original "Diana," possibly a meteor, has never been recovered, and the representations of the goddess that remain vary

The remains of the temple of Artemis at Sardis. Courtesy Dan Bahat.

greatly in form. Early coins from Ephesus depict the fertility goddess wearing a veil, covered by bands from the ankles to waist, and with many breasts on the upper torso. These physical features identify Diana (or Artemis) as having sprung from the many mother goddess cults of Asia Minor.[10] The process of syncretization had blended many deities into one.

Before Paul's arrival at Ephesus on his third journey, a dynamic orator, debater, and biblical scholar had begun a ministry to the Ephesians and Corinthians. The learned Apollos, having been educated in Alexandria, must have been knowledgeable about the teaching of Philo, who interpreted the Old Testament not only in its literal sense but also in an allegorical manner so that he could discover teachings consistent with Plato and other pagan philosophers. Luke describes Apollos as having "a thorough knowledge of the Scriptures" (Acts 18:24). Although Apollos preached with "great fervor" in Ephesus, he "knew only the baptism of John" (Acts 18:25). It is very likely that information about both John the Baptist and Jesus had reached Alexandria but evidently in an incomplete form. The lack of more perfect instruction in Egypt might help to account for the strong gnostic element that became so apparent among second-century Christians. How much Apollos understood is unclear from Luke's account, but Luke does say that Aquila and Priscilla further instructed Apollos in their home. The eloquent teacher then went to Corinth to present to the Jews evidence from their own Scriptures that Jesus was the Messiah. It was during his ministry there that Paul arrived in Ephesus.

At Ephesus Paul found a group of "disciples" who, like Apollos, had an imperfect knowledge of Christian teaching. It may be that these individuals were "disciples of John," though Luke himself does not directly assert this. He merely states that these "disciples" had received John's baptism and knew nothing of the Holy Spirit or of baptism in the name of Jesus. It is possible that they had heard something of the teaching of Jesus. Yet it would seem to be at odds with Pauline theology to consider anyone who had not received the Holy Spirit to be a member of the body of believers (Rom. 8:9). They might also have heard Apollos' teaching before the latter received further instruction from Aquila and Priscilla. It might be best to consider this group of about twelve men to have been "disciples" of John who had some limited knowledge of Jesus. Paul's preaching led to their conversion, to baptism in the name of Jesus, and to manifestations of the Holy Spirit's power through the gifts of tongues and prophecy.[11]

The Corinthian Correspondence

During Paul's stay at Ephesus, he wrote 1 Corinthians and, after resuming his journey, penned 2 Corinthians from somewhere in Macedonia. It is very probable that the two canonical letters were not the only letters Paul sent to Corinth. It also appears that the two journeys to Corinth recorded in Acts were not the only visits by Paul to the church there. It is probable that Paul made a quick trip to Corinth during the long Ephesian ministry. Paul apparently wrote four letters. Listed in chronological order, they were (1) a "previous letter," (2) 1 Corinthians, (3) the severe letter, and (4) 2 Corinthians.

1. *The Previous Letter.* In 1 Corinthians 5:9–11 Paul writes of a previous letter that the Corinthians had misunderstood. In this earlier epistle Paul had told the believers "not to associate with sexually immoral people," and they had interpreted this admonition to refer to association with immoral unbelievers. But in 1 Corinthians Paul explains that in his previous letter he had been speaking of discipline within the church, specifically the need to break fellowship with Christians guilty of serious immoral behavior. The so-called "previous letter" has been lost and is not to be identified with 2 Corinthians 6:14–7:1 as has sometimes been argued.

2. *1 Corinthians.* The first epistle to the Corinthians was actually Paul's second message to them; it was written about A.D. 55. The letter addressed rumors of misconduct brought to Paul's attention by "Chloe's household" (1:11). No information is given about the individual named Chloe, but the name itself suggests a few possibilities. "Chloe" originated as a designation for Demeter and was often given to female slaves. Chloe may have been a former slave, and she probably had become a convert. Because she had knowledge of the Corinthian situation, she might have lived in that city, but it is equally likely that she could have come from the area of Ephesus and had knowledge of Corinth from relatives or another source. Communication and commerce between Ephesus and Corinth were relatively easy. Ships could sail the island-studded Aegean

without losing sight of land. Thus news about problems at Corinth could readily come to Paul at Ephesus either from Chloe's family or from others. Paul wrote 1 Corinthians partly to deal with rumors of factionalism and glorification of human leaders (chaps. 1–4), of gross immorality that escaped church discipline (chap. 5), and of shameful litigation among believers (chap. 6). First Corinthians was also written as an answer to questions raised in a letter from the church at Corinth (7:1) about celibacy (chap. 7), food offered to idols (chaps. 8–10), behavior in congregational worship (chap. 11), spiritual gifts (chaps. 12–14), and whether the dead are resurrected (chap. 15).

Paul also told the Corinthians that he intended to visit them after a trip through Macedonia (4:19; 16:5), but he evidently decided to make a sudden trip directly to Corinth by sea, the so-called "painful visit." Probably this visit came about after Timothy returned to Ephesus with more discouraging news about Corinth. That Paul did make such an unscheduled hasty visit seems to be the import of the reference in 2 Corinthians 12:14 to visiting the Corinthians for the "third time," and in 2 Corinthians 13:1 to Paul's "third visit" to them.

3. *The Severe Letter.* A third epistle to Corinth, written from Ephesus and also not extant, has usually been called "the severe letter." Second Corinthians 2:1–4 speaks of this letter as one that followed the "painful visit." Paul's mood at the time of writing is characterized as one of "great distress and anguish of heart." His hope was that a letter that brought grief at the time of its reception would in the end produce joy. In 2 Corinthians 7:8–12 he speaks of this letter as having created not simply hurt but also the "godly sorrow [that] brings repentance." Both the "severe letter" and the earlier "painful visit" seem to have dealt with a wrong done by one of the Corinthians to an "injured party," probably Paul himself (2 Cor. 7:12)

4. *2 Corinthians.* Paul wrote his fourth letter, the canonical 2 Corinthians, after he had received good news from Titus about the repentance of the Corinthian church. But before his meeting with Titus, Paul experienced such intense pressure that he left Ephesus. Some unexplained peril suddenly befell him. "In our hearts," he explained, "we felt the sentence of death" (2 Cor. 1:8–9). This danger might have been the riot at the theater in Ephesus as described in Acts, or it could have been some more serious threat to Paul's life. At the insistence of friends, Paul had not entered the theater on the day of the tumult (Acts 19:30–31). Perhaps an incident at Ephesus or later at Troas, growing out of the earlier opposition faced at the theater, led to the threat to Paul's life. After Paul left Ephesus, he journeyed to Troas, where he had planned to meet with Titus. There he anxiously awaited the arrival of news from Corinth. But when Titus did not appear, Paul went on to Macedonia where his path finally crossed that of his co-worker, possibly at Philippi. There Titus presented the comforting news that the Corinthians had demonstrated repentance, a zeal for correcting problems in their church, and a warmth toward their spiritual father, Paul. The encouraging report

nearly overwhelmed the apostle, and he joyously penned 2 Corinthians.

Paul's purposes in writing 2 Corinthians were (1) to commend the believers for the comfort their response had given him even amid suffering and danger (2:3–11), (2) to explain the reasons for delaying his visit (1:15–17), (3) to encourage them to join with the Macedonians in generously contributing to the collection for the Jerusalem church, and (4) to defend his own integrity and office as an apostle against the attacks of a minority who still continued to oppose him despite the repentance of a majority (chaps. 10–13). The tone of the last four chapters of 2 Corinthians is so harsh and defensive that some scholars believe it was actually not part of 2 Corinthians originally but constituted the "severe letter." More likely Paul wrote the whole letter at one time. He chose to deal with the good news first and by conciliation prepare the way for the warnings he would have to direct to the minority opposition.

Paul's Travel Plans

Paul told the Corinthians in his first canonical letter that he planned to visit them by way of Macedonia. He advised that they take a collection each Sunday, so that by the time he arrived a delegation could be organized to carry the gift to the saints at Jerusalem (1 Cor. 16:1–4). In 2 Corinthians 9:1–11 he again encouraged them to be diligent and generous in their offering, following the example of the Macedonians, who had already given beyond their ability (2 Cor. 8:1–3). After his arrival at Corinth, Paul wrote to the Romans that the planned collection had been completed in the region of Macedonia and Achaia (Rom. 15:26). This gift must have been a means of mollifying the Jerusalem Christians who looked on Paul's Gentile work with a suspicious eye. It would be tangible evidence not only of the generosity of the Gentiles but also of the success of Paul's own ministry to them. Paul described the contribution as a debt owed by Gentiles to Jews: "For if the Gentiles have shared in the Jews' spiritual blessings, they owe it to the Jews to share with them material blessings" (Rom. 15:27). The immediate travel plan called for a trip from Corinth to Jerusalem to deliver the offering (Rom. 15:25). Afterward Paul hoped to be able to make a trip to Spain, with a stopover at Rome (Rom. 15:24). The trip to Rome would not come in the manner Paul expected, and whether he ever visited Spain is a debated question.

The missionary ministry had already taken Paul from Jerusalem to Asia Minor, the Balkan peninsula, and even "all the way around to Illyricum" (Rom. 15:19). The tour of the latter province is not mentioned in Acts, but it is easy to imagine that Paul might have traveled the Via Egnatia from the Hellespont to the Adriatic seaport of Dyrrhachium on this third journey. In his last epistle Paul mentioned that he had dispatched Titus to Dalmatia, the southern region of Illyricum (2 Tim. 4:10). It is possible that Titus' mission was to strengthen churches established by Paul in the province. Now, Paul told the Romans, there is "no more place for me to work in these regions" (Rom. 15:23). Paul's ministry bypassed some areas of Asia Minor such as Bithynia and Pontus. The reason seems to be his desire "to preach the gospel where Christ was not known, so that" he might not "be building on someone else's foundation" (Rom. 15:20). Christian communities existed in these provinces, according to 1 Peter 1:1. Perhaps they were founded by evangelists other than Paul or his immediate band of followers. A visit to Rome would not have been a ministry in virgin territory either since a body of believers already flourished there, but because Paul was a Roman citizen and, given the influence of a work in Rome's capital city, Paul was ready to establish an acquaintance with the believers there and to communicate to them his own understanding of the gospel.

The Letter to Rome

Paul wrote his famous Epistle to the Romans from Corinth. The place of origin is indicated by a comparison of statements about the collection—statements made in both the Roman and Corinthian epistles. In the latter the collection is anticipated while in Romans both the Macedonian and Achaian gifts were already in hand. Further evidence is provided by Paul's recommendation of Phoebe to the Romans. Phoebe was a Christian woman from Cenchrea, a village near Corinth (Rom. 16:1); Cenchrea was Corinth's harbor and lay on the coast just a few miles east. Paul's three-month stay in Corinth on his third journey provided sufficient time for the composition of the Roman letter.

The origin of the Roman church is unknown. It must have existed long before Paul wrote his letter, since he says he had "for many years" planned to visit the church (1:13; 15:23). Although there is no record of the introduction of Christianity into Rome, it is likely that believers arrived there within a few years after the Resurrection. Rome was such an important center that it drew people of all types, and members of any vital minority movement would not have been long without representatives there. Among the pilgrims who attended the Pentecost festival in Jerusalem and who heard Peter's call for repentance were "visitors from Rome (both Jews and converts to Judaism)" (Acts 2:10–11). Possibly there were Roman converts who returned to their city to form the early nucleus of believers. The Jews had a substantial population in Rome before the time of Christ. Cicero in 59 B.C. described them as "a big crowd" that was "influential . . . in informal assemblies."[12] Emperor Claudius (A.D. 41–54) hesitated to deal harshly with the Jews because of their numbers and influence. Dio Cassius, the Roman historian, asserts that Claudius did not drive the Jews out of Rome. He believed that the multitude of Jews had so increased as to make it "hard without raising a tumult to bar them from the city."[13] But Suetonius records that Claudius finally did expel the Jews from Rome because of the riots instigated by "Chrestus."[14] The expulsion is also recorded by Luke (Acts 18:2). Possibly the preaching of the *Christos* (Messiah) among the Jews by the believers created disturbances that led to a temporary expulsion. Among the Jews who returned afterward were Priscilla and Aquila (Rom. 16:3).[15] It seems unlikely that Peter could have been in Rome early enough to have been the founder of the church there. But the evidence strongly suggests that Peter did preach in Rome. The lack of any greeting to Peter in the letter of Paul to Rome indicates that he probably was not there before about A.D. 56 or 57. The original Christian community in Rome may have been primarily Jewish, but at least by the time of Paul's writing the Gentiles had become dominant (Rom. 1:5, 6, 13; 11:13). There is secular evidence for the conversion of a very highly placed Roman woman at about the time of Paul's letter (A.D. 56 or 57). Pompnia Graecina, wife of the leader of Rome's campaign in Britain, was accused of adopting an "alien superstition," a charge that has been interpreted to apply to one accepting Christianity.[16]

Remains of the Roman Forum, showing the temple of Antoninus Pius and Faustina, built by Antoninus in A.D. 141. Courtesy G. Nowotny.

The purpose of Paul's letter was (1) to prepare the Romans for Paul's projected visit and (2) to instruct them concerning his gospel of grace. His letter is the closest of any of his writings to a systematic exposition of his theology. While it is not exhaustive, in that it leaves many topics such as eschatology undeveloped, it does express in some detail the heart of the gospel: (1) that God's grace is received by faith and (2) that God's righteousness, which was made available through Christ's sacrifice rather than law keeping, is the only basis for justification.

To Jerusalem

Because of a plot against him, Paul suddenly dropped his original plans to sail directly to Syria after finishing his work at Corinth. Evidently the conspiracy against him involved an assassination during the ship voyage. For this reason Paul turned northeast toward Macedonia, pausing at Philippi, then moving on to Troas where he stayed for a week. A large party of Macedonians, Asians, and Galatians accompanied him on the trip from Philippi to Troas. Evidently Luke also joined the party at Philippi (Acts 20:6, "we"). At Troas on the Lord's Day the church gathered to eat a meal together and to celebrate the Lord's Supper. Luke provides the first biblical reference to the practice of gathering for worship on the first day of the week (Acts 20:7-8). The service included a message by Paul so lengthy that it was punctuated at midnight by the fall of a sleepy youth from a third-story window. After a miraculous restoration to life and another meal, Paul continued his discussion until daybreak. He then resumed his journey to Jerusalem. The port call at Miletus gave him an opportunity to meet with the elders of the Ephesian church, who came to see the apostle for what they believed would be their last meeting. Paul warned them to guard the flock against the danger of "savage wolves" that might lead them away from the truth (Acts 20:29–31). After reaching Palestine, Paul stayed with Philip the deacon, whose four daughters exercised the gift of prophecy (Acts 21:8–9). He received from Agabus the prophet a warning that if he went to Jerusalem he would be imprisoned by the Jews and betrayed into the hands of the Gentiles (Acts 21:11). None of those who conveyed their forebodings of ill could deter Paul from his fixed purpose of proceeding to Jerusalem to personally deliver the offering for the church there.

Chapter 12

Church and Empire in the Era of Claudius and Nero

The Assassination of Gaius

Words like *mad, foolish, tyrannical, autocratic, cruel,* and *sadistic,* have often been used to characterize Gaius, nicknamed Caligula ("little boots"). His handling of Jewish problems almost provoked insurrection in A.D. 41, twenty-five years before the famous Jewish revolt. Gaius liked to display the insignia of the gods on his garments. His divine pretensions annoyed his Jewish subjects. During his reign, the Jews of Alexandria demanded local civil rights and suffered pogroms instigated by the city's Greek population. One major disturbance occurred in A.D. 38 because the Greeks insisted on placing the emperor's statue in Alexandria's synagogues. Jews and Greeks both sent representatives to Gaius seeking relief. Philo, the Jewish philosopher, led one of the delegations, and he wrote a treatise telling of his experiences in dealing with the emperor. He also recorded an incident even more shocking to the Jews. Having desecrated the synagogues, the emperor devised a plan to convert the Jerusalem shrine into a temple bearing "the name of Gaius, 'the new Zeus made manifest.' "[1] Earlier Herod Agrippa I had risked his life to convince Gaius not to install the image in Jerusalem. Gaius temporarily agreed but then changed his mind and ordered the plans to proceed. The assassination of Gaius, by Latin rightists who wished to restore the Republic, ended the plan and averted rebellion in Palestine.

The Reign of Claudius (A.D. 41–54)

The Praetorian Guard established Gaius' Uncle Claudius as the new emperor in A.D. 41. Claudius seemed an unlikely prospect for leadership. A victim of paralysis, he shambled about, stuttering. Despite his outward appearance, he possessed a brilliant mind, and his witty remarks often sailed over the heads of his Philistine compatriots. He authored histories (no longer extant) of the reign of Augustus and of the Carthaginians. Because of his eccentricities, Claudius had been the frequent victim of Gaius' mockings. Suetonius records that when Claudius fell asleep on his couch after dinner, the emperor's friends would pelt him with olives and dates. Another favorite game involved placing slippers on the hands of the snoring uncle. A sudden blow of a cane would arouse him, and the jokesters would roar in laughter at the sight of Claudius rubbing his sleepy eyes with slippers.[2] Suetonius also records an amusing story explaining the way in which Claudius became emperor. According to this tale, when Claudius had heard the news of Gaius' assassination, he slipped away to a balcony and hid trembling behind the curtains. A palace guard who was wandering aimlessly by happened to notice feet protruding under the drapes. The reluctant Claudius suddenly "found himself acclaimed Emperor."[3]

Herod Agrippa I, who had won Gaius' friendship, and with it the tetrarchies of Philip and Herod Antipas, now ingratiated himself with Claudius. When the senate insisted that Claudius accede to demands that the republic be restored, Agrippa successfully negotiated instead a continuation of the authoritarian regime, with Claudius as princeps. As a reward Claudius installed Agrippa as king of all Palestine. When Agrippa died in A.D. 44, Claudius again restored the rule of the Roman governors. The return of the procurators after a hiatus of several years helped kindle strife that later led to the Jewish revolt of A.D. 66.

Claudius' foreign policy extended Roman influence and the *Pax Romana* into areas that had been less stable. Britain, Mauretania (the part of North Africa south of Spain), and Thrace came into the empire. The inclusion of Thrace, at the southeast tip of Europe, lying between Macedonia and Bithynia, encouraged the growth of population in the provinces near Thrace. As a result many of the cities where Paul established churches now gained population. Claudius generously extended rights of citizenship in the provinces. He also constructed new roads and aqueducts across the empire. On the home front he ably administered the government, depending primarily on freedmen to staff his bureaucracy. But his policy of increasing the powers of the princeps at the expense of the senate angered aristocrats.

A drawing of Emperor Claudius, from a statue now in the Vatican. Courtesy Carta, Jerusalem.

Domestic problems plagued Claudius. His wife Messalina led a profligate life. When she entered into a liaison and then marriage with a counsul-elect, with the intent of making him emperor, Claudius ordered the execution of them both. The problems with his next wife were even more serious. Agrippina, who succeeded Messalina, conspired to make Nero, her son by an earlier marriage, the designated heir. But Claudius already had a son with a prior claim. The son's name was Britannicus. In A.D. 54 when Claudius began considering disinheriting Nero, Agrippina poisoned the emperor. By her treachery she successfully insured the succession of her son to the throne.

The Reign of Nero (A.D. 54–68)

The Praetorian Guard established Nero (A.D. 54–68) as emperor and the sixteen-year-old boy promised to respect the privileges and powers of the senate and to end the treason trials that had bred suspicion and fear. Nero's first five years were a golden era of stable rule and good administration, at least in the provinces. Burrus, the prefect of the Praetorian Guard, and Seneca, Nero's tutor, gave sage advice to the youthful princeps during this period. In the imperial city murder and intrigue continued to be the fashion. Agrippina hounded all potential rivals for power as soon as her son entered upon his office. One of her early victims was Narcissus, a supporter of Britannicus. Agrippina also managed to have her image placed on the coinage, an indication she may have hoped to become regent. When Nero tried to free himself from his mother's power, she threw her weight behind Britannicus. But her favorable

attitude to Britannicus led directly to his assassination (A.D. 55), and Agrippina's intrigues brought on her own execution in 59. Three years after his mother's death, Nero faced another setback. He lost two able advisers who had brought him a measure of stability; Burrus died of natural causes, and Seneca retired.

In July of 64 a fire raged through the slums of Rome for over a week, leaving more than half the city a smoking ruin. Very few of Rome's districts escaped at least some damage. Nero's absence from the city at the time helped fuel the rumor that he had arranged for arson. Although he provided food and temporary shelters for victims of the fire, his relief efforts did not relieve him of the growing suspicion. The accusation that he initiated the holocaust was probably unfounded, but the emperor could not ignore the dangerous charge. He found a convenient scapegoat in the Christian community. Suetonius explicitly charges that Nero "brazenly set fire to the City" and that a group of exconsuls caught his attendants with "blazing torches" in hand.[4] But Suetonius' emotional tirades against Nero raise the suspicion that he may have been too willing to repeat any tale of the emperor's misconduct that came to him. Tacitus was more cautious and, though he was no admirer of Nero himself, admitted that it was not possible to determine whether the disaster was "accidental or treacherously contrived by the emperor."[5]

The persecution instituted by Nero is the first example of the Roman government's officially pursuing a repressive and violent policy toward

Christianity. Tacitus describes the persecution thus:

> Nero fastened the guilt and inflicted the most exquisite tortures on a class hated for their abominations, called Christians by the populace. Christus, from whom the name had its origin, suffered the extreme penalty during the reign of Pontius Pilatus, and a most mischievous persecution, thus checked for the moment, again broke out not only in Judea, the first source of the evil, but even in Rome, where all things hideous and shameful from every part of the world find their centre and become popular. Accordingly, an arrest was first made of all who pleaded guilty; then, upon their information, an immense multitude was convicted, not so much of the crime of firing the city, as of hatred against mankind. Mockery of every sort was added to their deaths. Covered with the skins of beasts, they were torn by dogs and perished, or were nailed to crosses, or were doomed to the flames and burnt, to serve as a nightly illumination, when daylight had expired. Nero offered his gardens for the spectacle, and was exhibiting a show in the circus, while he mingled with the people in the dress of a charioteer or stood aloft on a car. Hence, even for criminals who deserved extreme and exemplary punishment, there arose a feeling of compassion; for it was not, as it seemed, for the public good, but to glut one man's cruelty, that they were being destroyed.[6]

Nero's behavior betrays a dissolute and vicious character along with mental instability. He began to display divine pretensions and even planned to change the name of Rome to Neropolis. In 67 and 68 he decided to tour the eastern part of the empire, an area more accustomed to divine monarchs. In Greece he entered a host of competitions to demonstrate his superiority as an actor, athlete, and musician. The Greeks indulged his vanity by allowing him to win hundreds of contests, including some in which he did not even participate.

Meanwhile, troubles in the empire began to multiply. Judea had rebelled in 66, and that struggle continued. News of revolts in Africa, Spain, and Gaul against his authority increased the emperor's insecurity. Knowing that the senate intended to execute and replace him, the panicky Nero fled Rome and committed suicide.

Paul on Trial
at Jerusalem and Caesarea

Before the Sanhedrin

When Nero ascended the imperial throne in A.D. 54, Paul must have been near the end of his three-year Ephesian ministry. Paul arrived in Jerusalem at Passover season in 56. There he sought to scotch the rumor that he taught Hellenistic Jews to "turn away from Moses" and to leave their children uncircumcised (Acts 21:21). James induced Paul to prove his orthodoxy by undergoing certain purification rites in the temple. But when some of Paul's antagonists from Ephesus spotted him at the temple, they seized the evangelist, thus creating a riot. To keep order the Roman commander took Paul into custody. After Paul had his hearing before the Jewish Sanhedrin, the same Roman officer heard of a plot to take Paul's life. For his own protection Paul was sent to Caesarea to await disposition of his case. There he remained for two years while the

Roman procurators Felix and Festus tried to decide his fate.

Before Felix

The high priest Ananias appeared before Felix to argue the case against Paul. He charged that Paul was a "ringleader of the Nazarene sect" and that he had sought to "desecrate the temple" (Acts 24:5–6). Felix heard Paul's defense but chose to delay making any decision. Luke comments that Felix had already heard much about the new faith (Acts 24:22). A few days later Felix conducted another hearing, this time with his wife Drusilla, daughter of Herod Agrippa I, present. Drusilla had formerly been married to Azizus who ruled a small principality in Syria. Felix had persuaded her to leave Azizus and marry him. After the second hearing, Felix still put off making a decision during his two remaining years as procurator. Luke cites the delay as motivated by a desire to receive a bribe (Acts 24:26). The motivation ascribed by Luke fits the character of Felix. Tacitus, who was an aristocrat, disdained Felix because he was one of those freedmen whom Claudius had grown so fond of before becoming emperor. Yet Tacitus may not have been far from the mark when he described Felix as one who not only indulged "in every barbarity and lust," but also "exercised the power of a king in the spirit of a slave."[7]

It is not possible to date Felix's procuratorship with accuracy. He apparently replaced Ventidius Cumanus (A.D. 48–52) in 52, but the date of his own replacement by Festus has been variously estimated to be as early as 55 or as late as 60.[8] An estimate of A.D. 58 for Festus' accession fits well into the chronology of Paul's life.

Before Festus

Apart from the records in Josephus and Acts, nothing is known of Festus' life. He came to office during a turbulent era in Judea. Not long before his accession, an Egyptian terrorist had led four thousand *sicarii* (dagger-carrying revolutionaries) into the desert to begin an insurrection against Roman authority. According to Josephus, the procurator, Felix, slew four hundred of these rebels.[9] Festus followed a more moderate policy toward the dissident Jews, but his attempt to pour oil on the troubled waters did not have long-term success. Paul's trial by Festus comes during a brief respite from the more repressive policies of the procurators, policies that led to the Judean revolt of 66. But despite Festus' moderation, tensions continued. Josephus states that the sicarii grew especially numerous in Festus' reign and began to plunder and burn villages that opposed their movement.[10]

The political and religious situation facing Festus helped determine how he would handle Paul's case. At the beginning of his rule, the Jews from Caesarea went to Rome to appeal to Caesar to punish Festus and revoke his appointment.[11] Such pressures suggest the dilemma faced by Festus. He wished to deal with Paul in a legally respectable manner, but he also feared antagonizing the Jewish leadership. Luke states (Acts 25:1) that Festus went to Jerusalem to consult with the chief priests just three days after his arrival in Judea.

Apparently he wished to appease the Jewish leaders, but he hesitated to immediately agree to their demand that Paul be sent to Jerusalem for trial. Perhaps Festus feared for Paul's life. Luke asserts that the request for extradition was motivated by a plot against Paul's life (Acts 25:3). But when Festus later indicated to Paul that he might submit to demands to send him to Jerusalem, Paul perceived the danger and made his appeal to Caesar (Nero) (Acts 25:20–21). Festus could not ignore such an appeal, since as a Roman citizen Paul had an irrevocable right to take his case to Rome. Festus must have been greatly relieved by Paul's decision. It relieved him of a very ticklish case. If he sought to satisfy priestly demands for Paul's condemnation, he might be called himself to the bar of Roman justice, but the possibility of offending the Jewish leadership could also create a dangerous opposition that could press for his removal from office.

Before Herod Agrippa II

Festus could not perceive any justification for the accusations against Paul. The whole matter involved, in his words, "some points of dispute" about the Jewish "religion and about a dead man named Jesus who Paul claimed was alive" (Acts 25:19). To help him in preparing some kind of report to send to Rome with the prisoner, Festus called in King Herod Agrippa II. Agrippa's participation in the hearings encouraged Paul because he perceived the king to be "well acquainted with all the Jewish customs and controversies" (Acts 26:3), which had so puzzled Festus.

Unlike Festus, Agrippa and Berenice are mentioned in Roman historical sources such as Tacitus, Dio Cassius, and Juvenal.[12] They play a significant role in Palestinian history in the last half of the first century. Agrippa II was the son of Agrippa I who died suddenly in A.D. 44 (Acts 12:19–23). Claudius' advisers dissuaded him from appointing the seventeen-year-old Agrippa II to the kingship. Instead, Judea after a three-year hiatus came again under the rule of Roman governors, now called "procurators." But in 50 Claudius made Agrippa king of Chalcis. A few years later the emperor granted the territories of Philip the Tetrarch to Agrippa. Later Nero added to Agrippa's domain Tiberias and other cities in Galilee and Perea. Agrippa's rule over his scattered territories continued up until the time of his death sometime in the last decade of the century. He died sometime between 93 and 100. Not long before he received the title of king, Agrippa entered into an incestuous relationship with his sister Berenice who had been left a widow by the former king of Chalcis. Berenice's scandalous conduct later gained even more attention when she became the mistress of Titus, Roman conqueror of Jerusalem and eventually emperor.[13] Despite such conduct Agrippa held the power to invest the high priests with the robes of office.

Agrippa's influence over Jewish religious affairs explains why Festus found it useful to call him to participate in Paul's examination. Paul's defense before Agrippa in Acts 26:2–23 included an account of his own conversion and the message of Christ's resurrection. The king does not seem to have been impressed: "Do you think," he protested, "that in such a short time you can persuade me to be a Christian?" (Acts 26:28). But Agrippa was convinced that there was no basis for holding Paul. Paul could have been set free "if he had not appealed to Caesar" (Acts 26:32).

Paul at Rome

Festus sent Paul to Rome in the custody of a high-ranking Roman officer named Julius.[14] The stormy journey involved shipwreck and other hazards. Paul did not travel without Christian companionship. Aristarchus the Macedonian, mentioned in Acts 27:2 as a member of the entourage, was probably the Ephesian Christian mentioned in Acts 19:29. Whether he traveled all the way with Paul to Rome or disembarked at some point and later came to Rome is uncertain. But he did arrive at Rome. There Paul referred to him as his "fellow prisoner" (Col. 4:10). Luke also must have accompanied Paul (the pronoun "we" appears again beginning at Acts 27:1). Luke described the trip in great detail, using precise nautical terms. Final landfall came at Puteoli near Naples, and Paul met a reception party of Christian brethren there. Two other groups of believers traveled from Rome southward, one to the Three Taverns, and another to the Forum of Appius (both lie between Naples and Rome) to meet Paul as he journeyed toward the capital city.

There must have been a thriving church in Rome. Paul's own epistle to the church (Rom. 16:5, 14–15) had referred to several house churches there and acknowledged that the faith of the Roman believers had been "reported all over the world" (1:8). Tacitus describes the Christians at the time of the Neronian persecution in 64, about five years after Paul's arrival there, as "an immense multitude."[15] But Paul did not direct his first effort toward the church. As soon as he arrived in Rome, he followed his usual pattern of meeting with the Jewish leadership (Acts 28:17). He told the Roman Jews the circumstances of his unjust arrest. They had no message from Judea about Paul but agreed to hear him preach. For a full day he expounded on the messianic prophecies in the Jewish Scriptures that pointed to Jesus. Again as had happened first at Pisidian Antioch, some received the message, some rejected it, and Paul announced his intention to turn to the Gentiles with his message.

A section of the Appian Way. Paul may have walked here on his journey from Puteoli to Rome. Courtesy Gerald Nowotny.

Luke's account ends abruptly with the story of Paul's imprisonment. For two years he lived in a private home with the freedom to receive visitors, teach, preach, and write. Apart from his confinement and the presence of a guard, he enjoyed a large degree of freedom while awaiting trial. Acts does not suggest whether Paul was tried and executed, or tried and released, or exempted from trial altogether. It may be that he was released about A.D. 61; that he made further missionary trips, possibly including Spain; and that he was later imprisoned and executed in about 67.

The Prison Letters

Five of Paul's letters speak of his imprisonment: Ephesians, Philippians, Colossians, 2 Timothy, and Philemon. Since 2 Timothy fits neither the time period of Acts nor the Pauline itineraries described in Acts, it is usually considered to belong to a later period. It is not grouped with the four "prison epistles" but is categorized as one of the "pastoral epistles."

Philippians, like the other three "prison letters," probably belongs to the time period of the first Roman imprisonment, but it was most likely written near the end of Paul's imprisonment. Dating Philippians toward the end of the two years in Rome is supported by the fact that there were up to five journeys between Rome and Philippi occurring during the first imprisonment. Paul's period of imprisonment preceding the writing of Philippians had to cover a lengthy period of time for all of the journeys mentioned in Philippians to take place. These journeys include (1) Timothy's arrival at Rome in time to be co-author of the Philippian letter (1:1), (2) Philippi having heard the news of Paul's imprisonment

(4:10, 14, 18), (3) the journey of Epaphroditus to Rome with a gift for Paul (4:18), (4) Philippi having heard the news that Epaphroditus was ill (2:26), and (5) Rome having heard that the Philippians were distressed at the illness of Epaphroditus (2:26). Also it appears that Paul now anticipated that the final decision in his case would come shortly so that his future would involve either being with Christ or a journey to be with the Philippians (1:19–27).

Although Rome is traditionally favored as the source of the prison epistles, some scholars have argued for Caesarea or Ephesus. That Paul was imprisoned at Caesarea for two years is clearly stated in Acts, but the prison letters do not seem to fit that environment. Paul told Philemon, "Prepare a guest room for me, because I hope to be restored to you" (Philem. 22). At Caesarea Paul expected to go to Rome, not Colosse where Philemon lived (see Acts 23:11). The arguments for Ephesus as a place of imprisonment are slightly better. Paul's prison letters involve much communication and travel between prison on the one hand and Colosse and Laodicea on the other. These latter cities were close to Ephesus. But there is no definite evidence that Paul was in prison in Ephesus, and also the ease of sea and land travel in the Mediterranean of Paul's time weakens the argument that Paul could not have written the letters from a place so distant as Rome. Although 2 Corinthians 11:23 makes it clear that Paul was in bonds often, the events of his Ephesian ministry as recorded in Acts would not seem to leave enough time for the numerous trips and activities recorded in the prison letters. While it appears in Acts that Luke was not present with Paul during the Ephesian ministry, he clearly was with Paul at the time of the writing of Colossians (4:14). If Luke was with Paul at Ephesus, it is strange that he omitted so much information alluded to in the prison epistles from his record of events at Ephesus.[16]

It is not possible on the basis of references to the praetorium and Caesar's household to prove without doubt that Rome is intended. The term *praitōrion* (Greek) found in Philippians 1:13 may refer to a governor's residence in one of the provinces. If the context is understood to be the city of Rome, it would clearly mean the Praetorian Guard.[17] The phrase "those who belong to Caesar's household" in Philippians 4:22 could refer to those in the emperor's service in any part of the empire. Although the two latter passages cannot settle the argument, some scholars think they still should be understood as referring to Rome because this would be their most natural meaning. Rome seems to be the most likely candidate for the origin of the prison epistles. The argument can become quite complicated, and it should also be noted that Philippians need not have the same origin as the other three letters.

Philemon

Paul sent the letters to the Ephesians and Colossians to Asia by the hand of Tychicus (Eph. 6:21–22; Col. 4:8), his "dear brother . . . and fellow servant in the Lord" (Col. 4:7). Traveling with Tychicus to Colosse was Onesimus, the runaway slave who was now returning to his master Philemon. Onesimus carried a letter from Paul asking that the slave be granted mercy and restoration (Philem. 17). Onesimus had fled from Philemon's household to Rome, evidently taking some of his master's possessions with him. At Rome Onesimus heard and accepted Paul's message. He became a useful co-worker or servant to Paul. But not wishing to act improperly toward Philemon, who, like Onesimus, was a convert of Paul, Paul determined to send the slave back. Paul did not launch an attack on slavery. He evidently believed that time was too short and his work too urgent to be diverted into a social-reform movement. The apostle seems to tolerate slavery and to advocate passive acceptance of one's station in life. Yet he does warn Philemon to receive Onesimus "no longer as a slave, but better than a slave, as a dear brother" (v. 16). This and similar statements in the Pauline letters suggest concepts that could easily lead to recognition of the need for social change and greater equality.

Colossians

Paul's Colossian letter was sent to the same city where Philemon lived and to which Onesimus was returning. It is not surprising, then, that in the letter to Colosse Paul devoted five verses to the relationship of slaves to masters while giving only one to wives, husbands, children, and fathers (3:18–4:1). The Epistle to the Colossians does not encourage disobedience or revolution by slaves any more than does the letter to Philemon, but Paul calls for a type of relationship between slave and mas-

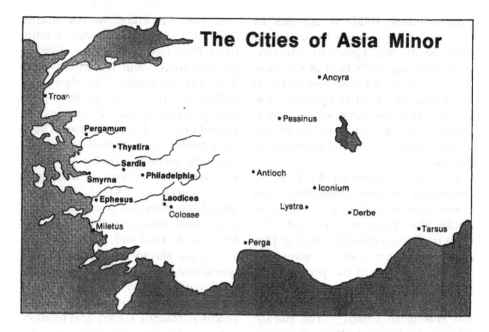

The Cities of Asia Minor

ter that differed much from the common miserable lot of slaves in the empire. While some slaves might have enjoyed a great deal more freedom and amenities of life than others, many experienced abuse, drudgery, and sometimes death at the whim of a master. But Paul called on masters to provide for slaves "what is right and fair, because you know that you also have a Master in heaven" (4:1). In Christ, distinctions between Greek and Jew or slave and free lack significance (3:11). This suggests that slaves have rights, deserve respect, and should be recompensed fairly for their work. Such ideas if carried to their logical outcome would bring slavery as practiced in the empire to an end. But again Paul stressed obedience on the part of the slave and the kind of diligence in labor that a Christian slave would wish to give to his heavenly Master (3:22–24).[18]

Heretical divergence from apostolic teaching had already disrupted the church at Colosse. Paul warned of teachers who would attempt to enslave the believer "through hollow and deceptive philosophy" (2:8). The precise character of the heresy (described in 2:9–23) is not fully explained, but it seems to be an amalgam of asceticism and Greek or Persian dualism. Some of the statements of Paul seem to speak of an undeveloped Gnosticism, but one needs to be careful not to take the more fully developed Gnosticism of the second century A.D. and read it back into this letter from the A.D. 60s. Some of the Persian religious concepts had reached Asia. Basic to Persian thought was the belief that matter is evil, and spirit is good. The antagonism between these good and evil forces was viewed as the cosmic struggle between the force of light and the power of darkness. As Gnosticism developed, it viewed man's struggle for salvation to involve gaining freedom for the soul from the prison of the physical body. This eventually led to two diverse tendencies in Gnosticism, one antinomian and the other ascetic. The libertine emphasis is not evident in the Colossian heretical teaching. Instead there is an emphasis on dietary regulations and ritual observances, such as circumcision and the keeping of special religious holidays. Although Gnosticism seems so diverse in its teachings, there is one common denominator that was present at Colosse also—the belief that salvation comes through the possession of esoteric knowledge. Some Gnostics believed that Christ had given secret oral information to the apostles and through them to others. Those who did not possess the "mystery" lacked the fullness of the gospel. Paul told the Colossians that they could all "have the full riches of complete understanding" and "know the mystery of God." This mystery was none other than Christ himself "in whom are hidden all the treasures of wisdom and knowledge" (Col. 2:2–3).

The element of angel worship in the heresy is reminiscent of the Gnostic belief that a hierarchy of aeons or emanations ranked below the Father. According to some of the Eastern religions (such as Mithraism, see chapter four), one had to appease each of the cosmic powers as the soul made its flight from darkness to light. Paul asserted that the saints already had the qualifications to share "in the kingdom of light" (Col. 1:12). "For he has rescued us from the dominion of darkness and brought us into the kingdom of the Son"

(1:13). Rather than exalting angelic powers, "in everything" Christ is to "have the supremacy" (1:18). He is the image of God, the agent of creation, the preexistent One, the head of the church, and the One in whom the fullness of God dwells (1:15–19). Christ is no mere aeon or spiritual force to be worshiped as one member of the angelic pantheon. In him "all the fullness of the Deity lives in bodily form, and you have been given fullness in Christ, who is the head over every power and authority" (2:9–10). The challenge of strange doctrines had moved Paul to pen a letter with advanced christological concepts.

Ephesians

The Ephesian epistle in subject matter, concepts, and phraseology is strikingly similar to Colossians. No other two Pauline letters are so alike. Yet while Colossians contains the specific references to individuals and situations in the local church so common to Paul's letters, Ephesians has very little of this. This is all the more surprising since Paul spent years at Ephesus but had not personally founded the Colossian church. Ephesians seems more like a general epistle than one directed to a specific locality. In style it is more like a sermon than a letter. Some scholars believe the epistle was written to a group of churches in Asia (Ephesus, Laodicea, Colosse) rather than to one church alone. The earliest manuscripts, such as the Beatty Papyrus (A.D. 200) and Vaticanus and Sinaiticus (fourth century), do not contain the phrase "in Ephesus" (1:1). Even if the letter was a circular epistle, the copy brought to Ephesus might have had the Ephesian address.

The amphitheater at Ephesus, with the Arcadian Way. Courtesy Duby Tal.

Those who deny the Pauline authorship of Ephesians suggest that the writer of the epistle was a follower of Paul who had so immersed himself in Pauline thought in general, and in the Colossian epistle particularly, that he could write a work that in many ways seemed Pauline, although lacking Paul's pastoral and personal touch. This is not the place for a full-scale discussion of the question of authenticity. The epistle itself purports to be from Paul, and this is supported by the fact that two early writers—Polycarp (A.D. 70–155), bishop of Smyrna, and Ignatius (d. 108/110), bishop of Antioch—made use of the letter.

Philippians

Paul's purpose in writing Philippians was to commend Epaphroditus to the church and to express gratitude for a generous gift. The Philippians had sent Epaphroditus to Rome with the gift (4:18), but he became so ill on his mission that he nearly died (2:26–30). Epaphroditus became distressed for the church at Philippi because of their deep concern for his well-being. Paul wished now to thank the church for the gift and for sending Epaphroditus to aid him during his time in prison (2:25; 4:10–19), but he wanted the Philippians to now welcome Epaphroditus home again and to give him the honor due such a selfless leader (2:29–30). Paul also wished to inform the Philippian church of his situation in prison. He had been able to preach the gospel and had seen fruit even among the "palace guard." His chains had encouraged other Christians to be more bold in speaking the Word. He also had experienced some danger and uncertainty about the outcome of his trial, but he now was convinced that he would be vindicated and be able to "continue with all of you for your progress and joy in the faith" (1:25). One of the constant themes of the letter is "joy." The word occurs sixteen times in either verb or noun form. Despite his own situation, Paul wanted the Philippians to be rejoicing rather than sorrowing. But there is also a rebuke in the letter because of disunity and quarreling. In calling for greater humility and selflessness, Paul appeals to the example of Christ's humbling himself as a servant even to the point of dying a criminal's death. The appeal to adopt the "mind of Christ," a mind of selflessness and sacrifice, leads into one of the most famous christological passages in the New Testament (Phil. 2:6–11). This description of Christ's humiliation and exaltation contains in a few phrases a wealth of doctrinal teaching on the person and work of Jesus Christ.

Chapter 13

The Church in Crisis

The decade of the sixties brought crisis for Christians, Jews, and the Roman Empire. For Christianity it was a period when the state under Nero launched an attack on believers in Rome, and it was also a time when heresy threatened from within. For Judaism, the decade witnessed a serious revolt in Palestine that led to the destruction of the temple and Jewish political influence. For the empire, the era brought the "year of the four emperors" in 68–69 when a succession of would-be rulers initiated a period of anarchy.

The Death of James the Just

Early in the decade the Jerusalem church experienced a severe crisis. It lost one of its most important leaders. Josephus records that after Festus' death, while Albinus was still making his way to Judea, the high priest, Ananias, "assembled the Sanhedrin of the judges, and brought before them the brother of Jesus, who was called Christ, whose name was

James, and some others, and when he had formed an accusation against them as breakers of the law, he delivered them to be stoned."[1] Eusebius of Caesarea, the church historian, quotes at length, from the work of Hegesippus, the story of James' piety and death. Most of this record cannot be used with full confidence, but there is very likely some basis for the account. The story that James had knees as hard as those of a camel because of his constant praying might be an exaggeration, but there is no reason to doubt that the leader of the Jerusalem church was a man of prayer. And Hegesippus is probably correct in saying that "because of his unsurpassable righteousness he was called the Righteous."[2] It is generally recognized that James stood for loyalty to the righteous demands of the Jewish law. Some of the details in the narrative of James' death as recorded by Hegesippus have been questioned. By his account, the scribes and Pharisees took James the Just to the sanctuary parapet and cast him

Pergamum, looking north over the Caicus Valley. Most extant remains date from the third to the second century B.C. Seats of the theater are in the foreground, and the temple of Dionysus is at the lower left. Courtesy Dan Bahat.

down to the pavement where they "pelted him with stones." While he was still alive, a fuller, taking his club, emerged from the crowd and delivered the fatal blow.[3] Whatever the precise circumstances, it is clear that James met a martyr's death probably in 61 or 62.

Eusebius cites a "firm tradition" that after James' death the apostles and the kinsmen of Jesus assembled to choose a successor for James, and "voted unanimously for Simeon, son of Clopas." According to tradition, Clopas was a brother of Joseph, and thus the new leader of the Jerusalem church was a cousin of Jesus.[4] Simeon supposedly continued to lead the church in Judea for many decades and finally met a martyr's death himself during the reign of Trajan (A.D. 98–117).[5]

Paul's Last Days

Nero's attack on the church has already been described. It was some-time during Nero's era that Paul entered his last phase of ministry. Without Acts to provide clear information about the events after Paul's Roman imprisonment, it is impossible to provide an unchallengeable account of his later activities. According to one scenario, the Roman supreme court condemned Paul to death and the imperial authorities beheaded him about A.D. 64. By this view Paul's execution was part of the Neronian persecution that came on the heels of the great conflagration in Rome. But if we are to assume that Paul was executed not long after the events recorded in Acts, then it becomes difficult to fit the pastoral letters (1 Timothy, 2 Timothy, and Titus) into the chronology. The descriptions of Paul's travels recorded in these epistles do not jibe with anything recorded in Acts. For this reason it seems probable that the authorities released Paul from his first Roman imprisonment, that he made the journeys alluded to in the pastoral letters, and then toward the end of Nero's reign that he was arrested and executed.

What was the outcome of Paul's first trial? We are left to conjecture about the answer to this question. There are three possibilities. (1) Probably the Jewish leadership did not wish to undertake the arduous journey to Rome to place their charges before the Roman court. It is clear from Acts that neither the Roman procurator Festus nor Agrippa II believed the charges to be valid (Acts 25:25; 26:32). Possibly the case then went by default, and the Roman court had no option but to release Paul. (2) If execution was the outcome of this trial, it is difficult to see how the pastoral epistles could be meshed with the travel accounts of Acts. For those who question the Pauline authorship of these letters, this difficulty is mitigated, but only partially. There still would remain the problem of explaining the origin of these letters, which in many respects seem genuine. (3) A third possibility is that Paul was exiled. Clement of Rome, writing in the last decade of the first century, speaks in a general way of exile but without explaining his precise meaning or giving a definite context. In a discussion of the persecution of the Christian leadership, Clement selected Peter and Paul as examples. He wrote of the latter:

> But, to pass from the examples of ancient days, let us come to those champions who lived nearest to our time. Let us set before us the noble examples which belong to our generation. By reason of jealousy and envy the greatest and most righteous pillars of the Church were persecuted, and contended even unto death. Let us set before our eyes the good Apostles. There was Peter who by reason of unrighteous jealousy endured not one nor two but many labours, and thus having borne his testimony went to his appointed place of glory. By reason of jealousy and strife Paul by his example pointed out the prize of patient endurance. After that he had been seven times in bonds, had been driven into exile, had been stoned, had preached in the East and in the West, he won the noble renown which was the reward of his faith, having taught righteousness unto the whole world and having reached the farthest bounds of the West; and when he had borne his testimony before the rulers, so he departed from the world and went unto the holy place, having been found a notable pattern of patient endurance.[6]

The mention of exile might have been a reference to the formal verdict handed down by the Roman authorities at Paul's hearing, or "exile" might have been nothing more than Clement's way of describing the manner in which unresponsive synagogues sometimes hounded Paul out of a town in the course of his missionary journeys. If the Romans actually did exile Paul to Spain, it would have been a providential answer to the prayer that he might carry the gospel there (Rom. 15:28). F. F. Bruce thinks exile is a possibility but opts in a tentative manner for the view that Paul's case was actually heard in Rome and resulted in his release.[7]

Clement's statement that Paul reached "the farthest bounds of the West" has often been taken as a witness to his having visited Spain, but the language is subject to different interpretations. Either Spain or

Britain could have been considered the western limit or boundary of the empire. (1) Those who see Rome, not Spain, as Paul's final destination make a point of the fact that the word *terma* could be translated "goal" rather than "boundary" or limit. The context in 1 Clement uses athletic terminology to describe apostolic heroism. For Clement, the final goal of Paul's life would be to reach Clement's own city, the capital of the empire where Paul would bear testimony (as a martyr) before the rulers. Rome then could be the limit of the west. (2) But others argue that Paul would have seen it differently. For him the goal was to visit Spain. While Clement's letter does not provide anything like definite proof that Paul went to Spain, it seems to be a natural interpretation of Clement's letter and to fit in with Paul's own stated plan to visit Spain as described in Romans 15:24.

The pastoral letters indicate that Paul visited Ephesus, Troas, Miletus, Corinth, Nicopolis (a city on the northwestern coast of Greece, just south of present-day Albania), the cities of Macedonia, and the island of Crete. Paul left Timothy in Ephesus to minister and defend the faith against heretical innovations (1 Tim. 1:3).

Paul's Final Challenge to Timothy and Titus

Paul wrote his two letters to Timothy to instruct the young pastor in his personal conduct and his leadership of God's people. He admonished Timothy not to allow others to disdain him because of his youthfulness (1 Tim. 4:12). Paul seems to have been fearful that Timothy might display a lack of discipline and firmness in his leadership of the church. He advises him (1) to "fan into flame the gift of God," which was in him "through the laying on of . . . hands. For God did not give us a spirit of timidity . . . " (2 Tim. 1:6–7); (2) to "endure hardship . . . like a good soldier of Christ Jesus" (2 Tim. 2:3); (3) to strive to present himself to God as "one approved, a workman who does not need to be ashamed . . . " (2 Tim. 2:15); (4) to "gently instruct" those who oppose his teaching (2 Tim. 2:25); and (5) to "correct, rebuke and encourage—with great patience and careful instruction" (2 Tim. 4:2).

Our information on Titus is restricted to Paul's letters. Luke never mentioned Titus in Acts, yet Titus seems to have been a frequent companion of Paul (2 Cor. 2:13; 7:6; 8:23; 12:18). Paul left Titus at Crete to minister to a troubled young church. Paul had no rebuke in his letter for his "true son in our common faith" (Titus 1:4). He had charged Titus to "straighten out what was left unfinished and appoint elders in every town" (v. 5). But Paul's confidence in Titus was not matched by high esteem for the Cretan church. Personality conflicts, legalism, indolence, and disobedience marked that troubled congregation. Paul advised Titus to give only two warnings to a "divisive person" before breaking fellowship (3:10). He instructed Titus to come to Nicopolis to spend the winter with him. Possibly Paul had visited this same area (in Epirus) during his missionary journeys to Greece. In 2 Timothy 4:10 Paul speaks of Titus as leaving him (evidently from Rome during the second imprisonment) to go to Dalmatia, a large undefined area along the eastern shores of the Adriatic.

The Pastoral Letters

The authorship of the pastoral letters has been a matter of long-standing debate. The full discussion of this complex subject belongs to the field of New Testament introduction. The name Paul is in the address of each of the three letters. The early church assumed their genuineness. During the last two centuries Bible scholars have sometimes questioned the Pauline authorship on the following grounds: (1) the events and journeys alluded to in the pastorals do not fit into Paul's life as recorded in Acts; (2) the vocabulary of the pastorals differs from that of Paul's other letters; (3) the advanced stage of church organization must call for a date of writing near the end of the first or into the second century; and (4) the pastorals seem to be attacking a form of Gnosticism common in the second century, a form that emphasized a vegetarian diet and prohibited marriage.

Let us consider these objections.

1. Dealing with the first objection very briefly, we may note that if one assumes the release of Paul and a late imprisonment, with execution about A.D. 67, then the travels of the pastorals can be placed in the era after the close of Acts.

2. Although in the Pastoral Epistles there are 175 *hapax legomena* (a Greek phrase meaning "occurring only once"), or terms occurring nowhere else in the New Testament, and though this is about twice as many as elsewhere in Paul's writings, arguments based on vocabulary are not so formidable as they may seem. Subject matter may drastically affect vocabulary. For example, Cicero would use as few as four hapaxes in one of his oratorical writings and as many as twenty-five in a philosophical work. The argument that the pastorals must belong to the second century because so many of the hapaxes found in them are also found in the apostolic fathers has serious problems. This argument is weakened by the fact that 74 percent of the hapaxes in 1 Timothy are not found in the apostolic fathers. Thus it is not so clear that the pastorals contain a second-century vocabulary. Also it should not be surprising that the pastorals contain a different vocabulary from that of Paul's earlier writings since this can be partially explained by his advancing age. Style and vocabulary change as one has new experiences and reaches maturity. The major champion of the linguistic argument against Pauline authorship is P. N. Harrison. An able summary of the problems in Harrison's view is found in the works of Donald Guthrie.[8]

3. There is insufficient evidence in the pastorals to support the view that they reflect the ecclesiastical situation of the second century. They actually have only a small amount of detail about church organization. This subject takes up only about 10 percent of the space in the pastorals. Also, 2 Timothy is a personal letter with very little in it that could qualify it as a pastoral epistle. None of the pastorals is a real manual of church discipline with discussion of conduct of worship and administrative proce-

dures. Therefore we do not have sufficient detail about church government in these letters to make a careful comparison with the apostolic fathers. First Timothy and Titus do not agree with the teaching of Ignatius (died c. 110) in his letters. Ignatius favored a monarchical bishop—one bishop to rule over the elders in a community. But Titus 1:5–7 uses the terms *elder* and *bishop* as synonyms. Also the pastorals do not indicate that a community should have only one bishop.[9]

4. The debate on Gnosticism is too complex for more than a brief comment. What Paul attacked in the pastorals was a first-century incipient Gnosticism that had Judaistic tendencies. The form of heresy alluded to in the pastorals is probably more akin to that found in Colossians than to the more fully developed Gnosticism of the second century.[10]

Paul's Arrest

Paul wrote 2 Timothy after being taken into custody again, possibly at Troas. He may have been taken by surprise since he had to request Timothy to go to Troas to pick up his cloak and scrolls (2 Tim. 4:13). That 2 Timothy records a second imprisonment is implied by a statement about Paul's "first defense," which resulted in his being "delivered from the lion's mouth" (4:16, 18). Paul did not anticipate release again. "For I am already being poured out like a drink offering," he states, "and the time has come for my departure" (4:6). Paul implored Timothy, "Do your best to come to me quickly" and "Get here before winter" (4:9, 21). Possibly Paul wished Timothy to hur-

ry from Ephesus to the coast and to set sail for Rome before the winter storms would threaten to prevent a voyage. One wonders if Timothy made the voyage so that Paul could have had a final opportunity to visit with him before suffering execution. According to tradition, both Peter and Paul died a martyr's death in Rome, Paul beheaded by the sword and Peter crucified upside down. But we have no contemporary testimony about the manner or specific timing of their deaths.

Peter's Epistles

Peter's activities after his confrontation with Paul (Gal. 2:11) remain obscure. In 1 Corinthians 9:5 Paul seems to imply that Peter became an itinerant evangelist and took his wife along on preaching tours. There is convincing evidence that Peter did go to Rome. In 1 Peter 5:13 he sends greetings from "Babylon" (a cryptic name for Rome). With him at the time was Mark, whom he referred to as "my son Mark." Clement and other early church fathers confirm Peter's association with Mark and the fact that together they ministered at Rome.[11]

Peter's first letter speaks of suffering "grief in all kinds of trials" (1:6). These difficulties probably do not refer to a systematic persecution organized by the state. Nero's sudden attack on the Christian community was unprecedented, and when it did occur there is no evidence that it reached beyond the bounds of Rome to the provinces. Peter might have written his letter before the conflagration and upheaval of 64. He may not have intended his words to be a reference to government opposition but rather to all kinds of persecution and trial that Christians may anticipate as a part of their normal experience; "Do not be surprised at the painful trial you are suffering, as though something strange were happening to you" (4:12). Peter admonished his hearers to avoid suffering the just penalty of the criminal but to praise God if they suffered as Christians (4:16).

Cappadocians bringing clothing as a tribute to the king (from the time of Xerxes, 485–465 B.C.). Courtesy B. Brandl.

The apostle Peter sent his first epistle to "the strangers in the world, scattered throughout Pontus, Galatia, Cappadocia, Asia and Bithynia," provinces in Asia Minor. Paul had ministered in Galatia and Asia, and perhaps Peter later followed Paul to those two provinces and the others mentioned. The recipients of the letter were primarily of Gentile background (2:10, 12; 4:3–4) though there may have been a Christian-Jewish minority among them. The reference to "strangers in the world, scattered" (1:1) suggests a reference to Jewish believers. The term "scattered" here is the Greek word *diaspora*, a word often used of Jews who had been dispersed or "sown" among the Gentile nations.

The authenticity of the letter designated 2 Peter in the New Testament has been the subject of controversy in both the early and the modern church. Eusebius of Caesarea in the fourth century recognized only Peter's first letter as genuine.[12] Origen was the first church father to refer to the letter by name, though it had been cited before his time. But 2 Peter has not lacked defenders. Those claiming authenticity point to the statement in 3:1: "Dear friends, this is now my second letter to you." The designation of the author as "Simon Peter, a servant and apostle of Jesus Christ," has been seen as consistent with the servant emphasis of Mark's Gospel, which bears traces of Peter's influence. Differences in style might be accounted for by a change in scribal aides. Peter's amanuensis for his first letter, Silas (1 Peter 5:12), is not mentioned as participating in the writing of the second. The inclusion of 2 Peter in the canon is in itself an evidence of belief in its apostolic origins.

One of the reasons given for assigning a second-century date to 2 Peter is that the author speaks of the letters of Paul ("all *his* letters") almost as if they had been collected and were to be placed in the same category with "the other scriptures" (3:15–16). While it is not likely that Peter could have had access to every letter of Paul, it is not necessary to interpret the statement as suggesting that they had been published as a *corpus*, i.e., as a full collection of the Pauline epistles by the time of 2 Peter. Peter may have written his second letter as late as 67 just before his death. Even by this date many of the letters of Paul could have been circulating among the believers as letters with divine authority behind them, and there is no reason to think that Peter could not have read some of these letters and also have known the basic thrust of some of those he had not seen.

Another statement in 2 Peter has raised doubts about its authenticity: the reference to "our dear [Greek *agapētos*, "beloved"] brother Paul" (3:16) has seemed to some an unlikely designation for Peter to use. But this doubt arises because of exaggeration of the difficulties between Peter and Paul that are mentioned in Galatians 2:11–14. It is important to remember that Peter and Paul are not always pictured as though they were in separate warring camps (see Acts 15:7–11, where Peter defended Paul's contention against the legalists). Just as Paul became reconciled to Mark, it seems likely that Paul and Peter also had enough of God's grace to look on one another as beloved brothers in Christ. The difficulties involved in the defense of the authenticity of 2 Peter deserve serious consideration but could not be fully examined here. The serious student will look to books on New Testament introduc-

tion for more detailed discussion of authorship.[13]

Peter wrote his second letter at a time of crisis in the church. Paul had warned of a primitive form of Gnosticism insinuating itself into the Colossian church. Now Peter also attacked a somewhat similar kind of perversion of the gospel—a teaching that had invaded a large area of Asia Minor. But the Gnosticlike heresy of 2 Peter was antinomian whereas that in Colossians was legalistic. Peter's corrective for the false *gnōsis* ("knowledge") of the deceivers was the true knowledge of God and Jesus Christ (1:3, 5–6, 8). "Knowledge" is a basic theme of 2 Peter. The writer accentuated his theme by repeated use of words based on the Greek roots *gnōsis* ("knowledge") and *epignōsis* ("knowledge," "recognition"). Peter's second epistle attacks an incipient form of Gnosticism that tended toward libertinism (perhaps akin to the antinomianism that Paul himself had condemned in his first letter to the Corinthians) for its adoption of the rallying cry "Everything is permissible" (1 Cor. 10:23). Paul feared the kind of arrogant knowledge that might cast off all restraint (1 Cor. 8:1–2, 4, 9). There were those at Corinth who had become puffed up with pride, knowing that an idol was "nothing at all in the world" (1 Cor. 8:4) and that the meat offered to such an idol was in itself not unwholesome. Paul knew that some would consider abundant grace as an excuse for licentious living (Rom. 6:1). It is not too surprising, then, that Peter also discovered in Asia Minor a perversion of Christian liberty that "ignorant and unstable people" had based on their own distortion of Paul's letters (2 Peter 3:16). Peter described the leaders of the movement as motivated by greed (2:3) and lustful desire (2:10, 14, 18). They were "lawless men" (3:17) who promised freedom (2:19) while making themselves and their followers slaves of depravity (2:19). The licentious conduct of these heretics suggests an early phase in the development of that second-century brand of Gnosticism that thought that a person could, by superior knowledge, become "spiritual" (free from the physical world) and thus unbound by moral limitations.

Relationship of Peter's Epistles to the Epistle of Jude

Jude attacked the same heretical tendencies in his time. In fact, the Epistle of Jude in its phraseology and content is surprisingly similar to 2 Peter. Over one-half of Jude's twenty-five verses can be substantially found in 2 Peter. It is evident that there is a dependency of one of the writers on the other, and scholars are not agreed on which epistle had the priority (or even on whether both might have borrowed from a third source). There were in ancient times no moral prohibitions against borrowing from or outright copying of sources. The question, then, does not involve one of improper use of another man's work, but rather simply the relationship of the two writings to one another. Clement of Alexandria believed the Epistle of Jude came from the hand of Jude, the brother of both Jesus and James. The writer of the brief letter identifies himself as "Jude, a servant of Jesus Christ and a brother of James" (v. 1).

Since the epistle is so short and since the only means of dating it is on the basis of internal evidence, there is not much information available for establishing the time of its composition. If one accepts the argument that Jude depends on 2 Peter (and not vice versa), then it must obviously be dated sometime after this letter. This might yield a date in the late 60s or possibly in the next two decades. One thing is clear, the Epistle of Jude—like Peter's letters, Colossians, 2 Timothy, and the Book of Hebrews—speaks to a church in crisis, a church facing suffering and the danger of heretical subversion.

The Danger of Spiritual Regression

Not all of the crises facing the church after mid-century stemmed from external threats from the state or even heretical movements within. There was always the danger of spiritual regression or the dulling of one's commitment. The letter to the Hebrews warns against remaining in a state of perpetual immaturity: "Let us leave the elementary teachings about Christ and go on to maturity" (Heb. 6:1). Some Christians might even abandon their commitment to the faith: "Let us hold unswervingly," adjures the writer, "to the hope we profess, for he who promised is faithful" (10:23). The great need was for a proper understanding of the divine origin and high-priestly mission of Jesus Christ. Perhaps some of the original recipients were Jewish Christians whose lack of knowledge might tempt them to revert to their former religion. They needed to know that in Christ all the symbolism of the Old Testament ritual has been fulfilled.

God's Son is superior to any of the Old Testament prophets or angels and to the levitical priesthood. His final sacrifice ends all need for further symbolic offering. Armed with an understanding of the better covenant, the young converts would be enabled to stand firm in their faith.

The recipients of the letter had at one time faced an external crisis in the form of persecution. Hebrews 12:3–4 suggests that in their struggle against sin and opposition, unlike their Savior, they had "not yet resisted to the point of shedding ... blood." The writer does, however, speak of a time when the church in its infancy stood its "ground in a great contest in the face of suffering" (10:32). The believers had accepted the confiscation of their property and encouraged those who were imprisoned (10:34). They were "publicly exposed to insult and persecution" (10:33). The references to a contest (*athlēsin*, "fight" or "struggle") and being "publicly exposed" (*theatrizomenoi*, "being publicly shamed") in the Greek text suggest the imagery of gladiatorial combat in the amphitheater, but perhaps the words are best understood in their symbolic sense, since none of the recipients had actually suffered death in their stand for Christ.

It is difficult to place the Book of Hebrews into a definite chronological or geographical context or even to identify its author. The book does not contain a salutation with Paul's name as all of his acknowledged epistles do. The style, expression, vocabulary, and manner of argument are strikingly different from any of Paul's writings. Only chapter 13 includes some statements that seem Pauline, such as a reference to "our brother Timothy" and the closing phrase "Grace be with you all" (13:23, 25). Nevertheless Pauline authorship has its defenders. In addition, Apollos, Barnabas, Clement of Rome, Luke, Priscilla and Aquila, and Silas have all been set forth as possible writers. Origen may be given the last word in this interminable debate. He once said that only God knows who wrote the letter. As to the recipients of the letter, we have little information. The statement in 13:24 that "those from Italy send ... their greetings" has been interpreted to mean either that the letter originated from Italy or that it was sent to Italy with greetings from those who had once resided there. The recipients appear to be Jewish believers who were wavering in their faith. The writer probably penned his letter before the destruction of the temple in the year 70. Timothy was still living (13:23), and the temple ritual receives so much attention that it would be very strange to omit reference to its physical destruction in such a context if the book postdated the siege by the Roman general Titus.

Ecclesiastical and Doctrinal Development of the Church

Although the church faced crises that threatened its doctrinal integrity and ethical standards, it did not succumb to these perils. The prison and pastoral letters, the Petrine epistles, Jude, and Hebrews demonstrate an increased understanding and development of Christian doctrine, ethics, and church order. As the synoptic Gospels were put in writing in the decades before A.D. 70 the church came into possession of the written explicit teachings of Jesus on morality and behavior.

The prison letters and Hebrews stated more clearly the church's christology. According to Philippians 2:6–7, Jesus Christ was "in very nature God" yet was able to empty himself of the external appearance of equality with God and took "the very nature of a servant, being made in human likeness." The letter to Colosse explained that the Son is the "image of the invisible God" (1:15) and that "God was pleased to have all his fullness dwell in him" (1:19). To the author of Hebrews "the Son is the radiance of God's glory and the exact representation of his being, sustaining all things by his powerful word" (1:3). To those tempted by the teachings of the antinomians, words of Jesus from the Gospels would come as clear admonitions. "Let your light shine before men," he admonished, "that they may see your good deeds and praise your Father in heaven" (Matt. 5:16).

The pastorals set forth more advanced and crystallized thinking on the character of church government. Elders and deacons are to be chosen from among those who are respectable, above reproach, temperate, experienced Christians who had proved themselves trustworthy both to society at large and to the church (1 Tim. 3:1–10). In addition to setting out general qualifications for holding office in the church, the pastorals specifically state the perquisites of office. The elder deserves honor and financial remuneration for his work and is not to be rebuked on the basis of frivolous charges (1 Tim. 5:17–20).

The duties and responsibilities of those in the ministry (represented by Timothy in particular) are expounded in 1 Timothy 4. Pastors should warn the flock against apostasy and legalistic heresy (4:1–6), read the Scripture publicly (v. 13), preach and teach (v. 13), and watch carefully their own life and doctrine (v. 16).

Some of the teachings of the church in this era came to be expressed in sayings or summaries that were similar to creedal formulations. Some examples are these: "Here is a trustworthy saying that deserves full acceptance: Christ Jesus came into the world to save sinners ... " (1 Tim. 1:15) and "Here is a trustworthy saying: If anyone sets his heart on being an overseer, he desires a noble task" (1 Tim. 3:1). See also 1 Timothy 4:8–9; 6:20; 2 Timothy 1:14; 2:11; Titus 2:11–14; 3:3–8. The two creedlike statements found in Titus teach that (1) God's grace brings salvation; (2) God's grace teaches us to reject former passions and live moral lives; (3) God's grace is based on his mercy, not on individual merit, and it is through his justification that we have hope of eternal life; (4) God's grace brings rebirth and renewal by the Holy Spirit; (5) Jesus is our great God and Savior; and (6) we are to await the blessed hope—the glorious appearing of Christ.

The church not only weathered the storms of the years after midcentury, it also emerged strong and vigorous. During this era many Christians must have taken courage in repeating these words of Jesus: "I will build my church, and the gates of Hades will not overcome it" (Matt. 16:18).

The ruins of ancient Laodicea in Asia Minor. Courtesy École Biblique et Archéologique Française, Jerusalem.

Chapter 14

The Last Decades

During the years from A.D. 68 to 96 the Roman administration moved from its brief period of anarchy at the end of Nero's reign to the more stable government of the Flavian rulers: Vespasian, Titus, and Domitian. For the church many of the same threats to its growth and stability that had surfaced in the earliest decades continued into the new era. Doctrinal deviations and ethical laxity remained problems, but the great trial of Nero's reign did not return until Domitian's persecution at the end of the century. Although Christians did endure hardship and oppression, the persecutions by first-century Roman leaders were sporadic and local rather than continuous, systematic, and universal.

The Jewish Revolt

The upheaval initiated by the Jewish rebellion against Roman authority in 66 had a dramatic effect not only on the Jewish nation and religion but also on the Jewish-Christian community of Judea and Galilee. The slaughter, the enslavement, and especially the dispersal of Jews to other lands took a heavy toll on the Christian-Hebrew community and drastically reduced the influence of the weakened mother church in Jerusalem.

The spirit of revolt had been brewing in Palestine for decades. Maccabean independence remained a cherished memory despite the brutalities and decadence of Hasmonean rule. Even Herod the Great, puppet ruler and Idumean though he was, could at least be remembered as a native ruler who stood between Rome and the Jewish nation. Some of the more zealous nationalists considered the payment of tribute to Rome a surrender of principle. Even more moderate Jews must have wished to be free of the Roman yoke. The avarice, corruption, and brutalities of the Roman governors accelerated the growth of the resistance movement. Josephus, having a pro-Roman bias, saw the conflict as the inevitable result of the fanaticism of the extreme nationalists, but also as the product of the misdeeds of the procurators. Bandits and marauders under the banner of patriotism had taken to the desert hills of Judea during the middle years of the century to begin a relentless assault on the Roman establishment.

Two of the procurators who could have competed for top place in the category of avarice and corruption were Albinus (A.D. 61 or 62 to 64), who succeeded Festus, and Gessius Florus (A.D. 64–69). It was during Florus' term that the revolt erupted. Albinus once initiated a novel form of prison reform, according to an account in Josephus. Having heard that his replacement, Florus, was on the way to take the helm, he cleared out the prisons of their inhabitants by executing the worst offenders and by releasing the remainder upon payment of bribes. Now the prisons were "emptied, but the country was filled with robbers."[1] With understandable exaggeration, Josephus charged that there was not "any sort of wickedness that could be named but" that Albinus "had a hand in it."[2] Florus did not rate much better with Josephus, who accused him of having "filled Judea with abundance of miseries."[3] While Albinus had been subtle in his crimes, Florus had "made a pompous ostentation of them," even becoming "a partner with the robbers themselves."[4]

One of the major incidents that helped precipitate the revolt occurred in Caesarea. The Jews there had frequently sought to buy a piece of land adjoining their synagogue property, but the Gentile owner not only refused to sell but proceeded to construct shops that nearly prevented access to the synagogue. Tempers flared on both sides. One of the Gentiles desecrated the Jewish place of worship by sacrificing birds on a piece of crockery at the synagogue entrance. A riotous confrontation of Jews and Gentiles in the city of Caesarea convinced a Roman cavalry officer that the offending sacrifice should be removed. But it was too late for a peaceful resolution. The Jews of Caesarea, taking their Torah with them, now determined to abandon their polluted sanctuary and the city itself. Florus, taking the riot to be an act of sedition, made a show of strength by marching to Jerusalem in May 66 with cavalry and foot soldiers. When the Romans seized seventeen talents from the temple treasury, a crowd of protesting Jews gathered before the temple. Florus responded by allowing his soldiers to pillage the city. Agrippa II and Berenice tried to calm Jewish passions, but the militants gained control of the situation. They captured the mountain fortress of Masada, near the Dead Sea, killing the Roman defenders. They ended the customary temple sacrifices that implored Jehovah's favor for Rome. These actions meant in effect a declaration of war against Roman authority. During the fall months of 66, massacres of Jews occurred both in Palestine and in Egypt.[5]

Victory seemed to be at hand for the rebels during the autumn. In September 66 Cestius Gallus, the governor of Syria, left Antioch for Palestine with a large army. At the Battle of Bethhoron the Jews slew thousands of the Roman soldiers and defeated the Roman governor. This temporary success seduced the rebels into thinking they could withstand the onslaught of Rome. They believed

God was on their side. Moderates now had to yield to the militants, and one of them, Josephus, took command of a Galilean force. Nero chose Vespasian, a former farm boy who had proved himself a capable general, to lead the Roman forces. The new commander quickly subdued Josephus and his Galilean forces, and within the years 67 and 68 gained control of most of Palestine, leaving to the rebels only the city of Jerusalem, Masada, and a few other centers of resistance.

Remains of an ancient church at Pella, one of the original ten cities of Decapolis. Courtesy Studium Biblicum Franciscanum, Jerusalem.

The Year of Anarchy and the Siege of Jerusalem

Nero's death in June 68 brought a lull in the fighting until the spring of 70 when Titus received Vespasian's former command. During the interval from 68 until T. Flavius Vespasian's accession on July 1, 70, the Roman state rocked from one crisis to another. Revolts in other provinces flared up as three emperors briefly claimed and then lost the imperial throne. Galba, Otho, and Vitellius ruled successively during the year of anarchy. The interval was not used to good advantage by the rebels in Jerusalem. Opposing factions in the city now threatened to devour each other with the same ferocity directed formerly at the Romans. Within the Jewish resistance movement itself the militants gained dominance. Despite dissension among the rebels, by the time the Romans began their assault in Jerusalem the besieged forces were able to unite against the common enemy.

The five-month siege of Jerusalem by Titus caused unimaginable suffering and horror and countless deaths. Even allowing for exaggeration of the story by Josephus, who claimed that almost one and a quarter million Jews died in the siege, the magnitude of the holocaust is mind boggling.

A view of the Citadel, from the southwest. It is popularly known as David's Tower and is near the Jaffa Gate. Courtesy Israel Government Press Office

The city could not easily be approached from the steep slopes on the east, west, or south. On the more accessible northern approach lay three defensive walls. Titus quickly took the first two defenses but discovered tenacious resistance as his army drew nearer to the third wall. He surrounded the city, making escape impossible, and mutilated and crucified in sight of the inhabitants of Jerusalem any who deserted the city and were taken prisoner. The corpses of thousands who had died of starvation were cast over the walls by the defenders. Finally, during July and August of 70 Titus captured the Antonia fortress and the temple itself. He himself entered the Holy of Holies, and his soldiers set fire to the temple area. Only three other strongholds remained: Herodium, Machaerus, and Masada. The siege of Masada took from mid-72 to the next spring. When the nearly impregnable fortress finally fell in A.D. 73, hundreds of its defenders committed suicide rather than face rape, torture, and slavery. The conquering Romans found only five children and two women alive when they broke into the fortress on the barren mountain top.

The Effect of the Revolt on Judaism and Christianity

The failure of the rebellion brought drastic consequences for the Jewish nation. The daily sacrifice had been discontinued in early August during the defense of the temple area against Titus' final mop-up operation in Jerusalem. Titus hoped to take the sanctuary without destroying it, but near the end of August 70, one of his soldiers threw a fire brand into the temple area and the uncontrollable flames destroyed the entire complex of buildings. With this act the temple ritual of Israel came to an end, and the priesthood could no longer func-

tion. More than ever the synagogues had to become the focus of worship. Although Judaism continued to be a *religio licita* (an authorized religion), it no longer enjoyed the political influence once exercised through the high priest and the Sanhedrin. The old priestly constitution ended. For six decades the Romans had permitted the Sanhedrin to exercise some control over national affairs. After A.D. 70 the authority of the Sanhedrin was transferred to the Roman procurator of the imperial province of Judea. A new Sanhedrin appeared at Jamnia (a city on the coastal plain just south of Joppa), but it was restricted to religious matters and had no political authority. The Sanhedrin of Christ and Paul's day no longer existed. Because the priestly function and Jewish political influence ceased, the Sadducees no longer had the basic supports that had given them a reason to exist. The Sadducean party now moved off the pages of history, and the Pharisees began to dominate Jewish intellectual and religious thought.

Judaism began to turn its attention more exclusively to the study and interpretation of the Torah. The new Sanhedrin with its seventy-two elders became a supreme court for interpretation of the law. The "ruler" of the Sanhedrin became a very prestigious figure in both Palestine and the Diaspora. The first such chairman of the Sanhedrin at Jamnia was Jochanan ben Zakkai. Still, the messianic fervor for national independence did not die easily. Other freedom struggles brought further defeats in later years. After the last such revolt in 132–135 the Jews more and more abandoned the inclination to seek political influence and turned inward to study their holy books. As the Jews withdrew into the seclusion of their rabbinical studies, the Christians surged forward to spread the message of the Cross.

What happened to the Christians at the time of the Roman siege of Jerusalem? Eusebius cites a tradition that before the war began the believers had been warned through a prophetic utterance to flee from Jerusalem to the city of Pella in Perea. It is possible that some of the details of this tradition could have arisen as a convenient way of showing God's judgment on the Jews and his favor to Christians for their acceptance of his Messiah. But despite scholarly suspicions about the accuracy of the tradition, there may be some truth in the story. Perhaps some Jerusalem believers remembered the words of Jesus (Matt. 24:15–16 [parallels Mark 13:14; Luke 21:20–21]): "So when you see standing in the holy place 'the abomination that causes desolation,' spoken of through the prophet Daniel—let the reader understand—then let those who are in Judea flee to the mountains." If the Jerusalem believers fled to Pella, the church would have diminished its place of leadership. Without a visible Jerusalem entity to speak with authority, its respected position as a guide would begin to fade. Even though this church did regain strength after the trial of A.D. 70, it never recaptured its former glory. The Christians of later decades gave less deference to the Jerusalem church.

The destruction of the temple had a dramatic impact on Christianity as a whole. The distinctive character of the faith became more apparent. Paul's teachings had demonstrated in the spiritual realm the unique and separate position of Christianity. But he had shown deference to James and the physical ceremonies of the temple. Now without a temple building the church would be able to proclaim its independence, and the pagan people would not be so likely to consider it nothing more than a Judaistic sect.

The Year of the Four Emperors (A.D. 68–69)

During the early years of the Jewish revolt Nero began a reign of terror that led to his fall. The revolt in Judea was only a prelude to other rebellions in other provinces—but these were aimed not so much at Roman authority in general as at Nero and his successors in particular. A new struggle for the imperial power brought a brief era of havoc, usually called "The Year of the Four Emperors."

In rapid succession four emperors ruled:

1. Galba was the first of these. In the spring of 68, Vindex, governor of part of Gaul, took up arms against Nero's leadership and gained the support of Galba, the governor of Spain. Vindex lost the leadership of the movement to Galba, the favorite of the senate and of the Praetorian Guard, who now claimed the emperorship. When the senate gave recognition to Galba, Nero fled the city in June 68 and committed suicide. But Galba did not enjoy a quiet rule. The example that armies in distant provinces might establish emperors was not lost on the legions defending the Danube and Rhine frontiers. They

proceeded to put forward their own pretenders, and a sorting-out process began, involving much disorder and suffering. The seventy-year-old Galba was stubborn, brutal, a strict disciplinarian, and parsimonious in rewarding his troops. Because of his harsh character a revolt broke out in lower Germany in January 69.

2. A second emperor, Otho, came to power during the German crisis. Before Galba could take action against the outbreak in lower Germany, the Praetorian Guard chose Otho, a senator, to replace Galba and to lead the struggle against the rebels (January 69). But Otho failed to defeat the rebels in the provinces, and not long after armies from the Rhine had come pouring through the Alpine passes, he committed suicide.

3. The third emperor, Vitellius, shocked the Romans by entering their city as a conqueror with his army of sixty thousand men in April 69. He spent his time gorging himself with food and was too lazy to try to restrain his troops from treating Italy like a conquered nation.

The armies of the Danube and the east had not had their turn at emperor making.

4. On July 1, 69, Vespasian, the fourth ruler within a year, was proclaimed emperor in Egypt. The armies from the Danube, on behalf of Vespasian, captured the city of Rome. Vitellius made a weak defense of the city, and during the struggle he was captured and executed by supporters of Vespasian.

The Flavians (A.D. 69–96)

The Julio-Claudian line ended with Nero, and the accession of Vespasian brought a new family to power, the Flavians, who ruled until 96. A group of Roman senators, commonly referred to as the Stoics, sought to bring an end to the concept of dynastic succession, but they failed to prevent the accession of Vespasian's sons, Titus (79–81) and Domitian (81–96).

Vespasian

Vespasian (69–79), the first of the new family line, came from the equestrian class. The first-century aristocratic senators viewed with disgust the increasing influence of this class. To them the coarse and plain-spoken Vespasian seemed as boorish as a peasant. He was not born a Roman but came from a bourgeois family in the Sabine hill-town of Reate. His plain, candid, and common-sense manners suggest at least superficial comparisons to the American president, Harry S Truman. Although Vespasian may not have been a brilliant leader, he was a good administrator and through strict economy managed to pay off a vast deficit hanging over from the days of Nero.

He sent a Roman army against the rebels in Gaul and Germany in 70 and ended the disorders that had flared so often on the Rhine. Titus, whom he left in command of his forces in Palestine, was welcomed home from the victorious siege of Jerusalem. Titus paraded his Jewish captives down the streets of Rome and displayed trophies such as the Menorah (the seven-branched lamp from the temple). The Arch of Titus, still standing in the Roman forum today, depicts in marble the new Jewish slaves carrying the Menorah with them. Vespasian's bid for power was accepted because, like Octavian, he seemed to have the potential to restore order and stability to the empire. He lived up to those expectations.

The Colosseum, or Flavian Amphitheater. Vespasian began construction in A.D. 70. An archaeological dig is in the foreground. Photograph by Richard L. Niswonger.

Despite his spartan economies, Vespasian did build new roads and public buildings. One of his most famous structures is the popular tourist attraction in Rome today, the Colosseum. He began construction of this building, also called the Flavian Amphitheater, on part of the site where Nero's "Golden House" stood. The elliptically shaped structure with its three stories held up to fifty thousand people. Eventually it would earn a special place in sacred history as the place where many early Christians fought with wild beasts and met martyrdom for the entertainment of frenzied mobs. Vespasian never lost his sense of humor, though many of his jests are not repeatable in polite company. Suetonius tells of his last clever line, a death-bed quip: "Dear me!" he said. "I must be turning into a god."[6]

Titus

Suetonius described the popular Titus (79–81), who succeeded his father Vespasian, as "an object of universal love and adoration."[7] A brief stint as co-regent with his father and his record in Judea suggested he may have been a ruthless and arbitrary tyrant. But these apprehensions were not fulfilled. Titus won approval from all quarters. If his reign had lasted more than his brief two years, the verdict of his contemporaries probably would have been less glowing. Two catastrophes rocked Italy during his rule—the eruption of Mount Vesuvius and another major fire in the city of Rome. The volcanic eruption in 79 buried the cities of Pompeii and Herculaneum under twenty feet of ash, leaving them almost intact. The remains of these cities, frozen in time, have been a boon for modern archaeologists. The fire destroyed the Capitoline temple and much of the northern part of the city. Titus showed great generosity in aiding the victims of both disasters, even reaching into his own funds to relieve suffering. Part of his popularity stemmed from lavish spending for entertaining the Roman populace. He dedicated the Flavian Amphitheater and celebrated the occasion with one hundred days of dramatic entertainments for the masses.

Domitian

Domitian (81–96) probably ruled more ably than his reputation suggests. He had no son to succeed him and hallow his memory. After his death, the senate and the next emperor denounced Domitian as a tyrant with no redeeming virtues. Since Domitian initiated a second persecution of Christianity, the church joined with secular writers to villify the last Flavian emperor. Domitian was no doubt tactless in openly boasting of the autocratic nature of his rule, and near the end of his tenure he became increasingly suspicious and brutal. Suetonius provides an example of the type of story Domitian's detractors repeated to each other after his death. According to this tale, Domitian, early in his reign, "would spend hours alone every day catching flies—believe it or not!—and stabbing them with a needle-sharp pen." Once when asked whether anyone was closeted with the emperor, an aide replied, "No, not even a fly."[8] But if allowances are made for prejudice in the record, it appears that Domitian was probably neither the monster of cruelty depicted by tradition nor a gifted administrator. Domitian was not prepared to take the reins in 81. Although he had held the consulship several times, he had seldom been permitted to hold the more important posts that would have fitted him for office. Titus had been groomed for the emperorship; Domitian was not. Once Domitian came to power, the effect of having been relegated to the background seems to have soured and embittered him.

Domitian in his role as administrator had both successes and failures. He proved fairly capable of controlling the provinces. His soldiers extended Roman control of Britain as far north as the Firth of Forth. Also a block of territory between the Upper Rhine and the Danube, which had been a constant source of irritation, now became part of the empire with a defensive wall to hold back marauders. He had less success in keeping the Danube frontier pacified. In the realm of finances Domitian demonstrated a tendency toward lavish spending, yet he did not actually bring the state to bankruptcy, and he did not resort to debasing the coinage. He sought to gain public support by imitating the lavish spending techniques used by Titus. He began entertaining the Romans with games and gladiatorial demonstrations, and he offered generous bonuses to soldiers and others. He completed construction work on the Flavian Amphitheater, which Vespasian had begun. He erected the Arch of Titus to celebrate his brother's successful siege of Jerusalem. Possibly there is some truth to the charges that to meet expenses for his lavish building programs he confiscated property as a means of punishing wealthy noblemen accused of crimes. He rigorously enforced the Jewish sanctuary tax first imposed by Titus. Although the temple lay in ruins, Titus had ordered all Jews to pay the tax to Rome in return for the privilege of practicing Judaism.[9] Some Jews tried to evade the tax by denying their link with Judaism. Suetonius records the brutal manner in which the Domitian administration enforced the Jewish tax. He tells of a boyhood experience when he attended a "crowded Court where the Procurator had a ninety-year-old man stripped to establish whether or not he had been circumcised."[10]

Head of Titus, who captured Jerusalem in A.D. 70 and Masada in 73. He succeeded his father as emperor in 79. Courtesy the Trustees of the British Museum.

Christianity in Domitian's Era

Christians and Jews, as well as the senatorial aristocracy, must have found Domitian's claim to be *Dominus et Deus* shocking. For Christians and Jews there was only one Lord and God. To Christians Jesus was the only man who should be worshiped as "King of Kings and Lord of Lords" (Rev. 19:16). Suetonius states that Domitian once began a letter to his procurators with the opening line "'Our Lord God instructs you to do this!'" "Lord God," Suetonius asserts, became Domitian's typical title.[11] It is not surprising that Domitian, who had not been groomed to be emperor, should feel a need to bolster his

dignity and demand respect. When he became emperor, it was clear to the Roman senate that he had gained the office solely by inheritance. He could not, like Titus, confirm his worthiness by demonstrated military leadership. Thus he blunderingly offended his subjects by demanding veneration. He never actually had the title *Dominus et Deus* formally conferred on himself, but by the last years of his reign the title had become customary, and Domitian began to use the phrase himself. Perhaps he had hoped for deification before death. Some of those who refused to worship his genius were condemned as atheists and put to death.

Actually, it cannot be proved with-

The Colosseum, exterior and interior views. The colosseum seated about 50,000 spectators. Geral Nowotny.

271

out doubt that Domitian initiated a persecution against Christians. Roman historical records provide no clear evidence of even a small-scale movement, let alone a concerted or large-scale persecution. While evidence for Nero's persecution is unambiguous, that for Domitian's consists of a few vague references to individuals who were executed. It was not stated specifically in the charges that these criminals were Christians, but they have been interpreted to be the kind of indictment that might have been made against believers.

Domitian's own cousin, Flavius Clemens, might have been one of the Christians martyred because of the emperor's quest for divine honors. The evidence for Clemens' conversion is suggestive, not conclusive. It is more certain that his wife Domitilla had become a Christian. Domitian, near the end of his life, when it was apparent he would have no natural son to succeed him, chose the two sons of Clemens and Domitilla to serve as his heirs. Despite this display of confidence in the family, Domitian, in his last year of life, executed Clemens and banished Domitilla. Suetonius provides a meager amount of information on the death of Clemens. Domitian, he states, had executed "his own extremely stupid cousin, Flavius Clemens, just before the completion of a consulship."[12] The phrase here translated "extremely stupid" has usually been understood to be a reference to laziness or inertia. It may mean that Clemens chose to avoid active involvement in the social and political affairs of the court. This certainly does not prove he was a Christian, but it would be consistent with the probable behavior of a Christian in such a situation. Clemens may have avoided contact with the corrupt and depraved social life of the empire. Dio Cassius records that Clemens and his wife Domitilla were accused of "atheism" (*atheotatos*), a charge on which many others who drifted into Jewish ways were condemned.[13] Some of the accused, he asserts, were executed or deprived of property, but Domitilla, the emperor's relative, "was merely banished to Pandateria." Also accused of the same crimes was a former consul and skilled gladiator named Glabrio.[14] While there is no way to prove absolutely that these individuals were Christians, the evidence can be easily interpreted in that way. Another statement from the time comes from one who was clearly a Christian leader. Clement of Rome, near the end of Domitian's reign, spoke of "the sudden and repeated misfortunes and calamities that have befallen us."[15]

That Domitian persecuted adherents of Judaism is not ambiguous. Dio Cassius records that from the time of the fall of Jerusalem "it was ordered that the Jews who continued to observe their ancestral customs should pay an annual tribute of two denarii to Jupiter Capitolinus."[16] Domitian broadened the Capitoline or temple tax that Vespasian and Titus had collected from the Jews. Domitian decreed that this tax would include all who were circumcised, whether professing Judaism or not, plus any uncircumcised Gentiles who did acknowledge practicing the Jewish faith.[17] Domitian also prohibited Jews from proselytizing Roman citizens. It is possible that Christian

Jews may have suffered along with other Jews if they resisted this tax. To a pagan like Domitian, Christians would appear to be atheists because they rejected veneration of the Roman gods, and while the Roman authorities by now probably began to recognize Christianity as a distinct movement, they might have continued to think of it as a sect with a strongly Jewish tradition. The anti-Semitic ruler Domitian probably thought of Christianity as both atheistic and Judaistic in its tendencies.

A stronger argument can be made for the theory that Domitilla, Domitian's niece, was executed as a Christian. The oldest Christian catacomb in Rome, on the Via Ardeatena, was dug out beneath land belonging to the family of Domitilla. Also her family name, Flavia, is found on inscriptions in the burial caverns. By Eusebius' day the tradition of a severe persecution by Domitian was well established. Eusebius speaks of Domitian as the "successor of Nero in enmity and hostility to God," and the "second to organize persecution against us."[18] Eusebius also records that Flavia Domitilla was one of many who were banished to the island of Pontia "because of their testimony to Christ."[19]

William M. Ramsay has concluded that "Domitian's persecution is as certain as that of Nero."[20] But even Ramsay admits that the only ancient pagan document referring to executions for specifically religious reasons was *The Epitome of the History of Rome* by Dio Cassius. An eleventh-century monk from Constantinople named Xiphilin abridged and paraphrased books 36 through 80 of the

work of Dio Cassius. The information on Domitian is found in this section of the late-second-century Roman historian's work, which Xiphilin compiled. Xiphilin's version is not a very reliable source. According to this version of Dio's history, as noted earlier, Clemens, Domitilla, and Glabrio were punished on a charge of *atheotēs* (a Greek term meaning "sacrilege" or "atheism"). Dio states that many others were exiled or executed on the same charge and that these same people had adopted Jewish traditions.[21] While such charges could fit either Judaism or Christianity, Ramsay concluded that other evidence that Domitilla was a Christian excluded the possibility that the religious persecution mentioned by Dio Cassius was Judaism. Although the situation may not be so clear as Ramsay portrays it, there is nevertheless some basis for the tradition of a persecution of Christianity under the last Flavian emperor.[22]

Church and State After Domitian

There is no evidence of an official or organized Roman policy of systematic persecution of Christianity until the reign of Decius (249–251). Until that time there were local, sporadic persecutions that might affect first one province, then another. This does not mean that the Christians did not continually face the potential threat of martyrdom. The Roman government on many occasions not only confiscated the property of Christians, but also executed, banished, and tortured them. Although no universal proscription of the faith was enforced as a matter of state policy before Decius, the whole social, religious, and political climate of the empire was antithetical to Christianity. The Roman authorities viewed Christians as subversives who threatened the established social order. There is some evidence that despite the absence of a systematic crusade, there was an understanding by Roman leaders that Christianity was something more than just another branch of the legally approved religion, Judaism, but was in fact an illegal cult and that to be a Christian was per se a serious criminal offense. This understanding could date back as early as the destruction of the temple (A.D. 70) when Christianity seemed to stand out more distinctly as a separate movement. Perhaps Domitian simply carried out with more severity a policy that was gaining favor under the earlier Flavians.

The strongest indication that profession of Christianity was considered inherently criminal is found in the correspondence of Pliny and Trajan. These letters reveal that there was an already-established policy for dealing with the Christians, though it still needed refinement and clarification. Pliny the Younger, who governed the province of Bithynia-Pontus about 111–113, wrote a letter to the emperor Trajan (98–117). In his epistle he assumed the illegality of the Christian religion but inquired as to policies on enforcement, whether to actively seek out the guilty, the nature of the evidence to be required for conviction, and the question of clemency on the basis of repentance or youth. Clearly, there still remained questions about details of policy, but nowhere did Pliny or Trajan suggest that any decision needed to be made on whether Christianity should be allowed to live in peace as would a legal faith like Judaism. They clearly perceived Christianity to be (1) an established and distinctive faith with an identity of its own and (2) an illegal religion.[23]

The Ministry of John at Ephesus

One of the apostles, John the beloved, lived on into the reign of Domitian. In the Book of Acts both he and Peter are portrayed as holding a prominent leadership position in the church from the outset (Acts 3:1–11; 4:1–23; 8:14–25). Paul's letter to Galatia mentions John along with Peter and James (the half-brother of Jesus) as "those reputed to be pillars" (Gal. 2:9). How long John continued to be associated with the Jerusalem church is unclear. Perhaps he left Judea at the time of the Jewish revolt (66–70) before the siege of Jerusalem. Early Christian tradition identifies him as being the leader of the church at Ephesus until nearly the end of the first century. Irenaeus says that "the church in Ephesus, founded by Paul," had "John remaining among them permanently until the times of Trajan."[24] Polycrates, bishop of Ephesus (189–198), as quoted by Eusebius, claimed that "John, who leant back on the Lord's breast, and who became a sacrificing priest wearing the mitre, a martyr and a teacher ... sleeps in Ephesus."[25] The term *martyr* in Greek means "witness" and indicates that John testified or witnessed for his faith. The term originally did not necessarily suggest that one suffered death for being a faithful witness. Possibly John's exile to Patmos constituted his testimony as a martyr. The mitre, a priestly garment, appears to have been a symbol of John's office as bishop of Ephesus. Polycrates also described the coming of Philip to the province of Asia, but the account is marred by his confusion of Philip the evangelist with Philip the apostle. He speaks of Philip the apostle as having daughters who had a very special life in the Holy Spirit, apparently a reference to Philip the evangelist's daughters who were "virgin prophetesses" (Acts 21:8–9). Eusebius claims that John lived in Asia, that he was exiled to Patmos, that he "directed the churches" of Asia after his return from exile following the death of Domitian, and that he did not die until Trajan's reign.[26] This would mean that John lived until 98 or shortly thereafter. By the traditional view, John was for perhaps one or two decades of his life the only apostle living. At Ephesus, the sole apostolic survivor during the last third of the first century could proclaim the Word of life "which we have heard, which we have seen with our eyes, which we have looked at and our hands have touched" (1 John 1:1).

Five books have been traditionally associated with the apostle John. These consist of the fourth Gospel, the three letters, and the Book of Revelation. But debates about the authorship of these books and their relationship to one another have given rise to an extensive body of literature on the Johannine question. Complex arguments have been presented in defense of one view or another, and these could not be examined here. A few facts and questions should be noted. Only one of the five books has a personal name

attached. The Book of Revelation consists of "The revelation of Jesus Christ," which God made known "by sending his angel to his servant John" (Rev. 1:1). John was a very common name, and the author does not differentiate himself from others with the name, leaving the possibility of debate about his actual identity. By simply using the well-known name of John, the writer may have assumed his reputation as an apostle would be enough to clarify authorship. The first letter has no name attached, while the second and third are written by "the elder" (2 John 1; 3 John 1). The writer of the fourth Gospel did not give his name, although he identified himself under the title of "the beloved disciple" or the "other disciple." As discussed in an earlier chapter, the designation seems to apply to one of the inner circle of disciples— Peter, James, or John—and can be narrowed down to John the apostle, whose name does not appear in the book, as the writer. The books themselves provide only a meager amount of precise information about the actual identity of the author or authors.

From the earliest days of the church some Bible students have wondered how the author of the fourth Gospel and the epistles could also have been the same person who wrote the Book of Revelation. The style of the Apocalypse is strikingly different from that of the other Johannine books. Eusebius quotes Dionysius (bishop of Alexandria and pupil of Origen) on the stylistic differences between the Gospel and 1 John as opposed to Revelation: "The first two are written not only without any blunders in the use of Greek, but with remarkable skill as regards diction, logical thought, and orderly expression. It is impossible to find in them one barbarous word or solecism, or any kind of vulgarism." But the Book of Revelation "uses barbarous idioms, and is sometimes guilty of solecisms."[27] A solecism is a syntactical or grammatical error such as the failure in Greek to use an adjective in the same gender, number, or case as the noun it modifies. Not all of the objections and questions can be considered here. But it may be suggested that an apocalyptic book might adopt a peculiar Greek style for a poetic purpose.[28] A book written "in the spirit" or in a state of exaltation, while the writer was being held to slave labor in a penal colony, possibly with an amanuensis, and with a subject content that included oracles and visions would very naturally have a different style.[29] Everett F. Harrison has pointed out some striking similarities of style and vocabulary common to both the Gospel and Revelation. Examples include the use of terms like *logos, lamb, true*, and *overcome*, the use of the name Jesus without the article, and other expressions.[30]

Although Dionysius of Alexandria and Eusebius, who reproduced much of Dionysius' work, both questioned the authority of the Book of Revelation, there is testimony from the early church that John the apostle did write the book. The witness of Irenaeus that the apostle John authored Revelation is important because Irenaeus was associated with Polycarp, who was personally acquainted with John.[31] Justin Martyr spoke of "John, one of the Apostles of Christ, who prophesied, by a revelation that was made to him, that those

who believed in our Christ would dwell a thousand years in Jerusalem."[32] Origen and Tertullian agreed with this view that the apostle wrote Revelation.[33]

Another theory discussed in both ancient and modern times is that the "elder" mentioned in 2 and 3 John was not the apostle but another John who might have been the apostle's disciple. Since some of the church fathers believed that two Johns lived at Ephesus, it is argued that the "elder John" may have written the Gospel and epistles, while the apostle wrote Revelation with its "Hebraic-Greek" style. But this theory is difficult to prove. It seems more likely that "elder" could have applied to the apostle's office, to his age, or possibly to both.

Heresy in the Johannine Era

The writings of Paul and Peter attest to a growing threat of heresy within the church in the seventh decade. During the Flavian era the need for defense of the faith and for sound teaching became even more crucial. John wrote his Gospel for an apologetic purpose, to persuade people to put faith in Jesus as Son of God. His epistles and Revelation also condemn the spread of error. Among Jewish Christians in Syria and Palestine were some whose view of Christ diverged from that which Paul's and John's writings upheld. In the second century the church fathers identified as heretical a sect of Jewish believers known as Ebionites (meaning "the poor") who, while being followers of Jesus, held that he was a mere man on whom God's Spirit came at his baptism. They stressed the necessity for believers to continue steadfastly in the observance of the Mosaic law. Irenaeus says that the Ebionites used only Matthew's Gospel and rejected Paul's letters, considering him a heretic. They "are so Judaic in their style of life," he asserted, "that they even adore Jerusalem as if it were the house of God."[34] There seems also to have been a Gnostic tendency among some of those called Ebionites. It is apparent in 1 John that docetism had already affected Asia. According to docetism God could not have literally been incarnated. His appearance was spiritual rather than fleshly. One of the key concepts of Gnosticism is the disdain for the material as evil. John speaks of such a view as "the spirit of antichrist" (1 John 4:3). "Every spirit," he asserts, "that acknowledges that Jesus Christ has come in the flesh is from God, but every spirit that does not acknowledge Jesus is not from God" (1 John 4:2–3).

Cerinthus, an Egyptian Jew, came into western Asia Minor during the last decade of John's life and began to preach an early brand of Gnosticism. The apostle John knew Cerinthus personally and, according to the church fathers, wrote 1 John to attack his views. According to Irenaeus, Cerinthus believed that the world had been created not by "the primary God, but by a certain Power separated from him, and at a distance from that Principality who is supreme over the universe." According to Irenaeus, Cerinthus denied the Virgin Birth, taught that Jesus was a mere human though "more righteous, prudent and wise than other men," that "Christ descended upon him in the form of a dove" after his

baptism, and that he then began preaching of "the unknown Father." But before Jesus was crucified, the Christ departed from him. The man Jesus arose but the Christ remained "impassible, inasmuch as he was a spiritual being."[35] These views suggest a dualistic view of the Savior. On the one hand, Christ was a pure spirit unaffected by the evil physical world, and, on the other hand, Jesus was a man on whom the spiritual power descended. In contrast to such tendencies, John asserted that those who are "born of God" are the ones who believe "that Jesus is the Christ" (1 John 5:1) and that the one who overcomes is the one "who believes that Jesus is the Son of God. This is the one who came by water and blood—Jesus Christ. He did not come by water only, but by water and blood" (1 John 5:5–6). The Apocalypse also denounces false doctrine (2:6, 14–24). False teaching combined with immoral behavior is perhaps the doctrine of the Nicolaitans mentioned in Revelation 2:15, at least this was the meaning of that term for some of the early church fathers.[36]

Persecution and Revelation

The Book of Revelation appears to be a book of comfort. It promises eventual triumph for the people of God who are undergoing persecution. John speaks of himself as their "brother and companion in the suffering and kingdom and patient endurance" and notes that he was exiled to Patmos as a result of his religious position—"because of the word of God" (1:9). He also tells of the martyrdom of a man named Antipas at Pergamum (2:13), and he speaks of deliverance for the church at Philadelphia from "the hour of trial that is going to come upon the whole world" (3:10). There are frequent references to the suffering and the shedding of the blood of the saints (16:6; 17:6; 18:24; 19:2; 20:4). The setting seems to be the reign of Domitian, although a minority of scholars would favor Nero's reign. But Nero did not seem to press himself forward as a deity with the same alacrity as Domitian did, nor did Nero's persecution reach beyond the city of Rome itself. The persecution alluded to in Revelation seems to be threatened or impending rather than a massive or systematic blood-letting of Christians. Some of the suffering described in Revelation may be more prophetic of a future cataclysm than descriptive of a contemporary situation. Perhaps the background of Revelation is one of occasional martyrdom, as in the case of Antipas, with the threat of serious trouble looming on the horizon.

Whatever the precise political situation in the Roman Empire at that time, it is clear that by John's last days the church faced a society that was hostile. Domitian sought, like Augustus, to revive the weakened ancient religion of Rome. Christians, like any unofficially approved society, seemed to be subversive and dangerous. A band of believers, united in worship of one master, with a growing body of followers in far-flung areas of the empire, and opposed to the cultural and moral patterns of the day, was bound to become the object of scorn, ridicule, and angry opposition.

Chapter 15

Conclusion

Geographic Spread of Christianity by A.D. 100

By the year A.D. 100 Christianity had spread to a vast region. Asia Minor with its large cities became one of the most thoroughly evangelized regions. Not only urban areas had major congregations of believers, but even the more resistant conservative pagan countryside saw converts coming into the faith. Pliny complained that in Bithynia "the contagion of this superstition has spread not only to the cities but also to the villages and farms."[1] The faith also reached Syria, Macedonia, Greece, Illyricum, Cyprus, Crete, Italy, and probably Egypt. Because of the veil of darkness covering the era from about A.D. 65 to 150, the exact boundaries of Christian expansion can only be approximated. There simply are not sufficient extant documents to bridge the gap of our ignorance about early Christian history for a period of about eight decades after the events recorded in Acts. From our knowledge of Chris-

tianity's existence in various regions in the centuries after A.D. 150, scholars have worked backward, speculating about the time and man-

The countryside of Crete, showing the slopes of Mount Ida, the legendary birthplace of Zeus. Courtesy Gerald Nowotny.

ner of the arrival of the gospel in particular regions. We also have traditions from later centuries that offer information about the travels of the apostles whose names and later lives are not recorded by Acts. These late memories of the church cannot be verified. One common tradition has

279

the apostle Thomas traveling as far as India with the message. The ancient church of India looks back to this disciple as the founder of its movement. Perhaps this tradition is based on a historical reality, but there is no way to corroborate such stories.

Elamite archers of the royal Persian guard at Susa, from the fifth century B.C.
Courtesy Réunion des Musées Nationaux.

According to Acts 2:9 the pilgrims who visited Jerusalem at Pentecost included "Parthians, Medes, and Elamites; residents of Mesopotamia ... Egypt and the parts of Libya near Cyrene ...." Perhaps some of these worshipers became converts and spread Christianity to their homeland. It is then a possibility, though it cannot be proved, that Christianity

within the earliest decades moved east from Jerusalem as well as west. But the historical record of the first century proves only a westward movement into the Roman regions. Equally uncertain is the question of whether the gospel message reached Spain, Gaul, and Britain within the first century. Even with the exact bounds unclear, it is certain that the early believers spread their message with phenomenal success over a wide region.

Development of Church Government and Doctrine by A.D. 100

By the beginning of the second century, the organization of the church had become more fully developed, although it appears that the form of church government was not uniform from place to place. Any attempt to understand the basic form of apostolic church government about A.D. 100 is doomed to partial failure for two reasons. There is a lack of documentary information from the era. Second, what is available has been obscured by controversy between proponents of different forms of church order. Although the surviving documents are few and provide only a limited amount of information, it is of great interest to Christians to be aware at least of what can be known.

Ignatius, bishop of Antioch, provides one view of ecclesiastical government. In no uncertain terms this bishop, who so eagerly awaited his martyrdom in Rome, asserted the authority of the local bishop over elders (presbyters) and deacons. It should not be assumed that his views were universally accepted. The congregation, he believed, "ought to regard the bishop as the Lord Himself."[2] He also spoke of "the bishop presiding after the likeness of God and the presbyters after the likeness of the council of the Apostles."[3] People should "respect the deacons as Jesus Christ, even as they should respect the bishop as being a type of the Father and the presbyters as the council of God and as the college of Apostles."[4] Ignatius believed that without the bishop it was unlawful for the Christians "to baptize or to hold a love-feast."[5]

But another Christian document from roughly about the turn of the century provides a different perspective. The *Didache*, or *The Teaching of the Twelve Apostles*, gives a much higher role to those who were recognized as true prophets. The firstfruit of grain and oxen should go to the prophets, "for they are your chief priests."[6] The *Didache* advises the appointment of bishops and deacons since "they also perform the service of the prophets and teachers."[7] There is very little information in this brief little book as to the distinctions between the various offices. All the officers of the church are to be considered worthy of respect, but the tone of the book does seem to give a special place to prophets, to those who display the power of speaking in the Spirit. A prophet may administer the Lord's Supper whenever he desires to do so.[8] An interesting test is suggested for winnowing out unworthy from true prophets. Any itinerant prophet who wants hospitality for more than two or three days and does not have a trade should be considered unworthy of his upkeep.[9]

The positions of prophet and teacher were among the earliest offices of the church, but by the time of the *Didache* they were beginning to diminish in influence as the offices of elder and deacon gained greater importance.

Another source of information from the period is *1 Clement*, but this work, while longer than the *Didache*, does not really offer much information about church government. Clement was concerned that the younger Corinthian leaders not expel the older church officers whose tenure had begun in the days of the apostles. Some scholars believe that *1 Clement* equates the terms *bishop* and *presbyter*, as seems to be the case also in Acts (compare Acts 20:17 with 20:28).

A more tightly organized church government and further definition of doctrine were needed in the second century as the church faced internal theological conflict. Almost as soon as Paul began his missionary journeys he had to combat heretical viewpoints. In the last decade of the first century, John battled incipient Gnosticism (discussed in the preceding chapter). During the course of the first century the church had begun the process of sorting out its theology so as to differentiate orthodox doctrine from the variations that consistently troubled it. The Gnostic tendencies that began to stir the waters of theological controversy in the latter decades of the first century would become a tidal wave in the second century. Paul's and John's writings established a foundation for the work of the apologists of the next century who would continue the struggle to defend doctrinal integrity.

Christianity and Judaism

The Christian faith, so deeply rooted in Judaism, began increasingly to assert its independence and distinctiveness by A.D. 100. Paul's battle against legalism, the development of large Gentile churches as at Rome, the destruction of the temple in 70 with the consequent weakening of the Jewish Christian movement centered in Jerusalem, all contributed to the separation of the two faiths. Hostilities between Christians and Jews increased as the church entered the second century. Judaism began to close the doors of the synagogues to those they considered tainted by the Nazarene heresy. Similarly, Christians began to warn against maintaining ties with Judaism. Ignatius, about A.D. 107, thundered, "It is monstrous to talk of Jesus Christ and to practice Judaism."[10] *The Epistle of Barnabas* sounded a hostile note when it asserted that when God gave Moses the law at Sinai, he determined that the people (the Jews) "were not worthy to receive it by reason of their sins."[11] Only Moses as an individual was found worthy of possessing a covenant relationship with God. In Barnabas' view the nation of Israel never came to possess the covenant blessings. God held these blessings in abeyance from the time of Moses until the Gentiles were brought out of darkness to receive them. Christianity and Judaism were increasingly understood to be distinct movements.

As the first century of the new era ended, Judaism began to turn away from the secular outside world. Jewish learning set aside its earlier attempts to establish points of contact with Greek and Roman intellectual traditions. The tendency to become absorbed in the study of their own detailed legal traditions seemed odd to outsiders. Elaborate discussions of ritualistic procedures that could not be practiced without a physical temple seemed archaic and of no utility to Judaism's critics. But for the Jew, the complex array of traditions became an object of devotion to be treasured. Christianity, by contrast, breaking loose from the confines of a religion tied to one people and nation, went out to preach a universal gospel to the vast Gentile world. Christians with their messianic message cast aside the more narrow nationalistic expectations that derived from the Maccabean memory. Instead of organizing a rebellion that would establish a Jewish independent kingdom, they preached a returning messianic Savior and King who would gather all nationalities into his fold.

Factors Contributing to Christianity's Growth

How did a seemingly obscure sect originating in one of the more distant Roman provinces gain a foothold in the empire by the first century's end? The following four suggestions may be offered:

1. Christianity very early became a missionary faith. Its inclusivism contrasted, as has been seen, with Judaism's exclusiveness.

2. The relationship to Judaism gave some initial aid. Christians could come under the umbrella of legal protection given by the Romans to the Jews. They also had access to Jewish synagogues in scattered cities around the Roman world. In these

Jewish communities there existed a ready-made though increasingly hostile audience. This audience, steeped in the Hebrew Scriptures and monotheistic tradition, provided a seedbed for the introduction of Christian teaching. Conversely, it could be argued that the tie to Judaism also hindered the spread of Christianity since the anti-Semitism aimed at Jews often snared Christians who were identified with them. The identification could well have been a millstone around the neck of the Christians, and by the year 100 they wanted to be free from it.

3. The failure of Roman religion, philosophy, and the mystery religions to satisfy the intellectual, moral, and spiritual needs of the empire left a vacuum that Christianity quickly filled. The desire for a personal relationship with God, for assurance of immortality, for a more ordered and disciplined life, for a meaning and purpose to one's earthly existence, all contributed to the appeal of Christianity.

4. Finally, no human logical analysis can fully explain the victory of the crucified Nazarene over the Roman world. In the final analysis one looks to the providential power of God as the ultimate reason for Christianity's rise from a fragile seedling to a mighty tree. The power of God manifested in the Resurrection event created the Resurrection faith that eventually would win the hearts and minds of vast multitudes.

APPENDIX A

THE PTOLEMIES, SELEUCIDS, AND HASMONEANS
(a partial list)

The Ptolemies to 145 B.C.

Ptolemy I Soter	305–282
Ptolemy II Philadephus	282–246
Ptolemy III Euergetes I	246–222
Ptolemy IV Philopator	222–205
Ptolemy V Epiphanes	204–180
Ptolemy VI Philometer	180–145

The Seleucids to 140 B.C.

Seleucus I Nicator	311–281
Antiochus I Soter	281–261
Antiochus II Theos	261–246
Seleucus II Callinicus	246–225
Seleucus III Soter	225–223
Antiochus III (the Great)	223–187
Seleucus IV Philopator	187–175
Antiochus IV Epiphanes	175–164
Antiochus V Eupator	163–162
Demetrius I Soter	162–150
Alexander Balas	150–145
Demetrius II Nicator	145–140

The Hasmonean Rulers to 63 B.C.

Matthias	167
Judas	167–161
Jonathan	161–143
Simon	143–135
John Hyrcanus	135–105
Aristobulus I	105–104
Alexander Janneus	104–78
Alexandra	78–69
Hyrcanus II	69–63*
Aristobulus II	69–63*

*NOTE: Aristobulus II died in 49 B.C. and Hyrcanus II in 30 B.C. Their conflicting claims to power led to Roman intervention in 63 B.C., but both continued to claim authority after the Roman seizure of Palestine in A.D. 63.

APPENDIX B

ASSYRIA	BABYLONIA	PERSIA	

722 B.C.   586 B.C.   537 B.C.   ALEXANDER
334–323 B.C.

PTOLEMIES	SELEUCIDS	HASMONEANS

320 B.C.   198 B.C.   142 B.C.   63 B.C.

287

APPENDIX C

THE HERODIAN DYNASTY

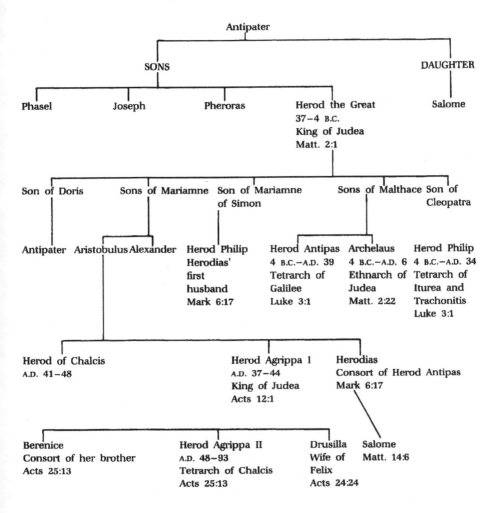

Antipater

SONS   DAUGHTER

Phasel   Joseph   Pheroras   Herod the Great   Salome
                                             37–4 B.C.
                                             King of Judea
                                             Matt. 2:1

Son of Doris   Sons of Mariamne   Son of Mariamne   Sons of Malthace   Son of
                                    of Simon   Cleopatra

Antipater   Aristobulus Alexander   Herod Philip   Herod Antipas   Archelaus   Herod Philip
                                    Herodias'   4 B.C.–A.D. 39 4 B.C.–A.D. 6   4 B.C.–A.D. 34
                                    first   Tetrarch of   Ethnarch of   Tetrarch of
                                    husband   Galilee   Judea   Iturea and
                                    Mark 6:17   Luke 3:1   Matt. 2:22   Trachonitis
                                                                                     Luke 3:1

Herod of Chalcis   Herod Agrippa I   Herodias
A.D. 41–48   A.D. 37–44   Consort of Herod Antipas
                                    King of Judea   Mark 6:17
                                    Acts 12:1

Berenice   Herod Agrippa II   Drusilla   Salome
Consort of her brother   A.D. 48–93   Wife of   Matt. 14:6
Acts 25:13   Tetrarch of Chalcis   Felix
                           Acts 25:13   Acts 24:24

APPENDIX D

ROMAN RULERS OF PALESTINE
63 B.C. to A.D. 138

Leaders of the Roman Republic

63–48 B.C.	Pompey, Caesar, and Crassus
48–44 B.C.	Julius Caesar
43–31 B.C.	Mark Antony, Octavian, Lepidus
31–27 B.C.	Octavian

Roman Governors of Judea

Roman Emperors

27 B.C.–A.D. 14	Augustus (same person as Octavian)

Roman Governors of Judea		Roman Emperors	
Coponius	A.D. 6–10		
M. Ambivius	A.D. 10–13		
Annius Rufus	A.D. 13–15	A.D. 14–37	Tiberius
Valerius Gratus	A.D. 15–26		
Pontius Pilate	A.D. 26–36		
Marcellus	A.D. 36–38	A.D. 37–41	Gaius (Caligula)
Maryllus	A.D. 38–41	A.D. 41–54	Claudius
(Herod Agrippa I ruled Judea as king, A.D. 41–44)			
Cuspius Fadus	A.D. 44–46		
Tiberius Alexander	A.D. 46–48		
Ventidius Cumanus	A.D. 48–52		
M. Antonius Felix	A.D. 52–58	A.D. 54–68	Nero
Porcius Festus	A.D. 58–61		
Albinus	A.D. 61–65		
Gessius Florus	A.D. 65–70	A.D. 68	Galba
		A.D. 69	Otho

		A.D. 69	Vitellius
Siege of Jerusalem	A.D. 70	A.D. 69–79	Vespasian
Vettulenus Cerialis	A.D. 72		
Lucilius Bassus	A.D. 72–75		
M. Salvienus and Flavius Silva	A.D. 75–86	A.D. 79–81	Titus
		A.D. 81–96	Domitian
Pompeius Longinus	A.D. 86		
		A.D. 96–98	Nerva
		A.D. 98–117	Trajan
		A.D. 117–138	Hadrian

APPENDIX E

TIMELINE: APOSTOLIC ERA TO A.D. 70

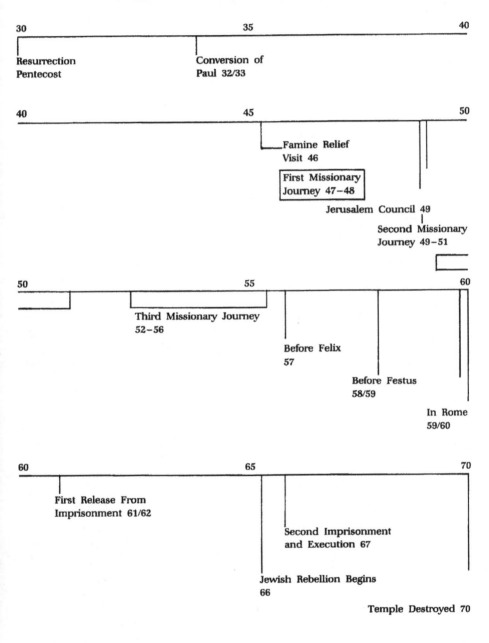

30	35	40

Resurrection
Pentecost

Conversion of
Paul 32/33

40	45	50

Famine Relief
Visit 46

First Missionary
Journey 47–48

Jerusalem Council 49

Second Missionary
Journey 49–51

50	55	60

Third Missionary Journey
52–56

Before Felix
57

Before Festus
58/59

In Rome
59/60

60	65	70

First Release From
Imprisonment 61/62

Second Imprisonment
and Execution 67

Jewish Rebellion Begins
66

Temple Destroyed 70

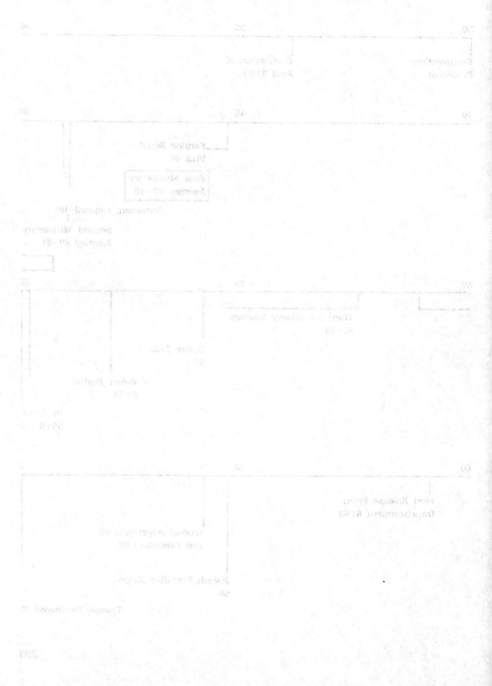

NOTES

Chapter 1

[1] For Josephus' version see *Antiquities of the Jews*, 11.8.4–5.; Most historians doubt Josephus' story. See, for instance, W. Stewart McCullough, *The History and Literature of the Palestinian Jews From Cyrus to Herod* (Toronto: University of Toronto Press, 1975), 87.

[2] For more information on Alexander a useful ancient source is Plutarch, *Life of Alexander*. Recent secondary works of value are N. Burich, *Alexander the Great: A Bibliography* (Ann Arbor: University Microfilms, 1970); A. R. Burn, *Alexander the Great and the Hellenistic Empire* (New York: AMS, 1948); J. F. C. Fuller, *The Generalship of Alexander the Great* (London: Eyre and Spottiswoode, 1958); J. R. Hamilton, *Plutarch-Alexander: A Commentary* (Oxford: Clarendon, 1969); W. W. Tarn, *Alexander the Great*, 2 vols. (Cambridge: the University Press, 1980); Ulrich Wilcken, *Alexander the Great*, trans. G. C. Richards (New York: Dial, 1932).

[3] For further reading on the Ptolemies and the Hellenistic era in Palestine see Edwyn R. Bevan, *A History of Egypt Under the Ptolemaic Dynasty* (London: Methuen, 1927); T. C. Skeet, *The Reigns of the Ptolemies*; Victor Tcherikover, *Hellenistic Civilization and the Jews*, trans. S. Applebaum (Philadelphia: Jewish Publication Society of America, 1959). In Martin Hengel, *Judaism and Hellenism*, trans. John Bowden (Philadelphia: Fortress, 1974) there is a detailed discussion of the political, economic, and cultural effect of Hellenism on Palestine and Judaism. On the Seleucids see Edwyn R. Bevan, *The House of Seleucus*, 4 vols. (London: Longmans, 1902).

[4] Moses Hadas, *Hellenistic Culture: Fusion and Diffusion* (Morningside Heights, N.Y.: Columbia University Press, 1959), 27; Louis Finkelstein, ed., *The Jews: Their History*, 4th ed. (New York: Schocken, 1970), 95.

[5] See 2 Maccabees 4:12.

[6] Wisdom of Solomon 14:17, 27. The New English Bible has been used for all Old Testament quotations from the Apocrypha.

[7] Elias Bickerman provides insight into the underlying historical forces leading to the revolt. See his book *From Ezra to the Last of the Maccabees* (New York: Schocken, 1962). Bickerman sees the clash between Jewish and Greek culture, as predating even Alexander's time.

[8] 1 Maccabees 1:11–15.

[9] 1 Maccabees 1:27.

[10] 1 Maccabees 3:4.

[11] See 1 Maccabees 9:23–31.

[12] 1 Maccabees 14:47.

[13] For further reading on the Pharisees see Louis Finkelstein, *The Pharisees*, 2 vols. (Philadelphia: Jewish Publication Society of America, 1962); R. Travers Herford, *The Pharisees* (New York: Macmillan, 1924); Emil Schürer, *The History of the Jewish People in the Age of Jesus Christ* (Edinburgh: T. & T. Clark, rev. ed., 1979), 381–414; Marcel Simon, *Jewish Sects at the Time of Jesus*, trans. James H. Farley (Philadelphia: Fortress, 1967); Ellis Rivkin in *A Hidden Revolution* (Nashville: Abingdon, 1978) argues that the Pharisees acted as revolutionaries by defending a second oral law that in effect modified the written law.

Chapter 2

[1] Josephus, *Wars* 1.21.13. The count may be exaggerated.

[2] Morton Scott Enslin, *Christian Beginnings* (New York: Harper & Brothers, 1938), 47.

[3] Michael Grant, *Herod the Great* (New York: American Heritage, 1971), 11–14; other useful secondary works on Herod the Great for the student to consult include S. Perowne, *The Life and Times of Herod the Great* (London: Hodder, 1956); S. Sandmel, *Herod: Profile of a Tyrant* (Philadelphia: Lippincott, 1967); Arnold

Jones, *The Herods of Judaea* (London: Oxford University Press, 1938).

[4] Josephus, *Wars* 1.21.1–12.

[5] Josephus, *Antiquities* 16.10.1.

Chapter 3

[1] See I. Howard Marshall, *The Acts of the Apostles* (Grand Rapids: Eerdmans, 1980), 129. See also F. F. Bruce, *Commentary on the Book of Acts* (Grand Rapids: Eerdmans, 1956), 133. Marshall argues for two synagogues, and Bruce for one.

[2] The whole of the reading known as the *Shema* originally included a larger Scripture portion: Deut. 6:4–9; 11:13–21; Num. 15:37–41.

[3] For a convenient summary of the question see D. A. Hagner, "Sanhedrin," in *The Zondervan Pictorial Encyclopedia of the Bible*, 5 vols. (Grand Rapids: Zondervan, 1975), 5:268–73.

[4] See Joachim Jeremias, *Jerusalem in the Time of Jesus*, trans. F. H. Cave and C. H. Cave (Philadelphia: Fortress, 1969), 354–55 for a discussion of the term *Cuthean*.

[5] Ibid., 353.

[6] Josephus, *Antiquities* 13.5.9.

[7] See Jeremias, *Jerusalem*, 246–52 for evidence of a well-defined and well-organized Pharisaic party.

[8] Josephus, *Antiquities* 18.1.6.

[9] F. F. Bruce, *New Testament History* (Garden City, N.Y.: Doubleday, 1971), 97–98.

[10] For an analysis of the Qumran community and its writings as they relate to the origin of Christianity see William S. LaSor, *The Dead Sea Scrolls and the New Testament* (Grand Rapids: Eerdmans, 1972). LaSor argues against the view that the Essenes rather than Jesus Christ originated the main themes of Christian faith. Other significant secondary works on the scrolls include J. M. Allegro, *The Dead Sea Scrolls: A reappraisal*, 2nd ed. (New York: Penguin, 1964); idem, *Search in the Desert* (Garden City, N.Y.: Doubleday, 1964); idem, *The Dead Sea Scrolls and the Christian Myth* (Buffalo: Prometheus, 1979); William H. Brownlee, *The Meaning of the Qumran Scrolls for the Bible* (New York: Oxford University Press, 1964); James H. Charlesworth, ed., *John and Qumran* (London: Geoffrey Chapman, 1972); James H. Charlesworth, *The Discovery of a Dead Sea Scroll* (Lubbock: Texas Tech University Press, 1985); G. R. Driver, *The Judean Scrolls* (Oxford: Blackwell, 1965); Roland de Vaux, *The Archae-*

ology of the Dead Sea Scrolls (London: Oxford University Press, 1973); Y. Yadin, *The Scroll of the War of the Sons of Light Against the Sons of Darkness* (New York: Oxford University Press, 1962); idem, *The Temple Scroll* (New York: Random, 1985).

[11] *Antiquities* 18.1.5.

[12] Josephus, *Wars* 2.8.4.

[13] John Allegro, *The Dead Sea Scrolls: A Reappraisal*, 2nd ed. (New York: Penguin, 1964), 88; Millar Burrows, *The Dead Sea Scrolls* (New York: Viking, 1955), 54–56.

[14] Allegro, *Reappraisal*, 94–96; Burrows, *Scrolls*, 64–67.

[15] A. Dupont-Sommer, *The Essene Writings From Qumran*, trans. G. Vermes (Cleveland: World, 1962), 198–201.

[16] W. Stewart McCullough, *History and Literature of the Palestinian Jews From Cyrus to Herod* (Toronto: University of Toronto Press, 1975), 221.

[17] Josephus, *Wars* 2.8.13.

[18] Aboth 1:1. For a translation of the Mishnah see Herbert Danby, *The Mishnah* (Oxford: Oxford University Press, 1933). See page 446 for Aboth 1:1.

[19] Ibid., Sanhedrin 11.3.400.

[20] Ibid.

[21] Ibid., Tohoroth 4.4.

[22] T. W. Manson, *The Servant-Messiah* (Cambridge: Cambridge University Press, 1953), 5–8. A similar view is expressed by W. R. Farmer, *Maccabees, Zealots, and Josephus* (New York: Columbia University Press, 1956), 121–23. For further reading on the messianic hope see Joseph Klausner, *The Messianic Idea in Israel*, trans. W. F. Stinespring (New York: Macmillan, 1955); Sigmund Mowinckel, *He That Cometh*, trans. G. W. Anderson (Oxford: Blackwell, 1956).

[23] For the text of 1 Enoch and a discussion of its history see R. H. Charles, *The Apocrypha and Pseudepigrapha of the Old Testament in English*, vol. 2, *Pseudepigrapha* (Oxford: Clarendon, 1913), 163ff. The Psalms of Solomon found in 2:625–52 also demonstrate the character of the messianic expectation.

[24] R. H. Charles, *The Apocrypha and Pseudepigrapha*, 1 Enoch 62:5–7, 2:228.

[25] Ibid., 1 Enoch 105:2:277.

Chapter 4

[1] Edward V. Arnold, *Roman Stoicism* (Freeport, N.Y.: Books for Libraries, 1971), 64–65.

[2]George Panichas, *Epicurus* (New York: Twayne, 1967), 124.

[3]Ibid., 124–27.

[4]Ibid., 129.

[5]An example of the argument that Paul adopted Epicurean modes of thought and transformed them into Christian conceptions can be found in Norman DeWitt, *St. Paul and Epicurus* (Minneapolis: University of Minnesota Press, 1954), 3–20.

[6]Harold Mattingly, *Roman Imperial Civilization* (New York: Norton, 1971), 210–12.

[7]Ibid., 219.

[8]Moses Hadas, *Hellenistic Culture: Fusion and Diffusion* (Morningside Heights, N.Y.: Columbia University Press, 1959), 191–92.

[9] For further reading on emperor worship see L. Sweet, *Roman Emperor Worship* (Boston: Badger, 1919); on Roman and Greek religion see F. Altheim, *A History of Roman Religion*, trans. Harold Mattingly (London: Methuen, 1938); Samuel Angus, *The Religious Quests of the Graeco-Roman World: A Study in the Historical Background of Early Christianity* (London: Murray, 1929); Franz Cumont, *After Life in Roman Paganism* (New Haven: Yale University Press, 1922); idem, *Astrology and Religion Among the Greeks and Romans* (New York: Putnam, 1912); idem, *The Mysteries of Mithra* (New York: Dover, 1956); idem, *The Oriental Religions in Roman Paganism* (New York: Dover, 1956); John Ferguson, *The Religions of the Roman Empire* (Ithaca: Cornell University Press, 1970); Frederick C. Grant, ed., *Hellenistic Religions* (New York: Liberal Arts, 1953); Frederick C. Grant, ed., *Ancient Roman Religion* (New York: Liberal Arts, 1957); Michael Grant, *Roman Myths* (New York: Scribner, 1971); R. Graves, *The Greek Myths*, 2 vols. (New York: Penguin, 1955); Moses Hadas and Morton Smith, *Heroes and Gods* (New York: Harper & Row, 1965); R. Ogilvie, *The Romans and Their Gods in the Age of Augustus* (New York: Norton, 1970).

[10]Tacitus, *Annals* 4.38.

[11]Suetonius, *Lives of the Caesars: Tiberius* 26.

[12]James G. Frazer, *The Golden Bough: A Study in Magic and Religion* (New York: Macmillan, 1953), 213, 403–5.

[13]Ferguson, *Religions of the Roman Empire*, 13–26; 106–8.

[14] Ibid., 47–48.

[15] Ibid., 121.

[16] Franz Cumont, *The Mysteries of Mithra* (New York: Dover, 1956), 179–99; Frazer, *Golden Bough*, 415–16.

[17] Galatians 4:4, King James Version.

Chapter 5

[1]Earle E. Cairns, *God and Man in Time, A Christian Approach to Historiography* (Grand Rapids: Baker, 1979), 53, 76.

[2]Harold Lindsell, *The Battle for the Bible* (Grand Rapids: Zondervan, 1976), 82; for a similar view see John Warwick Montgomery, "The Fuzzification of Biblical Inerrancy," in John Warwick Montgomery, ed., *Faith Founded on Fact: Essays in Evidential Apologetics* (Nashville: Nelson, 1978), 220–21.

[3]George Eldon Ladd, *The New Testament and Criticism* (Grand Rapids: Eerdmans, 1967), 171–79.

[4]Ibid., 186–94.

[5]F. F. Bruce, *The New Testament Documents: Are They Reliable?* 5th ed. (Grand Rapids: Eerdmans, 1980), 31.

[6]See William R. Farmer, *The Synoptic Problem: A Critical Analysis* (Macon: Mercer University Press, 1976), and Hans-Herbert Stoldt, *History and Criticism of the Marcan Hypothesis*, trans. Donald I. Niewyk (Macon: Mercer University Press, 1980).

[7]See Farmer, *The Synoptic Problem*, 268–69, for a discussion of other theoretical possibilities than the six indicated. Given what we know about the parallel features of the Synoptics, he does not consider any but the six to be practical possibilities. Stoldt thinks thirty or more possibilities could exist if we consider other variables such as a postulated Q document. See Stoldt, *History and Criticism*, 4.

[8]Charles H. Dyer, "Do the Synoptics Depend on Each Other?" *Bibliotheca Sacra* 138 (July-September 1981): 230–45.

[9]H. Stoldt, *History and Criticism*, xiii.

[10]Rudolf Bultmann, *The History of the Synoptic Tradition*, trans. John Marsh, 2nd ed. (Bristol: Blackwell, 1972), 11–54.

[11]For an example of a form critic who has used form criticism in a much more moderate manner than Bultmann see Vincent Taylor, *The Formation of the Gospel Tradition*, 2nd ed. (London: Macmillan, 1935). Taylor maintains a high degree of respect for the authenticity of the content of the Synoptics.

[12]F. F. Bruce, *New Testament Documents*, 33.

[13]Robert L. Thomas, ed., and Stanley N. Gundry, assoc. ed., *A Harmony of the Gospels* (Chicago: Moody, 1978), 287–94.

[14] Grant R. Osborne, "The Evangelical and Redaction Criticism: Critique and Methodology," *Journal of the Evangelical Theological Society* 22:4 (December 1979): 305–22; see also Osborne's earlier article, "Redaction Criticism and the Great Commission: A Case Study Toward a Biblical Understanding of Inerrancy," *Journal of the Evangelical Theological Society* 21:2 (1978): 117–30. For an example of an Evangelical scholar who has used critical tools in a cautious and conservative manner see I. Howard Marshall, *Luke: Historian and Theologian* (Grand Rapids: Eerdmans, 1972). Marshall explains his approach in his book, *I Believe in the Historical Jesus* (Grand Rapids: Eerdmans, 1977). Osborne has also provided an example of the technique in *The Resurrection Narratives: A Redactional Study* (Grand Rapids: Baker, 1984).

[15] Ladd, *New Testament and Criticism*, 150–52.

[16] Eusebius, *Ecclesiastical History* 3.39.

[17] Ibid.

[18] For a more complete discussion see Donald Guthrie, *New Testament Introduction*, 3 vols. (London: Tyndale, 1965), 1:212–302.

[19] John A. T. Robinson, *Redating the New Testament* (Philadelphia: Westminster, 1976), 1–30, 254–311.

[20] F. F. Bruce, *Jesus and Christian Origins Outside the New Testament* (Grand Rapids: Eerdmans, 1977), 99–109.

[21] Some scholars believe the Gospel of Thomas may contain authentic sayings of Jesus even when it uses sources independent of the Synoptics. For this viewpoint see Hugh Montefiore and H. E. W. Turner, *Thomas and the Evangelists* (Naperville, Ill.: Allenson, 1962), 78. For a translation of the Coptic Gospels see James M. Robinson, ed., *The Nag Hammadi Library in English* (New York: Harper & Row, 1977). F. F. Bruce provides a small amount of commentary on each of the sayings of the Gospel of Thomas in his book *Jesus and Christian Origins*, 110–56; Robert M. Grant, in his article "Two Gnostic Gospels" in the *Journal of Biblical Literature* 79 (March 1960): 4, warns that despite the fascination with the Gospel of Thomas we should remember that its sayings are mainly a witness to Gnostic christology rather than to the historical Jesus.

[22] F. F. Bruce, *New Testament Documents*, 13–18.

[23] Suetonius, *Lives of the Caesars: Claudius* 25.

[24] Suetonius, *Lives: Nero* 16.

[25] Tacitus, *Annals* 15.44.

[26] Pliny, *Epistles* 10.96.

[27] Ibid., 10.97.

[28] Josephus, *Antiquities* 20.9.1.

[29] Ibid., 18.3.3. See also F. F. Bruce's discussion of this in *Jesus and Christian Origins*, 32–41.

Chapter 6

[1] For a more thorough discussion of the date when Christ began His ministry see Harold Hoehner, *Chronological Aspects of the Life of Christ* (Grand Rapids: Zondervan, 1979), 29–44, and Jack Finegan, *Handbook of Biblical Chronology* (Princeton: Princeton University Press, 1964), 259–80.

[2] Finegan, *Biblical Chronology*, 231–33.

[3] Hoehner, *Chronological Aspects*, 11–12.

[4] Ibid., 26–27; Finegan, *Biblical Chronology*, 258–59.

[5] Josephus, *Antiquities* 18.1.1.

[6] William M. Ramsay, *Was Christ Born at Bethlehem?* (Grand Rapids: Baker, 1979 reprint of 1898 ed.), 227–29.

[7] Ibid., 231–46; Finegan, *Biblical Chronology*, 258–59.

[8] A. N. Sherwin-White, *Roman Society and Law in the New Testament* (Grand Rapids: Baker, 1978 reprint of 1963 ed.), 162–71; Tacitus, *Annals* 3.48.

[9] Hoehner, *Chronological Aspects*, 18–23.

[10] A photocopy of the papyrus is found in Adolf Deissmann, *Light From the Ancient East*, 4th ed. (New York: Harper and Brothers, 1927), 270–71. The original is now located in the British Museum.

[11] William F. Arndt and F. Wilbur Gingrich, *A Greek-English Lexicon of the New Testament and Other Early Christian Literature*, 4th ed. (Chicago: University of Chicago Press, 1952), 486.

[12] Harold W. Hoehner, *Herod Antipas* (Grand Rapids: Zondervan, 1980), 102.

[13] Edgar J. Goodspeed, *A Life of Jesus* (New York: Harper & Brothers, 1950), 32–33, 38.

[14] Josephus, *Antiquities* 18.2.3.

[15] Hoehner, *Herod Antipas*, 50.

[16] Ibid., 220–21.

[17] Ibid., 346–47; Bo Reicke, *The New Testament Era*, trans. David E. Green (Philadelphia: Fortress, 1974), 124–25.

[18] Josephus, *Antiquities* 18.4.6.

[19] Josephus, *Wars* 2.1.3.

[20] Sherwin-White, *Roman Society and Law*, 6.

[21] Josephus, *Antiquities* 18.6.5.

Chapter 7

[1] Jack Finegan, *Handbook of Biblical Chronology* (Princeton: Princeton University Press, 1964), 193, 409.

[2] Tacitus, *Annals* 6.19.

[3] For the view that Tiberius held to a moderate policy see H. H. Scullard, *From the Gracchi to Nero*, 2nd ed. (London: Methuen, 1963), 282–85.

[4] Suetonius, *Lives of the Caesars: Tiberius* 75.

[5] Josephus, *Antiquities* 18.3.1–5; 18.4.1–2; idem, *Wars* 2.9.2–4; Tacitus, *Annals* 15.44; Philo, *Legation to Gaius* 38. Significant articles on Pilate and Sejanus include S. Liberty, "The Importance of Pontius Pilate in Creed and Gospel," *Journal of Theological Studies* 15 (1944): 38–56; P. Maier, "Sejanus, Pilate and the Date of the Crucifixion," *Church History* 38 (1968): 3–13.

[6] On John the Baptist's relationship to Qumran see W. H. Brownlee, "John the Baptist in the New Light of Ancient Scrolls," *Interpretation* 9 (1955): 71–90; A. S. Geyser, "The Youth of John the Baptist," *Novum Testamentum* 1 (1956): 70ff.

[7] Josephus, *Antiquities* 18.5.2.

[8] Harold W. Hoehner, *Herod Antipas* (Grand Rapids: Zondervan, 1980), 136–46.

[9] On the meaning of the baptism of Jesus see Everett F. Harrison, *A Short Life of Christ* (Grand Rapids: Eerdmans, 1979), 71–75; Donald Guthrie, *Jesus the Messiah* (Grand Rapids: Zondervan, 1972), 39–42; G. Campbell Morgan, *The Crises of the Christ* (New York: Revell, 1936), 149–210.

[10] For a description of views on the location of the Temptation see Robert D. Culver, *The Life of Christ* (Grand Rapids: Baker, 1976), 71. Jack Finegan offers a description of the traditional site of the Temptation, Jebel Quarantania, in *The Archaeology of the New Testament* (Princeton: Princeton University Press, 1969), 82.

[11] The view that lack of food made Jesus more vulnerable to temptation is expressed in Frederic William Farrar, *The Life of Christ* (Cleveland: World, 1965), 57–59.

[12] R. V. G. Tasker sees the testing process as a lifelong ordeal for Jesus in his commentary, *The Gospel According to St. Matthew: An Introduction and Commentary* (Grand Rapids: Eerdmans, 1979), 54–56.

[13] See T. W. Manson's study of the Lord's Prayer in his book, *The Teaching of Jesus: Studies of Its Form and Content*, 2nd ed. (Cambridge: Cambridge University Press, 1963), 113–15. Other useful works on the teaching of Christ are E. C. Colwell, *An Approach to the Teaching of Jesus* (New York: Abingdon, 1947); W. A. Curtis, *Jesus Christ the Teacher* (London: Oxford University Press, 1943); H. H. Horne, *Jesus The Master Teacher* (Grand Rapids: Kregel, 1964); J. Dwight Pentecost, *The Words and Works of Jesus Christ* (Grand Rapids: Zondervan, 1981); J. S. Stewart, *The Life and Teaching of Jesus Christ* (Nashville: Abingdon, 1982); R. H. Stein, *The Method and Message of Jesus' Teachings* (Philadelphia: Westminster, 1978).

[14] William M. Ramsay, *Was Christ Born at Bethlehem?* (Grand Rapids: Baker, 1979 reprint of 1898 ed.), 197–98.

[15] Ibid., 189–202; Harold Hoehner, *Chronological Aspects of the Life of Christ* (Grand Rapids: Zondervan, 1979), 31–37.

[16] Hoehner, *Chronological Aspects*, 31–37.

[17] Finegan, *Handbook of Biblical Chronology*, 282–83.

[18] Robert L. Thomas, ed., and Stanley N. Gundry, assoc. ed., *A Harmony of the Gospels* (Chicago: Moody, 1978), 326–27; Johnston M. Cheney, *The Life of Christ in Stereo*, ed. Stanley A. Ellisen, 2nd ed. (Portland: Western Baptist Seminary, 1971), 226–28.

[19] For an example of the view that the Galilee mission was a failure see Michael Grant, *Jesus: An Historian's Review of the Gospels* (New York: Scribner, 1977), 128–29.

Chapter 8

[1] Alfred Edersheim, *The Life and Times of Jesus the Messiah*, one-vol. ed. (Grand Rapids: Eerdmans, 1971), 2:364.

[2] R. Alan Cole, *The Gospel According to St. Mark* (Grand Rapids: Eerdmans, 1981), 176–77.

[3] Ethelbert Stauffer, *Christ and the Caesars, Historical Sketches*, trans. K. and R. Gregor Smith (Philadelphia: Westminster, 1955), 122–28.

[4] Harold Hoehner, *Chronological Aspects of the Life of Christ* (Grand Rapids: Zondervan, 1979), 90–93.

[5]Jack Finegan, *Handbook of Biblical Chronology* (Princeton: Princeton University Press, 1964), 288–90; Robert L. Thomas, ed., and Stanley N. Gundry, assoc. ed., *A Harmony of the Gospels* (Chicago: Moody, 1978), 320–22.

[6]For a brief discussion of the varying viewpoints on this problem see J. Jocz, "Passover," in *The Zondervan Pictorial Encyclopedia of the Bible*, 5 vols. (Grand Rapids: Zondervan, 1975), 4:605–11.

[7]Hoehner, *Chronological Aspects*, 65–74.

[8]Josephus, *Antiquities* 16.6.2.

[9]Hoehner, *Chronological Aspects*, 95–114.

[10]C. H. Dodd, *More New Testament Studies* (Grand Rapids: Eerdmans, 1968), 94–101.

[11]Thomas and Gundry, *Harmony*, 335–36.

[12]A. N. Sherwin-White, *Roman Society and Law in the New Testament* (Grand Rapids: Baker, 1978 reprint of 1963 ed.), 36.

[13]Ibid., 36–40; Leon Morris, *The Gospel According to John* (Grand Rapids: Eerdmans, 1971), 786–88.

[14]Harold W. Hoehner, *Herod Antipas* (Grand Rapids: Zondervan, 1980), 236–37.

[15]Ibid., 245.

[16]Adolf Deissman, *Light From the Ancient East*, 4th ed. (New York: Harper and Brothers, 1927), 378.

[17]Harold Hoehner ably argues for the A.D. 33 date. He believes the picture of Pilate in the Gospel of John as a weak figure who wished to avoid offending the Jews could not fit Pilate as he is known in the records before A.D. 31. See *Chronological Aspects*, 95–114. For testimony of Pilate's arrogant and cruel treatment of the Jews see Philo, *Legation to Gaius*, 301–2; Josephus, *Antiquities* 18.3.1–2; idem, *Wars* 2.9.2–4.

[18]For the view that John and Mark contradict each other see J. E. Bruns, "Use of Time in the Fourth Gospel," *New Testament Studies* 13 (1967): 289.

[19]In defense of the view that John followed a special Roman method of counting the hours from midnight see N. Walker, "The Reckoning of Hours in the Fourth Gospel," *Novum Testamentum* 4 (1960): 69–73.

[20]Johnny V. Miller, "The Time of the Crucifixion," *Journal of the Evangelical Theological Society* 26:2 (June 1983): 157–66.

[21] For this view see Merrill C. Tenney, "The Historicity of the Resurrection," in *Jesus of Nazareth: Savior and Lord*, ed. Carl F. H. Henry (Grand Rapids: Eerdmans, 1966), 138–44.

[22]On the historical evidence for the Resurrection see also F. Morison, *Who Moved the Stone?* (London: Faber and Faber, 1944); J. Orr, *The Resurrection of Jesus* (London: Hodder and Stoughton, 1908); Merrill C. Tenney, *The Reality of the Resurrection* (New York: Harper & Row, 1963), 105–44.

[23]John Wenham, *Easter Enigma* (Grand Rapids: Zondervan, 1984), 64–67.

[24]Ibid.

[25]Ibid., 97–99.

[26]George Eldon Ladd, *I Believe in the Resurrection of Jesus* (Grand Rapids: Eerdmans, 1975), 87–88.

Chapter 9

[1]William M. Ramsay, St. Paul the Traveller and Roman Citizen (Grand Rapids: Baker, 1979 reprint of 1897 ed.), 207–10.

[2]William M. Ramsay, *The Bearing of Recent Discovery on the Trustworthiness of the New Testament* (Grand Rapids: Baker, 1979 reprint of 1915 ed.), 35–52. For a scholarly analysis of Ramsay's defense of Acts see W. Ward Gasque, *History of the Criticism of the Acts of the Apostles* (Grand Rapids: Eerdmans, 1975), 136–42; see also idem, *Sir William Ramsay: Archaeologist and New Testament Scholar.*

[3]I. Howard Marshall, *Luke: Historian and Theologian* (Grand Rapids: Zondervan, 1971), 69–76.

[4]A. N. Sherwin-White, *Roman Society and Law in the New Testament* (Grand Rapids: Baker, 1963), 189. For an example of a more negative view on Luke's reliability see Martin Hengel's chapter "Luke the Historian" in his book *Between Jesus and Paul* (Philadelphia: Fortress, 1983), 96–128. See also C. K. Barrett, *Luke the Historian in Recent Study* (London: Epworth, 1961); W. W. Gasque, "The Book of Acts and History," in R. A. Guelich, ed., *Unity and Diversity in New Testament Theology* (Grand Rapids: Eerdmans, 1978), 54–72.

[5]For the view that the church had its origin in Galilee see Sean Freyne, *Galilee From Alexander the Great to Hadrian* (Wilmington and Notre Dame: Michael Glazier and University of Notre Dame Press, 1980), 346–47.

[6]Arthur Darby Nock, *Early Gentile Christianity and Its Hellenistic Background* (New York: Harper Torchbooks, 1964), 105–7.

[7]Marshall, *Luke: Historian and Theologian*, 209–11.

[8] Ibid., 204–6.

[9] F. J. Foakes-Jackson and Kirsopp Lake, eds., *The Beginnings of Christianity, Part I, The Acts of the Apostles*, 5 vols. (Grand Rapids: Baker, 1979), 1:304.

[10] Eric M. Meyers and James F. Strange, *Archaeology, The Rabbis and Early Christianity* (Nashville: Abingdon, 1981), 52.

[11] The identity of the Hellenists has been much debated. The view presented here is discussed more fully in C. F. D. Moule, "Once More, Who Were the Hellenists?" *The Expository Times* 70:4 (January 1959): 100; on the Hellenists see also Richard N. Longenecker, *Paul, Apostle of Liberty* (Grand Rapids: Baker, 1964), 27–30, 273–76.

[12] Philo, *On the Migration of Abraham* 92.

[13] For an example of the approach that sees a sharp distinction between Hellenist and Hebraic Christians see Foakes-Jackson and Lake, *The Beginnings*, 1:308–9.

[14] *The Epistle of Barnabas* 16:1, 2, 7–9.

[15] F. F. Bruce, *Peter, Stephen, James and John: Studies in Early Non-Pauline Christianity* (Grand Rapids: Eerdmans, 1980), 56–57, 62–64.

[16] I. Howard Marshall, *The Acts of the Apostles* (Grand Rapids: Eerdmans, 1980), 131–32.

[17] F. F. Bruce, *Commentary on the Book of Acts* (Grand Rapids: Eerdmans, 1956), 156–57.

[18] William F. Arndt and F. Wilbur Gingrich, *A Greek-English Lexicon of the New Testament and Other Early Christian Literature*, 4th ed. (Chicago: University of Chicago Press, 1952), 483.

[19] Leonhard Goppelt, *Apostolic and Post—Apostolic Times*, trans. Robert A. Guelich (New York: Harper Torchbooks, 1970), 93.

[20] Justin Martyr, *Apology* 1.26.56.

[21] For this viewpoint see I. Howard Marshall, *The Acts*, 354, and F. F. Bruce, *New Testament History* (Garden City, N.Y.: Doubleday, 1972), 237. See Bruce's punctuation in *Commentary on the Book of Acts*, 438.

[22] Archibald T. Robertson, *A Grammar of the Greek New Testament in the Light of Historical Research* (Nashville: Broadman, 1934), 506.

[23] A useful summary of the problem is found in E. M. Blaiklock, "Aretas," in *The Zondervan Pictorial Bible Encyclopedia*, 5 vols., ed., Merrill C. Tenney, (Grand Rapids: Zondervan, 1975), 3:299–300.

[24] Josephus, *Antiquities* 18.6.5.

[25] Ibid., 19.8.2

Chapter 10

[1] Compare 1 Clement 5:3–4 with 6:1; Irenaeus, *Heresies* 3.1.1.

[2] Bruce M. Metzger, "Antioch-on-the-Orontes," *The Biblical Archaeologist* 11 (December 1948): 81. For more information on Antioch see Glanville Downey, *A History of Antioch in Syria From Seleucus to the Arab Conquest* (Princeton: Princeton University Press, 1961).

[3] See Floyd Filson's explanation of this in *A New Testament History* (Philadelphia: Westminster, 1964), 206.

[4] Josephus, *Antiquities* 20.2.5. and 20.5.2.

[5] F. J. Foakes-Jackson and Kirsopp Lake, eds., *The Beginnings of Christianity, Part I, The Acts of the Apostles*, 5 vols. (Grand Rapids: Baker, 1979), 5:454–55.

[6] Eusebius, *Ecclesiastical History* 3.39.15. Papias' earlier tradition is quoted here by Eusebius.

[7] William F. Arndt and F. Wilbur Gingrich, *A Greek-English Lexicon of the New Testament and Other Early Christian Literature*, 4th ed. (Chicago: University of Chicago Press, 1952), 850.

[8] For the more traditional view see F. F. Bruce, *New Testament History* (Garden City, N.Y.: Doubleday, 1972), 273. For a different view see B. van Elderen, "Some Archaeological Observations on Paul's First Missionary Journey," in W. W. Gasque and R. P. Martin, eds. *Apostolic History and the Gospel* (Exeter, 1970), 151–61.

[9] Josephus, *Antiquities* 12.3.4. Josephus records that Antiochus the Great sent two thousand families of Jews to Phrygia to help stabilize the region under his control.

[10] I. Howard Marshall, *The Acts of the Apostles* (Grand Rapids: Eerdmans, 1980), 236–37.

[11] For one such ancient characterization of the Gauls see Julius Caesar, *The Gallic Wars* 2.1; 4.5; 6.16.

[12] F. F. Bruce, *The Epistle to the Galatians* (Grand Rapids: Eerdmans, 1982), 7–8.

[13] For the traditional view see J. B. Lightfoot, *The Epistle of St. Paul to the Galatians* (Grand Rapids: Zondervan, 1957, reprint of 1865 ed.), 18–35. On the south Galatian theory see William M. Ramsay, *The Church in the Roman Empire* (Grand Rapids: Baker, 1979 reprint of 1897 ed.), 8–15, 97–111; idem, *A Historical Commentary on St. Paul's Epistle to the Gala-*

tians (Grand Rapids: Baker, 1979 reprint of 1900 ed.).

¹⁴Ramsay, *Church in the Roman Empire*, 98–100.

¹⁵Ibid., 102–4.

¹⁶J. Gresham Machen, *The Origin of Paul's Religion* (Grand Rapids: Eerdmans, 1947), 83.

Chapter 11

¹William F. Arndt and F. Wilbur Gingrich, *A Greek-English Lexicon of the New Testament and Other Early Christian Literature*, 4th ed. (Chicago: University of Chicago Press, 1952), 778.

²William M. Ramsay, *St. Paul the Traveller and Roman Citizen* (Grand Rapids: Baker, 1979, reprint of 1897 ed.), 214.

³W. J. Conybeare and J. S. Howson, *The Life and Epistles of St. Paul* (Grand Rapids: Eerdmans, 1949), 229–31.

⁴Arndt and Gingrich, *A Greek–English Lexicon*, 736.

⁵Ramsay, *St. Paul the Traveller*, 219.

⁶Arndt and Gingrich, *A Greek–English Lexicon*, 692.

⁷Ibid., 856.

⁸Seneca, *Naturales Quaestiones* 4A, Praefatio 11.

⁹F. J. Foakes-Jackson and Kirsopp Lake, eds., *The Beginnings of Christianity, Part I, The Acts of the Apostles*, 5 vols. (Grand Rapids: Baker, 1979), 5:460–64.

¹⁰Ibid., 251–56.

¹¹For further discussion of Apollos' faith and the nature of John's disciples see I. Howard Marshall, *The Acts*, Tyndale New Testament Commentaries (Grand Rapids: Eerdmans, 1980), 302–8; see also Arthur C. McGiffert, *A History of Christianity in the Apostolic Age* (Edinburgh: T. & T. Clark, 1897), 290–92.

¹²Cicero, *Pro Flacco* 28.

¹³Dio Cassius, *Roman History* 60.6.

¹⁴Suetonius, *Life of Claudius* 25.

¹⁵This statement is based on the assumption that all of Romans 16 as it stands in the "Received Text" belongs there and is not part of an Ephesian letter as some textual critics believe.

¹⁶Tacitus, *Annals* 13.32.

Chapter 12

¹Philo, *The Embassy to Gaius*, 346. The Greek term *epiphanēs*, translated "manifest," suggests the appearance in bodily form of a deity. Coins of Antiochus Epiphanes bore the Greek inscription *antiochou theou epiphanous* (Antiochus, God manifest).

²Suetonius, *Lives of the Caesars: Claudius* 8.

³Ibid., 10.

⁴Suetonius, *Lives: Nero* 38.

⁵Tacitus, *Annals* 15.38.

⁶Ibid., 15.44.

⁷Tacitus, *Histories* 5.9.

⁸See Kirsopp Lake, "The Chronology of Acts," in F. J. Foakes-Jackson and Kirsopp Lake, eds., *The Beginnings of Christianity, Part I, The Acts of the Apostles*, 5 vols. (Grand Rapids: Baker, 1979), 5:466, for an argument for an early date (A.D. 55). For the more common view that Festus' accession belongs in the latter part of the time span from 55–60 see E. M. Blaiklock, "Porcius Festus" in *The Zondervan Pictorial Encyclopedia of the Bible*, 5 vols., ed. Merrill C. Tenney (Grand Rapids: Zondervan, 1975), 2:532–33.

⁹Josephus, *Antiquities* 20.8.6.

¹⁰Ibid., 20.8.10.

¹¹Ibid., 20.8.9.

¹²See Juvenal, *Satires* 6.156–60; Tacitus, *Histories* 2.2 and 5.1; Dio Cassius, *History* 56.18.

¹³Juvenal, *Satires* 6.156–60; Dio Cassius, *History* 56.18.

¹⁴The exact nature of the "imperial regiment" is uncertain. The theory that it may have been a Samaritan regiment is probably incorrect. For the theory that it was instead a Syrian cohort see Foakes-Jackson and Lake, *Beginnings*, 5:443–44.

¹⁵Tacitus, *Annals* 15.44.

¹⁶For a defense of Ephesus as the place of imprisonment see G. S. Duncan, *St. Paul's Ephesian Ministry* (New York: Scribner, 1930). For an argument in support of Rome see C. H. Dodd, *New Testament Studies* (Manchester: University of Manchester Press, 1953), 95–96.

¹⁷William F. Arndt and F. Wilbur Gingrich, *A Greek-English Lexicon of the New Testament and Other Early Christian Literature*, 4th ed. (Chicago: University of Chicago Press, 1952), 704.

¹⁸Herbert M. Carson, *The Epistles of Paul to the Colossians and Philemon* (Grand Rapids: Eerdmans, 1960), 21–24, 93–95.

Chapter 13

[1] Josephus, *Antiquities* 20.9.1.
[2] Eusebius, *Ecclesiastical History* 2.23.
[3] Ibid.
[4] Ibid., 3.11.
[5] Ibid., 3.32.
[6] 1 Clement 5.
[7] F. F. Bruce, *Paul: Apostle of the Heart Set Free* (Grand Rapids: Eerdmans, 1977), 441–45; J. J. Gunther, *Paul: Messenger and Exile* (Valley Forge: Judson, 1972), 144ff. (Gunther argues that Paul did not visit Spain.)
[8] See P. N. Harrison, *The Problem of the Pastorals* (Oxford: Milford, 1921); Donald Guthrie, *The Pastoral Epistles: An Introduction and Commentary* (Grand Rapids: Eerdmans, 1957), 46–52, 212–28. See also idem, *The Pastoral Epistles and the Mind of Paul* (London: Tyndale, 1956).
[9] Guthrie, *Pastoral Epistles: An Introduction,* 24–32.
[10] Ibid., 32–38.
[11] Eusebius in *Ecclesiastical History* 2.15; 3.39; 5.8; 6.14.
[12] Ibid., 3.1.
[13] A helpful summary of the problem is found in Everett F. Harrison, *Introduction to the New Testament* (Grand Rapids: Eerdmans, 1964), 411–28. See also Michael Green, *2 Peter Reconsidered* (London: Tyndale, 1961); D. Edmond Hiebert, *An Introduction to the Non-Pauline Epistles* (Chicago: Moody, 1962), 139–57.

[11] Ibid., 13.
[12] Ibid., 15.
[13] Dio Cassius, *Roman History* 67.14.1–3.
[14] Ibid., 67.14.3–4.
[15] 1 Clement 1.1.
[16] Dio Cassius, *Roman History* 65.7.2.
[17] Suetonius, *Lives: Domitian* 2.
[18] Eusebius, *Ecclesiastical History* 3.18.
[19] Ibid.
[20] William Ramsay, *The Church in the Roman Empire* (Grand Rapids: Baker, 1979, reprint of 1897), 260.
[21] Dio Cassius, *Roman History* 67.14.1–3.
[22] Ramsay, *Church in the Roman Empire,* 259–78.
[23] Pliny, *Epistles* 96 and 97.
[24] Irenaeus, *Against Heresies* 3.3.4.
[25] Eusebius, *Ecclesiastical History* 3.31.
[26] Ibid., 2.18; 3.1, 23.
[27] Ibid., 7.25.
[28] See Leon Morris, *The Revelation of St. John* (Grand Rapids: Eerdmans, 1980), 29–30.
[29] Ibid.
[30] Everett F. Harrison, *Introduction to the New Testament* (Grand Rapids: Eerdmans, 1967), 468–69.
[31] Irenaeus, *Against Heresies* 5.35.2.
[32] Justin Martyr, *Dialogue With Trypho* 81.
[33] Origen, *Against Celsus* 6.6; 8.17; Tertullian, *Against Praxeas* 17.
[34] Irenaeus, *Against Heresies* 1.26.2.
[35] Ibid., 1.26.1.
[36] Ibid., 1.26.3.

Chapter 14

[1] Josephus, *Antiquities* 20.9.5.
[2] Josephus, *Wars* 2.14.1.
[3] *Antiquities* 20.11.1.
[4] Ibid.
[5] *Wars* 2.14–18.
[6] Suetonius, *Lives of the Caesars: Vespasian* 23.
[7] Ibid., *Titus* 1.
[8] Ibid., *Domitian* 3.
[9] See Exodus 30:13; Matthew 18:25.
[10] Suetonius, *Lives: Domitian* 12.

Chapter 15

[1] Pliny, *Letters.* 10.96.
[2] Ignatius, *Epistle to the Ephesians* 6.
[3] Ignatius, *Epistle to the Magnesians* 6.
[4] Ignatius, *Epistle to the Trallians* 3.
[5] Ignatius, *Epistle to the Smyrneans* 8.
[6] *Didache,* 13.3.
[7] Ibid., 15.2.
[8] Ibid., 10.7.
[9] Ibid., 12.1–5.
[10] Ignatius, *Epistle to the Magnesians.* 10.
[11] *Epistle of Barnabas.* 14.1.

A LIST OF ANCIENT WORKS

Note: These writings can be found in various editions and translations. This list will make the student aware of some of the more important works relevant to New Testament history.

The Book of Enoch.
Cicero. *Pro Flacco.*
Dio Cassius. *Roman History.*
The Epistle of Barnabas.
The Epistles of Ignatius.
The Epistle of Polycarp to the Philippians.
Eusebius. *Ecclesiastical History.*
The Gospel of Thomas.
Irenaeus. *Against Heresies.*
Josephus, Flavius. *Antiquities of the Jews.*
————. *Wars of the Jews.*
Justin Martyr. *The Dialogue With Trypho.*
————. *The First and Second Apologies.*
Juvenal. *Satires.*
1 and 2 Maccabees.
The Mishnah.
Origen. *Against Celsius.*
Philo of Alexandria. *Allegorical Interpretation.*
————. *The Legation to Gaius.*
Pliny the Younger. *Epistles.*
Plutarch. *Lives.*
Seneca. *Naturales Quaestiones.*
The Shepherd of Hermas.
Strabo. *Geography.*
Suetonius. *Lives of the Caesars.*
Tacitus. *The Annals.*
————. *The Histories.*
The Teaching of the Twelve Apostles (Didache).
Tertullian. *Against Praxeas.*
The Talmud.
The Wisdom of Solomon.

BIBLIOGRAPHY OF MODERN WORKS

Books

Allegro, John M. *The Dead Sea Scrolls and the Christian Myth.* Buffalo: Prometheus, 1979.

_____. *The Dead Sea Scrolls: A Reappraisal.* 2nd ed. New York: Penguin, 1964.

_____. *The People of the Dead Sea Scrolls in Text and Pictures.* Garden City, N.Y.: Doubleday, 1958.

_____. *Search in the Desert.* Garden City, N.Y.: Doubleday, 1964.

Altheim, F. *A History of Roman Religion.* Translated by Harold Mattingly. London: Methuen, 1938.

Anderson, Hugh. *Jesus and Christian Origins: A Commentary on Modern Viewpoints.* New York: Oxford University Press, 1964.

Angus, Samuel. *The Environment of Early Christianity.* New York: Scribner, 1921.

_____. *The Religious Quests of the Graeco-Roman World: A Study in the Historical Background of Early Christianity.* London: Murray, 1929.

Arndt, William F., and F. Wilbur Gingrich. *A Greek-English Lexicon of the New Testament and Other Early Christian Literature.* 4th ed. Chicago: University of Chicago Press, 1952.

Arnold, Edward V. *Roman Stoicism.* Freeport, N.Y.: Books for Libraries, 1971.

Bailey, Cyril. *Phases in the Religion of Ancient Rome.* Berkeley: University of California Press, 1932.

Barrett, Charles K. *Luke the Historian in Recent Study.* London: Epworth, 1961.

_____. *The New Testament Background: Selected Documents.* London: SPCK, 1958.

Bauer, W. *Orthodoxy and Heresy in Earliest Christianity.* Translated and edited by R. A. Kraft and G. Krodel et al. 2nd ed. Philadelphia: Fortress, 1971.

Bevan, Edwyn R. *A History of Egypt Under the Ptolemaic Dynasty.* London: Methuen, 1927.

_____. *Jerusalem Under the High Priests.* London: Edward Arnold, 1904.

_____. *The House of Seleucus.* 4 vols. London: Longmans, 1902.

Bickerman, Elias. *From Ezra to the Last of the Maccabees.* New York: Schocken, 1962.

_____. *The Maccabees.* New York: Schocken, 1947.

Black, M. *The Scrolls and Christian Origins: Studies in the Jewish Background of the New Testament.* New York: Scribner, 1961.

Blaiklock, E. M. *The Century of the New Testament.* London: Inter-Varsity Fellowship, 1962.

_____. *Cities of the New Testament.* London: Pickering & Inglis, 1965.

_____. *Rome in the New Testament.* London: Inter-Varsity Fellowship, 1959.

Boak, A. E. R. *A History of Rome to 565 A.D.* 4th ed. New York: Macmillan, 1953.

Bogue, Robert H. *The Dawn of Christianity.* New York: Vantage, 1985.

Borsch, H. *The Son of Man in Myth and History.* Philadelphia: Westminster, 1967.

Brandon, S. G. F. *The Fall of Jerusalem and the Christian Church.* 2nd ed. London: SPCK, 1957.

————. *Jesus and the Zealots.* New York: Scribner, 1967.

————. *The Trial of Jesus.* London: Batsford, 1968.

Brown, Raymond E. *The Birth of the Messiah.* New York: Doubleday, 1977.

————. *The Gospel According to John.* 2 vols. Garden City, N.Y.: Doubleday, 1966.

Brownlee, William H. *The Meaning of the Qumran Scrolls for the Bible.* New York: Oxford University Press, 1964.

Bruce, F. F. *The Acts of the Apostles.* 2nd ed. Grand Rapids: Eerdmans, 1953.

————. *Commentary on the Book of Acts.* Grand Rapids: Eerdmans, 1956.

————. *The Epistle to the Galatians.* Grand Rapids: Eerdmans, 1982.

————. *Jesus and Christian Origins Outside the New Testament.* Grand Rapids: Eerdmans, 1977.

————. *The New Testament Documents: Are They Reliable?* 5th ed. Grand Rapids: Eerdmans, 1980.

————. *New Testament History.* Garden City, N.Y.: Doubleday, 1971.

————. *Paul: Apostle of the Heart Set Free.* Grand Rapids: Eerdmans, 1977.

————. *Peter, Stephen, James and John: Studies in Early Non-Pauline Christianity.* Grand Rapids: Eerdmans, 1980.

————. *Second Thoughts on the Dead Sea Scrolls.* Grand Rapids: Eerdmans, 1961.

————. *The Spreading Flame.* Grand Rapids: Eerdmans, 1953.

Buchan, John. *Augustus.* Boston: Houghton, 1937.

Bultmann, Rudolf. *The History of the Synoptic Tradition.* Translated by John Marsh. 2nd ed. Bristol: Basil Blackwell Oxford, 1972.

————. *Jesus Christ and Mythology.* New York: Scribner, 1958.

Burich, Nancy J. *Alexander the Great: A Bibliography.* Ann Arbor: University Microfilms, reprint of 1970 edition.

Burn, Andrew R. *Alexander the Great and the Hellenistic Empire.* New York: AMS, reprint of 1948 edition.

Burrows, Millar. *The Dead Sea Scrolls.* New York: Viking, 1955.

————. *More Light on the Dead Sea Scrolls.* New York: Viking, 1958.

Busch, Fritz-Otto. *The Five Herods.* Translated by E. W. Dickes. London: Robert Hale, 1958.

Cadbury, Henry J. *The Book of Acts in History.* New York: Harper & Row, 1955.

————. *The Making of Luke-Acts.* 2nd ed. London: SPCK, 1958.

Carcopino, Jerome. *Daily Life in Ancient Rome.* Edited by Henry T. Rowell. Translated by E. O. Lorimer. New Haven: Yale University Press, 1940.

Carrington, Philip. *The Early Church.* Vol. 1, *The First Christian Century.* Cambridge: Cambridge University Press, 1957.

Carson, Herbert M. *The Epistles of Paul to the Colossians and Philemon.* Grand Rapids: Eerdmans, 1960.

Cary, M. *A History of Rome Down to the Reign of Constantine.* 2nd ed. London: Macmillan, 1957.

Catchpole, David R. *The Trial of Jesus.* Leiden: Brill, 1971.

Charles, R. H. *The Apocrypha and Pseudepigrapha of the Old Testament in English.* Oxford: Clarendon, 1913.

Charlesworth, James H. *The Discovery of a Dead Sea Scroll: Its Importance in the History of Jesus Research.* Lubbock: Texas Tech University Press, 1985.

Charlesworth, James H., ed. *John and Qumran.* London: Geoffrey Chapman, 1972.

Charlesworth, M. P. *Documents Illustrating the Reigns of Claudius and Nero*. Cambridge: Cambridge University Press, 1951.

Cheney, Johnston M. *The Life of Christ in Stereo*. Edited by Stanley A. Ellisen. 2nd ed. Portland: Western Baptist Seminary, 1971.

Cole, R. Alan. *The Gospel According to St. Mark*. Grand Rapids: Eerdmans, 1981.

Colwell, E. C. *An Approach to the Teaching of Jesus*. New York: Abingdon, 1947.

Cornfeld, Gaalyahu, ed. *Daniel to Paul: Jews in Conflict with Graeco-Roman Civilization*. New York: Macmillan, 1962.

Cross, F. M., Jr. *The Ancient Library of Qumran and Modern Biblical Studies*. Rev. ed. Grand Rapids: Baker, 1980.

Cullman, Oscar. *Peter: Disciple, Apostle, Martyr*. Translated by F. V. Filson. New York: Living Age Books, 1958.

Culver, Robert D. *The Life of Christ*. Grand Rapids: Baker, 1976.

Cumont, Franz. *After Life in Roman Paganism*. New Haven: Yale University Press, 1922.

_____. *Astrology and Religion Among the Greeks and Romans*. New York: Putnam, 1912.

_____. *The Mysteries of Mithra*. New York: Dover, 1956.

_____. *The Oriental Religions in Roman Paganism*. New York: Dover, 1956.

Curtis, W. A. *Jesus Christ the Teacher*. London: Oxford University Press, 1943.

Danby, Herbert. *The Mishnah*. Oxford: Oxford University Press, 1933.

Dancy, J. C. *A Commentary of 1 Maccabees*. Oxford: Blackwell, 1954.

Daniel-Rops, Henry. *Daily Life in the Time of Jesus*. Translated by Patrick O'Brian. Ann Arbor: Servant, 1980.

Davies, William D. *Christian Origins and Judaism*. Salem, N.H.: Ayer, 1962.

_____. *Paul and Rabbinic Judaism*. 4th ed. Philadelphia: Fortress, 1948.

Deissmann, Adolf. *Bible Studies*. Edinburgh: T. & T. Clark, 1901.

_____. *Light From the Ancient East*. 4th ed. New York: Harper and Brothers, 1927.

DeWitt, Norman. *St. Paul and Epicurus*. Minneapolis: University of Minnesota Press, 1954.

Dibelius, Martin. *From Tradition to Gospel*. Translated by B. L. Woolf. New York: Scribner, 1935.

_____. *The Message of Jesus Christ*. Translated by F. C. Grant. New York: Scribner, 1939.

Dill, Samuel. *Roman Society from Nero to Marcus Aurelius*. London: Macmillan, 1905.

Dodd, C. H. *The Apostolic Preaching and Its Developments*. London: Hodder and Stoughton, 1936.

_____. *The Interpretation of the Fourth Gospel*. Cambridge: Cambridge University Press, 1953.

_____. *More New Testament Studies*. Grand Rapids: Eerdmans, 1968.

_____. *New Testament Studies*. Manchester: University of Manchester Press, 1953.

Downey, Glanville. *Antioch in the Days of Theodosius the Great*. Norman, Okla.: University of Oklahoma Press, 1962.

_____. *A History of Antioch in Syria from Seleucus to the Arab Conquest*. Princeton: Princeton University Press, 1961.

Driver, G. R. *The Judean Scrolls*. Oxford: Blackwell, 1965.

Duncan, G. S. *St. Paul's Ephesian Ministry*. New York: Scribner, 1930.

Dupont-Sommer, A. *The Essene Writings from Qumran*. Translated by G. Vermes. Cleveland: World, 1962.

Edersheim, Alfred. *The Life and Times of Jesus the Messiah*. Grand Rapids: Eerdmans, 1971.

Enslin, Morton Scott. *Christian Beginnings.* New York: Harper and Brothers, 1938.

Fairweather, William. *The Background of the Epistles.* Edinburgh: T. & T. Clark, 1935.

Farmer, William R. *Jesus and the Gospel.* Philadelphia: Fortress, 1982.

——————. *Maccabees, Zealots and Josephus.* New York: Columbia University Press, 1956.

——————. *The Synoptic Problem: A Critical Analysis.* Macon: Mercer University Press, 1976.

Farrar, Frederic William. *The Life of Christ.* Cleveland: World, 1965.

Ferguson, John. *The Religions of the Roman Empire.* Ithaca: Cornell University Press, 1970.

Filson, Floyd. *A New Testament History.* Philadelphia: Westminster, 1964.

Finegan, Jack. *The Archaeology of the New Testament.* Princeton: Princeton University Press, 1969.

——————. *Handbook of Biblical Chronology.* Princeton: Princeton University Press, 1964.

Finkelstein, Louis. *The Pharisees: The Sociological Background of Their Faith.* 3rd ed. 2 vols. Philadelphia: Jewish Publication Society of America, 1962. Reprint of 1938 edition.

Foakes-Jackson, F. J., and Kirsopp Lake, eds. *The Beginnings of Christianity.* 5 vols. Grand Rapids: Baker, 1979. Reprint of 1920 edition.

Frazer, James G. *The Golden Bough: A Study in Magic and Religion.* Abridged ed. New York: Macmillan, 1953.

——————. *The Golden Bough.* 3rd ed. 2 vols. (1913; reprint ed., London: Macmillan, 1980).

Freyne, Sean. *Galilee From Alexander the Great to Hadrian.* Wilmington and Notre Dame: Michael Glazier and the University of Notre Dame Press, 1980.

Friedlander, Ludwig. *Roman Life and Manners Under the Early Empire.* Translated by Leonard A. Magnus. 2nd ed. 4 vols. London: Dutton, n.d.

Fuller, J. F. C. *The Generalship of Alexander the Great.* London: Eyre and Spottiswoode, 1958.

Fuller, Reginald H. *The Formation of the Resurrection Narratives.* 2nd ed. Philadelphia: Fortress, 1980.

Gaffin, R. B. *The Centrality of the Resurrection.* Grand Rapids: Baker, 1978.

Gasque, W. Ward. *History of the Criticism of the Acts of the Apostles.* Grand Rapids: Eerdmans, 1975.

Gasque, W. Ward, and Ralph P. Martin, eds. *Apostolic History and the Gospel.* Grand Rapids: Eerdmans, 1970.

Gaster, Theodore H., ed. *The Dead Sea Scriptures in English Translation.* 2nd ed. Garden City, N.Y.: Doubleday, 1976.

Goguel, Maurice. *The Life of Jesus.* Translated by O. Wyon. New York: Macmillan, 1933.

——————. *The Primitive Church.* Translated by H. C. Snape. London: Allen and Unwin, 1964.

Goodspeed, Edgar J. *A Life of Jesus.* New York: Harper and Brothers, 1950.

Goppelt, Leonhard. *Apostolic and Post-Apostolic Times.* Translated by Robert A. Guelich. New York: Harper Torchbooks, 1970.

Gough, Michael. *The Early Christians.* London: Thames and Hudson, 1961.

Grant, Frederick C., *The Economic Background of the Gospels.* London: Oxford University Press, 1926.

——————. *An Introduction to New Testament Thought.* Nashville: Abingdon, 1950.

——————. *Roman Hellenism and the New Testament.* New York: Scribner, 1962.

Grant, Frederick C., ed. *Ancient Roman Religion.* New York: Liberal Arts, 1957.

——————. *Hellenistic Religions.* New York: Liberal Arts, 1953.

Grant, Michael. *Herod the Great*. New York: American Heritage, 1971.

_____. *Jesus: An Historian's Review of the Gospels*. New York: Scribner, 1977.

_____. *Roman Myths*. New York: Scribner, 1971.

Grant, Robert M. *Augustus to Constantine: The Thrust of the Christian Movement into the Roman World*. New York: Harper & Row, 1970.

_____. *The Formation of the New Testament*. New York: Harper & Row, 1965.

Graves, R. *The Greek Myths*. 2 vols. New York: Penguin, 1955.

Green, Michael. *2 Peter Reconsidered*. London: Tyndale, 1961.

Green, Peter. *Alexander the Great*. New York: Praeger, 1970.

Guignebert, Charles. *The Jewish World in the Time of Jesus*. Translated by S. H. Hooke. New York: K. Paul, Trench, Turbner, 1939.

Guelich, R. A., ed. *Unity and Diversity in New Testament Theology*. Grand Rapids: Eerdmans, 1978.

Gundry, Robert H. *Matthew: A Commentary on His Literary and Theological Art*. Grand Rapids: Eerdmans, 1982.

Gunther, John J. *Paul: Messenger and Exile: A Study in the Chronology of His Life and Letters*. Valley Forge: Judson, 1972.

Guthrie, Donald. *Jesus the Messiah*. Grand Rapids: Zondervan, 1972.

_____. *New Testament Introduction*. 3 vols. London: Tyndale, 1965.

_____. *The Pastoral Epistles and the Mind of Paul*. London: Tyndale, 1956.

_____. *The Pastoral Epistles, An Introduction and Commentary*. Grand Rapids: Eerdmans, 1957.

Hadas, Moses. *Hellenistic Culture: Fusion and Diffusion*. Morningside Heights, N.Y.: Columbia University Press, 1959.

Hadas, Moses, and Morton Smith. *Heroes and Gods*. New York: Harper & Row, 1965.

Haddad, George. *Aspects of Social Life in Antioch in the Hellenistic-Roman Period*. New York: Hafner, 1949.

Hagner, Donald A., and Murray J. Harris. *Pauline Studies: Essays presented to Professor F. F. Bruce on His 70th Birthday*. Exeter: Paternoster, 1980.

Haines, C. R. *Heathen Contact with Christianity During Its First Century and a Half*. Cambridge: Deighton, 1923.

Hamilton, J. R. *Plutarch-Alexander: A Commentary*. Oxford: Clarendon, 1969.

Harding, G. Lankester. *The Antiquities of Jordan*. New York: Crowell, 1959.

Hardy, E. G. *Christianity and the Roman Government*. London: G. Allen; New York: Macmillan, 1925.

Harrison, Everett F. *Introduction to the New Testament*. Grand Rapids: Eerdmans, 1964.

_____. *A Short Life of Christ*. Grand Rapids: Eerdmans, 1979.

Harrison, P. N. *Polycarp's Two Epistles to the Philippians*. Cambridge: Cambridge University Press, 1936.

_____. *The Problem of the Pastorals*. Oxford: Humphrey Milford, 1921.

Head, Eldred Douglas. *New Testament Life and Literature as Reflected in the Papyri*. Nashville: Broadman, 1952.

Hedrick, Charles W., and Robert Hodgson, Jr., eds. *Nag Hammadi, Gnosticism and Early Christianity*. Peabody, Mass.: Hendrickson, 1987.

Hengel, Martin. *Acts and the History of Earliest Christianity*. Translated by John Bowden. Philadelphia: Fortress, 1980.

_____. *Between Jesus and Paul*. Philadelphia: Fortress, 1983.

_____. *Judaism and Hellenism*. Translated by John Bowden. Philadelphia: Fortress, 1974.

Hennecke, E. *New Testament Apocrypha.* Translated by R. McL. Wilson. Edited by W. Schneemelcher. Philadelphia: Westminster, 1963.

Herford, R. Travers. *The Pharisees.* New York: Macmillan, 1924.

Hiebert, D. Edmond. *An Introduction to the Non-Pauline Epistles.* Chicago: Moody, 1962.

Hoehner, Harold W. *Chronological Aspects of the Life of Christ.* Grand Rapids: Zondervan, 1979.

_____. *Herod Antipas.* Grand Rapids: Zondervan, 1980.

Horne, H. H. *Jesus the Master Teacher.* Grand Rapids: Kregel, 1964.

Howlett, Duncan. *The Essenes and Christianity.* New York: Harper, 1957.

Jeremias, Joachim. *Jerusalem in the Time of Jesus.* Translated by F. H. and C. H. Cave. Philadelphia: Fortress, 1969.

Jocz, Jakob. *The Jewish People and Jesus Christ.* Grand Rapids: Baker, 1979. Reprint of 1949 edition.

Jones, Arnold H. *The Herods of Judaea.* London: Oxford University Press, 1938.

Kee, Howard C. *Jesus in History.* 2nd ed. New York: Harcourt, Brace Jovanovich, 1977.

Klausner, Joseph. *Jesus of Nazareth: His Life, Times, and Teaching.* Translated by Herbert Danby. New York: Macmillan, 1944.

_____. *The Messianic Idea in Israel.* Translated by W. F. Stinespring. New York: Macmillan, 1955.

Knox, John. *Chapters in a Life of Paul.* New York, Nashville: Abingdon, 1950.

Koch, Klaus. *The Growth of the Biblical Tradition.* Translated by S. M. Cupitt. New York: Scribner, 1969.

Kümmel, W. G. *The New Testament: The History of the Investigation of Its Problems.* Translated by S. M. Gilmour and H. C. Kee. Nashville: Abingdon, 1972.

Ladd, George Eldon. *I Believe in the Resurrection of Jesus.* Grand Rapids: Eerdmans, 1975.

_____. *The New Testament and Criticism.* Grand Rapids: Eerdmans, 1967.

_____. *A Theology of the New Testament.* Grand Rapids: Eerdmans, 1974.

Lane, W. L. *The Gospel According to Mark.* Grand Rapids: Eerdmans, 1974.

LaSor, William Sanford. *The Dead Sea Scrolls and the New Testament.* Grand Rapids: Eerdmans, 1972.

Lietzmann, Hans. *The Beginnings of the Christian Church.* Translated by Bertram Lee Woolf. 2nd ed. New York: Meridian, 1949.

Lightfoot, J. B. *The Epistle of St. Paul to the Galatians.* Grand Rapids: Zondervan, 1957. Reprint of 1865 edition.

Lightfoot, J. B., and J. R. Harmer, eds. *The Apostolic Fathers.* Grand Rapids: Baker, 1984 reprint of 1891 edition.

Lods, Adolphe. *The Prophets and the Rise of Judaism.* New York: Dutton, 1937.

Loewe, H., ed. *Judaism and Christianity.* London: Sheldon, 1937.

Longenecker, Richard N. *The Christology of Early Jewish Christianity.* Grand Rapids: Baker, 1970.

_____. *Paul, Apostle of Liberty.* Grand Rapids: Baker, 1964.

McGiffert, Arthur C. *A History of Christianity in the Apostolic Age.* Edinburgh: T. & T. Clark, 1897.

Machen, J. Gresham. *The Origin of Paul's Religion.* Grand Rapids: Eerdmans, 1947.

Mahaffy, John Pentland. *A History of Egypt Under the Ptolemaic Dynasty.* New York: Scribner, 1899.

Manson, Menaham. *The Dead Sea Scrolls.* 2nd ed. Grand Rapids: Baker, 1983.

Manson, T. W. *The Teaching of Jesus: Studies of Its Form and Content.* 2nd ed. Cambridge: Cambridge University Press, 1963.

Manson, W. *Jesus the Messiah.* London: Hodder and Stoughton, 1943.

Marsh, Frank Burr. *The Reign of Tiberius.* Oxford: Oxford University Press. London: Humphrey Milford, 1931.

Marshall, I. Howard. *The Acts of the Apostles.* Grand Rapids: Eerdmans, 1980.

_____. *I Believe in the Historical Jesus.* Grand Rapids: Eerdmans, 1977.

_____. *Luke: Historian and Theologian.* Grand Rapids: Zondervan, 1971.

Marxsen, Willi. *The Resurrection of Jesus of Nazareth.* Translated by Margaret Kohl. Philadelphia: Fortress, 1970.

Mattingly, Harold. *Roman Imperial Civilization.* New York: Norton, 1971.

Meinardus, Otto F. *St. Paul in Ephesus and the Cities of Galatia and Cyprus.* New Rochelle, N.Y.: Caratzas, 1979.

Montefiore, Hugh. *Josephus and the New Testament.* London: Mowbray, 1962.

Montefiore, Hugh, and H. E. W. Turner. *Thomas and the Evangelists.* Naperville, Ill.: Allenson, 1962.

Moore, Frank G. *The Roman's World.* New York: Columbia University Press, 1936.

Moore, George Foot. *Judaism in the First Centuries of the Christian Era.* 3 vols. Cambridge, Mass.: Harvard University Press, 1927–1930.

Morgan, G. Campbell. *The Crises of the Christ.* New York: Revell, 1936.

Morison, F. *Who Moved the Stone?* London: Faber and Faber, 1944.

Morris, Leon. *The Gospel According to John.* Grand Rapids: Eerdmans, 1971.

_____. *The Revelation of St. John.* Grand Rapids: Eerdmans, 1980.

Moulton, James Hope, and George Milligan. *The Vocabulary of the Greek New Testament.* Grand Rapids: Eerdmans, 1949.

Mowinckel, Sigmund. *He That Cometh.* Translated by G. W. Anderson. Oxford: Blackwell, 1956.

Murray, Gilbert. *Five Stages of Greek Religion.* 3rd ed. Boston: Beacon, 1951.

Mylonas, George E. *Eleusis and the Eleusinian Mysteries.* Princeton: Princeton University Press, 1961.

Neusner, Jacob. *The Foundations of Judaism: Method, Teleology, Doctrine.* Philadelphia: Fortress, 1983–1985.

_____. *From Politics to Piety: The Emergence of Pharisaic Judaism.* Englewood Cliffs, N.J.: Prentice-Hall, 1973.

_____. *The Rabbinic Traditions About the Pharisees Before 70.* 3 vols. Leiden: Brill, 1971.

Nock, Arthur Darby. *Conversion: The Old and New in Religion From Alexander the Great to Augustine of Hippo.* Oxford: Oxford University Press, 1933.

_____. *Early Gentile Christianity and Its Hellenistic Background.* New York: Harper Torchbooks, 1964.

_____. *Essays on Religion and the Ancient World.* 2 vols. Oxford: Clarendon, 1972.

_____. *St. Paul.* New York: Harper and Brothers, 1938.

Oates, Whitney J., ed. *The Stoic and Epicurean Philosophers.* New York: Modern Library, 1940.

Ogilvie, R. M. *The Romans and Their Gods in the Age of Augustus.* New York: Norton, 1970.

Olmstead, Albert Ten Eyck. *History of Palestine and Syria to the Macedonian Conquest.* New York: Scribner, 1931.

Orr, James. *The Resurrection of Jesus.* London: Hodder and Stoughton, 1908.

Osborne, Grant R. *The Resurrection Narratives: A Redactional Study.* Grand Rapids: Baker, 1984.

Otto, Walter Friedrich. *The Homeric Gods: The Spiritual Significance of Greek Religion.* New York: Pantheon, 1954.

Panichas, George. *Epicurus.* New York: Twayne, 1967.

Pentecost, J. Dwight. *The Words and Works of Jesus Christ.* Grand Rapids: Zondervan, 1981.

Perowne, S. *The Life and Times of Herod the Great.* London: Hodder and Stoughton, 1956.

Perrin, Norman. *The Kingdom of God in the Teaching of Jesus.* Philadelphia: Westminster, 1963.

Plutarch. *The Parallel Lives.* Translated by Bernadotte Perrin. 11 vols. New York: Putnam, 1922–1927.

Ramsay, William M. *The Bearing of Recent Discovery on the Trustworthiness of the New Testament.* Grand Rapids: Baker, 1979 reprint of 1915 edition.

—————. *The Church in the Roman Empire.* Grand Rapids: Baker, 1979 reprint of 1897 edition.

—————. *A Historical Commentary on St. Paul's Epistle to the Galatians.* Grand Rapids: Baker, 1979 reprint of 1900 edition.

—————. *St. Paul the Traveller and Roman Citizen.* Grand Rapids: Baker, 1979 reprint of 1897 edition.

—————. *Was Christ Born at Bethlehem?* Grand Rapids: Baker, 1979 reprint of 1898 edition.

Reicke, Bo. *The New Testament Era.* Translated by D. E. Green. Philadelphia: Fortress, 1974.

Ringgren, Helmer. *The Faith of Qumran.* Translated by Emilie T. Sander. Philadelphia: Fortress, 1963.

Rivkin, Ellis. *A Hidden Revolution.* Nashville: Abingdon, 1978.

Robertson, Archibald T. *A Grammar of the Greek New Testament in the Light of Historical Research.* Nashville: Broadman, 1934.

Robinson, James M. *A New Quest of the Historical Jesus.* London: SCM, 1959.

Robinson, James M., ed. *The Nag Hammadi Library in English.* New York: Harper & Row, 1977.

Robinson, John A. T. *Redating the New Testament.* Philadelphia: Westminster, 1976.

Rose, H. J. *Religion in Greece and Rome.* New York: Harper & Row, 1959.

Sanders, E. P. *Paul and Palestinian Judaism.* Philadelphia: Fortress, 1977.

Sandmel, Samuel. *Herod: Profile of a Tyrant.* Philadelphia: Lippincott, 1967.

—————. *Philo's Place in Judaism.* Cincinnati: Hebrew Union College Press, 1956.

Schlatter, Adolf. *The Church in the New Testament Period.* Translated by Paul P. Levertoff. London: SPCK, 1955.

Schoeps, Hans J. *Jewish Christianity.* Translated by D. R. A. Hare. Philadelphia: Fortress, 1976.

Schonfield, Hugh J. *A History of Jewish Christianity.* London: Duckworth, 1936.

Schürer, Emil. *The History of the Jewish People in the Age of Jesus Christ.* Rev. ed. 2 vols. Edinburgh: T. & T. Clark, 1979.

Schweitzer, Albert. *The Quest of the Historical Jesus.* Translated by W. Montgomery. New York: Macmillan, 1910.

Scullard, H. H. *From the Gracchi to Nero.* 2nd ed. London: Methuen, 1963.

Sherwin-White, A. N. *Roman Society and Law in the New Testament.* Grand Rapids: Baker, 1963.

Simon, Marcel. *Jewish Sects at the Time of Jesus.* Translated by James H. Farley. Philadelphia: Fortress, 1967.

Simpson, E. K. *The Pastoral Epistles.* London: Tyndale, 1954.

Smallwood, Mary. *The Jews under Roman Rule.* Leiden: Brill, 1970.

Sparks, H. F. D. *A Synopsis of the Gospels: The Synoptic Gospels with the Johannine Parallels.* Philadelphia: Fortress, 1964.

Stauffer, Ethelbert. *Christ and the Caesars, Historical Sketches.* Translated by K. Smith and R. Gregor Smith. Philadelphia: Westminster, 1955.

Stein, R. H. *The Method and Message of Jesus' Teachings.* Philadelphia: Westminster, 1978.

Stendahl, Krister. *Paul Among Jews and Gentiles.* Philadelphia: Fortress, 1976.

Stewart, J. S. *The Life and Teaching of Jesus Christ.* Nashville: Abingdon, 1982.

Stoldt, Hans-Herbert. *History and Criticism of the Marcan Hypothesis.* Translated by Donald I. Niewyk. Macon: Mercer University Press, 1980.

Stone, Michael E. *Scriptures, Sects and Visions.* Philadelphia: Fortress, 1980.

Stonehouse, N. B. *The Witness of Luke to Christ.* London: Tyndale, 1951.

Streeter, B. H. *The Primitive Church.* New York: Macmillan, 1929.

Sweet, Louis Matthews. *Roman Emperor Worship.* Boston: Badger, 1919.

Tarn, W. W. *Alexander the Great.* 2 vols. Cambridge: Cambridge University Press, 1948.

Tarn, W. W., and G. T. Griffith. *Hellenistic Civilization.* 3rd ed. London: Arnold, 1952.

Tasker, R. V. G. *The Gospel According to St. Matthew: An Introduction and Commentary.* Grand Rapids: Eerdmans, 1979.

Taylor, Vincent. *The Formation of the Gospel Tradition.* 2nd ed. London: Macmillan, 1935.

_____. *The Life and Ministry of Jesus.* New York: Abingdon, 1955.

Tcherikover, Victor. *Hellenistic Civilization and the Jews.* Translated by S. Applebaum. Philadelphia: Jewish Publication Society of America, 1959.

Tenney, Merrill C. *New Testament Times.* Grand Rapids: Eerdmans, 1965.

_____. *The Reality of the Resurrection.* New York: Harper & Row, 1963.

Thackery, H. St. John. *Josephus, the Man and the Historian.* New York: Jewish Institute of Religion, 1929.

Thomas, Robert L., ed., and Stanley N. Gundry, associate ed. *A Harmony of the Gospels.* Chicago: Moody, 1978.

Throckmorton, B. Jr., ed. *Gospel Parallels: A Synopsis of the First Three Gospels.* 4th ed. Nashville: Nelson, 1979.

Vaux, Roland De. *Ancient Israel: Its Life and Institutions.* New York: McGraw-Hill, 1961.

_____. *The Archaeology of the Dead Sea Scrolls.* London: Oxford University Press, 1973.

Vermes, Geza. *The Dead Sea Scrolls: Qumran in Perspective.* Philadelphia: Fortress, 1981.

_____. *Jesus and the World of Judaism.* Philadelphia: Fortress, 1984.

Wallbank, F. W. *The Hellenistic World.* Sussex, N.J.: Humanities, 1981.

Wenham, John. *Easter Enigma.* Grand Rapids: Zondervan, 1984.

Wilcken, Ulrich. *Alexander the Great.* Translated by G. C. Richards. New York: Dial, 1932.

Willoughby, H. R. *Pagan Regeneration.* Chicago: University of Chicago Press, 1929.

Winter, Paul. *On the Trial of Jesus.* Berlin: de Gruyter, 1961.

_____. *On the Trial of Jesus.* Edited by T. A. Burkill and G. Vermes. Rev. ed. Berlin: de Gruyter, 1973.

Wrede, W. *The Messianic Secret.* Translated by J. C. G. Greig. Cambridge: Clarke, 1971.

Yadin, Yigael. *Bar-Kokhba: The Rediscovery of the Legendary Hero of the Last Jewish Revolt Against Imperial Rome.* London: Weidenfeld and Nicholson, 1971.

——————. *Masada: Herod's Fortress and the Zealots' Last Stand.* London: Weidenfeld and Nicholson, 1966.

——————. *The Temple Scroll: The Hidden Law of the Dead Sea Sect.* New York: Random, 1985.

Yadin, Yigael, ed. *The Scroll of the War of the Sons of Light Against the Sons of Darkness.* New York: Oxford, 1962.

Yamauchi, Edwin M. *Pre-Christian Gnosticism: A Survey of the Proposed Evidences.* Grand Rapids: Eerdmans, 1973.

Zeitlin, Solomon. *The Rise and Fall of the Jewish State.* 2 vols. Philadelphia: Jewish Publication Society, 1967.

Articles

Blaicklock, E. M. "Aretas.' *The Zondervan Pictorial Bible Encyclopedia.* Edited by Merrill C. Tenney. Grand Rapids: Zondervan, 1975. 3:299–300.

——————. "Porcius Festus." *The Zondervan Pictorial Bible Encyclopedia.* Edited by Merrill C. Tenney. Grand Rapids: Zondervan, 1975. 2:532–33.

Brownlee, W. H. "John the Bapitst in the New Light of the Ancient Scrolls." *Interpretation* 9 (1955): 71–90.

Bruns, J. E. "Use of Time in the Fourth Gospel." *New Testament Studies* 13 (1967): 285–90.

Dyer, Charles H. "Do the Synoptics Depend on Each Other?" *Bibliotheca Sacra* 138 (July-September 1981): 230–45.

Geyser, A. S. "The Youth of John the Baptist." *Novum Testamentum* 1 (1956): 70–75.

Grant, Robert M. "Two Gnostic Gospels." *Journal of Biblical Literature* 79 (March 1960): 1–11.

Jocz, J. "Passover." *The Zondervan Pictorial Bible Encyclopedia.* Edited by Merrill C. Tenney. Grand Rapids: Zondervan, 1975. 4:605–11.

Liberty, S. "The Importance of Pontius Pilate in Creed and Gopspel." *Journal of Theological Studies* 15 (1944): 38–56.

Maier, P. "Sejanus, Pilate and the Date of the Crucifixion." *Church History* 38 (1968): 3–13.

Metzger, Bruce M. "Antioch-on-the-Orontes." *The Biblical Archaeologist* 11 (December 1948): 69–88.

Miller, Johnny V. "The Time of the Crucifixion." Journal of the Evangelical Theological Society 26/2 (June 1983): 157–66.

Moule, C. F. D. "Once More, Who Were the Hellenists?" *The Expository Times* 70/4 (January 1959): 100–102.

Osborne, Grant R. "Redaction Criticism and the Great Commission: A Case Study Toward a Biblical Understanding of Inerrancy." *Journal of the Evangelical Theological Society* 21/2 (1978): 117–30.

——————. "The Evangelical and Redaction Criticism: Critique and Methodology." *Journal of the Evangelical Theological Society* 22/4 (December 1979): 305–22.

Walker, N. "The Reckoning of Hours in the Fourth Gospel." *Novum Testamentum* 4 (1960): 69–73.

INDEX OF PERSONS

INDEX OF SUBJECTS

323

NEW TESTAMENT HISTORY

INDEX OF BIBLICAL REFERENCES

9 780310 312017